THE COMPLETE OPERAS OF
RICHARD
WAGNER

THE COMPLETE OPERAS OF
RICHARD WAGNER

CHARLES OSBORNE

DA CAPO PRESS • NEW YORK

Library of Congress Cataloging in Publication Data

Osborne, Charles, 1927-
   The complete operas of Richard Wagner / Charles Osborne. — 1st
Da Capo Press ed.
     p.   cm.
   Originally published: London: M. O'Mara Books, 1990. With new
introd.
   Includes bibliographical references and index.
   ISBN 0-306-80522-7
   1. Wagner, Richard, 1813-1883 — Operas. 2. Opera. I. Title.
[ML410.W1308   1993]   92-34417
782.1'092 — dc20   CIP

Music examples are reproduced by kind permission of
Boosey & Hawkes Music Publishers Limited

First Da Capo Press edition 1993

This Da Capo Press paperback edition of *The Complete Operas of Richard Wagner*
is an unabridged republication of the book published in London in 1990. It
is reprinted by arrangement with Trafalgar Square Publishing.

Published by Da Capo Press, Inc.
A Subsidiary of Plenum Publishing Corporation
233 Spring Street, New York, N.Y. 10013

Manufactured in the United States of America

Contents

To the memory
of
EVA METZLER

Introduction

THIS volume completes a series which I began more than twenty years ago with *The Complete Operas of Verdi* and which continued with similarly titled guides to the operas of Mozart, Puccini and Strauss. There are, of course, many other important composers of opera, among them Tchaikovsky, Massenet, Meyerbeer, Janácek, Handel, Britten, Tippett, and the three great composers of the *bel canto* era: Rossini, Donizetti and Bellini. However, it will surely be generally agreed that the five composers I chose to include in this series are the pre-eminent creators of opera. Of them, the most controversial still, and the most complex, is Richard Wagner.

That Wagner's racial and other theories were either evil or absurd or both is irrelevant to his stature as an artist. In his own day, and immediately after his death, he was extremely influential, although his influence is apparent less in the work of other composers than in that of poets and painters. Those composers whose operas can be called Wagnerian—Humperdinck and Reyer, for example—are not of the first rank, with the exception of Debussy, whose *Pelléas et Mélisande* is deeply indebted to Wagner and in particular to *Parsifal*. However, there is hardly a major poet of the turn of the century who did not walk in the valley of the shadow of the master.

In Paris, the Symbolists came under Wagner's sway. French poets such as Gérard de Nerval and Théophile Gautier were enthusiastic Wagnerians, and both Baudelaire and Mallarmé wrote essays on the composer. Wagnerian references abound, too, in the painting of the time. Cézanne painted an *Overture to Tannhäuser*, Renoir painted the composer's portrait, and artists such as Fantin-Latour, Odilon Redon and, in England, Whistler and Aubrey Beardsley produced lithographs of scenes from Wagner operas.

Wagner's only peers as creators of opera are Mozart in the preceding century and his own contemporary, Verdi. He was the greatest of the nineteenth-century German romantics, and the creator of music dramas of unique emotive power and compulsion.

I am grateful for permission to quote from the following: Eduard Hanslick: *Music Criticisms 1846–99* (Penguin Books); Ernest Newman: *Wagner Nights* (Putnam); Ernest Newman: *Wagner as Man and Artist* (Jonathan Cape); Robert Donington: *Wagner's 'Ring' and its Symbols* (Faber and Faber).

C.O.

ONE

Die Feen

(The Fairies)

Romantic Opera in Three Acts

Dramatis personae:
The Fairy King   (bass)
Ada, a Fairy   (soprano)
Farzana, a Fairy   (soprano)
Zemina, a Fairy   (soprano)
Arindal, Prince of Tramond, later King   (tenor)
Lora, his Sister   (soprano)
Morald, Lora's Lover and Arindal's Friend   (baritone)
Gernot, Arindal's Huntsman   (bass)
Drolla, Lora's Maid   (soprano)
Gunther, a Courtier of Tramond   (tenor)
Harald, Arindal's General   (bass)
A Messenger   (tenor)
The Voice of the Sorcerer Groma   (bass)

LIBRETTO by the composer, based on the play, *La Donna Serpente*,
by Carlo Gozzi

TIME: The mythical past

PLACE: Tramond, and the fairy realm

FIRST PERFORMED at the Hoftheater, Munich, 29 June 1888, with Lili
Dressler (Ada) and Franz Mikorey (Arindal), conducted by Franz Fischer.

I

OF all the great composers, Wagner appears to be the only one to have written an autobiography. Unfortunately, *My Life* (*Mein Leben*), which he wrote and printed privately towards the end of his life, is an even less truthful piece of work than the usual volume of memoirs, its first direct lie appearing in the opening sentences of the book in which the composer states unequivocally that he was baptized two days after his birth, and that his father was 'Friedrich Wagner [who] was at the time of my birth a clerk in the police service at Leipzig'.

It is true that Carl Friedrich Wagner was the legal father of the child who was born on 22 May 1813, and who three months (not 'two days') later was baptized Wilhelm Richard Wagner in Bach's old church, St Thomas's. However, the father of Johanna Wagner's ninth child was not her husband but Ludwig Geyer, an unsuccessful portrait painter who had become an actor and who used to lodge with the Wagners whenever he was in Leipzig. Carl Friedrich Wagner died of typhoid fever in November, six months after Richard's birth. Nine months after the death of her husband, Johanna married Ludwig Geyer, who took on the burden of supporting not only a wife but also her seven surviving children, only one of whom was his. The family moved to Dresden, the Saxon capital, where Geyer was employed as an actor. Six months after their marriage, a second child was born to the Geyers, a girl, Cäcilie, who became the fond companion of her brother Richard's childhood.

Geyer died when young Richard was eight years of age, but the lad continued to be known as Wilhelm Richard Geyer until his confirmation six years later, when he reverted to his legal name of Wagner. It is not known exactly when Richard (as he was always called) realized that his stepfather was actually his real father, but he was certainly aware of the fact several years before he produced his autobiography. He referred to it in a letter to his sister Cäcilie when they were in their fifties, and he had most probably already suspected the truth while he was still in his teens. But the adult Wagner, virulently and hysterically anti-Semitic, could never have brought himself to reveal in his memoirs that his father bore a Jewish surname, and may indeed have been Jewish. No proof has been discovered of Geyer's racial ancestry, but young Richard Geyer would no doubt have been assumed by his schoolmates to be Jewish. He was born in the Jewish quarter of Leipzig, and his features, especially the prominent nose and the high, intellectual brow, would not have helped to belie the assumption.

After Ludwig Geyer's death, young Richard and his half-brother Julius were sent to live with Geyer's brother, Karl Friedrich Geyer, a goldsmith in the small town of Eisleben. The following year, Richard returned home to Dresden. Later, when his stepsister Luise accepted a theatre engagement in Leipzig, the family moved back to that city, where Richard attended the

Nicolaischule for two and a half years. Here he made his first contacts with students from Leipzig University, and began to take an active interest in literature, theatre, music, politics and philosophy. At the age of sixteen, he began seriously to learn the technique of musical composition, taking lessons in harmony from a theatre violinist named Müller. Before long, he was composing music: a piano sonata, an aria, a string quartet and incidental music for a pastoral play he himself had written.

For a time, frustrated no doubt by the general lack of interest shown in his earliest compositions, the young Wagner threw himself into a wide range of student activities. After his enrolment at Leipzig University as a music student, he pursued a hectic social life, drinking, gambling and even duelling. He became a strongly opinionated and argumentative young man, given to haranguing his acquaintances in the thick Saxon accent which he was never to lose.

Finally emerging from this period of adolescent confusion, Wagner returned to the study of harmony and counterpoint in earnest with Christian Theodor Weinlig, the cantor of St Thomas's Church. After a year, he began to produce compositions for piano, orchestral pieces and songs. Two overtures and a symphony by the eighteen-year-old composer were performed at concerts in Leipzig. With a friend, Wagner visited Brünn (now Brno), the capital of Moravia, and then travelled on alone to Vienna, the Mecca for all musicians, where he succumbed to the apparently carefree frivolity of the Viennese temperament, found himself entranced by the waltzes of Strauss and Lanner, and made his first acquaintance with the Viennese magic plays with music by Raimund and other composers. The influence of this unique Viennese genre can be traced not only in Wagner's first completed work for the stage, *Die Feen*, but also throughout his entire *oeuvre*, up to his final opera, *Parsifal*.

In the summer of 1832, passing through Prague on his way home from Vienna, he began work on an opera, writing the libretto himself, as well as the music. Even at this early stage of his career, Wagner gave no serious thought to the possibility of collaborating with a librettist. For him, a work of art such as an opera was the product of one creative mind, and it was therefore essential for him to be the author of the words as well as the composer of the music. The libretto of *Die Hochzeit* (The Wedding) was the outcome of his thwarted passion for a girl in Prague named Jenny Pachta. Its plot, about a young woman who pushes an importunate admirer off her balcony to his death, and finally confesses to the crime at his funeral, was taken partly from Johann Gustav Busching's book *Ritterzeit und Ritterwesen* (The Knights: their times and customs) and a play, *Cardenio und Celinde*, by Karl Immermann.

Wagner completed the libretto of *Die Hochzeit* in Prague, and on his return

11

to Leipzig began to write the music. However, after composing an orchestral introduction, a chorus, a recitative and a septet, he abandoned the work, possibly because his sister Rosalie considered it excessively gloomy. The completed pieces reveal that his choral writing was assured, if hardly individual, and his passages of accompanied recitative both sensitive and flexible. His teacher Weinlig praised the 'clarity and singableness' of the septet. Though not yet twenty, Wagner was clearly already equipped to compose a full-length opera, and he was to do so before his twenty-first birthday. (More than a hundred years later, the fragments of *Die Hochzeit* were first performed at the Neues Theater, Leipzig, on 13 February 1938.)

In February 1833, through the influence of his half-brother Albert, who was the leading tenor of the opera company in Würzburg in neighbouring Bavaria, the twenty-year-old Richard secured a position as coach for the chorus and soloists at the theatre in Würzburg. He was pleased to be leaving the state of Saxony and thus avoiding the military service he would shortly have been required to undertake there. In Würzburg he began to acquaint himself with the opera company's repertoire, and for Marschner's *Der Vampyr* he composed an alternative cabaletta for the tenor aria, '*Doch jetzt wohin ich blicke*' (But now, wherever I look), possibly to suit his brother Albert's capabilities. Though in Marschner's style, it is a more dramatic piece than the cabaletta which it was composed to replace.

Wagner remained with the Würzburg company for most of 1833, and then stayed on in the town for some months to finish the composition of his first complete opera, *Die Feen* (The Fairies), to his own libretto based on a play by the eighteenth-century Venetian playwright Carlo Gozzi. Excerpts from the opera were played at a concert in Würzburg, and Wagner's sister Rosalie attempted to have it staged in Leipzig, but *Die Feen* was never produced during its composer's lifetime. It first reached the stage in Munich in 1888. Over the following half-century it received no more than a handful of performances, in Prague (1893), Munich (1910), Zurich (1914) and Stuttgart (1932). Although it has never been staged at the Festival Theatre in Bayreuth, since the Wagner family apparently does not consider the three operas which precede *Der fliegende Holländer* to be worthy of inclusion in its repertory, *Die Feen* was given two performances in Bayreuth in the modern Stadthalle (Town Hall) in August 1967, by students of the International Youth Festival.

The opera was given its British première by amateurs in Birmingham at the University of Aston on 17 May 1969, and was first seen in London at the Fulham Town Hall on 3 May 1973. On 2 May 1977 it was broadcast by the BBC, conducted by Edward Downes. The opera was revived in Wuppertal in 1981. The following year, a concert performance was given in New York by the New York City Opera on 24 February. In 1983, the Wagner centenary year, concert performances of *Die Feen* were given in Vienna and Munich.

II

CARLO Gozzi (1720–1806), the Venetian playwright on whose *La Donna Serpente* (The Serpent Woman), written in 1762, Wagner's opera of 1833 was based, was the author of a number of charming and witty plays, many of which were dramatized versions of fairy tales. Two of Gozzi's plays were to provide subjects for well-known twentieth-century operas: Prokofiev's *The Love for Three Oranges*, which was based on Gozzi's *Fiaba dell' Amore delle Tre Melarance* of 1761, and Puccini's *Turandot*, which derives from Gozzi's 1762 play of the same title. Among Wagner's many changes to Gozzi's play were his removal of the action from the Orient to a legendary land which is Germanic in character, and his renaming of the characters. For some of the characters in *Die Feen*, he chose names which he had already allotted to personages in the abandoned *Die Hochzeit*: Ada, Lora, Arindal and Harald.

In his autobiography, Wagner had this to say of *Die Feen*:

I had borrowed the plot from a dramatic fairy-tale by Gozzi, *La Donna Serpente*, and called it *Die Feen*. The names of my heroes I chose from different poems by Ossian and others. My prince was called Arindal. He was loved by a fairy called Ada, who held him under her spell and kept him in fairyland, away from his realm, until his faithful friends at last found him and induced him to return, for his country was going to rack and ruin, and even its capital had fallen into the enemy's hands.

The loving fairy herself sends the prince back to his country, for the oracle has decreed that she shall lay upon her lover the severest of tasks. Only by performing this task triumphantly can he make it possible for her to leave the immortal world of fairies in order to share the fate of her earthly lover, as his wife. In a moment of deepest despair about the state of his country, the fairy queen appears to Arindal and deliberately destroys his faith in Ada by deeds of the most cruel and inexplicable nature.

Driven mad by a thousand fears, Arindal begins to imagine that all this time he has been dealing with a wicked sorceress, and tries to escape the fatal spell by pronouncing a curse upon Ada. Wild with sorrow, the unhappy fairy sinks down, reveals their mutual fate to the lover who is now lost to her for ever, and tells him that, as a punishment for having disobeyed the decree of Fate, she is doomed to be turned into stone. (In Gozzi's version she becomes a serpent.)

Immediately afterwards it appears that all the catastrophes which the fairy queen had prophesied were but deceptions: victory over the enemy as well as the growing prosperity and welfare of the kingdom now follow in quick succession. Ada is taken away by the Fates, and Arindal, a raving madman, remains behind alone. The terrible sufferings of his madness do not, however, satisfy the Fates. To bring about his utter ruin, they appear

13

before the repentant man and invite him to follow them to the nether world, on the pretext of enabling him to free Ada from the spell.

Through the treacherous promises of the wicked fairies, Arindal's madness grows into sublime exaltation. One of his household magicians, a faithful friend, having in the meantime equipped him with magic weapons and charms, Arindal now follows the traitresses. The latter cannot get over their astonishment when they see how Arindal overcomes one after the other of the monsters of the infernal regions. Only when they arrive at the vault in which they show him the petrified figure of his beloved do they recover their hope of vanquishing the valiant prince, for, unless he can break the charm which binds Ada, he must share her fate and be doomed to remain a statue of stone forever.

Arindal, who until then has been relying on the dagger and the shield given him by the friendly magician, now makes use of an instrument—a lyre—which he has brought with him, but whose meaning he had not yet understood. To the sounds of this instrument he now expresses his plaintive moans, his remorse, and his overpowering longing for his enchanted queen. The statue is moved by the magic of his love: the beloved one is released. Fairyland with all its marvels opens its portals, and the mortal learns that, owing to his former inconstancy, Ada has lost the right to become his wife on earth, but that her beloved, through his great and magic power, has earned the right to live for ever by her side in fairyland.

Although I had written *Die Hochzeit* in the darkest vein, without operatic embellishments, I painted this new subject with the utmost colour and variety. In contrast to the lovers out of fairyland, I depicted a more ordinary couple, and I even introduced a third pair who belonged to the coarser and more comical servant world. I deliberately took no pains in the matter of the poetic diction and the verse. My idea was not to encourage my former hopes of making a name as a poet. I was now really a musician and a composer, and I wished to write a decent opera libretto myself simply because I was sure that nobody else could write one for me: the reason being that such a book is something quite unique which cannot be written either by a poet or by a mere man of letters. . . . In a German style similar to Marschner, I wrote the music to *Die Feen* in the course of the year 1833.

III

CLEARLY there are similarities between the libretto of *Die Feen* and that of Mozart's *Die Zauberflöte*; not in the details of plot but in the underlying meaning. Indeed, *Die Feen*, though an immature work by the standards of later Wagnerian music drama, is an important landmark in the progression of German fairy-tale operas from Mozart and *Die Zauberflöte* to Strauss and

Die Frau ohne Schatten, and its plot looks forward to Strauss (the spouse turned to stone) as much as it looks backward to Mozart. The juxtaposition of royal and bourgeois couples links all three operas, but Schikaneder wrote for Mozart, and Hofmannsthal for Strauss, with, in the one case, more wit and, in the other, more style than Wagner the librettist was able to summon up for Wagner the composer.

With *Die Feen*, Wagner plunged into that world of myth and fairy-tale which he was creatively to inhabit for the remainder of his life. Musically, however, the opera represents a false start, for Wagner not only chose the kind of subject which the more established German composers of his day tended to favour, but also imitated their style. This is not especially surprising when one bears in mind the composer's extreme youth: he was only twenty. But in view of the direction his mature genius was to take, and the grandiose scale of his later achievement, it is perhaps a trifle odd to find so few traces of originality or individuality in Wagner's first completed opera.

When one examines *Die Feen* now with the benefit of hindsight, it is not difficult to discern adumbrations of musical and dramatic themes which were to be more fully worked out in the operas of Wagner's maturity. At the time of its composition, however, there was nothing in *Die Feen* to indicate to Wagner's fellow-musicians and colleagues that this was the work of a powerful and original talent. Wagner's libretto, which makes use of only a very limited vocabulary, is repetitious, and much of it is puerile and nonsensical. Some of the orchestral writing in the opera is pastiche Mendelssohn, while certain effects are borrowed from Beethoven, from Weber and, in particular, from Marschner, whose three operas *Der Vampyr*, *Der Templer und die Jüdin* and *Hans Heiling* clearly had deeply impressed the young Wagner. As we have seen, the composer himself admitted that he had written *Die Feen* in what he thought of as the style of Marschner, a composer who at that time was widely performed in the opera houses of Germany. Nevertheless, although there may be only few traces of the artistic personality of the mature Wagner to be found in this, his first work for the stage, it is in many ways an attractive and not unenjoyable opera of its time.

IV

THE Overture to *Die Feen* is a large-scale romantic tone-poem, full of tunes (one of which anticipates a motif from Elisabeth's '*Dich, teure Halle*' in *Tannhäuser*), scored with assurance and warmth, and well constructed, though perhaps a trifle too long. When the curtain rises on the first scene of Act I, a fairy-tale garden is revealed, in which a group of fairies, among them Farzana and Zemina (sopranos), dance and sing in praise of the beauty of their realm. The music of their dance is a stately *andante*; their chorus

('*Schwinget euch auf*': Wing your way here) paints a charming picture of the enchanted world they inhabit, a solo horn adding a certain melancholy tone to the overall colour.

In a passage of accompanied recitative, Farzana and Zemina express their sorrow at the thought that one of their number, Ada, born of a fairy mother and a mortal father, is about to leave them, having renounced her immortality for love of a mortal, Arindal, Crown Prince of Tramond. Farzana reminds Zemina that the Fairy King in his displeasure has set such difficult conditions upon the union of Ada and Arindal that the mortal Arindal will never be able to meet them, and that Ada will consequently return to the fairy kingdom forever. Farzana and Zemina now summon up all the fairies and sprites, who, in another chorus ('*Reicht Hilfe uns zu unsrem Werk*': Give us your help in our work), pledge to do all in their power to bring about the separation of the couple and thus ensure Ada's continuing immortality. The recitative is pedestrian, as much of Wagner's recitative was to remain, throughout almost his entire *oeuvre*, but the chorus, a stirring *allegro con brio*, makes a strong ending to the opening scene, the sprites adding their male voices to the hitherto all-female chorus.

The scene now changes to a rocky wilderness. Three friends of Arindal enter: from one side Gernot, Arindal's huntsman (bass), and from the other Gunther, a courtier from Tramond (tenor), accompanied by Morald (baritone). Gunther and Morald greet Gernot, whom they have not seen since the day, eight years previously, when he had disappeared in company with the Crown Prince Arindal. Morald explains that he and Gunther have been sent by Groma, a sorcerer and the protector of the royal family, to find Arindal. His father having died, Arindal is now King, but a longtime enemy has laid siege to Tramond and is claiming the hand in marriage of Arindal's sister, Lora, to whom Morald is betrothed. Arindal must return to protect his kingdom.

Gernot tells Gunther and Morald that, on that day eight years ago, he and Arindal had pursued a beautiful doe until it plunged into a river and vanished. Leaping in after it, they had suddenly found themselves in a magnificent castle where they had encountered a beautiful woman. Arindal and the woman had fallen in love, and she had agreed to marry him on one condition: that, for eight years, he refrain from asking her name. Arindal had agreed, and over the years the woman had borne him two children. The two lovers had lived happily together until the previous day when, no longer able to suppress his curiosity, Arindal had asked his consort who she was and whence she had come. At this, she and her maidservants and the entire castle had disappeared in a clap of thunder. Arindal and Gernot had found themselves in the wilderness, and Arindal was now desperately searching for his lost love. After Gernot has been assured by Gunther that his own wife, Drolla (Lora's maid), is still alive, and grieving for him, the three men conceal themselves as Arindal is seen approaching.

The scene has until now progressed entirely in rather leaden accompanied recitative, but with the entrance of Arindal (tenor), which is heralded by a phrase repeated in great agitation, it gains in interest, broadening into what Wagner in his score describes as an aria, though its first section is more like a long passage of arioso. It becomes a more formal aria only at the words '*Wo bist du, ach, wo bist du?*' (Where are you, ah, where are you?), in which Arindal voices his desperation at the loss of his beloved Ada. The tempo quickens again in a cabaletta-like conclusion to the aria. Here, and elsewhere in *Die Feen*, Wagner makes use of motifs and occasionally longer phrases and themes from some of his teenage compositions, among them a C major symphony and an F sharp minor fantasy for piano.

Arindal's huntsman Gernot re-enters and, by asserting that Ada was in fact an evil old witch, attempts to persuade his master to return to his own country. In a dull little song, '*War einst 'ne böse Hexe wohl*' (There was once an evil witch), he tells Arindal the story of Dilnovaz, an old and ugly sorceress who possessed a magic ring which gave her the power to make herself beautiful. In her guise of beauty she enchanted a king who, when he later discovered her embracing another man, lunged at her with his dagger. He succeeded only in cutting off the little finger on which she wore the magic ring. Sudddenly, in place of his beloved, there stood before him the ugly old witch.

Unconvinced by Gernot's tale, Arindal is about to leave him when Gunther returns, disguised as a venerable priest. While Gernot comments *sotto voce* on the brilliance of this ploy, Gunther announces hmself as a holy man who has come to warn Arindal that he has been ensnared by an evil woman. Whoever yields to her is lost to the kingdom of heaven forever. The wild animals who dwell in the surrounding cliffs, says Gunther, were once human beings who fell under the spell of the sorceress. Unless Arindal renounces Ada, a similar fate awaits him.

Shaken by these revelations, Arindal is on the point of following the holy man when a clap of thunder and a flash of lightning suddenly transform Gunther back into his real appearance. Outraged by Gunther's deception, Arindal thanks Ada, through the power of whose love he is convinced Gunther was unmasked. However, Morald now enters in the guise of Arindal's dead father. Gernot and Gunther murmur to each other that his disguise is thoroughly convincing, and indeed Arindal is convinced as Morald explains that he is the spirit of the dead king. He castigates Arindal for having wasted his youth by wandering about in a lovesick trance while his sister was attempting to save their kingdom from the attacks of 'savage King Murold'. He pleads with Arindal to return and protect the kingdom.

As Arindal is about to comply, another burst of thunder and lightning transforms Morald into himself again. But Morald, in *propria persona* as an old friend of Arindal, is able to convince him that the king, his father, is really dead, and that the kingdom is under threat. Arindal realizes that he must give up his search for Ada and return with his companions to his own country.

The scene in which his companions appear in disguise to Arindal had begun as a trio, and developed into a lively quartet. When the others depart, night having now fallen, Arindal remains alone, lamenting his eternal separation from Ada. His only hope now, he exclaims, is that he will die in battle, defending his homeland. A sudden drowsiness overtaking him, he lies down by a large rock and falls asleep, lulled by the orchestra's lower strings. One is reminded of the scene in *Die Walküre* in which Siegmund rests before his fight with Hunding, and is visited by Brünnhilde.

Arindal's brief soliloquy, which follows the quartet, formally begins the finale to the opera's first act. The finale continues with a miraculous change of scene, as the landscape around Arindal is transformed into Ada's fairy garden with a magnificent palace in the background. Ada (soprano), gorgeously attired, her dress covered in sparkling jewellery, emerges from the palace and, in a graceful and exquisitely scored cavatina with echoes not only of Weber but also of '*Porgi amor*' from Mozart's *Le Nozze di Figaro*, declares that she is willing to renounce her fairy immortality in order to become the mortal wife of Arindal.

When Arindal awakens, overjoyed to find Ada standing before him, she warns him that their happiness is still threatened. He swears he will never leave her, to which she replies sadly that he will forsake her on the morrow. Arindal's three fellow-countrymen now appear, with a number of their companions from Tramond. They are bemused to find themselves in the fairy kingdom but determined to take Arindal back with them to the world of mortals, even though they themselves are dazzled by Ada's beauty.

A procession of fairies headed by Farzana and Zemina arrives with the news that Ada's mortal father has died, and that she is now Queen of the Fairies. The fairies all greet her as their new sovereign, and Farzana and Zemina tell each other that Ada's ascension to the fairy throne will surely prevent her from choosing to live as a mortal.

When an understandably perplexed Arindal asks Ada what is happening, she begs him not to question her further but to return home with his friends. She is forbidden by her destiny to confide further in him, but they will meet on the morrow when, as she puts it, he will encounter her to his own misfortune. Despite what he may see then, he must not curse her. Arindal swears that, of course, he will never curse her. The lovers part, to fulfil their duties in their separate kingdoms, fairy and mortal, and Ada is borne away in a magnificent carriage.

The Arindal–Ada duet which begins the finale proper is clearly the work of someone who has heard the Florestan–Leonore duet of reunion in Beethoven's *Fidelio*. The ensemble which develops after the arrival of Arindal's fellow mortals is inappropriately four-square, in the style of Lortzing rather than Marschner, but with the appearance of the chorus of fairies Wagner's music takes on an air of greater confidence. The *adagio* septet which follows Arindal's declaration that he will never curse Ada would not sound out of place in *Lohengrin*, and the ensuing *allegro* ensemble makes an exciting conclusion to Act I.

Act II takes place in the great hall of the royal palace of Tramond. After a few bars of agitated orchestral introduction, the curtain rises to reveal a crowd of warriors and citizens who, in a fine opening chorus, bewail the fact that they are being attacked by an enemy whose forces are already massed outside the city walls. They call on heaven for protection, and are not greatly reassured when Arindal's sister Lora (soprano) enters, clad in armour, to castigate them for their cowardice. Lora reminds them of the sorcerer Groma's prediction that their empire could never be overthrown as long as Arindal returned to them, but the crowd points out that there is no indication that Arindal will ever return.

Depressed by this thought, Lora sings a mournful but rather featureless aria, '*O musst du Hoffnung schwinden?*' (Oh, hope, must you disappear?) When a messenger (tenor) enters to announce the imminent return of Morald accompanied by Arindal, Lora's mood immediately changes, and she embarks upon a joyous cabaletta in which she is joined by the chorus. She hurries out, returning with Arindal and Morald who are greeted by the chorus in a happy *allegro*. In a trio, whose lively tempo the mature Wagner could with advantage have emulated more frequently than h : did, Lora and Morald look forward to a happy future together once victory (ver the enemy has been achieved, while Arindal bemoans his separation fron Ada and the wretched condition of his country. The trio, especially Lora' part in it, is decidedly Beethovenian. The soprano's vocal line soars to a high C in her penultimate bar.

When everyone has left, Gernot and Gunther enter, discussing the strange events of the morning in drab and heavy-handed recitative. Gernot attempts to discover from Gunther whether his beloved Drolla (Lora's maid) has been faithful to him throughout his years of absence, and whether she is still young and pretty. But Gunther suggests that Gernot should ask the lady these questions himself, for he sees her approaching them. Gunther departs, and Gernot and Drolla (soprano) embark upon a comic duet in which, after they have expressed their joy at seeing each other again, Gernot boasts of his romantic conquests among the maidens in Ada's castle, while Drolla responds by attempting to make him jealous with stories of the many knights who have courted her. Finally, they both confess they have been lying, and that each has longed only for the other. The reminiscence this time is of Mozart's Papageno and Papagena (*Die Zauberflöte*), or his Blondchen and Pedrillo (*Die Entführung aus dem Serail*). The duet, though it is perhaps too lengthy, is not without charm and, in its scoring, distinct originality.

Gernot and Drolla depart, and Ada enters with Farzana and Zemina, her two companions, who urge her to renounce her mortal lover. The choice, Farzana points out to the Fairy Queen, is between protracted death and eternal life. Farzana and Zemina abruptly disappear, and Ada is left alone to contemplate her desperate situation in a weighty recitative ('*Weh' mir*': Alas, for me) and *allegro* aria ('*Ich haufe selbst die Schrecken an*': I myself heap these terrors upon him). The latter is a dramatic scena which, though its shape may be somewhat unwieldy, is extraordinarily impressive. The influence of Beethoven, and in particular of the great '*Abscheulicher!*' scena of Leonore in *Fidelio*, is still strongly in evidence, and the phrase from *Die Feen's* Act I that was later to appear in '*Dich, teure Halle*' (*Tannhäuser*) is rather overused, but there is no denying the effectiveness of this, the most extended solo number in the score.

At the conclusion of her aria, Ada departs, and the huge, unsatisfactory, complicated rather than complex finale of Act II is launched with a portentous figure in the orchestra, leading to a call on the horns which heralds the arrival of Arindal, Morald, Gunther, Gernot, Lora, Drolla, and a chorus of citizens and warriors. Morald leads the warriors off to do battle with the invaders, but Lora is surprised when her brother Arindal hesitates to accompany them. Suddenly, Ada makes one of her unexpected appearances. Confronting Arindal, she conjures up their two small children, who rush into Arindal's arms. When he exclaims that he will never be parted from them again, Ada causes a fiery abyss to appear, into which she throws the children. The abyss immediately disappears. All are aghast, but to Arindal's horrified questions Ada replies only that he must remain steadfast. The ensemble in which everyone exclaims at the beauty of the children is charmingly sentimental; the melodramatic outburst which follows verges on the risible, though it also displays a certain rough power.

Fugitives from the battle raging outside the city walls now appear, announcing the imminent defeat of Tramond's army. Arindal turns to Ada, asking for comfort, but she tells him that she has come not to console but to torment him. Lora wonders what can have happened to the additional troops which a Tramond general, Harald, had gone to a neighbouring country to raise. More fugitives arrive, with the news that Morald, who had been leading the army, has disappeared and must have been either captured or slain. Harald (bass) now arrives, but without any troops, for they had been attacked by a superior army, led by a woman who, when she had scattered Harald's soldiers, told him she was Ada. Harald now recognizes her, and confirms her identity. Convinced that his wife is an evil sorceress, Arindal curses her. Harald's music is dull, and Wagner unfortunately fails to rise to the challenge of Arindal's curse.

As soon as the curse is uttered, Zemina and Farzana miraculously reappear, announcing to Ada that the bond with Arindal has now been broken and that she is returned to the immortal fairy world The damage having been done, Ada is now free to reveal to Arindal that, by cursing her, he has ensured their eternal separation. She explains her half-fairy, half-mortal parentage, and confesses that Arindal had been put to a cruel test by the Fairy King. He was to remain in ignorance of his wife's name and status for eight years, and then on the last day to be subjected by her to such torments that it would be impossible for him not to be tricked into cursing her.

Ada goes on to reveal that she has really been acting in the best interests of Arindal and his country. The warriors she had slain were not friends but enemy troops with whom Harald had sought to conspire. Harald is forthwith seized and led away, as Ada continues to provide satisfactory answers to Arindal's questions. Was Morald not killed? No, he is even now defeating the enemy. 'But the murder of my children condemns you,' cries Arindal, at which both children reappear from nowhere and rush into their father's arms. A magnificent destiny awaits the children, Ada tells Arindal. It is only she who will suffer endless misery.

Trumpets announce the return of the triumphant army led by Morald, and the act ends with a chorus of jubilation for all but Ada and Arindal as she tells him that, as punishment, she will that day be turned to stone. The scene darkens, Ada sinks out of sight with Zemina and Farzana amid thunder and lightning, and the curtain falls. The general effect throughout the Act II finale has been of a botched shot at something that Wagner was later to achieve superbly in *Lohengrin*.

The first scene of Act III is set in a great hall of the royal palace of Tramond. The curtain rises on a festive scene, with Morald and Lora on the throne, and Drolla, Gernot and Gunther near them. A chorus of gaily dressed citizens sings a hymn of victory and peace, greeting Morald and Lora as King and Queen. In a passage of leaden and undramatic recitative, Morald bids them cease their celebrations. His heart is heavy, he tells the assembled company, for Arindal, after handing the throne over to him and to Lora, has lost his reason. When the chorus resumes, it is with an *adagio* prayer, in which Morald, Lora and the others join, that the curse of madness be lifted from Arindal.

Everyone leaves, slowly and sadly, and for a few moments the stage is empty. Then the voice of Arindal is heard calling from the distance, and the young prince enters, deranged. He imagines he is hunting a deer which, when

21

he shoots it, turns into Ada. Exhausted he falls, unconscious, by the steps to the throne. This mad scene for Arindal is musically disappointing and dramatically ineffective: Wagner has not yet acquired the experience and wisdom to be able to depict madness convincingly.

Ada's voice calls as though from a great distance. She has been turned into stone, and implores Arindal to hasten to her side and free her. From another direction, the voice of the sorcerer Groma exhorts Arindal to rescue Ada. A shield, a sword and a lyre suddenly appear by the young prince's side, and Groma's voice announces that with their aid Arindal can achieve his highest goal. The fairies Farzana and Zemina now enter. In a rather clumsily constructed trio ('*Auf! Auf! Auf!*': Up! Up! Up!) they awaken Arindal and agree to accompany him to Ada. They are aware that their expedition will lead to Arindal's death, but it will also free Ada, which is their only concern. At the conclusion of the trio, all three sink out of sight, but not before Arindal has remembered to take shield, sword and lyre with him.

The second scene of Act III comprises the finale of the opera, a musical segment lasting over twenty minutes in performance, and incorporating a pantomime-like transformation scene towards the end. The curtain rises on what the libretto describes as 'a frightening cavern in an underground kingdom, inhabited by spirits with hideous features'. Descending scales on the trombones above an urgent tremolo in the strings introduce an awkwardly written, melodramatic but mercifully brief chorus, in which the spirits sing of their duty to guard the 'dark and dreadful door which protects this cavern'. When Farzana and Zemina enter, leading Arindal, their utterance is punctuated by threatening growls from the chorus. The two fairies encourage Arindal to fight the hideous spirits, which he dutifully proceeds to do, although, as he points out, he is greatly outnumbered. He is on the point of collapse when the voice of Groma is heard reminding him to use his shield. Arindal holds the shield up before him, and the spirits instantly disappear.

Somewhat inconsistently, Zemina and Farzana are displeased that Arindal has dispelled the guardians of the portal so easily. In a brief trio, they assure each other that Arindal will not triumph any further, while he gives thanks to Groma for his timely assistance. The voices of Groma's benign spirits are now heard encouraging Arindal in a few graceful phrases as the scene miraculously changes to another part of the subterranean realm. A chorus of men of bronze in close formation bars the way, asking in threatening monotones what the stranger wants. Zemina issues a challenge on behalf of Arindal, who again begins to do battle. Although he holds the shield before him, however, he is soon forced to yield. Groma's voice comes in on cue, this time with the words '*Das Schwert!*' (The sword!). Thus reminded, Arindal draws his sword, and the men of bronze are defeated.

After another brief trio, followed again by encouragement from the voices of Groma's spirits, Wagner damagingly lessens the dramatic momentum momentarily by reverting to his amateurish recitative for a few bars, in which Arindal asks where he is to find his wife, and Zemina draws his attention to a rock which opens up to reveal a magically illuminated grotto within which one can see a stone of human dimensions. 'There, Arindal,' Zemina takes pleasure in informing him, 'your wife languishes.'

The recitative gives way to arioso and, by the time the malicious spirits have told Arindal that he can free Ada only by breaking the spell by which she is imprisoned, the forward movement of the music has been resumed in a return to the trio. Encouragement is offered for the third time by the voices of Groma's spirits, and the still-invisible sorcerer himself instructs Arindal to pick up the lyre which he had laid aside.

The power of sweet music having been recalled to him, Arindal takes up his lyre. The two fairies mutter that this is Groma's work, as the prince embarks upon a plaintive, almost Schubertian song, accompanying himself on the lyre (the sound of which is provided by the orchestra's harp). In his song, Arindal summons up his deepest feelings of love and desire, imploring the stone to restore his wife to him. As he sings and plays, the stone gradually transforms itself into Ada, who sinks joyfully into Arindal's arms. 'No power can take me from you now,' she exclaims in an ecstatic phrase, as Farzana and Zemina turn away, horrified.

The scene is transformed into a magnificent fairy palace, high in the clouds. Seated on a throne, surrounded by a chorus of fairies and spirits, the Fairy King (bass) informs Arindal that Ada will remain immortal and that he, Arindal, has achieved immortal status as well, by the immense power of his love for her. Arindal confirms that he has renounced his earthly kingdom in favour of Morald and Lora, who have entered together with Gunther, Gernot and Drolla, Ada leads her husband to the fairy throne and, in a brisk and brief final chorus, all join in celebrating Arindal's immortality.

ALTHOUGH its third act is decidedly inferior to the earlier two, there is much to enjoy in *Die Feen*, especially if one thinks of it not as early and immature Wagner but as a typical German romantic opera of its time. Its libretto, nonsensical though much of it may be, is no worse than several which Schubert deigned to set, and its music, though oddly lacking in the kind of dramatic impulse which Wagner's exact contemporary, the young Verdi, displayed from the very beginning in his first opera, *Oberto* (1839), nevertheless compares favourably with that of most other German operas written in the early 1830s by composers such as Kreutzer and Spohr. Had *Die Feen* managed to reach the stage at the time when it was written, in 1833, it might even have been able to compete successfully with such operas by the popular and prolific Marschner (its composer's chief model) as *Der Vampyr* (1828), *Der Templer und die Jüdin* (1829), *Des Faulkners Braut* (1832) and *Hans Heiling* (1833).

The occasional adumbrations, both dramatic and musical, of aspects of *Lohengrin* and other works of the mature Wagner that are to be discerned in *Die Feen* make the opera fascinating to the dedicated Wagnerian. Its arias are for the most part conventional, and its ensembles contain many passages that are no more than pedestrian; but occasionally something of the fresh breeze of *Der fliegende Holländer* blows through the choruses, and in the role of Gernot there is even the germ of a characterization which was to reach its culmination in Kurwenal in *Tristan und Isolde*. The opera's libretto may be beyond repair, despite the crypto-Jungian examination it has undergone at the hands of some twentieth-century Wagner commentators, but some of the music of *Die Feen* by no means disgraces the composer of *Tannhäuser* and *Lohengrin*.

Oddly, Wagner himself, who was usually not at all backward in promoting his own works, seems to have lost interest in this, his first completed opera, after it became clear that it was not going to be produced in Leipzig as he had hoped. More than thirty years later, in 1865, the composer presented his manuscript score of *Die Feen* to Ludwig II of Bavaria as a Christmas gift, the first of his early operas to be given away. Later still, in 1882, according to Cosima Wagner's diary, he declared that he was opposed to the publication or performance of 'these early works' which, as he put it, 'did not derive from the loftiest of circumstances.'

Therefore, it was not until five years after Wagner's death that *Die Feen* reached the stage, in Munich, on 29 June 1888. Rehearsals were conducted by the young Richard Strauss, but the public performances were entrusted to Franz Fischer. (The distinguished critic and Wagner scholar Ernest Newman was mistaken in identifying the conductor as Hermann Levi, and later writers have tended simply to copy his error.) Though the sucessful Munich production led to other performances, *Die Feen* did not make its way into the standard repertoire, and has yet to be staged in Wagner's own Festival Theatre at Bayreuth.

TWO

Das Liebesverbot

(The Ban on Love)

Grand Comic Opera in Two Acts

Dramatis personae
Friedrich, a German, Viceroy of Sicily during the
    absence of the King   (bass)
Luzio, a Young Nobleman   (tenor)
Claudio, a Young Nobleman   (tenor)
Antonio, Friend of Luzio and Claudio   (tenor)
Angelo, Friend of Luzio and Claudio   (bass)
Isabella, Claudio's Sister, a Novice in the
    Convent of St Elizabeth   (soprano)
Mariana, another Novice   (soprano)
Brighella, Captain of the Watch   (buffo bass)
Danieli, an Innkeeper   (bass)
Dorella, in Danieli's service, formerly
    Isabella's chambermaid   (soprano)
Pontio Pilato, in Danieli's service   (buffo tenor)

LIBRETTO by the composer, based on Shakespeare's *Measure for Measure*

TIME: The sixteenth century

PLACE: Palermo

FIRST PERFORMED at the Stadttheater, Magdeburg, 29 March 1836, with
Karoline Pollert (Isabella), Traugott Krug (Friedrich), Herr Freimüller
(Luzio), and Herr Schreiber (Claudio), conducted by the composer.

I

IT was while he still had hopes that *Die Feen* would be staged by the opera company in Leipzig that the young Wagner began to turn his thoughts toward the composition of another opera, but this time in the Italian rather than the German manner. Almost before he had completed *Die Feen*, he had begun to be disillusioned with the prevailing German style of Gothic romanticism. During his year at Würzburg, he had come to know some of the more recent Italian operas in the company's repertoire and, although throughout his life he affected to despise the simpler orchestration and the melodic prodigality of the Italian composers, it was clear to him that the Italian operatic style was aesthetically superior to the laboured pedantry of what was being composed in Germany. In March 1834, he attended in Leipzig a performance of Bellini's *I Capuleti ed i Montecchi* (The Capulets and Montagues) in which Wilhelmine Schröder-Devrient, the dramatic soprano whom he greatly admired, sang the role of Romeo. Years later, in his memoirs, he wrote that her performance

> carried everyone by storm. The effect of it was not to be compared with anything that had been witnessed theretofore. To see the daring romantic figure of the youthful lover against a background of such obviously shallow and empty music prompted one, at all events, to meditate doubtfully upon the cause of the great lack of effect in solid German music as it had been applied hitherto to the drama. Without for the moment plunging too deeply into this meditation, I allowed myself to be borne along with the current of my youthful feelings, then roused to ardour, and turned involuntarily to the task of working off all that brooding seriousness which in my earlier years had driven me to such pathetic mysticism.

The practical outcome of this enthusiasm was that Wagner now turned his thoughts towards the composition of an opera in what he considered to be the Italian style. With his friend Theodor Apel, the son of the poet August Apel, he spent a holiday in Bohemia in May. The two young men drove about the country in their carriage, seeing all there was to be seen, drinking a great deal, and indulging in fierce theoretical arguments. In Prague, Wagner introduced his friend to the Pachta household and its nubile daughters, and seems to have been in high spirits throughout the whole of his stay in the city. His escapades included climbing along the second-floor window ledge of his hotel in his underwear, and leading a party of drunken revellers in a noisy rendition of the forbidden revolutionary 'Marseillaise' in the middle of the night.

One morning in Teplitz, however, the young composer took time off from larking about to do a little work: he sketched a draft of the libretto for his next opera. Perhaps Bellini's *Romeo and Juliet* opera had set him thinking of Shakespeare (though Shakespeare's *Romeo and Juliet* was not the principal

26

source of *I Capuleti ed I Montecchi*), for the play on which Wagner loosely based his libretto was *Measure for Measure*.

On his return home to Leipzig, the twenty-one-year-old Wagner found that, on the recommendation of the chief conductor there, he had been offered a job as conductor at the theatre in Magdeburg, a small town on the Elbe. He joined the Magdeburg company at Lauchstädt, a spa where operas and plays were performed during the summer, and made his debut conducting what must have been a dreadful performance of Mozart's *Don Giovanni*, with poor singers and an inadequate orchestra which had never rehearsed the opera. Wagner had been so little impressed by the slothful manager of the company that he had intended to reject the engagement and return immediately to Leipzig. It was only when he met, at his lodging house, the company's leading actress, Minna Planer, a beautiful young woman who was three years his senior, that he decided to stay. Before long, he and Minna had become lovers.

As was usual in small German towns, the drama and opera companies were integrated into one unit, sharing a theatre, with operas and operettas alternating in the repertoire with plays. After he had steered *Don Giovanni* to a more or less successful conclusion, Wagner found himself in charge of the music for Nestroy's Viennese farce, *Lumpacivagabundus*. 'The fact that I submitted without bitterness and even with some cheerfulness to this unworthy use of my musical talent', he wrote in *My Life*,

> was due less to my taste being at this period in its salad days than to my intercourse with Minna Planer, who was employed in that magic trifle as the Amorous Fairy. Indeed, in the midst of this dust-cloud of frivolity and vulgarity, she always seemed very much like a fairy, the reasons for whose descent into this giddy whirl, which indeed seemed neither to carry her away nor even to affect her, remained an absolute mystery. For while I could discover nothing in the opera singers other than the familiar stage caricatures and grimaces, this fair actress differed wholly from those around her in her unaffected soberness and dainty modesty, as also in the absence of all theatrical pretence and stiltedness.

As he rapidly gained experience during the winter months in Magdeburg, Wagner began to acquire a local reputation as a reliable conductor. Unfortunately, he also acquired a reputation for extravagance, loose living, and reluctance to pay his debts. Before long he was being pressed by a large number of tradesmen, to whom he referred contemptuously as a 'cursed rabble of Jews'. He had one hope of satisfying his creditors: with the proceeds of a concert he was allowed to give for his own benefit. He persuaded the famous Wilhelmine Schröder-Devrient to appear, but the concert turned out to be a fiasco. Refusing to believe that the distinguished soprano was really likely to sing at a concert for the benefit of the disreputable young Wagner, and suspecting that they were being made the victims of a hoax, the citizens of Magdeburg stayed away. Madame Schröder-Devrient sang to a sparse audience, and Wagner fled to Leipzig.

After a summer of unemployment at home, the young conductor returned to Magdeburg in the autumn of 1835 and resumed his relationship with Minna. He also continued to work on his Shakespeare-based opera, *Das Liebesverbot* (The Ban on Love). Wagner completed his score by the beginning of the new year, 1836, and the Magdeburg management agreed to allow him to stage his opera at the end of the winter season, as his benefit performance. Because of the expense involved in mounting the work, an arrangement was arrived at whereby the management would take the entire proceeds of the first performance, the second performance constituting the composer's benefit. When the police took exception to the title of the opera as being too frivolous for a work to be performed in the week before Easter, Wagner retitled it *Die Novize von Palermo* (The Novice of Palermo).

The composer left, in his memoirs, the following account of what was obviously a disaster:

I did not consider it altogether unsatisfactory that the time for the rehearsals was postponed until the very end of the season, for it was reasonable to suppose that our company, which was often greeted with unusual applause, would receive special attention and favour from the public during its concluding performances. Unfortunately, however, contrary to our expectations, we never reached the proper close of this season, which had been fixed for the end of April; for already in March, owing to irregularity in the payment of salaries, the most popular members of the company, having found better employment elsewhere, tendered their resignations to the management. The director, who was unable to raise the necessary cash, had to bow to the inevitable.

Now, indeed, my spirits sank, for it seemed more than doubtful whether my *Liebesverbot* would ever be produced at all. I owed it entirely to the warm affection felt for me personally by all members of the opera company, that the singers consented not only to remain until the end of March, but also to undertake the task of studying and rehearsing my opera, a task which, considering the very limited time, promised to be extremely arduous . . . we had but ten days before us. And since we were concerned not with a light comedy or farce, but with a grand opera, and one which, in spite of the trivial character of its music, contained numerous and powerful concerted passages, the undertaking might have been regarded almost as foolhardy . . .

[At the first performance] the singers, especially the men, were so extraordinarily uncertain that from beginning to end their embarrassment crippled the effectiveness of every one of their parts. Freimüller, the tenor, whose memory was most defective, sought to patch up the lively and emotional character of his imperfectly learned role of the madcap Luzio by means of pieces of routine business learned in *Fra Diavolo* and *Zampa*, and especially by the aid of an enormously thick, brightly coloured and fluttering plume of feathers. Consequently, as the management failed to have the libretto printed in time, it was impossible to blame the public for not being able to understand the main outline of the story, as they had only the sung words to guide them.

With the exception of a few passages performed by the female singers, which were favourably received, the whole performance, which I had fashioned to depend largely upon bold, energetic action and speech, remained but a musical shadow-play, to which the orchestra contributed its own inexplicable effusions, sometimes with exaggerated noise. . . .

Feeling sure that my opera had made no impression, and had left the public completely undecided about its merits, I reckoned that, in view of [its second performance and the composer's benefit] being the opera company's farewell, we should have satisfactory, not to say large, takings. Consequently, I did not hesitate to charge full prices for admittance. I cannot rightly judge whether, up to the commencement of the overture, any people had taken their places in the auditorium, but at about a quarter of an hour before the time we were due to begin I could see only Madame Gottschalk [a Jewish money-lender who had befriended Wagner] and her husband, and, curiously enough, a Polish Jew in full dress, seated in the stalls.

Despite this, I was still hoping for an increase in the audience, when suddenly the most incredible commotion occurred behind the scenes. Herr Pollert, the husband of my prima donna who was singing the role of Isabella, was assaulting Schreiber, the very young and handsome second tenor who was taking the role of Claudio, and against whom the injured husband had for some time been nursing a secret rancour born of jealousy. It appeared that the soprano's husband, who had surveyed the theatre from behind the drop-scene with me, had satisfied himself as to the size of the audience, and had decided that the longed-for hour was at hand when, without damaging the operatic enterprise, he could wreak vengeance on his wife's lover.

Schreiber was so severely injured by him that the unfortunate fellow had to seek refuge in his dressing-room, his face covered with blood. When Isabella was told of this, she rushed despairingly to her raging spouse, only to be so soundly cuffed by him that she went into hysterics. The confusion that ensued amongst the company soon knew no bounds. They took sides in the quarrel, and it turned into a general fight as everybody seemed to regard this unhappy evening as particularly favourable for the paying off of any old scores and supposed insults.

It was clear that the soprano and tenor suffering from the effects of Herr Pollert's conjugal resentment were unfit to appear that evening. The manager had to go before the drop-scene to inform the small and oddly assorted audience gathered in the theatre that, owing to unforeseen circumstances, the performance would not take place. This was the end of my career as conductor and composer in Magdeburg, which to begin with had seemed so full of promise, and which had been begun at the cost of considerable sacrifice. The serenity of art now gave way completely to the stern realities of life.

II

SHAKESPEARE'S comedy, *Measure for Measure*, written around 1604, is set in a mythical Vienna. After leaving Angelo as his deputy to enforce the city's laws, which have for some time been ignored, Duke Vincentio purports to leave Vienna, but actually remains, disguised as a friar, to observe what happens. Angelo revives an old statute against fornication, and sentences Claudio to death for having seduced Juliet. When Claudio's sister, Isabella, a novice in a nunnery, pleads for her brother's life, her beauty stirs Angelo's repressed passions. He offers to spare Claudio's life if she will yield herself to him, an offer which Isabella indignantly rejects.

Although he at first approves of his sister's attitude, Claudio weakens as the thought of his approaching death weighs more heavily upon him, and begs her to comply. Overhearing their conversation, Vincentio, still disguised as a monk, proposes that Isabella should pretend to agree to Angelo's proposal. In her place, however, he intends to send Mariana, who had been betrothed to Angelo but whom he had spurned after the loss of her dowry. The plan is successful, Vincentio returns as Duke, castigates Angelo for his hypocrisy, orders him to marry Mariana and makes it clear that he himself intends to marry Isabella.

The main source of Shakespeare's play is George Whetstone's *Promos and Cassandra*, which in turn is based on an Italian tale, related by Giovanni Battista Giraldi in his *Hecatommithi*, published in Sicily in 1565. Wagner removes the story from Vienna to Sicily, changing Angelo into Friedrich, a German, and reducing Shakespeare's ironic comedy to the level of rumbustious farce. What follows below is a detailed synopsis of the opera's plot as provided by the composer in *My Life*:

An unnamed king of Sicily leaves his country for a journey to Naples, and hands over to the Regent he has appointed—whom I have called Friedrich

30

in order to make him appear as German as possible—full authority to exercise all the royal power in order to effect a complete reform in the social habits of his capital city, which had provoked the indignation of the Council.

At the opening of the play we see the servants of the public authority, busily employed either in shutting up or in pulling down the houses of popular amusement in a suburb of Palermo, and in carrying off the inmates, including hosts and servants, as prisoners. The populace oppose this first step, and much scuffling ensues. In the thickest of the throng, the Captain of the Watch, Brighella, after a preliminary roll of drums for silence, reads out the Regent's proclamation, according to which the acts just performed are declared to be directed towards establishing a higher moral tone in the manners and customs of the people. A general outburst of scorn and a mocking chorus meet this announcement.

Luzio, a high-spirited young nobleman, seems inclined to thrust himself forward as leader of the mob, and immediately finds an occasion for playing a more active role in the cause of the oppressed people on seeing his friend Claudio being led away to prison. From his friend, Luzio learns that, in pursuance of some musty old law unearthed by Friedrich, Claudio is to suffer the penalty of death for a certain amorous escapade in which he is involved. His sweetheart, marriage with whom had been prevented by the enmity of their parents, has borne him a child. Friedrich's puritanical zeal joins cause with the parents' hatred.

Claudio fears the worst, and sees no way of escape except through mercy, provided his sister Isabella may be able, by her entreaties, to melt the Regent's hard heart. Claudio implores his friend at once to seek out Isabella in the Convent of the Sisters of St Elizabeth, which she has recently entered as a novice. There, between the quiet walls of the convent, we first meet this sister, in confidential intercourse with her friend Mariana, also a novice.

Mariana reveals to her friend, from whom she has long been parted, the unhappy fate which has brought her to the convent. Under vows of eternal fidelity she had been persuaded to a secret relationship with a man of high rank. But finally, when in extreme need she found herself not only forsaken, but threatened by her betrayer, she discovered him to be the most powerful man in the realm, none other than the Regent himself.

Isabella gives vent to her indignation in impassioned words. She is more determined now than ever to retreat from a world in which so vile a crime can go unpunished. When Luzio now brings her tidings of her own brother's fate, her disgust at Claudio's conduct is replaced by scorn for the villainy of the hypocritical Regent, who presumes so cruelly to punish the comparatively venial offence of her brother, which at least was not stained by treachery.

31

Her violent outburst imprudently reveals Isabella to Luzio in a seductive aspect. Smitten with sudden love, he urges her to quit the convent for ever and to accept his hand. She contrives to check his boldness, but resolves at once to avail herself of his escort to the Regent's court of justice. Here the trial scene is prepared, and I introduce it by a burlesque hearing of several persons charged by the Captain of the Watch with offences against morality.

The seriousness of the situation becomes more marked when the solemn figure of Friedrich strides through the unruly crowd, commanding silence, and he himself undertakes the hearing of Claudio's case in the severest manner possible. This implacable judge is already on the point of pronouncing sentence when Isabella enters, requesting, before them all, a private interview with the Regent. In this interview she behaves with noble moderation towards the dreaded, yet despised man before her, and appeals at first only to his mildness and mercy. His interruptions merely serve to stimulate her ardour. She speaks of her brother's offence in melting accents, and implores forgiveness for so human and by no means unpardonable a crime.

Seeing the effect of her moving appeal, she continues with increasing ardour to plead with the judge's hard and unresponsive heart, which can certainly not have remained untouched by sentiments such as those which had actuated her brother, and she calls upon his memory of these to support her desperate plea for pity. At last the ice of his heart is broken. Friedrich, deeply stirred by Isabella's beauty, can no longer contain himself, and promises to grant her petition at the price of her own love.

Scarcely has she become aware of the unexpected effect of her words when, filled with indignation at such incredible villainy, she cries to the people through doors and windows to come in, that she may unmask the hypocrite before the world. The crowd is already rushing tumultuously into the hall of judgement when, by a few significant hints, Friedrich, with frantic energy, succeeds in making Isabella realize the impossibility of her plan. He would simply deny her charge, boldly pretend that his offer was made merely to test her, and would doubtless be readily believed as soon as it became only a question of rebutting a charge of lightly making love to her.

Isabella, ashamed and confounded, recognizes the madness of her first step, and gnashes her teeth in silent despair. As Friedrich once more announces his stern resolve to the people, and pronounces sentence on the prisoner, it suddenly occurs to Isabella, spurred by the painful recollection of Mariana's fate, that what she has failed to procure by open means she might possibly obtain by craft. This thought suffices to dispel her sorrow, and to fill her with the utmost gaiety.

Turning to her sorrowing brother, her agitated friends, and the perplexed crowd, she assures them all that she is ready to provide them with the most amusing of adventures. She declares that the carnival festivities, which the Regent has just strictly forbidden, are to be celebrated this year with the utmost licence. She assures them that the dreaded ruler only pretends to be so cruel, in order the more pleasantly to astonish them by himself taking a merry part in all that he has just forbidden.

Everyone believes that Isabella has gone mad, and Friedrich in particular reproves her incomprehensible folly with passionate severity. But a few words on her part suffice to transport the Regent himself with ecstasy, for in a whisper she promises to grant his desire, and swears that on the following night she will send him such a message as shall ensure his happiness. And so ends the first act in a whirl of excitement.

We learn the nature of the heroine's hastily formed plan at the beginning of the second act, in which she visits her brother in his cell, with the object of discovering whether he is worthy of rescue. She reveals Friedrich's shameful proposal to him, and asks if he would wish to save his life at the price of his sister's dishonour. Claudio expresses his fury and fervently declares his readiness to die; whereupon, bidding farewell to his sister, at least for this life, he makes her the bearer of the most tender messages to the dear girl whom he leaves behind.

After this, sinking into a softer mood, the unhappy man declines from a state of melancholy to one of weakness. Isabella, who had already determined to inform him of his rescue, hesitates in dismay when she sees him fall in this way from the heights of noble enthusiasm to a muttered confession of a love of life still as strong as ever, and even to a stammering query as to whether the suggested price of his salvation is altogether impossible.

Disgusted, Isabella springs to her feet, thrusts the unworthy man from her, and declares that to the shame of his death he has further added her most hearty contempt. After having handed him over again to his gaoler, her mood once more changes swiftly to one of wanton gaiety. True, she resolves to punish the waverer by leaving him for a time in uncertainty as to his fate, but she stands firm by her resolve to rid the world of the abominable seducer who dared to dictate laws to his fellow-men.

Isabella asks Mariana to take her place at the nocturnal rendezvous, at which Friedrich so treacherously expected to meet her (Isabella), and sends Friedrich an invitation to this meeting. In order to entangle Friedrich more deeply in ruin, she stipulates that he must come disguised and masked, and fixes the rendezvous in one of those pleasure resorts which he has just suppressed. To the irresponsible Luzio, whom she also desires to punish for his saucy suggestion to a novice, she relates the story of Friedrich's proposal, and her pretended intention of complying, from sheer necessity, with his desires. This she does in a fashion so incredibly light-hearted that the otherwise frivolous man, first dumb with amazement, ultimately yields to a fit of desperate rage.

Luzio swears that, even if the noble maiden herself can endure such shame, he will himself strive by every means in his power to avert it, and would prefer to set all Palermo on fire and in tumult rather than allow such a thing to happen. And, indeed, he arranges everything in such a manner that on the appointed evening all his friends and acquaintances assemble at the end of the Corso, as though for the opening of the prohibited carnival procession. At nightfall, as things are beginning to grow wild and merry, Luzio appears, and sings an extravagant carnival song, with the refrain 'Who joins us not in frolic jest/Shall have a dagger in his breast,' by means of which he seeks to stir the crowd to bloody rebellion.

When a band of watchmen approaches, under Brighella's leadership, to scatter the merry throng, the mutinous project seems on the point of being accomplished. But for the present Luzio prefers to yield, and to scatter his forces about the neighbourhood, as he must first of all win the real leader of their enterprise. Isabella had revealed to him that it was on this spot that her pretended meeting with the Regent would take place. For the Regent, therefore, Luzio lies in wait. Recognizing him in an elaborate disguise, he blocks his way and, as Friedrich violently breaks loose, is on the point of following him with shouts and drawn sword when, on a signal from Isabella who is hidden among some bushes, he is himself stopped and led away.

Isabella then advances, rejoicing in the thought of having restored the betrayed Mariana to her faithless spouse. Believing that she holds in her hand the promised pardon for her brother, she is just on the point of abandoning all thought of further vengeance when, breaking the seal, to her intense horror she recognizes by the light of a torch that the paper contains yet a still more severe order of execution which, owing to her desire not to disclose to her brother the fact of his pardon, a mere chance had now delivered into her hand, through the agency of the bribed gaoler. After a hard fight with the tempestuous passion of love, and recognizing his helplessness against the enemy of his peace, Friedrich has in fact already resolved to face his ruin, even though as a criminal, yet still as a man of honour. An hour on Isabella's breast, and then his own death by the same law whose implacable severity shall also claim Claudio's life.

Isabella, perceiving in this conduct only a further proof of the hypocrite's villainy, breaks out once more into a tempest of agonized despair. Upon her cry for immediate revolt against the unscrupulous tyrant, the people collect together and form a motley and passionate crowd. Luzio, who also returns, counsels the people with stinging bitterness to pay no heed to the woman's fury. He points out that she is only tricking them, as she has already tricked him, for he still believes in her shameless infidelity. Fresh confusion. Increased despair of Isabella. Suddenly from the background comes the absurd cry of Brighella for help, who, himself suffering from the pangs of jealousy, has by mistake arrested the masked Regent, and thus led to the latter's discovery.

Friedrich is recognized, and Mariana, trembling on his breast, is also unmasked. Amazement, indignation! Cries of joy burst forth all round, the necessary explanations are quickly given, and Friedrich sullenly demands to be set before the judgement-seat of the returning King. Claudio, released from prison by the jubilant populace, informs him that the sentence of death for crimes of love is not intended for all times.

Messengers arrive to announce the unexpected arrival in the harbour of the King. It is resolved to march in full masked procession to meet their beloved ruler, and joyously to pay him homage, all being convinced that he will heartily rejoice to see how ill the gloomy puritanism of Germany is suited to his hot-blooded Sicily. Of him it is said, 'Your merry festals please him more/Than gloomy laws or legal lore.' Friedrich, with his freshly affianced wife, Mariana, must lead the procession, followed by Luzio and the novice, who is for ever lost to the convent.

It is clear even from Wagner's synopsis of his own libretto that, although his plot outline was derived from Shakespeare's play, the moral tone of his opera was intended to be completely different, a youthfully impetuous discarding of the shackles of German puritanism, in favour of what Wagner perceived to be a southern Italian licentiousness.

After its single performance on 29 March 1836 in Magdeburg, *Das Liebesverbot* appears not to have been staged again until 1923, when it was produced in Munich. A Berlin production followed in 1933, strongly cast with Käthe Heidersbach, Marcel Wittrisch, Theodor Scheidl and Martin Abendroth, and there were other German performances during the thirties. The opera was seen in London for the first time on 15 February 1965, in a University College student production, conducted by George Badacsonyi. It reached Bayreuth (though not, of course, the Festival Theatre) when it was staged in the Stadthalle on 18 August 1972, by students at an International Youth Festival.

Das Liebesverbot has yet to be fully staged in the USA, though excerpts were performed by students of the Metropolitan Opera Studio in 1965. An almost complete concert performance of the score was given at the Waterloo Music Festival, in Waterloo Village, New Jersey, on 9 July 1983, conducted by Gerard Schwarz.

III

IN later life, Wagner professed to find most of *Das Liebesverbot* 'horrible', possibly because its models had been Italian instead of German. The lively Overture is boisterously Italianate, rather like Rossini but heavier, with a great deal of bustle and high-spirited noise. At its conclusion, the curtain rises on a suburban fairground in Palermo, with a number of pleasure booths and, in the foreground, a tavern run by one Danieli (bass). The entire scene is in an uproar, with police destroying the booths and kiosks, tearing down the signs, and destroying all the furniture and crockery. A crowd of citizens attempts to stop the police, and fighting breaks out.

As they are ejected from Danieli's tavern, the young nobleman Luzio (tenor) and his friends Antonio (tenor) and Angelo (bass) are torn between amusement and indignation. When Danieli himself, and his employees, the oddly named Pontio Pilato (Pontius Pilate: tenor) and Dorella (soprano), are brought out from the tavern under arrest by the Captain of the Watch, Brighella (bass), and his men, Dorella appeals to her ex-lover Luzio to help her. Luzio asks Brighella what authority he has for his action, and the Captain of the Watch reads out the Viceroy's proclamation, which is greeted with derisive laughter by the Sicilians, who refer scathingly to the Viceroy, Friedrich, as a 'German fool'.

Until this point, the action has been advanced in a lively chorus with solo vocal lines incorporated for the leading characters, in the manner of a typical Donizetti opera. When Luzio's friend, the young nobleman Claudio (tenor), is brought in under guard as the first person to be sentenced to death under the new laws prohibiting extramarital love-making, the mood of the music quietens somewhat. Claudio's song in which he implores Luzio to visit his (Claudio's) sister, Isabella, in her convent is a tolerable imitation of a graceful Italian cavatina, though its melody is hardly appropriate to the dramatic situation. Following Italian convention, a cabaletta-like conclusion to Claudio's quasi-aria utilizes all the solo singers and the chorus. As Luzio rushes off to visit Isabella, Brighella and his police make their way through the crowd with their prisoners, and the curtain falls. The whole of this opening scene has been musically conventional, although its orchestral conclusion, after the voices have ceased singing, offers Claudio's theme played expressively by the cellos before the full orchestra interrupts with a *fortissimo* flourish.

The second scene is set in a cloister in the convent of St Elizabeth. On one side is the garden of the cloister, and on the other the church. In the middle is a door. As the curtain rises, there is heard in the orchestra Wagner's first use of a theme which he was later to employ in *Tannhäuser* as the motif of Heavenly Grace. To this theme, a chorus of nuns can be heard in the church, singing the words '*Salve Regina coeli*'. The two novices, Isabella and Mariana, enter from the garden and sing a duet ('*Göttlicher Frieden, himmlische Ruh*': Divine peace, heavenly repose) in which they rejoice in the peace and security of life in the convent. In a scene in which passages of melody alternate with recitative, Mariana confesses to her friend that she had sought refuge in the convent because she had been deserted by the man to whom she had been secretly married. When Mariana tells her that the man is none other than Friedrich, now appointed by the King as Viceroy, Isabella denounces him as a hypocrite. The two women resume their tranquil duet, though Isabella's vocal line is now more agitated.

A bell rings at the cloister door, and Mariana slips away while Isabella admits the visitor, who is Luzio. When he identifies himself, Isabella tells him she has heard stories of her brother's dissolute friend, but she listens as Luzio informs her of Claudio's arrest for the crime of having made love to a girl named Julia, whom he now wishes to marry, and of the sentence of death which threatens him under the new law introduced by Friedrich.

In her agitation, Isabella allows her veil to fall, at which Luzio exclaims at her beauty and immediately professes his love for her. Isabella peremptorily and indignantly rejects his proposal, but agrees to leave the convent with him, and to confront Friedrich. This duet scene is lively and, while it is not particularly distinguished musically, it at least mirrors appropriately the state of mind of the two characters: Isabella agitated and Luzio reverting to irresponsible type.

The scene now changes to a hall of justice, with platforms and galleries. Brighella stands at the entrance with a detachment of the watch, whom he orders to their places. As the Viceroy has not yet arrived, Brighella decides to take unto himself the reponsibility of acting as judge. In a not very successful attempt at a comic song, he orders the guards to bring the prisoners in, one at a time. The first is a terrified Pontio Pilato who, mainly because of his unfortunate name, is sentenced to banishment in a scene which has something of the flavour of the exchanges between Osmin and Pedrillo in *Die Entführung aus dem Serail*, though Wagner is unlikely to have known Mozart's opera at this time.

Brighella's next victim is Dorella but, as she is aware that he finds her attractive, she laughs at Brighella, flirts a little, and thoroughly confuses him. Wagner successfully imitates the light comic patter of Italian opera in this quite engaging little scene, which comes to an end only when the other prisoners waiting outside grow impatient and begin to hammer on the door. Despite their impatience, however, their off-stage chorus goes on for rather too long before they finally burst the door open and rush in.

The finale of Act I is launched with a lively ensemble as the crowd storms into the courtroom. The harrassed Brighella is saved only by the sudden arrival of Friedrich (bass) with several officers of state. Friedrich quietens the crowd, and is about to proceed with the trial when a deputation of young noblemen, headed by Antonio, comes forward. Antonio hands Friedrich a petition, begging for the reinstatement of the annual carnival on the ground that the life of Palermo simply could not continue in a world without joy. The chorus of citizens adds its voice to the plea of the young noblemen; but in a stern recitative, punctuated by passages of grim orchestral comment, Friedrich makes it clear that he is determined to lead the populace away from what he describes as their sinful and depraved ways. He had been commissioned by the King to improve the morals of the citizens, and it is his intention to return them to the King in a purified state.

After a hushed response from the crowd, Friedrich orders that the trial continue, and Claudio is brought in. Rejecting Claudio's excuse that he was young and in love, Friedrich summarily sentences both him and the absent Julia to death. As the crowd reacts in horror, Isabella enters with Luzio, and forces her way through to Friedrich. Announcing herself as Claudio's sister, she asks for a private audience with the Viceroy. At first Friedrich refuses her, but when she suggests that he is afraid of a woman, he angrily orders the crowd to leave. A solo clarinet introduces Isabella's aria, '*Kennst du das Leid der Elternlosen?*' (Do you know the suffering of an orphan?), a rather trite *adagio* which fails to affect Friedrich.

As the scene progresses, the musical interest quickens with the drama. Friedrich makes his shocking proposal that he will set Claudio free in exchange for Isabella's favours, and she, horrified at his hypocrisy, rushes to the window and calls the citizens back, determined to expose his villainy. The people rush in, filling the hall and the galleries, and Isabella is about to unmask Friedrich when he warns her that she will not be believed. If she were to accuse him of cruelty, the populace might listen, but if she talks of his lust they will merely laugh at her, and he will have no difficulty in convincing them that he was merely testing her virtue.

Realizing the truth of his words, Isabella remains silent. When the people ask what has happened, she simply waves them back, and they assume that her behaviour is the result of her grief at the fate of her brother. But a sudden idea comes to Isabella, as she thinks of her friend Mariana, betrayed by Friedrich. She decides to accept the Viceroy's proposal, but to send his wife Mariana to him in her place. She gives Friedrich her promise that she will meet him secretly.

The exchanges between Friedrich and Isabella are dull and musically unilluminating, but the ensemble that builds up after Isabella indicates her inability to address the populace is effective. Though Isabella articulates her plan to ensnare Friedrich in phrases reminiscent of Leonore plotting the downfall of Pizarro in Beethoven's *Fidelio*, her subsequent duet with him is clumsily written and unconvincing, and the ensemble which closes the act is far too lengthy for its meagre content.

Act II is preceded by an *andante* orchestral introduction which begins sombrely, the oboe enunciating the theme which Claudio had employed when he urged Luzio to seek Isabella's help. The orchestra's mood inappropriately lightens to a tender wistfulness as the curtain rises on the garden of Claudio's prison. Claudio is discovered alone, contemplating his fate in a graceful arioso. The tempo quickens as Isabella enters, and the scene in which her brother's courage momentarily falters can be made to sound exciting, though Wagner's tunes hardly do justice to the dramatic situation, and his harmonic changes parallel the shifting emotions of the two characters only superficially. This key scene is disappointingly conventional. One cannot help feeling that Donizetti, whose style Wagner is attempting to imitate here, would have written considerably more attractive tunes and injected a greater degree of emotional intensity into them.

Claudio is taken back to his cell while Isabella, left alone in the garden, resorts to recitative to plan her next moves, which involve keeping Claudio in uncertainty as to his fate and instructing Mariana how to regain Friedrich as a husband. The plot is unnecessarily complicated by the arrival in the prison garden of Dorella and, later, Luzio. The dialogue between Isabella and Dorella is conducted in *recitativo secco* which, according to the score, can be spoken if preferred.

When Luzio, who has eyes only for Isabella, arrives, a charming trio ensues which, though it is hardly essential to the action, is one of the more attractive numbers in the opera. A passage of spoken dialogue follows—equally inessential—in which Pontio Pilato, now no longer a prisoner but a gaoler, has an altercation with Luzio. A number of policemen appear in answer to Pontio's call for help, but Luzio knocks him down and escapes over the prison wall. One has the impression that Wagner intended to compose a light-hearted duet at this point, but either did not get round to it or perhaps noticed that his comic opera was already far too long.

The scene changes to a room in Friedrich's palace, where the Viceroy impatiently awaits a message from Isabella, and broods on the fact that his life has been thrown into disorder by her beauty. After the usual deadening recitative, introduced by the orchestra's statement of the motif associated with Friedrich's stern puritanism, his aria, '*Ja, glühend wie des Südens Hauch*' (Yes, warm as a breath of the south), comes as a welcome relief. Rather curiously, the aria's vocal line is marked '*vibrato*' in Wagner's score—a direction which it seems quite unnecessary to give to the average Wagnerian bass.

At the conclusion of Friedrich's aria, Brighella enters with Dorella who delivers to the Viceroy the letter of assignation from Isabella. This encourages Friedrich to indulge in a cabaletta, in the first verse of which he exults in his good fortune, and in the second of which he confirms Claudio's death sentence and accepts that he too must die in punishment for the sin he hopes to commit with Isabella. He leaves, and the scene ends tamely with an exchange of spoken dialogue in which Dorella persuades Brighella to accompany her to the forbidden carnival that evening, disguised as Pierrot to her Columbine.

The opera's finale takes place in the gardens of the city that evening. Danieli has set up a refreshment tent, and among the amusement booths and shrubberies a number of citizens are strolling, most of them in masks or carnival costumes. Angelo, Antonio and Luzio are among the crowd, which is in a merry mood and determined to participate in the carnival despite the Viceroy's ban. As the curtain rises, a lively orchestral *allegro* leads into the opening ensemble, followed by a light-hearted carnival song and dance contributed by Luzio.

When Brighella arrives with his officers of the watch, Luzio advises the revellers to discard their masks and observe the law. They all wander off in various directions, Brighella donning his Pierrot costume before he departs in search of Dorella. Next, Isabella and Mariana enter, wearing identical costumes. From here to the end of the opera, the action follows Wagner's synopsis closely. Friedrich is unmasked, reluctantly accepts that Mariana is his lawful wife, and leads the carnival procession which welcomes back the King. Isabella forsakes the convent for Luzio. Except for a touching little cavatina sung by Mariana ('*Welch' wunderbar erwarten*': What strange awaiting) and a quite lively quartet for Isabella, Dorella, Luzio and Brighella, the remainder of the finale is unexceptional and, again, somewhat too prolonged.

ALTHOUGH, in later life, Wagner was to describe *Das Liebesverbot* as 'atrocious, abominable, nauseating', it is none of these things—though it contains few, if any, traces of Wagner's mature genius. It is a not very successful German imitation of Italian opera buffa. Wagner's flirtation with Italian methods here resulted, musically, in an even less satisfactory work than *Die Feen*, though in some respects *Das Liebesverbot* is a more interesting opera than the earlier one. Its libretto, a travesty of Shakespeare's play, is actually better planned and shaped than some of the libretti of Wagner's mature operas, for which the composer did not have the advantage of a play already in existence whose structure he could utilize.

Musically, *Das Liebesverbot* is shamelessly eclectic, even more so than *Die Feen*. The Marschner influence, though much less strong, is still apparent, but Wagner's fussily uninventive score is more reminiscent of Rossini, Donizetti and Bellini, composers whose operas he had been conducting.

THREE

Rienzi, der Letzte der Tribunen

(Rienzi, the Last of the Tribunes)

Grand Tragic Opera in Five Acts

Dramatic personae
Cola Rienzi, Papal Notary   (tenor)
Irene, his Sister   (soprano)
Stefano Colonna, Roman Patrician   (bass)
Adriano, his Son   (mezzo-soprano)
Paolo Orsini, Roman Patrician   (bass)
Raimondo, Papal Legate   (bass)
Baroncelli, a Roman Citizen   (tenor)
Cecco del Vecchio, a Roman Citizen   (bass)
A Messenger of Peace   (soprano)
A Herald   (tenor)

LIBRETTO by the composer, based on the novel, *Rienzi, the Last of the Roman Tribunes*, by Edward Bulwer-Lytton

TIME: The middle of the fourteenth century

PLACE: Rome

FIRST PERFORMED at the Hoftheater, Dresden, 20 October 1842, with Joseph Tichatschek (Rienzi), Henriette Wust (Irene), Wilhelm Dettmer (Colonna), Wilhelmine Schröder-Devrient (Adriano), and Michael Wächter (Orsini), conducted by Carl Gottlieb Reissiger

I

WAGNER'S time at Magdeburg had ended ignominiously. After the failure of *Das Liebesverbot*, his creditors decided to take action, as a result of which he found a summons nailed to his door. When Minna left to take up an engagement in Königsberg, Wagner departed for Berlin in May 1836, in an attempt to have *Das Liebesverbot* accepted for performance there. By July, however, it was clear to him that he was not going to achieve his object, so he joined Minna in Königsberg, where he had been promised an appointment as conductor as soon as the temporary occupant of the post, Ludwig Schuberth, had left to resume his job in the Livonian (now Latvian) capital city of Riga, where the theatre was undergoing reconstruction. Unfortunately the reopening of the theatre in Riga was delayed, and in any case Schuberth, who was in love with the prima donna of the Königsberg company, was in no hurry to return to his wife in Riga.

Eventually the Königsberg management agreed to set a date, April of the following year, for the start of Wagner's engagement as conductor, on the strength of which Wagner and Minna married on 24 November. When the preacher who married them assured the composer that there was 'an unknown friend' to whom they could turn for help, Wagner envisaged a rich benefactor, but was distinctly depressed when the preacher revealed that the unknown friend's name was Jesus.

The day after the wedding, the composer had to appear at a magistrate's court to answer the claims of his Magdeburg creditors. Before long, his Königsberg creditors began to put pressure upon him as well. The situation in the newly-wed couple's household was not improved when an eleven-year-old child, Natalie, introduced locally as Minna's sister, came to live with them. Wagner was aware that Natalie was, in fact, the illegitimate child of Minna and a Saxon guards officer who had forcibly seduced her when she was fifteen.

After some months Minna, taking Natalie with her, ran away to her parents' home in Dresden, unable to face her husband's way of life which entailed continual hiding from creditors. Wagner, thinking she had eloped with a Königsberg merchant named Dietrich, whom he knew to be interested in her, immediately instituted divorce proceedings, but then as quickly withdrew them. Shortly afterwards, Minna again disappeared, and this time there could be no doubt that Dietrich was involved. Wagner had by now been offered an engagement at the opera house in Riga, a town which, although at that time governed by Russia, as it has been again in recent years, was nevertheless a prosperous Baltic outpost of German culture. He accepted the offer and, while waiting to go to Riga, spent several weeks with his sister Ottilie and her husband Hermann Brockhaus, an authority on Eastern languages.

Having failed to achieve success with either his German or his Italian opera, Wagner had for some time been toying with the idea of attempting to write a French grand opera *à la* Meyerbeer. At his sister's house he read, in German translation, *Rienzi, the Last of the Roman Tribunes*, by the English novelist Edward Bulwer-Lytton, and was so taken with the novel that he immediately began to plan an opera to be based on it. He decided to begin the composition of *Rienzi* as soon as he had settled in at his new post in Riga.

When, in due course, Wagner arrived in Riga, he found that his wife was willing to return to him. In October 1837, Minna and her sister Amalie, a mezzo-soprano, made the journey to Riga. For a time the family was a relatively happy one. Wagner, bored with the light French and Italian operas he was given to conduct, devoted much of his time and energy to the composition of *Rienzi*. That he decided to cast this, his third opera, in the mould of Meyerbeerian grand opera was due rather to opportunism than to admiration of the German–Jewish composer who had conquered Paris. Wagner was impressed as much, if not more, by the huge profits that Meyerbeer's *Les Huguenots* was reputed to be making as by the merits of that opera's score. Setting his sights high, he determined that *Rienzi* would be composed not for Riga but for Paris.

It was not long, however, before the domestic situation in Riga began to deteriorate. First, the sisters began to quarrel, apparently because a young Russian officer fell in love with Amalie, whom he eventually married. During the year in which he was courting her, the two sisters managed to live in the same house without addressing a single word to each other. Then the theatre manager, Holtei, while openly displaying his antipathy to Wagner, began to make unwelcome advances to Minna. Finally, Wagner's old creditors from Magdeburg and Königsberg caught up with him, and demanded justice under Russian law. In addition, Wagner had contracted a number of fresh debts in Riga. At the instigation of his creditors, the composer's passport was confiscated, and to make matters worse he learned that his contract at the theatre would not be renewed. Flight appeared to be the only way out of his difficulties.

At this point, Abraham Möller, an old friend of Wagner's from Königsberg, came to his aid. In July 1839, Möller conveyed Wagner and Minna in his carriage at top speed across the Russian frontier to an East Prussian port. The family pet was now a large Newfoundland dog called Robber, who had also to be squeezed into the carriage. Near the frontier they were forced to wait until sundown, 'and had ample leisure in which to realize that we were in a smugglers' drinking den, which gradually became filled to suffocation point with Polish Jews of most forbidding aspect.' During the night, the fugitives ran across the ditch which stretched the entire length of the frontier, managing to avoid the Cossack guards.

At the Prussian port of Pillau, where the coach overturned and deposited

Wagner on a pile of manure, they boarded a small sailing vessel, the *Thetis*, whose captain agreed to take them to London without passports. The journey should have taken no more than eight days, given the good weather which was reasonably to be expected in summer. But it turned out to be three weeks before the travellers reached London after a singularly adventurous and eventful voyage. Part of Wagner's account of the sea journey is worth quoting for the light it throws on one of his most popular operas, which he was to compose after *Rienzi*:

There was an elderly and peculiarly taciturn sailor named Koske whom we observed carefully, because Robber, who was usually so friendly, had taken an irreconcilable dislike to him. Oddly enough, this fact was to add in some degree to our troubles in the hour of danger. After seven days' sailing, we were no further than Copenhagen where, without leaving the vessel, we seized an opportunity of making our very spare diet on board more bearable by various purchases of food and drink. In good spirits we sailed past the beautiful castle of Elsinore, the sight of which brought me into immediate touch with my youthful impressions of *Hamlet*.

We were sailing all unsuspecting through the Cattegat to the Skagerack when the wind, which had at first been merely unfavourable, and had forced us to a process of weary tacking, changed on the second day to a violent storm. For twenty-four hours we had to struggle against it under disadvantages which were quite new to us. In the captain's painfully narrow cabin, in which one of us was without a proper berth, we were a prey to sea-sickness and endless alarms. Unfortunately, the brandy cask, at which the crew fortified themselves during their strenuous work, was let into a hollow under the seat on which I lay at full length.

Now it happened to be Koske who came most frequently in search of the refreshment which was such a nuisance to me, and this in spite of the fact that on each occasion he had to encounter Robber in mortal combat. The dog flew at him with renewed rage each time he came climbing down the narrow steps. I was thus compelled to make efforts which, in my state of complete exhaustion from sea-sickness, rendered my condition every time more critical. At last, on 27 July, the captain was compelled by the violence of the west wind to seek a harbour on the Norwegian coast. And how relieved I was to behold that far-reaching rocky coast, towards which we were being driven at such speed!

A Norwegian pilot came to meet us in a small boat and, with experienced hand, assumed control of the *Thetis*, whereupon in a very short time I was to have one of the most marvellous and most beautiful impressions of my life. What I had taken to be a continuous line of cliffs turned out on our approach to be a series of separate rocks projecting from the sea. Having sailed past them, we perceived that we were surrounded, not only in front and at the sides, but also at our back, by these reefs, which closed in behind us so near together that they seemed to form a single chain of rocks.

At the same time, the hurricane was so broken by the rocks in our rear that the further we sailed through this ever-changing labyrinth of projecting rocks, the calmer the sea became, until at last the vessel's progress was perfectly smooth and quiet as we entered one of those long sea-roads running through a giant ravine—for such the Norwegian fjords appeared to me. A feeling of indescribable content came over me when the enormous granite walls echoed the hail of the crew as they cast anchor and furled the sails. The sharp rhythm of this call clung to me like an omen of good cheer, and shaped itself presently into the theme of the seamen's song in my *Flying Dutchman.*

In mid-August, the *Thetis* reached the mouth of the Thames. When Richard and Minna finally arrived in London with Robber, they took lodgings at the King's Arms boarding-house in Old Compton Street, Soho, for a week. Wagner tried to contact Sir George Smart, conductor of the Philharmonic Society, to whom he had previously sent an Overture, *Rule, Britannia*, which he had composed in Königsberg. Smart was out of town, so Wagner next went to the House of Commons in an attempt to meet Bulwer-Lytton, the author of *Rienzi* and Member of Parliament for Lincoln:

My total ignorance of the English language stood me in good stead here, and I was treated with unexpected consideration; for, as none of the lower officials in that vast building could make out what I wanted, I was sent, step by step, to one high dignitary after the other, until at last I was introduced, as an entirely unintelligible individual, to a distinguished-looking man, who came out of a large hall as we passed. (Minna was with me all the time, but Robber had been left behind at the King's Arms.) He asked me very civilly, in French, what I wanted, and seemed favourably impressed when I enquired for the celebrated author. He was obliged to tell me, however, that he was not in London.

I went on to ask whether I could not be admitted to a debate, but was told that, in consequence of the old Houses of Parliament having been burnt down, they were using temporary premises where the space was so limited that only a few favoured visitors could procure cards of admittance. But on my pressing more urgently, he relented, and shortly afterwards opened a door leading direct into the strangers' seats in the House of Lords. It seemed reasonable to conclude from this that our friend was a Lord in person.

I was immensely interested to see and hear the Premier, Lord Melbourne, and Brougham (who seemed to me to take a very active part in the proceedings, prompting Melbourne several times, as I thought), and the Duke of Wellington, who looked so comfortable in his grey beaver hat, with his hands diving deep into his trousers pockets, and who made his speech in so conversational a tone that I lost my feeling of excessive awe. He had a curious way, too, of underlining his points of special emphasis by shaking his whole body. I was also much interested in Lord Lyndhurst, Brougham's particular enemy, and was amazed to see Brougham go across several times to sit down coolly beside him, apparently with a view to prompting even his opponent.

The matter in hand was, as I learned afterwards from the newspapers, the discussion of measures to be taken against the Portuguese Government to ensure the passing of the Anti-Slavery Bill. The Bishop of London, who was one of the speakers on this occasion, was the only one of these gentlemen whose voice and manner seemed to me stiff or unnatural, but possibly I was prejudiced by my general dislike of parsons.

After a week in London, the Wagners made their way by channel steamer to Boulogne, where they stayed for a month and where they met Meyerbeer, who received the young composer graciously, allowed him to read aloud a large part of the libretto of *Rienzi*, and agreed to examine the score, whose composition Wagner had not yet completed. Meyerbeer also gave Wagner introductions to men of influence in the musical world of Paris, among them both the administrator and the chief conductor of the Paris Opéra. This was a generous and disinterested gesture, for Meyerbeer was the reigning idol of Parisian grand opera and might well not have wished to encourage younger rivals or potential successors.

Displeased at finding himself once again indebted to a Jew (a situation which was to be repeated endlessly throughout his entire lifetime), Wagner many years later in his memoirs repaid his debt to the older composer in characteristic fashion. Describing his first meeting with Meyerbeer, he wrote, 'The years had not yet given his features the flabby look which sooner or later mars most Jewish faces, and the fine formation of his brow around the eyes gave him an expression of countenance that inspired confidence.' In journalistic articles he wrote anonymously and scurrilously of Meyerbeer, referring to him on one occasion as a scoundrel.

Wagner and Minna, still accompanied by their giant Newfoundland, Robber, finally arrived in Paris on 16 September 1839, and Wagner immediately began to seek contact with people of influence in musical and operatic circles. Short of money, he began borrowing from Eduard Avenarius, who was shortly to marry Wagner's sister Cäcilie, and who had found lodgings in Paris for the Wagners. Most of the composer's close friendships were with members of the German community, for his knowledge of French was virtually non-existent: he remained monolingual throughout his life. Though he met Heine, Berlioz and several other prominent artists in Paris, his attitude towards them was too envious to allow him to benefit from their friendship or advice.

After he had pawned Minna's jewellery, her clothes and finally her wedding-ring, and had then sold the pawn tickets, Wagner resorted to borrowing further from in-laws and acquaintances, and even accepted money from friends of his friends, among them a wealthy Jewish merchant named Axenfeld. He was not in the habit of repaying any of these debts. Indeed, Wagner may have been the first artist to put into successful practice the theory that the world owed him a living.

Out of respect for Meyerbeer, Duponchel, the Director of the Opéra, agreed to see Wagner, though it was not to be expected that the Paris Opéra would rush to commission an opera from a young and completely unknown foreign composer. Yet, at Meyerbeer's urging, the Opéra's chief conductor, Habeneck, accepted for concert performance Wagner's *Columbus* overture, which had been written for a play of that title by the composer's friend from Leipzig, Theodor Apel. Despite his lack of familiarity with the language, Wagner began to compose songs to French texts, and attempted, though without conspicuous success, to sell them to French singers.

Wagner managed to get his opera *Das Liebesverbot* accepted by the Théâtre de la Renaissance, once again through the influence of Meyerbeer, but the theatre became bankrupt before the opera could be produced, and Wagner decided that Meyerbeer was somehow to be held responsible. A new Director of the Paris Opéra was prevailed upon to listen to parts of the opera played on the piano by its composer, an audition which was also attended by the famous librettist Scribe. But *Das Liebesverbot* made no effect, and Wagner began work on a new opera which he at first envisaged as a short, one-act curtain-raiser. This was in due course to become *Der fliegende Holländer* (The Flying Dutchman).

The financial situation was now desperate, Avenarius was no longer prepared to support the Wagners, and even Robber had run away to find a master better able to feed him. Months after he had disappeared, Wagner caught sight of Robber in the distance and called him. When the dog recognized his old master, he fled for the second time. The lowest point of the family misfortunes was reached in October 1840, when Wagner was imprisoned for debt. He remained in prison for several weeks until Minna's begging letters, drafted by the composer himself, to Theodor Apel bore fruit. After his release he attempted to earn a living by making arrangements of operas and other music, and accepted journalistic assignments, most of which came his way through the good offices of the German–Jewish music publisher Moritz Schlesinger, a friend of Meyerbeer. But journalism paid little, and

47

Wagner's German had to be translated for publication.

Though jealous of any composer who had achieved success in Paris, Wagner entertained a healthier respect for Berlioz than for Meyerbeer, who continued to be helpful to him. Berlioz and Wagner met in Paris on several occasions. Berlioz praised some of Wagner's journalism, and Wagner, in *My Life*, professed a guarded admiration for the French composer: 'But while admiring this genius who was absolutely unique in his methods, I could never quite shake off a certain peculiar feeling of anxiety. His works left me with a sensation as of something strange, something with which I felt I should never be able to be familiar, and I was often puzzled at the strange fact that, though ravished by his compositions, I was at the same time repelled and even wearied by them.' (Berlioz, in his *Memoirs*, referred to the German composer's 'intellectual laziness, against which he should be more on his guard'.) Obviously, the artistic ideals of the two composers were in fundamental opposition to each other. The classical discipline which lay securely at the heart of Berlioz's romanticism seemed bland and soulless to Wagner, while Berlioz must have thought Wagner's view of the roles of drama and music in opera completely wrong-headed.

In June 1841, Wagner learned that *Rienzi*, which he had managed to complete, probably while he was in the debtors' prison, and which he had submitted to the Dresden Opera, had been accepted for performance in Dresden. He had been recommended to the management by Meyerbeer. By this time, Wagner had exhausted every possibility of finding success in Paris, yet he remained in Meudon, a village outside the city, for most of the year to work on *Der fliegende Holländer*, which had now grown beyond the proportions of a mere curtain-raiser. When he had finished composing this opera, Wagner sent it to Berlin. He and Minna were now living in the city of Paris again, and as usual their debts were being paid by patient and generous friends. Wagner managed to attract one or two minor commissions, among them one from a Jewish composer, Josef Dessauer, who paid him 200 francs to write a libretto. Wagner also found the time to draft the synopsis of a drama, to which he gave the title *Die Sarazenin* (The Saracens), for his own possible future use as a libretto.

Although *Rienzi* had been accepted by Dresden, it had not yet been produced, and further delays were now imposed. Wagner began to realize that, if his opera were ever to reach the stage, it would be necessary for him personally to agitate for its production. In March 1842 he learned that the Berlin Opera had accepted *Der fliegende Holländer* at the suggestion of Meyerbeer, to whom, therefore, Wagner was once again indebted. Clearly the time was ripe for his return to Germany. Borrowing the funds for the journey, Richard and Minna set off by coach for Dresden.

Almost as soon as they arrived in Dresden, in April 1842, Wagner went off

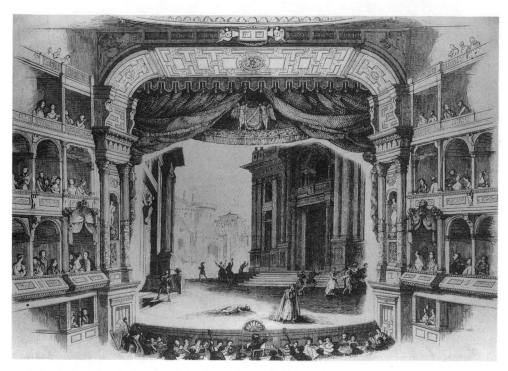

Woodcut of the final scene of Act IV of *Rienzi* at its Dresden première in 1842

The final scene of *Der fliegende Holländer* as seen at its Dresden première in 1843

left: Lotte Lehmann as Elsa in
Lohengrin, Vienna, 1921

right: Nicolai Gedda as Lohengrin,
Stockholm, 1966

opposite: Hans Hotter in the title-role
of *Der fliegende Holländer*, New York,
1950

Geraint Evans as Beckmesser in Act III of *Die Meistersinger von Nürnberg* at the Royal Opera House, Covent Garden, 1982

to Leipzig to visit his mother, whom he had not seen for some years. By the end of the month, having also visited Berlin to find out how plans for the projected production of *Der fliegende Holländer* were advancing, Wagner was back in Dresden. In June, he and Minna visited the spa town of Teplitz (now Teplice in Czechoslovakia), where Minna took the waters. At the end of June, Wagner left his wife at Teplitz while he set out alone on a hiking tour in the Bohemian mountains, during the course of which he began to sketch the libretto for a new three-act opera which he called *Der Venusberg*, but which was eventually to become *Tannhäuser*.

By the middle of July, Wagner had returned to Dresden and was actively involved in preparations for the forthcoming première of *Rienzi*. The opera cannot have been an easy one for the recently opened Dresden opera house to stage, for it was inordinately long, its large cast and its choruses were expensive to dress, and the orchestra found Wagner's music extremely difficult to play. Fortunately, the principal singers were first-rate. Joseph Tichatschek sang the title-role, and the famous Wilhelmine Schröder-Devrient was cast as Adriano, despite the fact that she did not care for the role and that her ample figure was hardly seen to its best advantage in the costume of a male youth.

The first performance on 20 October began at six in the evening, and did not end until shortly before midnight. On this occasion, the stamina of performers and audience appears to have been greater than that of the composer, who wrote in *My Life*:

> . . . when I try to recall my condition during that evening, I can only picture it as a kind of dream. Of real pleasure or agitation I felt nothing at all. I seemed to stand quite aloof from my work. But the sight of the thickly crowded auditorium upset me so greatly that I was unable even to glance at the body of the audience, whose presence merely affected me like some natural phenomenon—something like a continuous downpour of rain— from which I sought shelter in the farthest corner of my box as under a protecting roof.
>
> . . . one great anxiety filled me with growing alarm: I noticed that the first two acts had taken as long as the whole of *Der Freischütz*, for instance. On account of its warlike calls to arms, the third act begins with an exceptional uproar, and when, at its close, the clock pointed to ten, which meant that the performance had already lasted a full four hours, I became perfectly desperate. The fact that, after this act also, I was loudly called for, I regarded merely as a final courtesy on the part of the audience, who wished to signify that they had had quite enough for one evening, and would now leave the house in a body.

As we had still two acts to go, I thought it was certain that we should not

49

be able to finish the piece, and apologized for my lack of wisdom in not having previously effected the necessary curtailments. Now, thanks to my folly, I found myself in the unheard-of predicament of being unable to finish an opera, otherwise extremely well received, simply because it was absurdly long. I could only explain the undiminished zeal of the singers, and particularly of Tichatschek, who seemed to grow lustier and cheerier the longer it lasted, as an amiable device to conceal from me the inevitable catastrophe.

However, my astonishment at finding the audience still there in full muster, even in the last act towards midnight, filled me with unbounded perplexity. I could no longer trust my eyes or ears, and regarded the entire events of the evening as a nightmare. It was past midnight when, for the last time, I had to obey the thunderous calls of the audience, side by side with my faithful singers.

There can be no doubt of the success of *Rienzi*'s première. At a few performances in Dresden the following year, the opera was given in two parts, as *Rienzis Grösse* (Rienzi's Greatness) and *Rienzis Fall* (Rienzi's Fall), one part per evening. But audiences complained at having to pay twice for what had originally been one opera, so the management reverted to performing the work on one evening, though with substantial cuts. This shortened *Rienzi* of 1842 remained for many years Wagner's most popular opera. (It is interesting to note that, born in the same year as Verdi, Wagner also had his earliest success in the same year as his Italian contemporary, whose first real breakthrough had come seven months earlier with *Nabucco*.)

The first American performance of *Rienzi* was given in New York at the Academy of Music on 4 March 1878. The opera reached London on 27 January 1879, when it was staged at Her Majesty's Theatre in an English translation. Though it is still occasionally revived, *Rienzi* is no longer a popular Wagner opera, and it has yet to be produced at the Wagner Festival Theatre in Bayreuth.

II

THE English novelist Edward George Earle Lytton (the first Baron Lytton), usually known as Bulwer-Lytton, was born in 1803 and died in 1873. A member of Parliament for fifteen years, he served as colonial secretary in 1858–9 and was created a peer in 1866. He was a prolific writer whose collected works run to a large number of volumes, but he is remembered today for no more than two of his historical novels: *The Last Days of Pompeii* and *Rienzi, the Last of the Roman Tribunes*. The former has twice been filmed, but the latter, an immensely long novel first published in 1835, lives on only as the source of Wagner's opera.

Wagner read *Rienzi* a year or two after its initial publication, in a German translation by G. N. Baermann. It has been suggested that another source of the opera was a successful English play on the same subject by Mary Russell Mitford, which appeared seven years before Bulwer-Lytton's novel. This is possible, for there are certain similarities between play and opera. Both give more prominence to a love affair between Rienzi's sister Irene and Adriano Colonna than Bulwer-Lytton does, both combine Rienzi's two careers as Tribune and Senator, which the novelist does not, and both play and opera are in five acts.

When Wagner met Bulwer-Lytton's son in Vienna in 1863, he assured him that his father's novel had been his only source, yet a letter written in 1840 to his old schoolfriend Theodor Apel suggests that the idea of an opera about Rienzi had originated with Apel before Wagner had encountered Bulwer-Lytton's novel. As his friends usually discovered to their cost, however, one could not place one's trust in anything Wagner said or wrote.

The historical Cola di Rienzi was born in 1313, the son of an innkeeper and a washerwoman. In 1347, with the support of the Roman populace, he overthrew the rule of the patricians, set himself up as Tribune, and called together an Italian national parliament. Expelled by his opponents in the following year, he returned in 1352 and in 1354 was appointed Senator by the Pope. However, he could no longer maintain his hold over the Romans, and in the same year was assassinated.

In his Preface to the first edition of *Rienzi*, Bulwer-Lytton wrote:

... having had occasion to read the original authorities from which modern historians have drawn their accounts of the life of Rienzi, I was led to believe that a very remarkable man had been superficially judged, and a very important period crudely examined. And this belief was sufficiently strong to induce me at first to meditate a more serious work upon the life and times of Rienzi. Various reasons concurred against this project—and I renounced the biography to commence the fiction. I have still, however, adhered, with a greater fidelity than is customary in Romance, to all the leading events of the public life of the Roman Tribune; and the reader will perhaps find in these pages a more full and detailed account of the rise and fall of Rienzi than in any English work of which I am aware. I have, it is true, taken a view of his character different in some respects from that of Gibbon ... but ... as I have given the facts from which I have drawn my interpretation of the principal agent, the reader has suffcient data for his own judgment. In the picture of the Roman populace, as in that of the Roman Nobles of the fourteenth century, I follow literally the descriptions left to us. They are not flattering, but they are faithful likenesses.

Preserving generally the real chronology of Rienzi's life, the plot of this work extends over a space of some years, and embraces the variety of characters necessary to a true delineation of events. The story, therefore, cannot have precisely that order of interest found in fictions strictly and genuinely *dramatic*, in which (to my judgement at least) the time ought to be as limited as possible, and the characters as few, no new character of importance being admissible towards the end of the work. If I may use the word Epic in its most modest and unassuming acceptation, this Fiction, in short, though indulging in dramatic situations, belongs as a whole, rather to the Epic than the Dramatic school.

Bulwer-Lytton's novel is written in such turgid prose as to be virtually unreadable today. It was the character of the Roman leader, Cola di Rienzi, that attracted Wagner, rather than the novelist's skill, and his libretto substitutes the usual terse operatic shorthand for the flowery and more leisurely style of the novel. Bulwer-Lytton's Adrian and Irene fall in love thus, after Adrian has rescued Irene from abduction at the hands of the Orsini family:

'Where am I?' cried Irene, rising from the couch. 'This room—these hangings—Holy Virgin! do I dream still!—and you! Heavens!—it is the Lord Adrian di Castello!'

'Is that a name thou hast been taught to fear?' said Adrian; 'if so, I will forswear it.'

If Irene now blushed deeply, it was not in that wild delight with which her romantic heart might have foretold that she would listen to the first words of homage from Adrian di Castello. Bewildered and confused,—terrified at the strangeness of the place, and shrinking even from the thought of finding herself alone with one who for years had been present to her fancies,— alarm and distress were the emotions she felt the most, and which most were impressed upon her speaking countenance; and as Adrian now drew nearer to her, despite the gentleness of his voice and the respect of his looks, her fears, not the less strong that they were vague, increased upon her: she retreated to the further end of the room, looked wildly round her, and then, covering her face with her hands, burst into a paroxysm of tears.

Moved by these tears, and divining her thoughts, Adrian forgot for a moment all the more daring wishes he had formed.

'Fear not, sweet lady,' said he earnestly: 'recollect thyself, I beseech thee; no peril, no evil can reach thee here; it was this hand that saved thee from the outrage of the Orsini—this roof is but the shelter of a friend! Tell me, then, fair wonder, thy name and residence, and I will summon my servitors, and guard thee to thy home at once.'

Perhaps the relief of tears, even more than Adrian's words, restored Irene to herself, and enabled her to comprehend her novel situation; and as her senses, thus cleared, told her what she owed to him whom her dreams had so long imaged as the ideal of all excellence, she recovered her self-possession, and uttered her thanks with a grace not the less winning, if it still partook of embarrassment.

'Thank me not,' answered Adrian passionately. 'I have touched thy hand—I am repaid. Repaid! nay, all gratitude—all homage is for me to render!'

Blushing again, but with far different emotions than before, Irene, after a momentary pause, replied, 'Yet, my Lord, I must consider it a debt the more weighty that you speak of it so lightly. And now, complete the obligation. I do not see my companion—suffer her to accompany me home; it is but a short way hence.'

'Blessed, then, is the air that I have breathed so unconsciously!' said Adrian. 'But thy companion, dear lady, is not here. She fled, I imagine, in the confusion of the conflict; and not knowing thy name, not being able, in thy then state to learn it from thy lips, it was my happy necessity to convey thee hither;—but I will be thy companion. Nay, why that timid glance? my people, also, shall attend us.'

'My thanks, noble Lord, are of little worth; my brother, who is not unknown to thee, will thank thee more fittingly. May I depart?' and Irene, as she spoke, was already at the door.

'Art thou so eager to leave me?' answered Adrian, sadly. 'Alas! when thou hast departed from my eyes, it will seem as if the moon had left the night!—but it is happiness to obey thy wishes, even though they tear thee from me.'

A slight smile parted Irene's lips, and Adrian's heart beat audibly to himself, as he drew from that smile, and those downcast eyes, no unfavourable omen.

In Wagner's *Rienzi*, Adriano and Irene first address each other in these words:

> Adriano: O fair one, tell me, do you trust me?
> Irene: Hero of my honour, of my life,
>   I trust you with my greatest treasure.
> Adriano: You are aware that I am a Colonna,
>   yet you do not flee from me, whose entire family
>   is abhorrent to you and to your brother?
> Irene: Oh, why do you mention your ancestry?
>   I fear for you, my rescuer,
>   when I think of those proud nobles
>   who will never forgive you for having rescued
>   a plebeian maiden from dishonour.

Adriano: Ah, do not remind yourself of the misery
that threatens us and Rome!
Your brother has such a great spirit, but alas
I forsee that he will fall!
The mob itself will betray him,
and the nobles will punish him.
And you, Irene? What will be your fate?
But ah, may your misfortune be my password,
and let all other ties be dissolved!
I will give my life, my all, for you!

Irene: And if I am fortunate?

Adriano: Oh, be silent!
I tremble at the prospect of your good fortune!
Come night and death,
I shall be yours forever!

Both: Yes, a world full of suffering
will be sweetened by your lovely gaze.
To part from it, with you,
is my sacred destiny!
Should the whole world collapse,
and all hope perish,
the realms of love
offer us a new Fatherland!

The historical Rienzi has been claimed as a precursor by both of the great modern totalitarian ideologies, communism and fascism. When the Soviet Republic celebrated its tenth anniversary in 1928, the proceedings were opened with the Overture to Wagner's *Rienzi*, an acknowledgment of Cola di Rienzi as a champion of the proletariat. Adolf Hitler told a former schoolfriend that the idea of National Socialism came to him during a performance of *Rienzi* that he and his friend attended together in Linz in 1906. Mussolini's state, too, paid homage to the fourteenth-century Roman Tribune, and a book on Rienzi was found in Napoleon's baggage after his defeat at the battle of Waterloo.

In *The Decline and Fall of the Roman Empire*, Edward Gibbon said of Cola di Rienzi, 'Posterity will compare the virtues and failings of this extraordinary man; but in a long period of anarchy and servitude, the name of Rienzi has often been celebrated as the deliverer of his country, and the last of the Roman patriots.'

III

IN *A Communication to My Friends*, in 1851, Wagner described Rienzi as the result of his longing to attempt something 'on a grand and inspiring scale'. 'This mood', he wrote,

was fed and fostered by my reading of Bulwer's *Rienzi*. From the misery of modern private life, from which I could nowhere discover anything worth using as material for art, I was led away by this picture of a great historical and political event, in lingering on which I needs must find a salutary distraction from cares and conditions that appeared to me as nothing else than absolutely fatal to art . . . This Rienzi with great thoughts in his head, great feelings in his heart, amid an entourage of coarseness and vulgarity, set all my nerves quivering with sympathy and love. Yet my plan for a work of art based thereon sprang first from the perception of a purely lyric element in the hero's atmosphere . . .

To do something grand, to write an opera for whose production only the most exceptional means should suffice—a work, therefore, which I should never feel tempted to bring before the public amid such cramping relations as those which then oppressed me, and the hope of whose eventual production should thus incite me to make every sacrifice in order to extricate myself from those relations—this is what resolved me to resume and carry out with all my might my former plan for *Rienzi*. In the preparation of this text, also, I took no thought for anything but the writing of an effective operatic libretto. The 'grand opera' with all its scenic and musical display, its sensationalism and massive vehemence, loomed large before me; and not merely to copy it, but with reckless extravagance to outbid it in its every detail, became the object of my artistic ambition.

However, I should be unjust to myself, did I represent this ambition as my only motive for the conception and execution of my *Rienzi*. The material really aroused my enthusiasm, and I put nothing into my sketch which had not a direct bearing on the grounds of this enthusiasm. My chief concern was my Rienzi himself; and only when I felt quite contented with him, did I give rein to the notion of a grand opera. Nevertheless, from a purely artistic point of view, this grand opera was the pair of spectacles through which I unconsciously regarded my *Rienzi* material; nothing in that material did I find enthrall me but what could be looked at through these spectacles. True, that I always fixed my gaze upon the material itself, and did not keep one eye open for certain ready-made musical effects which I might wish to father on it by hook or crook; only, I saw it in no light other than that of a five-act opera, with five brilliant finales, and filled with hymns, processions, and musical clash of arms. Thus I bestowed no greater care upon the verse and diction than seemed needful for turning out a good, and not a trivial, opera text.

I did not set out with the object of writing duets, trios, and so on, but they found their own way in, here and there, because I looked upon my subject exclusively through the medium of opera. For instance, I by no means hunted about in my material for a pretext for a ballet; but with the eyes of the opera composer. I perceived in it a self-evident festival that Rienzi must give to the people, and at which he would have to exhibit to them, in dumbshow, a drastic scene from their ancient history: this scene being the story of Lucretia and the consequent expulsion of the Tarquins from Rome. (That this pantomime has had to be omitted from the stage performances of *Rienzi* has been a serious drawback to me; for the ballet that replaced it has obscured my nobler intentions, and turned this scene into nothing more nor less than ordinary operatic spectacle.) Thus in every department of my plan I was certainly ruled by the material alone; but on the other hand, I ruled this material according to my only chosen pattern, the form of the grand opera. My artistic individuality, in its dealings with the impressions of life, was still entirely under the influence of purely artistic, or rather art-formalistic, mechanically operating impressions.

The original manuscript score of *Rienzi*, in four volumes, no longer exists. Wagner presented it to the Bavarian King Ludwig II as a Christmas present in 1868, but by 1939 it had come into the possession of the President of the Reichsarbeitskammer, who, on 20 April of that year, presented it to Adolf Hitler. The score appears not to have survived its last owner. It is unlikely that the work has been staged in its entirety since its first performance in Dresden in October 1842. Wagner himself authorized various cuts in the light of practical experience gained in performance of the opera, and these were incorporated into the first edition of *Rienzi*, which was published in Dresden in 1845.

IV

THE Overture, a vigorous and large-scale affair, incorporates a number of themes which will be heard again during the opera. Beginning with three sustained trumpet notes which later are to become a signal for revolt, it soon introduces the broadly flowing and stately tune of Rienzi's Prayer in the final act (Ex. 1), and moves through more martial themes, among them a stirring battle-hymn, to an emphatic, if crude, finale.

Ex.1

56

The curtain rises on a street in Rome, at night. In the foreground to the right is Rienzi's house. In the background can be seen the Church of St John Lateran. Paolo Orsini (bass), the head of a patrician family, arrives with his followers, two of whom enter Rienzi's house through a window to abduct his sister Irene (soprano). Before they can leave with her, Stefano Colonna (bass), head of a rival house, enters with members of his faction, and a fight breaks out between the two families. Adriano (mezzo-soprano), Colonna's youthful son, now appears with armed followers, forces his way to Irene, and sets her free.

The citizens, or plebeians, who have now assembled, try to stop the nobles from fighting, using stones, clubs, axes, hammers and other improvised weapons when exhortation proves powerless. But not even the appearance on the scene of Raimondo (bass), the Papal Legate, with his attendants, can quell the violence. The plebeian Rienzi (tenor), a Papal Notary, enters with his friends Baroncelli (tenor) and Cecco del Vecchio (bass), and restores order, at least temporarily, simply by using his natural authority. He upbraids the Colonnas and Orsinis, who decide to fight one another the following day, outside the city walls.

When the nobles have departed, Rienzi, with the support of Raimondo, promises to restore law and order to Rome. He commands the citizens to return to their homes, but to arm themselves. When the nobles march out of the city on the morrow to fight, they will find the gates locked against their return. The citizens are to wait, next day, for the sound of the trumpets which will call them to rise against the patricians. The citizens now depart, leaving Rienzi, Irene and Adriano, who has not left with his father.

Wagner's *Rienzi*, like his earlier two operas, is made up of separate numbers. The action up to this point has been carried forward in an Introduction which is disappointingly pedestrian both in its ensemble passages and its recitative, until Rienzi's call to arms ('*Doch, höret ihr der Trompete Ruf*': But when you hear the trumpet call). This at least is lively, though hardly memorable.

(It was in order to emphasize Adriano's youth that Wagner wrote the role for a female mezzo-soprano. This was an error of judgment, for Adriano, who must be at least eighteen, is taken seriously as Irene's suitor, and would have his credibility improved considerably by being given a male voice. The opera is sometimes performed with a tenor Adriano, when the advantage gained in dramatic verisimilitude easily outweighs the occasional musical adjustments that have to be made to a score which is, after all, not exactly Holy Writ. The composer's grandson, Wieland Wagner, in his production of the opera in Stuttgart in 1957, successfully used a tenor Adriano.)

Irene tells her brother Rienzi that it was Adriano, a Colonna, who had saved her from the Orsinis. Though he disapproves of the lawless behaviour of the nobles, Adriano finds it difficult to ally himself with the plebeians, until he is reminded that it was a member of his own family, a Colonna, who had murdered Rienzi's brother, a deed which Rienzi has sworn to avenge. Adriano then pledges himself to the cause of the plebeians in a noisy, undistinguished trio, at the conclusion of which Rienzi entrusts his sister to Adriano's protection and goes off at the call of what he refers to as his lofty duty.

Adriano and Irene declare their love for each other in a lightly Italianate duet, interrupted by the sound of the trumpet signalling the plebeian revolt and also the beginning of the Act I finale. From all sides citizens rush in, welcoming the day of their liberation. When an organ is heard playing in the nearby church, the crowd outside falls to its knees, while the congregation within is heard singing a hymn to freedom. Suddenly, the great doors of the church are flung open, and Rienzi appears in full armour, his head uncovered, with Raimondo, the Papal Legate, by his side, and the leaders of the people's army. Acclaimed by the crowd, Rienzi declares that Rome henceforth shall be free. He is hailed by the populace as Emperor of Rome, but refuses the title, announcing that the city is to be governed by a Senate and that he himself will act as the people's Tribune. His friends Baroncelli and Cecco lead the crowd in an oath of allegiance to their new leader. Victory over the patricians, it seems, has been easily won.

The initial chorus of citizens is suitably plebeian, and the hymn sung by a double chorus in the church somewhat ungainly, but Rienzi's address to the citizens (*'Die Frieheit Roms sei das Gesetz'*: Rome's freedom shall be the law) goes with a swing, after which the rest of the finale limps along to its conclusion.

Act II, which takes place in a great hall of the Capitol, is preceded by a brief but graceful orchestral introduction. When the curtain rises, the hills of Rome can be seen through the open portals at the back of the hall. The *'Gesang der Friedensboten'* (Song of the messengers of peace), an unaccompanied hymn of peace, is heard, and the singers themselves enter through the portals. They are youths from what Wagner's libretto calls 'the best Roman families', dressed in white silk garments of semi-antique style, with wreaths in their hair and silver batons in their hands. These patrician youths had been sent by Rienzi to spread his message of peace throughout the land. Greeted by him and by the Senators now, the messengers of peace report on the success of their mission, in a charming chorus with an important solo part for the chief messenger (soprano). They are then bidden by Rienzi to spread the tidings through the streets of Rome. The messengers of peace depart, singing. The patricians, headed by Orsini and Colonna, all dressed in the vestments of peace, now enter to pay grudging tribute to Rienzi, though Colonna is the only one of the group actually to utter. Rienzi tells them firmly that they must

58

in future abide by the law. He then graciously invites them to a banquet, and leaves with Cecco, Baroncelli and the Senators. This last section of the opening number of Act II is composed in the stiff recitative to which Wagner too frequently resorted in his early operas.

In a mundane trio with ensemble (the latter provided by the patricians), Colonna and Orsini join forces to plot the death of their common enemy, Rienzi, while Adriano, who has overheard them, attempts in vain to dissuade his father from so dishonourable an act. The patricians depart, leaving Adriano to agonize over whether to betray Colonna, his father, or Rienzi, the brother of his beloved Irene.

The finale to Act II is the opera's most extended section. An attractive festive chorus accompanies the procession of Senators, patricians and citizens, who enter through the portals to fill the great hall. Rienzi arrives with Irene, accompanied by Baroncelli and Cecco. After Rienzi has greeted the assembled crowd, the Ambassadors of Lombardy, Naples, Hungary. Bavaria and Bohemia are announced, and enter with scrolls which they hand over to Rienzi, the ceremony accompanied by a stately march. Rienzi stirs up indignation and wrath among the Ambassadors when he declares that, not only should all Italy be united but also the citizens of Rome should that day be allowed to elect the next Holy Roman Emperor. Adriano whispers to Rienzi that he should be on his guard against traitors, but Rienzi replies that he is protected by a breastplate which he is wearing beneath his cloak.

There follows a spectacular balletic representation of a subject from ancient Rome: the rape of Lucretia by Tarquinius, Lucretia's death, the rout of Tarquinius and his troops by Brutus and Collatinus, and finally a mock battle in which the ancient Romans are seen to defeat knights dressed in the style of Rienzi's day. The performance ends with a ceremonial dance of peace, during which Orsini attempts to plunge a dagger into Rienzi's breast. The coup fails, the patricians are arrested, the populace disperse, and a court of justice is hastily assembled. The senators condemn the patricians to death by the axe, but Rienzi, moved by the pleading of Irene and Adriano on behalf of Adriano's father, pardons them all.

The music accompanying the ballet–pantomime fulfils its purpose adequately, the Dance of the Women possessing a certain gracious charm, and the Pyrrhic Dance a suitable vigour, though the final Festive Dance is more than a trifle bombastic. The ensemble with which the act ends, the humiliated patricians still muttering vengeance while everyone else gives voice to more exalted sentiments, is effective in its inflated, Meyerbeerian style, the familiar march tune from the Overture bringing the curtain down with an agreeable flourish.

Act III takes place in the ruins of the old Roman Forum. An alarm bell is heard tolling as the curtain rises on a scene of great commotion, with a wildly excited crowd calling for Rienzi. The patricians, despite the oath of loyalty they were obliged to swear in order to save their lives, have armed themselves again and are about to attack. Rienzi appears, admits that he was wrong to have exercised clemency, and calls the people to arms. This opening number has an engaging though perhaps misplaced jollity.

Adriano enters in distress, torn between conflicting emotions. He laments his situation in a noble recitative ('*Gerechter Gott*': O Just God) and aria ('*In seine Blüte bleicht mein Leben*': My life is decaying in its springtime). The aria is Italianate in its structure, an almost cabaletta-like conclusion following the repeated sound of the alarm bell at which Adriano decides to make his way to his father and attempt to effect a reconciliation between him and Rienzi.

The finale to the act begins as the citizens return—armed—followed by a procession of priests and monks, accompanied by women and girls. Cecco, Baroncelli and the Senators enter on horseback, and finally Rienzi, clad in armour, arrives on horseback, accompanied by Irene on foot. Rienzi exhorts the citizens to avenge a thousand years of shame, and the citizens respond with a spirited battle-hymn, already familiar from the Overture, in whose refrain of '*Santo Spirito, Cavaliere*' Rienzi, the priests and the monks all join. Wagner notes in his score that the words of this '*Schlachthymne*' are taken directly from Bulwer-Lytton's novel. The scene is described thus in *Rienzi, the Last of the Roman Tribunes*:

Within an hour the Roman army—vast, miscellaneous—old men and boys, mingled with the vigour of life, were on their march to the Gate of San Lorenzo; of their number, which amounted to twenty thousand foot, not one-sixth could be deemed men-at-arms; but the cavalry were well equipped, and consisted of the lesser Barons and the more opulent citizens. At the head of these rode the Tribune in complete armour, and wearing on his casque a wreath of oak and olive leaves, wrought in silver. Before him waved the great gonfalon of Rome, while in front of this multitudinous array marched a procession of monks, of the order of St Francis (for the ecclesiastical body of Rome went chiefly with the popular spirit, and its enthusiastic leader)—slowly chanting the following hymn, which was made inexpressibly startling and imposing at the close of each stanza, by the clash of arms, the blast of trumpets, and the deep roll of the drum; which formed, as it were, a martial chorus to the song:

ROMAN WAR-SONG
March, march for your hearths and your altars!
Cursed to all time be the dastard that falters,
Never on earth may his sins be forgiven.
Death on his soul, shut the portals of heaven!
A curse on his heart, and a curse on his brain!—

Who strikes not for Rome, shall to Rome be her Cain!
Breeze fill our banners, sun gild our spears,
Spirito Santo, Cavaliers! . . .

(Rienzi's battle-cry was '*Spirito Santo, Cavaliere*', i.e. 'Cavalier' or horseman in the singular. Bulwer-Lytton made the noun plural, but Wagner reverted to the original.)

Adriano tries to persuade Rienzi not to attack the nobles but instead to send him as an emissary to his father. Rienzi refuses, and he and his troops march off, singing their song of battle, leaving a despairing Adriano to remain behind with Irene and the women. Adriano attempts to rush off to join his father, but Irene holds him back, and finally he joins her and the women in a prayer to the Virgin. He and Irene pray for help, while the women ask the Virgin to send death to the enemies of the people. Their prayer is punctuated by the off-stage noise of battle.

As the sounds of battle cease, the '*Schlachthymne*' can be heard, at first in the distance and then nearer, as Rienzi's troops return. The victorious citizens greet their womenfolk, and Rienzi announces the defeat of the enemy and the deaths of Colonna and Orsini. The body of Colonna, Adriano's father, is carried in, and Adriano with a cry of horror flings himself upon it. Then, after cursing Rienzi and vowing to avenge his father's death, he rushes out.

The messengers of peace enter, bearing wreaths of laurel. Rienzi steps into the triumphal chariot they have brought with them and is crowned with a laurel wreath. Irene, broken-hearted at the departure of Adriano, is supported by women as Rienzi is acclaimed, and the citizens rejoice at having achieved their freedom. This Act III finale contains some of *Rienzi*'s most effective music, both in its solo passages and in its lively ensembles.

In Act IV, which takes place in a square outside the Lateran Church, the citizens, led by Baroncelli and Cecco, discuss the political situation and express their concern at the fact that the Germans have withdrawn their Ambassador from Rome and that both the Pope and the new Holy Roman Emperor are opposed to Rienzi. Baroncelli tells the citizens that Rienzi intends to attempt a reconciliation with the nobles by allowing his sister to marry Adriano. When the crowd asks if this accusation can be proved, Adriano steps forward. In a trio with chorus, he, Baroncelli and Cecco attempt to incite the people against their former hero, and Adriano announces his intention of killing Rienzi. A gloomily portentous orchestral introduction has set the mood of the scene before the rise of the curtain, the action is carried forward tersely and swiftly, and the trio itself has an exciting urgency.

As the citizens are about to disperse, they are surprised to see a procession, headed by the Papal Legate, Raimondo, cross the square and enter the church. A second procession now arrives, headed by Rienzi, who leads Irene by the hand. Adriano cannot bring himself to assassinate Rienzi in Irene's presence, and the others are won over by the Tribune's speech in which he reminds them of all that he has achieved on their behalf. The fickle crowd cheers Rienzi, but suddenly the doors of the church are flung open and the priests and monks can be heard within, pronouncing a malediction upon Rienzi. Raimondo appears, and announces that Rienzi has been excommunicated. The crowd slinks off in confusion, leaving Rienzi, Irene and Adriano alone. Adriano tries to persuade Irene to flee with him, but she refuses to leave her brother. 'Mad woman! Perish with him!' Adriano exclaims as he rushes off. Irene and Rienzi stand clasping each other and listening to the chanting of the monks as the curtain falls.

Rienzi's utterance in this act reverts to its earlier stiffness, and the priests' malediction fails to make much of an effect. The finale is perfunctory, and one has the distinct impression that the composer is running out of steam.

After a slow and pensive orchestral introduction, the curtain rises on the first scene of Act V, a hall in the Capitol, in which Rienzi, alone, kneels before a small domestic altar. In an aria, '*Allmächt'ger Vater*' (Almighty Father), whose expressive tune (Ex. 1) was heard first in the Overture to the opera and next in the introduction to this act, Rienzi prays to be allowed to continue the work he has begun. Irene enters and embraces her brother, who tells her that she is the only one not to have deserted him. Even his great love, the city of Rome, has turned against him. Rienzi advises Irene to leave him and join Adriano, but Irene refuses. Brother and sister embrace once more, and Rienzi hurries away to attempt to sway the citizens by his oratory. Both Rienzi's cavatina, as he sings of his love for Rome, and his duet with Irene are among the opera's weaker numbers.

Irene is about to leave when Adriano enters in a state of intense emotion, his sword drawn, and implores her to escape with him. Darkness begins to fall, and the noise of tumult in the streets outside can be heard as a crowd rages through the city, smashing windows and starting fires. Adriano tries to drag Irene away by force, but she breaks free of him and hurries off. In a frenzy, Adriano exclaims that he will find his way to her, even through the flames of burning Rome. Their scene, though hardly memorable in musical terms, at least moves with a dramatic swiftness.

For the finale, the scene changes to the square in front of the Capitol. Citizens arrive from all directions with firebrands. When Rienzi appears on the highest balcony, the mob, led by Cecco and Baroncelli, threatens to stone him. Lighted torches are flung into the Capitol, which is soon ablaze. Adriano, entering at the head of the returning nobles, rushes into the Capitol in an attempt to save Irene, but part of the building collapses, burying him with her and Rienzi. As the nobles begin to attack the citizens, the curtain falls. All of this happens with almost indecent haste, to music which does not rise above the banal.

Compared with Wagner's earlier two operas, *Rienzi* seems curiously lifeless. Most of its thematic material is banal, its instrumentation in general is coarse, and its interminable recitative is conventional and ploddingly undramatic. The opera's greatest disadvantage, however, is its immense and wildly impractical length, which is certainly not justified by the work's very slight dramatic and musical interest. By cutting nearly half of the score one could make the rest of it tolerable in performance, but it seems obvious, with hindsight, that, in choosing to turn away from his former German and Italian models in order to strike out in the direction of Meyerbeer and French grand opera in his desire to achieve a quick success, Wagner had seriously misjudged the nature of his own burgeoning genius.

Years later, the composer referred to *Rienzi* in a letter to Liszt, in these terms: 'Neither as artist nor as man do I feel the urge to reconstruct that, to my taste, superannuated work which, because of its immoderate dimensions, I have had to remodel more than once. I no longer have the heart for it, and desire with all my soul to do something new instead.'

FOUR

Der fliegende Holländer
(The Flying Dutchman)

Romantic Opera in Three Acts

Dramatis personae
Daland, a Norwegian Sea Captain   (bass)
Senta, his Daughter   (soprano)
Erik, a Hunter   (tenor)
Mary, Senta's Nurse   (mezzo-soprano)
Daland's Helmsman   (tenor)
The Dutchman   (baritone)

LIBRETTO by the composer

TIME: The early nineteenth century

PLACE: The Norwegian coast

FIRST PERFORMED at the Hoftheater, Dresden, 2 January 1843, with Michael Wächter (the Dutchman), Wilhelmine Schröder-Devrient (Senta), Herr Reinhold (Erik) and Carl Risse (Daland), conducted by the composer.

I

IT was in July 1841, a good fifteen months before the première of *Rienzi*, that Wagner began the composition of his next opera, *Der fliegende Holländer* (The Flying Dutchman), the first concrete musical and dramatic ideas for which had been put into his mind by his hazardous journey by sea from Riga to London in 1839 (described in the previous chapter). While still in Riga, Wagner had read in Heine's *Memoirs of Herr von Schnabelewopski* the story of the Flying Dutchman. The legend was not created by Heine; it had been widely known for many years. A Dutch sea captain swears that he will round a certain dangerous cape in rough weather, even if he should go on sailing until the day of judgement. His oath is noted in high places, and he and his ship are thereafter condemned to sail on throughout eternity. A detail in several accounts of the legend involves the phantom ship hailing other vessels, and asking their seamen to deliver letters from the crew to relatives in Holland. But the letters turn out to be addressed to people long since dead.

Wagner's first intention was to compose a one-act opera on the subject of the Flying Dutchman, a short work which he hoped might be performed as the curtain-raiser to a ballet at the Paris Opéra, and it was in this form that he wrote the synopsis of a libretto while he was still also at work on the composition of *Rienzi*. He sought the advice of Meyerbeer, who introduced him to Léon Pillet, the new director of the Opéra. Pillet in due course bought Wagner's plot, but handed it over to another composer. Although furious at this, Wagner accepted the sum of 500 francs for his synopsis, deciding to write his Flying Dutchman opera as a full-length work (though still in one uninterrupted act) for a German opera house. His original sketch became *Le Vaisseau Fantôme*, an opera by the French composer Pierre Dietsch, which was staged at the Paris Opéra in November 1842. (At least, Wagner claimed that this work was based on his idea, although Dietsch's two librettists appear to have used another source of the Flying Dutchman legend.)

In April 1841, Wagner and Minna left their lodgings in Paris and moved outside the city to Meudon, where the composer worked first on his libretto and then on the music of *Der fliegende Holländer*, the composition of which he had completed by September. The Wagners returned to Paris in the autumn, to a cheaper apartment than the one they had earlier occupied, for money was even scarcer than usual: Wagner remained indoors for most of the time because his shoes no longer had much of their soles left. He orchestrated his opera, and composed its Overture, and in November he sent his score to Count Redern, the director of the Berlin Hofoper.

Again, Meyerbeer came to Wagner's aid, by paying a visit to Redern to recommend *Der fliegende Holländer*, and following this up with a letter to the opera director: 'The day before yesterday I had the honour to speak to Your Excellency about this interesting composer, whose talent and extremely straitened circumstances make him doubly worthy of not having the doors of the great Court Theatre, the protector of German art, closed to him.'

As a result of Meyerbeer's recommendation, *Der fliegende Holländer* was accepted for production by the Berlin Hofoper. However, after the not unsuccessful première of *Rienzi* in Dresden in October 1842, the Dresden Opera acquired the rights in *Der fliegende Holländer* from the Berlin Hofoper, which had not yet got round to staging the work. The opera was given its first performance at the Dresden Hoftheater on 2 January 1843.

Despite what Wagner referred to as the 'magnificent performance of my great artist [Wilhelmine Schröder-Devrient]', the occasion was not a blazing success. The composer blamed Michael Wächter, the singer of the title-role, for this:

Unfortunately even Schröder-Devrient saw only when the rehearsals were too far advanced how utterly incapable Wächter was of realizing the horror and supreme suffering of my Mariner. His distressing corpulence, his broad, fat face, the extraordinary movements of his arms and legs, which he managed to make look like mere stumps, drove my passionate Senta to despair. At one rehearsal, when in the great scene in Act II she comes to him in the guise of a guardian angel to bring the message of salvation, she broke off to whisper despairingly in my ear, 'How can I say it when I look into those beady eyes? Good God, Wagner, what a muddle you have made!'

Although only four performances of *Der fliegende Holländer* were given in Dresden in 1843, after which it was not revived in that city until 1865, the opera made its way on to other German stages. and eventually was produced in a number of foreign countries. In London, at the Theatre Royal, Drury Lane, in 1870, it became the first Wagner opera to be performed in Great Britain. (It was sung in Italian, as *L'Olandese Dannato*.) The first American performance, also in Italian, was given in Philadelphia in 1876.

It was for a production in Zurich in April 1852 that Wagner, who conducted, revised some of the orchestration and changed the ending of the Overture to the form in which it is known today. The opera reached Covent Garden, still in Italian but this time as *Il Vascello Fantasma*, in 1877. It was not staged at Bayreuth until 1901, since which time it has been produced there at frequent intervals. It is, in fact, the earliest Wagner opera in the Bayreuth repertoire.

Wagner had planned the opera to be performed without intervals, but this was found not to be practicable in Dresden. Indeed, it was not until the Bayreuth production of 1901, staged by Wagner's widow, Cosima, that the composer's wishes were respected and the opera was presented in one continuous act. In that form, however, *Der fliegende Holländer* plays for nearly two and a half hours, and most opera houses, not surprisingly, prefer to perform it in three acts, each of manageable length.

II

THE story of the Flying Dutchman is sometimes referred to as 'the English legend'; and, although it may not have originated there, it certainly did make several appearances in English literature and drama in the early nineteenth century. An anonymous story, 'Vanderdecken's Message Home, or The Tenacity of Natural Affection', appeared in *Blackwood's Magazine* in May 1821, and in 1827 a three-act play by Edward Fitz-Ball, called *The Flying Dutchman or The Phantom Ship* was produced in London at the Adelphi Theatre. Two years later, on the other side of the Thames at the Surrey Theatre, another play about the Flying Dutchman, by Douglas Jerrold, was performed. In 1839, Captain Marryat's novel *The Phantom Ship*, based on the legend, was published. This introduces the character of Philip, the son of the Dutchman, Vanderdecken, who after many wondrous adventures finally catches up with his father's ship. He saves Vanderdecken from eternal damnation, but at the cost of both their lives. As they go down with the ship, 'all nature smiled as if it rejoiced that a charm was dissolved for ever, and that THE PHANTOM SHIP WAS NO MORE.' (The capitals are Captain Marryat's.)

(In 1878, two years after Wagner's opera had finally reached London at the Lyceum Theatre, Henry Irving played at the same theatre in yet another stage adaptation of the legend, a play called *Vanderdecken*, by W. G. Wills and Percy Fitzgerald. The play's incidental music was 'selected from the works of Eminent Composers, and also from Norwegian Airs', and selections from Wagner's opera were played during one of the intervals.)

Heine's *Memoirs of Herr von Schnabelewopski*, a crypto-autobiographical work of fiction which he published in his *Salon* in serial form in 1834, mentions the Flying Dutchman in two instalments. In Chapter VI the eponymous hero describes how he saw, in Hamburg one night, 'a big ship looking like a sombre giant in a great scarlet cloak', and wonders if this could be the Flying Dutchman. In the next chapter, Schnabelewopski has this to say about the legend:

> You surely know the legend of the Flying Dutchman. It is the story about the doomed ship which can never come into harbour, and which has been roaming the seas since time immemorial. When it encounters another vessel, some of its ghostly sailors row across in a boat and beg the others to take letters home for them. These letters have to be nailed to the mast, otherwise some misfortune will strike the ship, especially if there is no Bible on board or no horse-shoe nailed to the foremast. The letters are always addressed to people whom no one knows, and who have been dead for

years, so that some distant descendant receives a letter addressed to a great-great-grandmother who for centuries has been slumbering in the grave.

That wooden spectre, that grim and grisly ship owes its name to its captain, a Dutchman, who once swore by all the devils in hell that he would sail round a certain cape, whose name escapes me, even if he had to sail until the day of judgement. The devil took him at his word, and so he must roam the seas forever, until he is redeemed by a woman's fidelity. Being stupid, the devil does not believe in the fidelity of women, so he has allowed the doomed captain to come on shore once every seven years, and get married in an attempt to achieve redemption. Poor Dutchman! Time and time again he has been only too glad to be set free from marriage and his redeemer, and get back on board his ship.

The play which I saw in Amsterdam was based on that legend. Another seven years have passed; the poor Dutchman, wearier than ever of his endless voyaging, lands, becomes friendly with a Scottish merchant to whom he sells diamonds at an absurdly low price and, when he hears that his customer has a beautiful daughter, asks for her hand in marriage. They agree on this bargain as well.

The scene changes to the Scotsman's house, where the maiden awaits her bridegroom with the greatest anxiety. She keeps looking sorrowfully at a large and very old painting hanging in the room, which depicts a handsome man in the costume of the Spanish Netherlands. It is a family heirloom which, according to her grandmother, is a faithful portrait of the Flying Dutchman as he was seen in Scotland a hundred years before, in the time of William of Orange. There is a tradition attached to the painting, warning the women of the family to beware of the original.

For this very reason the man's features have impressed themselves on the heart of the romantic girl. Thus, when the Dutchman himself enters the room, she is startled, but not afraid. He, too, is moved, on seeing the picture, but when he is informed whose portrait it is, he disarms suspicion with an easy tactfulness, making fun of the legend of the Flying Dutchman, the Wandering Jew of the ocean. Nevertheless, as though affected by it, he becomes gloomy, brooding on how terrible must be the life of someone condemned to endure unimaginable tortures on the wild ocean, how his body itself must be a living coffin in which his soul is so horribly imprisoned. Rejected by both life and death, like an empty cask thrown by the sea on to the shore, and contemptuously thrust back into the sea, his agony is as deep as the ocean on which he must sail, his ship without anchor and his heart without hope.

I think that these were almost exactly the words with which the bridegroom ends. The bride gazes upon him with deep seriousness, continuing to cast glances at his portrait. It would appear that she has discovered his secret, for when he later asks her, 'Katherine, will you be true to me?', she replies, 'True until death.'

I remember that, just then, I heard a laugh, and that it came not from the pit but from the gallery of the gods up above. When I looked up, I saw a marvellously beautiful Eve in that paradise, gazing seductively at me, with huge blue eyes. Her arm hung over the gallery, and in her hand she held an apple, or rather an orange. But instead of symbolically sharing it with me, she instead dropped the peel on my head. Was this done on purpose or by accident? That I wanted to know. But when I went up into paradise to make her acquaintance, I was more than a trifle surprised to find a white, soft creature, a marvellously tender woman . . .

Schnabelewopski goes on to describe his adventure with the young woman. Afterwards, he returns to the theatre:

When I went back into the theatre, I was just in time to see the final scene of the play, at the beginning of which the Flying Dutchman's wife, Mrs Flying Dutchman, is seen standing on a steep cliff above the sea, wringing her hands in despair, while her unhappy husband, out at sea, paces the deck of his phantom ship. He loves his wife, and is leaving her in order not to condemn her to perdition with him. He tells her of the dreadful curse laid upon him, and of his awful fate. But she cries out to him, 'I have been faithful to you until now, and I know how to remain true until death.' And with those words the faithful woman throws herself into the sea. Immediately, the curse on the Dutchman is lifted, he is redeemed, and the phantom ship sinks to the bottom of the sea.

The play which Schnabelewopski saw in Amsterdam included an element lacking in earlier accounts of the legend: the possibility of redemption for the Dutchman through the love of a faithful woman. It was this element of redemption through love which aroused Wagner's creative interest in the Dutchman, for this concept was thereafter to pervade almost every opera he wrote. Wagner commentators have speculated as to whether the Amsterdam play was a figment of the imagination of Heinrich Heine, or whether he had actually seen some such play. Heine had visited London in 1827, when Edward Fitz-Ball's play *The Flying Dutchman* was playing at the Adelphi Theatre, so it would have been possible for him to have seen it. But Heine told Wagner in Paris, in 1840, that the 'Amsterdam play' was his own invention, and that the theme of redemption through love, to which he could see the composer attached great significance, was his, Heine's, original contribution to the myth.

Wagner revealed what the precise significance of the Flying Dutchman myth was to him, in *A Communication to My Friends*:

The figure of the Flying Dutchman is a mythical creation of the folk: a primal trait of human nature speaks out from it with heart-enthralling force. This trait, in its most universal meaning, is the longing for respite from the storms of life. In the blithe world of Greece we meet with it in the wanderings of Ulysses and his longing for home, house, hearth, and wife: the attainable, and at last attained, reward of the city-loving son of ancient Hellas. The Christian, without a home on earth, embodied this trait in the figure of the Wandering Jew: for that wanderer, forever doomed to a long-since outlived life, without an aim, without any joy, there bloomed no earthly ransom; death was the sole remaining goal of all his strivings; his only hope, the laying down of being.

At the close of the Middle Ages a new, more active impulse led the nations to fresh life: in the world-historical direction its most important result was the urge to voyages of discovery. The sea, in its turn, became the soil of life; yet no longer the narrow, landlocked sea of the Grecian world, but the great ocean that engirdles all the earth. The fetters of the older world were broken; the longing of Ulysses, for home and hearth and wedded wife, after feeding on the sufferings of the 'never-dying Jew' until it became a yearning for death, had mounted to the craving for a new, an unknown home, invisible as yet, but dimly boded. This vast-spread feature confronts us in the myth of the Flying Dutchman—that seaman's poem from the world-historical age of journeys of discovery. There we light upon a remarkable mixture, a blend, effected by the spirit of the folk, of the character of Ulysses with that of the Wandering Jew.

The Dutch mariner, in punishment for his temerity, is condemned by the Devil (here, obviously the element of flood and storm) to do battle with the unresting waves, to all eternity. Like Ahasuerus, he yearns for his sufferings to be ended by death; the Dutchman, however, may gain this redemption, denied to the undying Jew, at the hands of a woman who, for love alone, shall sacrifice herself for him. The yearning for death thus spurs him on to seek this woman; but she is no longer the home-tending Penelope of Ulysses, as courted in the days of old, but the quintessence of womankind; and yet the still unmanifest, the longed-for, the dreamed-of, the infinitely womanly woman—let me out with it in one phrase: the woman of the future.

This was that Flying Dutchman who arose so often from the swamps and billows of my life, and drew me to him with such resistless might; this was the first folk-poem that forced its way into my heart, and called on me as man and artist to convey its meaning, and mould it as a work of art.

From here begins my career as poet, and my farewell to the mere concoctor of opera texts. And yet I took no sudden leap. In no way was I influenced by reflection; for reflection comes only from the mental combination of existing models: whereas I nowhere found the specimens which might have served as beacons on my road. My course was new; it was bidden me by my inner mood, and forced upon me by the pressing need to impart this mood to others. In order to enfranchise myself from within, that is, to address myself to the understanding of like-feeling men, I was driven to strike out for myself, as an artist, a path as yet not indicated to me by any outward experience; and that which drives a man hereto is necessity, deeply felt, not recognizable by practical reason but overmastering necessity.

It is curious that Wagner should have discovered elements of the Wandering Jew in the Dutchman myth, but in a sense it is understandable, for to him the Jew was someone greatly in need of a redemption which, in the Christian world, he could never find. Wagner's Dutchman, then, embodies the composer's earliest thoughts on the character and dilemma of the Wandering Jew, just as Kundry in *Parsifal* many years later represents his mature attitude to the subject. His Dutchman carries on his own shoulders the *Weltschmerz* of his race, and what he flees from is responsibility for the betrayal and murder of Jesus.

Unlike the Wandering Jew, however, the Dutchman can be redeemed by the love of a faithful woman, and it is in contemplating this touch added by Heine to the legend that Wagner not only takes a creative leap into the world of the Goethean *Ewigweibliche*, but also anticipates Ibsen in bringing into existence the new woman. The woman sought by Wagner's Dutchman is, as the composer himself pointed out, no longer the home-tending Penelope of ancient Greece, but the woman of the future.

Of course, the Dutchman is not only the Wandering Jew. He is also, and most importantly, the artist; and not just the artist in general, but Wagner in particular: Wagner, at this stage of his life, willing to accept his wife, Minna, as his redeemer. In his first sketch for the opera, the heroine's name is not Senta but Minna. Much of his own self-pity finds its way into the mouth of the Dutchman, for example in the *maestoso* section of his Act I aria, at the words '*War ich unsel'ger Spielwerk deines Spottes, als die Erlösung du mir zeigtest an?*' (Was I the unhappy plaything of your mockery when you showed me the possibility of redemption?). Heine's cynically frivolous conclusion, in his *Memoirs of Herr von Schnabelewopski*, that the moral of the play is that women should never marry Flying Dutchman, and that men can expect no better from women than to go down and perish, even if under favourable circumstances, is not one which Wagner would have had the humour to endorse. It is, in fact, his lack of humour, his ability to accept every aspect of the myth with the greatest seriousness, that enabled him to compose so hypnotically compelling an opera on the subject. When, many years later, he came to see himself as Parsifal, or as Tristan—even not so many years later when he saw himself as Lohengrin—a certain garrulity and lack of proportion had begun to obtrude themselves upon Wagner's artistic instincts, even in his greatest works. In his twenties when he wrote *Der fliegende Holländer*, composing the music in seven weeks, he was young enough for this not to be the case.

Wagner's involvement in the myth of the Dutchman, and his intensifying and humanizing of it, did not end with the composition of the opera. He has left detailed and fascinating notes on how the characters are to be conceived and performed. In an essay, 'Remarks on performing the opera *The Flying Dutchman*', he takes the reader, bar by bar, through the Dutchman's first scene, and almost move by move through his Act II scene with Senta, instructing the performers how and where to move, and on which bar to make what gesture:

Throughout the lengthy first *fermata* he [the Dutchman] stays motionless beside the door. At the commencement of the drum solo he slowly strides downstage. With the eighth bar of that solo, he halts. (The two bars *accelerando* for the strings relate to the gestures of Daland, who still stands wondering in the doorway, awaiting Senta's welcome, and impatiently invites it with a movement of his outstretched arms.) During the next three bars for the drum, the Dutchman advances to the extreme front of the stage, at the side, where he now remains without moving, his eyes bent fixedly on Senta. (The recurrence of the figure for the strings relates to the emphatic repetition of Daland's gesture.) At the *pizzicato* on the next *fermata*, Daland ceases inviting her, and shakes his head in amazement. With the entry of the basses, after the *fermata*, he himself comes down to Senta.

And so on.

Wagner is most interesting, in more general terms, on the character of Senta:

The role of Senta will be hard to misread. One warning alone have I to give: let not the dreamy side of her nature be conceived in the sense of a modern, sickly sentimentality. Senta, on the contrary, is an altogether robust Northern maid, and even in her apparent sentimentality she is thoroughly naïve. Only in the heart of an entirely naïve girl, surrounded by the idiosyncrasies of northern nature, could impressions such as those of the ballad of the Flying Dutchman and the picture of the pallid seaman call forth so wondrously strong a response as the impulse to redeem the doomed man. With her this takes the outward form of an active monomania, such as can be found, indeed, only in quite naïve natures. We have been told of Norwegian maids of such a force of feeling that death has come upon them through a sudden rigour of the heart. Much in this wise may it go with the seeming 'morbidness' of pale Senta.

'Nor must Erik', continues the composer, 'be a sentimental whiner. On the contrary, he is stormy, impulsive and sombre, like every man who lives alone (particularly in the northern highlands).' Of Senta's father, Wagner writes:

I beseech the exponent of Daland not to drag his role into the region of the positively comic. He is a rough-hewn figure from everyday life, a sailor who scoffs at storms and danger for the sake of gain, and with whom, for instance, the (as it appears to him) sale of his daughter to a rich man ought not to seem at all disgraceful. He thinks and acts, like a hundred thousand others, without the least suspicion that he is doing anything wrong.

III

VIEWED today in the light of Wagner's later achievements, and especially of *Tristan und Isolde, Der Ring des Nibelungen* and *Parsifal, Der fliegende Holländer* may seem a rather conventional work, revealing more in common with earlier German operas than with the masterpieces of Wagner's maturity. At the time of its composition and its first performances, however, it was thought to indicate a radical departure from the composer's usual practice. It is, in fact, the first opera in which Wagner made significant use of the device of the leitmotiv or leading motif, a musical theme specifically associated with either an individual character or an element in the drama.

Der fliegende Holländer is also a transitional work in the sense that, though it is not a 'number' opera, as Wagner's first three works for the stage were, it is not yet a fully fledged *durchkomponiert* or through-composed music drama. Separate numbers, such as the Dutchman's aria, Senta's ballad or Erik's cavatina, can be easily discerned, but the numbers are not formally separated from one another by recitative. Although, for the sake of convenience, Wagner divided his score into an Overture and eight numbers, *Der fliegende Holländer* was really conceived in larger units. Four of the score's eight numbers are, in fact, scenes which can be broken down into smaller components, as will become apparent in the following pages. As a result Wagner's melodic writing displays a greater fluency and freedom than in his earlier operas. *Der fliegende Holländer* is the first of Wagner's operas to adopt a three-act structure, a shape which the composer was subsequently to adhere to throughout his entire *oeuvre*, with the exception of *Das Rheingold*, the one-act prelude to the operas of *Der Ring des Nibelungen*.

It is not only in the music of his new opera that a distinct advance upon his three earlier stage works can be noticed. Wagner the librettist finds his individual voice for the first time in *Der fliegende Holländer*, no longer describing his characters conventionally, from the outside, but making them almost extensions of certain aspects of his own personality. The Dutchman, and even Senta, are considerably closer to Wagner than were any of the characters in *Die Feen, Das Liebesverbot* or *Rienzi*. As the composer himself wrote:

> The modern division into arias, duets, finales and so on, I had at once to give up, and in their stead narrate the saga in one breath, just as should be done in a good poem. In this manner, I brought forth an opera, of which, now that it has been performed, I cannot conceive how it could have pleased. For in its every external feature, it is so completely unlike that which one now calls opera, that I see indeed how much I demanded of the public, namely, that they should with one blow dissever themselves from all that which had hitherto entertained and appealed to them in the theatre.

When *Der fliegende Holländer* was being rehearsed for a production in Munich in 1864, the conductor, Franz Lachner, complained of 'the wind that blows out at you wherever you open the score'. His is a poetic and graphically penetrating description of the opera, which is imbued with the spirit of the storm-tossed ocean, from the first bars of its Overture until the final curtain. The Overture, a tone-poem which summarizes the action of the entire opera, contains all of the work's leading motifs, that of the anguished figure of the Dutchman (Ex. 2) making an immediate appearance, soon followed by the

Ex.2

theme associated with his redemption through Senta's love, later to be heard in Senta's Act II ballad, but here played on the cor anglais. The tempo quickens again, and other themes associated with the stormy ocean and the Dutchman's wandering over the seas are heard, juxtaposed against the vigorous, blunt tune which Daland's crew sing to keep their spirits up. The latter part of the overture is dominated by the redemption motif (Ex. 3).

Ex.3

Wagner's original version of the Overture had ended, after a final statement of the Dutchman's motif, with a few conventionally emphatic chords. In its revised, definitive form, it comes to an almost serene close with the redemption theme. The curtain rises on a seashore, with steep cliffs. A violent storm is raging, which has forced Daland's fishing vessel to take shelter in the bay, and Daland has gone ashore to reconnoitre. Sailors are busy furling sails and throwing ropes to secure the ship to land. Daland (bass) descends to the shore from the cliff, having ascertained that they are no more than seven miles from their home port. He laments that the storm has delayed his homecoming, especially as he had been able to glimpse his house where his daughter Senta is awaiting his return.

After being satisfied by his helmsman (tenor) that their ship is safely moored, Daland allows the rest of the crew to go below to rest, instructing the helmsman to keep watch. Daland himself goes below, and a fragment of what later becomes a dance-tune for the sailors is heard briefly as the exhausted helmsman begins his watch. He tries to keep awake by singing a song to himself, but finally succumbs to sleep. As the sky darkens and the storm threatens again, the blood-red sails and black masts of a phantom ship loom up on the horizon. The Flying Dutchman's ship rapidly approaches, and drops anchor with a tremendous crash close to the Norwegian ship. The helmsman momentarily half-awakens, murmuring a few bars of his song but sinking back into sleep. The ghostly crew of the Dutchman's vessel furl their sails, and the Dutchman himself steps ashore.

The music of this opening section sets the scene superbly, from the sailor's cries of 'Hojohe! Hallojo!' as they work—Wagner was to become increasingly fond of these elemental exclamations—through Daland's brisk arioso and his lyrical references to his house and daughter, and the simple song of the helmsman, to the eerie sounds of the Dutchman's motif as his ship mysteriously appears.

The Dutchman (baritone) now steps ashore. In a magnificent piece of dramatic and flexible recitative ('*Die Frist ist um*') and an exciting and moving aria ('*Wie oft in Meeres tiefsten Schlund*'), he broods on his fate. The following is a translation of Wagner's text:

(*Recitative*) The term is up. Another seven years have passed. Full of weariness, the ocean throws me on to land. Ha, proud ocean! In a short time you will carry me again. Your challenge is ever-changing, but my torment is eternal. The grace that I seek on land, I shall never find. To you, tides of the ocean, I shall remain true, until your last wave breaks and your last drop of water dries.

(*Aria*) How often into the sea's gloomiest depths have I hurled myself in yearning, but, alas, I could not find death. On to the rocks where many a ship has found its fearsome grave, I drove my vessel. But, alas, my grave would never close. With taunts I challenged pirates, hoping for death in fierce combat. 'Here,' I cried, 'show me your courage. My ship is full of treasure.' Alas, the sea's barbaric sons anxiously crossed themselves and fled. Nowhere a grave! Never my death! This is the dreadful decree of damnation.

I ask you, most blessed angel of God, who won for me the terms of my salvation, was I the unhappy plaything of your mockery when you showed me the possibility of redemption? Vain hope! Dreadful, empty fancy! There is no eternal fidelity to be found on earth.

Only one hope remains to me, only one remains unshattered. Although earth's seeds may continue to flourish, one day it must all come to an end. Day of judgement! Last day! When will you come to end my night? When will the knell of doom sound with which the earth shall be destroyed? When all the dead arise, then shall I become nothingness. Planets, end your course! Eternal oblivion, take me.

With the Dutchman's great monologue, Wagner's writing for the stage takes an immense leap forward into maturity. The expressive recitative conveys in its complexity all of the character's hopelessness, his desperate *Weltschmerz* and his longing for oblivion. The aria begins in a fierce *allegro molto agitato*, the baritone's voice heard above the undulating motif that represents the restless wandering to which he is doomed. In a slower *maestoso* ('*Dich frage ich, gepriesner Engel Gottes*': Tell me, I pray, Oh Angel sent from heaven), over *tremolando* chords in the cellos and basses he makes his impassioned plea for release from his torment, but in the final section of the aria ('*Nur eine Hoffnung*': One hope alone) he realizes that he must await the day of judgement before he can achieve the peace of non-existence. '*Ew'ger Vernichtung, nimm mich auf!*' (Eternal oblivion, take me!), he cries, and his plea is repeated in hollow, empty tones by the seamen on his ship, condemned to share his fate.

Daland now emerges from his cabin, sees the strange ship at anchor close to his own vessel, and reprimands his helmsman for having slept on duty. The helmsman hails the other ship, but gets no reply. However, Daland now catches sight of the Dutchman, who, in reply to his questions, explains that he is Dutch, that his ship has suffered no damage in the storm, but that he has been sailing for years without having found his homeland. His ship, he says, is heavily laden with treasures from many lands, priceless pearls and precious stones. At his signal, two members of his crew emerge, bearing a casket of jewels which the Dutchman offers to Daland in return for one night's shelter. He asks if Daland has a daughter, and then immediately offers all his riches for Senta's hand in marriage.

Excited at the prospect of acquiring so wealthy a son-in-law, Daland agrees, and invites the Dutchman to follow him to harbour as soon as the wind changes. The wind obligingly changes, but the Dutchman asks Daland to go on ahead. His own crew are tired, and need more rest, but his ship is fast and will soon overtake the Norwegian vessel. Daland boards his ship to pipe his crew, and they cast off to the strains of the helmsman's song, now sung by all the crew. The curtain falls.

After the intensity of the Dutchman's aria, his conversational exchanges with Daland can sound a trifle mundane. The *allegro giusto* section of their duet is attractive, Daland's opportunistic mutterings blending neatly with the Dutchman's more sympathetic and more broadly phrased sentiments, but the tune ('*Wohl, Fremdling, hab' ich eine schöne Tochter*': True, Stranger, I have a beautiful daughter) to which Daland sells off his daughter might be thought inappropriately jaunty.

When *Der fliegende Holländer* is performed in one act, a cut of 24 bars at the end of Act I and 21 bars at the beginning of Act II is all that is required to allow postlude to blend into prelude. The curtain is lowered for the scene change, and when it rises again it reveals a room in Daland's house. On one wall is a portrait of a pale man with a dark beard, wearing a black costume. Senta's old nurse, Mary (mezzo-soprano), and a number of village maidens sit spinning. A little apart from them, Senta sits, contemplating the portrait.

While the girls work, they sing of their sweethearts, the fishermen out at sea, who will bring them presents of gold from exotic lands if they spin industriously. Mary chides Senta for not spinning like the others, warning her that if she does not work she will not be brought a present by her beloved. At this the other girls point out that Senta has no need to hurry with her spinning. Her beloved is not a fisherman, but a hunter. Game, rather than gold, is all he is likely to bring her. Senta pays no heed, as she is lost in contemplation of the portrait. When Mary rebukes her for dreaming her young life away in front of a picture, Senta (soprano) asks Mary why she ever told her about the Dutchman in the first place.

The girls tease Senta by remarking that her betrothed, Erik, is hot-blooded. He may become jealous, and shoot his rival off the wall. They finally succeed in arousing Senta's anger, and she tells them to stop singing their stupid spinning chorus. If they want her to join them, they should find a better song. She suggests that Mary sing them the Ballad of the Flying Dutchman. Mary refuses, and Senta herself sings it, in the hope that it will move the girls to sympathy for his fate. Her song recounts the legend, ending with the Dutchman's search, every seven years, for a faithful wife.

When the girls ask where the Dutchman's saviour is to be found, Senta leaps from her chair, exclaiming ecstatically that it is she who will redeem the unhappy man. Unfortunately, Erik (tenor) arrives just in time to hear this rash promise. He has seen Daland's ship approaching the harbour, and has come to inform Senta of her father's imminent return. The other girls rush out to greet the returning sailors, leaving Senta and Erik alone. Erik, who is in love with Senta, fears that Daland will prefer to choose a wealthy husband for her. Senta refuses to listen to him, saying that she must go to welcome her father. Erik reproaches her for her apparent indifference to his feelings, and accuses her of having become obsessed with the portrait of the Dutchman.

Senta confesses that she is moved by the fate of the Flying Dutchman, and when Erik asks her to show some sympathy for his sufferings as well she scornfully rejects the comparison. Erik then tells her of a dream he has had, in which he saw her father's ship approaching. Two men came ashore from it, Daland and a stranger: the man in the portrait. Senta came out of the house to greet her father, but when she saw the stranger she embraced him. She and he sailed away together.

Rather than being disconcerted, Senta is excited by Erik's dream, and exclaims that she must find the Dutchman and perish with him. Erik rushes out of the house in horror, and, as Senta prays that his dream may become reality, Daland and the Dutchman suddenly appear at the door.

At the rise of the curtain, the orchestra had made a transition from the sea music concluding Act I to the domestic sounds of the spinning-party. The spinning chorus itself is a charming piece, with an attractive, drowsily lilting melody, the humming of the spinning-wheels portrayed by the strings of the orchestra. Senta's ballad which follows it is a splendidly dramatic account of the legend of the Dutchman, its vocal melody preceded in the orchestra by the motifs of the stormy sea and the Dutchman. Of the ballad, Wagner wrote later, in *A Communication to My Friends*:

> I remember that, before I began to write *Der fliegende Holländer*, I first sketched out Senta's Act II ballad, composing both the words and the melody. In this piece I unconsciously planted the thematic germ of the music of the entire opera: it was an image in microcosm of the whole drama, as I saw it in my mind, and when I was about to give a title to the finished work I felt strongly tempted to call it 'a dramatic ballad'. In the eventual composition of the music, the thematic image I had already evoked instinctively spread itself over the entire drama as one continuous tissue. All that I had to do was allow the various thematic germs contained in the ballad to develop to their legitimate conclusions, and I had all the principal features of the text in definite shapes before me. I should have had to doggedly follow the example of the self-willed composer if I had chosen to invent a fresh motif for each recurrence of the same mood in different contexts, a course I did not feel at all inclined to adopt, since what I had in mind was the most intelligible portrayal of the subject matter, rather than a mere collection of operatic numbers.

The duet for Erik and Senta is fairly conventional, though not unattractive. In essence, it is a lyrical aria for Erik ('*Mein Herz, voll Treue bis zum Sterben*': My heart, faithful until death), with interjections from Senta. Erik's dream narrative has a dramatic trance-like intensity, making a fitting bridge to the finale of the act which begins with the arrival of the Dutchman and Senta's father. When Erik describes the stranger accompanying Daland, the Dutchman's motif creeps in on bassoons and cellos against a background of violas *tremolando*, to immense effect. Senta, her eyes fixed on the portrait, sings the redemption motif softly to herself, but ends with a scream as she sees the original of the portrait suddenly appear in the doorway with her father.

At the sight of the Dutchman, Senta seems transfixed. Her father asks her to give a courteous welcome to the stranger, and indeed to accept him as her bridegroom. At the same time, he praises Senta's virtues and her beauty to the Dutchman. Senta and the Dutchman continue to gaze at each other as though in mutual recognition. When Daland leaves them alone together, they finally express their thoughts. He sees before him the image he has been seeking for years, that of an angel who will bring him salvation, while she sees the man for whom she has always felt deep compassion. Asked by the Dutchman if she could give herself to him for ever, she swears to remain faithful to him until death. Daland returns, delighted to find that they have agreed to marry, and hastens to announce the happy event at the festivities for the sailors' homecoming which are about to begin.

The Act II finale consists of a progression of aria, duet and trio. Daland's aria, '*Mögst du, mein Kind, den fremden Mann willkommen heissen?*' (Will you, my child, offer this stranger a warm welcome?), is a pleasantly hearty *allegro moderato* in conventionally Italianate style, appropriate to Daland's uncomplex nature. The duet for Senta and the Dutchman, '*Wie aus der Ferne längst vergang'ner Zeiten*' (As from the depths of long-forgotten times), is the centrepiece of the opera, a solemn declaration of love and yearning. This deeply felt outpouring of emotion is one of Wagner's finest creations, despite its resorting at one point to a conventional Italianate cadenza. The duet becomes increasingly impassioned until it ends in a state of radiant exaltation, initiated by Senta's '*Was ist's, das mächtig in mir lebet?*' (What is this powerful feeling that lives in me?).

The conclusion of the duet is followed precipitately by Daland's return, and the act ends with a short *allegro* trio which brings the curtain down in a flurry of excitement.

When the opera is performed in one act, a cut of twelve bars is made: the last eight bars of the postlude to Act II and the first four of the introduction to Act III. The curtain rises on the harbour, at night. Daland's ship is lit up, and its crew are dancing and singing on board. Close to it is the Dutchman's ship, dark and silent. The Norwegian sailors call out to the Dutchman's crew to come and join in their festivities, but they receive no reply. The village girls arrive with food and drink; but, when they offer to share their refreshments with the crew of the strange vessel, they too meet with no response. The Norwegian sailors mockingly suggest that the strangers must be dead if they have no need of food and drink. Becoming somewhat frightened when their sweethearts point out that the foreign ship could well be that of the notorious Flying Dutchman, the girls leave, promising to return later, and advising the local lads meanwhile to let their weary neighbours rest in peace.

The Norwegians taunt the strange crew, daring them to show themselves. At length, the sea, otherwise calm, begins to heave around the Dutchman's ship, and a violent wind whistles through its rigging. A faint, blue flame illuminates the hitherto invisible crew, who now drown out the singing of the Norwegians with their own ghostly chorus in which they call on their captain either to produce his promised bride or to put out to sea again. The Norwegians attempt to counter their eerie chanting, but the song of the Dutchman's crew overwhelms their singing and dancing, and the Norwegians flee in terror, at which the crew of the Dutchman's ship burst into scornful laughter. Suddenly, their ship becomes deathly still again, with the sea and sky completely calm.

The vigorous sailors' song dominates proceedings at the beginning of the act, but soon gives way, first to a more general merriment when the girls arrive, and then eventually to the sinister chorus of the Dutch sailors. Wagner paints this scene vividly: there is no hint of the conventional operatic chorus in this dramatic confrontation between the live Norwegians and the ghostly Dutch crew.

Senta appears, followed by Erik, who can hardly believe that the girl to whom he considered himself betrothed could have agreed to marry a man she has just met. Senta replies that it is her duty to do so, at which Erik reminds her of her duty to him, and of the happy days of the past when she assured him of her love. This conversation has been overheard by the Dutchman, who now comes forward crying that all is lost, and that he must return to sea for all eternity. 'Farewell, I will not destroy you,' he calls to Senta.

Erik tries to warn Senta that she is in the clutches of Satan, as the Dutchman announces that countless victims have suffered eternal damnation through breaking their vows to him, but that Senta will be saved because, although she promised to be faithful, she did not swear an oath before God.

Terrified, Erik calls for help, while Senta attempts to stop the Dutchman from returning to his ship. Mary, Daland and the villagers all arrive in time to hear the Dutchman declare his identity as he swiftly boards his ship, which immediately puts out to sea. They are unable to restrain Senta as she rushes to the top of a cliff, calling to the Dutchman, 'Praise your angel and his decree. Here I stand, true to you till death!' She throws herself into the sea, and immediately the Dutchman's ship sinks beneath the waves. In the glow of the rising sun, the transfigured forms of the Dutchman and Senta are seen in close embrace, rising from the wreck of the ship and soaring upwards to heaven.

The scene between Senta and Erik is exciting and swiftly paced, though it is perhaps a trifle surprising that Wagner should have chosen to insert a lyrical aria for Erik ('*Willst jenes Tags du nicht dich mehr entsinnen?*': Do you no longer remember the day?) which jeopardizes the dramatic momentum which has been built up. The Dutchman's arrival leads to a brief trio, and on to the almost brutally swift finale. As the souls of the Dutchman and Senta ascend to heaven, the motif of redemption is heard in the orchestra in the transfigured form in which it appeared at the close of the Overture.

SEEN in the light of the later music dramas of Wagner, *Der fliegende Holländer* is clearly a transitional work, though it is, nevertheless, an enormous step forward from *Rienzi*. It is the composer's first encounter with folk-myth, which was to form the basis of so much of his mature *oeuvre*, but he came to it fully fledged, and the fruit of the encounter is an opera which is in no sense an apprentice-work. That he was to deal differently with the world of myth in his masterpieces *Tristan und Isolde*, *Parsifal* and *Der Ring des Nibelungen* does not invalidate the fresher, crisper, more Italianate approach of *Der fliegende Holländer*, a work so filled with strong passions that it has simply no time for weak *longueurs*.

FIVE

Tannhäuser und der Sängerkrieg auf dem Wartburg

(Tannhäuser and the Song Contest on the Wartburg)

Grand Romantic Opera in Three Acts

Dramatis personae
Hermann, Landgrave of Thuringia   (bass)
Tannhäuser   (tenor)
Wolfram von Eschenbach   (baritone)
Walter von der Vogelweide   (tenor)
Biterolf   (bass)   Minstrel-knights
Heinrich der Schreiber   (tenor)
Reinmar von Zweter   (bass)
Elisabeth, the Landgrave's Niece   (soprano)
Venus, Goddess of Love   (soprano)
A Shepherd Boy   (soprano)

LIBRETTO by the composer

TIME: The early thirteenth century

PLACE: Thuringia, near Eisenach

FIRST PERFORMED at the Hoftheater, Dresden, 19 October 1845, with Johanna Wagner (Elisabeth), Wilhelmine Schröder-Devrient (Venus), Joseph Tichatschek (Tannhäuser) and Anton Mitterwurzer (Wolfram), conducted by the composer. Revised version first performed at the Paris Opéra, 13 March 1861, with Marie Saxe (Elisabeth), Fortunata Tedesco (Venus), Albert Niemann (Tannhäuser) and Signor Morelli (Wolfram), conducted by Pierre Dietsch.

I

ALTHOUGH the Dresden première of *Der fliegende Holländer* can hardly be described as a blazing success, with the opera achieving only four performances, Wagner was nevertheless offered the post of music director at the theatre. He declined to accept, however, since the position was subordinate to that of Kapellmeister to the Saxon Court. Fortunately, the King of Saxony admired, with reservations, both *Rienzi* and *Der fliegende Holländer*, and when his Kapellmeister, Francesco Morlacchi, died while on leave, Wagner was offered the lifelong position of Royal Kapellmeister, which he accepted, although not all that gracefully. 'The decision', the composer wrote in *My Life*,

> came as a kind of surprise. On 2 February 1843, I was very politely invited into the director's office, and there met the general staff of the royal orchestra, in whose presence Lüttichau [Director of the Court Opera] . . . solemnly read out to me a royal decree appointing me forthwith conductor to His Majesty, with a salary for life of four thousand five hundred marks a year.
>
> Lüttichau followed the reading of this document by a more or less ceremonious speech, in which he assumed that I would gratefully accept the King's favour. At this polite ceremony it did not escape my notice that all possibility of future negotiations over the figure of the salary was cut off. On the other hand, a substantial exemption in my favour, the omission of the condition which had been enforced upon Weber in his time, of having to serve a year's probation under the title of mere music director, was calculated to secure my unconditional acceptance.
>
> My new colleagues congratulated me, and Lüttichau with the politest phrases accompanied me home, where I fell into the arms of my poor wife who was giddy with delight. Therefore I fully realized that I must put the best face I could on the situation and, unless I wished to give unheard-of offence, I must even congratulate myself on my appointment as royal conductor.

Now that Wagner was in an established position and earning a decent salary, his creditors began to reassemble around him, even from as far away as Riga. 'I also heard from people in the most distant parts,' he wrote in his autobiography, 'who thought they had some claim on me, dating even from my student, indeed my school days, until at last I exclaimed in my astonishment that I expected to receive a bill next from the nurse who had suckled me.' Highly indignant that those tradesmen to whom he owed money now expected to be paid, he borrowed 3000 marks from Wilhelmine Schröder-Devrient to satisfy them.

All was not plain sailing at the theatre. When he attempted to appoint a

Darmstadt musician to the orchestra to fill a vacancy, Wagner discovered that he was not allowed to do so. The Dresden system required him to fill the vacancy from within the ranks, in a strict order of priority which took no account of the competence of the players concerned. And when his method of rehearsing *Don Giovanni* met with the disapproval of the leader of the orchestra, the Kapellmeister received no support from the director, who, on the contrary, made him promise, in writing, 'to alter nothing in the hitherto accepted interpretation of tempo, etc., when conducting older operas, even when it goes against my artistic judgement, leaving myself nevertheless free, when studying newer operas, to exercise my best judgement with the object of getting as perfect an interpretation as possible.'

Nevertheless, once he had settled in at Dresden, Wagner found time to work on his next opera, despite the fact that he was also obliged to compose a certain amount of occasional music. For the Dresden Liedertafel (or Choral Society) he composed *The Love Feast of the Apostles*, which he conducted at a festival of all the Saxon choral societies, when it was performed by a chorus of twelve hundred male voices and an orchestra of one hundred. To celebrate the unveiling of a statue of the late King Friedrich August I, he wrote another male-voice chorus. What chiefly occupied his attention, however, was his next work for the stage.

It was in the previous summer, during a hiking holiday in the mountains of Bohemia, that Wagner had begun to plan the libretto for his new opera, which at that time he thought of calling *Der Venusberg* (The Mount of Venus). 'One day,' he wrote, 'when climbing the Wostrai [the highest peak in the vicinity], I was astonished, on rounding a bend and entering a valley, to hear a merry dance tune whistled by a goatherd perched up on a crag. I seemed immediately to be standing among a chorus of pilgrims filing past the goatherd in the valley. However, I could not later recall the goatherd's tune, so I was obliged to help myself out in the matter, in my usual fashion.'

In due course the opera's title, which had given rise to ribald comments among the students and professors of the medical school in Dresden, was changed to *Tannhäuser und der Sängerkrieg auf dem Wartburg* (Tannhäuser and the Song Contest on the Wartburg). 'Bad enough', said Wagner's publisher, 'that some of the action be located on the Mountain of Venus.' By May 1843, the libretto had been completed, and in August Wagner began to compose the music. By the end of the following January, he had finished Act I. 'I have no recollections of any importance', he was to write in *My Life*, 'regarding my activities in Dresden during this winter.' Clearly, all his energies were devoted to the creation of the new opera.

The second act of *Tannhäuser* was composed during the summer of 1844, and completed by mid-October. Wagner later claimed that, during this time, his relationship with the theatre director, Baron von Lüttichau, which had previously been friendly though formal, began to deteriorate. 'Nevertheless,' he wrote, 'a certain peculiar tenderness towards me on the part of this singular man was always clearly perceptible. Indeed, I might almost say that much of his subsequent abuse of me sounded more like the strangely perverted plaints of an unrequited lover.'

By the end of 1844 Wagner had completed the composition of *Tannhäuser*, and by early the following April had finished scoring the entire work. It was decided that the opera should be given its première in Dresden in the autumn: after some preliminary rehearsals, the company dispersed for the summer. With Minna, Wagner travelled to Marienbad to take the water cure, on the advice of his doctor who had advised him to relax. Here he found his thoughts turning to his next opera, *Lohengrin*, which, he wrote later, 'stood suddenly revealed before me, complete in every detail of its dramatic construction'. In order to avoid over-exerting himself and to distract his attention from the Lohengrin project, he began to draft a humourous scene involving the sixteenth-century Nuremberg poet, Hans Sachs.

In mid-August, Wagner and Minna returned to Dresden, and in September rehearsals for *Tannhäuser* were resumed in earnest. The principal roles were undertaken by Joseph Tichatschek as Tannhäuser, the composer's young niece Johanna Wagner as Elisabeth, the famous Wilhelmine Schröder-Devrient as Venus, and a young baritone named Mitterwurzer as Wolfram.

We had now got so far, at least with the musical side of the production, that a possible opening date seemed not far off. Schröder-Devrient was one of the first to realize the extraordinary difficulties which the production of *Tannhäuser* would entail. And, indeed, she saw these difficulties so clearly that, to my great discomfiture, she was able to lay them all before me. Once when I called upon her, she read the principal passages aloud with great feeling and force, and then she asked me how I could have been so simple-minded as to have thought that so childish a creature as Tichatschek would be able to find the proper tones for Tannhäuser. I tried to bring her attention and my own to bear upon the nature of the music, which was written so clearly in order to bring out the necessary accent, that, in my opinion, the music actually spoke for the tenor who interpreted it, even if he were no actor. She shook her head, saying that this would be so only in the case of an oratorio.

She now sang Elisabeth's prayer, from the piano score, and asked me if I really thought that this music would achieve the effect I desired if sung by a young and pretty voice without any soul or without that experience of life which alone could give real expression to the interpretation. I sighed and said that, in that case, the youthfulness of the voice and its possessor must make up for what was lacking. At the same time, I asked her as a favour to me to see what she could do towards helping my niece, Johanna, to understand her part. All this, however, did not solve the problem of the role of Tannhäuser, for any attempt to teach Tichatschek would only have resulted in confusion. I was therefore obliged to rely entirely on the singer's peculiarly incisive 'speaking' tone.

Schröder-Devrient's anxiety about the principal parts arose partly out of concern about her own. She did not know what to do with the role of Venus. She had undertaken it to help ensure the success of the performance for, although it was a small part, so much depended upon its being ideally interpreted. Later on, when the work was given in Paris, I became convinced that I had written this part in too sketchy a manner, and this induced me to reconstruct it by making extensive additions and by supplying all that which I felt it lacked. For the moment, however, it looked as if no art on the part of the singer could give to this sketchy role anything to help it become what it ought to be.

The only thing that might have helped towards a satisfactory impersonation of Venus would have been the singer's confidence in her own great physical attraction, and in the effect it would help to produce by appealing to the public on that level. But the certainty that these means were no longer at her disposal paralysed this great singer, who could disguise her age and matronly appearance no longer. She therefore became self-conscious, and unable to use even her normal means of gaining an effect. On one occasion, with a little smile of despair, she expressed herself incapable of playing Venus, for the very simple reason that she could not appear dressed as the goddess ought to be dressed. 'What on earth am I to wear as Venus?' she exclaimed. 'After all, I cannot be clad in a girdle alone. A nice figure of fun I should look, and you would laugh on the other side of your face!'

The first performance of *Tannhäuser* was given at the Dresden Hoftheater on 19 October 1845, conducted by the composer, without most of the scenery, which had been ordered from Paris and which failed to arrive in time. The opera's reception was lukewarm, press criticism was unfavourable, and a rumour that the work was Catholic propaganda began to circulate, which of course did nothing to help *Tannhäuser* achieve popularity in a Protestant country. By the second performance, the role of Tannhäuser had been shortened, the scenery had arrived from Paris, and a far from full house gave the work a warmer reception than the first-night audience had accorded it. For the third performance, the theatre was packed.

Four years were to elapse before Tannhäuser was staged elsewhere, and ten years or more before it was seen on such important stages as those of Berlin, Munich and Vienna. Wagner's essay on sacred and profane love was in general thought to be too slow and stately for its subject matter. The composer himself realized that the work was unsatisfactory, and almost immediately began to revise it. When *Tannhäuser* was revived in Dresden in 1847, a number of changes were made to Act III. Further revision found its way into the vocal score of 1852 and a newly engraved orchestral score in 1860. By the time he received his first copies of this full score, Wagner had already decided to revise the opera again, for its production at the Paris Opéra.

Wagner and Minna were at this time living in Paris, where the composer was doing his best to promote himself by giving concerts of his music and attempting to persuade the Opéra to stage *Tannhäuser*. In due course, the Opéra agreed to produce the work. The management, however, did not mount a production immediately. Months went by, and it was not until Princess Metternich, the wife of the Austrian ambassador, used her influence with the Empress, that a performance was commanded and the newly revised *Tannhäuser* finally reached the stage.

Wagner had altered the opening scene of the opera, developing and expanding the ballet music. That he should have done this especially for Paris was not only desirable but obligatory, since all operas produced at the Paris Opéra had to contain ballets. Yet there was still a problem: in *Tannhäuser* the ballet music occurred in the first act, but the dictators of Parisian taste were quite specific in their requirement that the ballet should be in Act II. This was an unwritten rule enforced by the fashionable young men of the Jockey Club, an immensely conservative and philistine organization. Its members liked to turn up at the Opéra just in time to see the ballet, or at any rate to appreciate the charms of the female dancers; besides, they had to be given time to finish dining at a properly elegant late hour before strolling to the theatre.

M. Royer, the manager of the Opéra, attempted to impress upon Wagner the necessity of providing a ballet in Act II. He explained, as did several of the composer's friends, that it would be folly to incur the displeasure of the Jockey Club by failing to cater for its members' tastes. Wagner, however, was adamant that his *Tannhäuser* required no ballet in its second act. He hoped instead to please the Parisians with the rewritten and expanded sequence in Act I. If that was too early for the Jockey Club, he was willing to stage a separate ballet at the end of the evening, after the opera.

Dismissing the problem from his mind, Wagner turned his attention to two new tasks: the supervision of a French translation of his libretto and the selection of a suitable cast of singers. The principals eventually chosen were Albert Niemann, a tenor from Hanover, as Tannhäuser; Fortunata Tedesco, a voluptuously Junoesque soprano, as Venus; the twenty-one-year-old Marie Saxe as Elisabeth; and an Italian baritone, Morelli, as Wolfram. Rehearsals began. There were to be 163 before the first night, most of them conducted by Wagner himself.

However, since the tradition of the Paris Opéra forbade a composer from conducting his own work, the première was entrusted to a mediocre musician named Pierre Dietsch (he who, in 1842, had composed an opera about the Flying Dutchman and had been accused by Wagner of having stolen his libretto). Dietsch took over only at the final rehearsals of *Tannhäuser*. In due course, after a number of delays, arguments about the ballet and difficulties with the singers, dates were announced for the public performances, and a satisfactory dress rehearsal was held.

On the first night, 13 March 1861, despite the presence of the Emperor and Empress and the leaders of Paris society, the performance was disrupted by organized demonstrations by members of the Jockey Club, furious that the composer had disregarded their wishes concerning the ballet. At the second performance, five nights later, they continued their attack. Wagner recalled the occasion in *My Life*:

> The first act promised well. The Overture was loudly applauded without a note of opposition. Madame Tedesco, who had been completely won over to her role of Venus by a wig powdered with gold dust, called out triumphantly to me in the manager's box that everything was now all right. But when shrill whistling was suddenly heard in the second act, Royer the manager turned to me with an air of complete resignation and said, '*Ce sont les Jockeys. Nous sommes perdus.*' From that time he gave up all attempt to resist them.
>
> The impression made by this scene had a disastrous effect upon my friends. After the performance, von Bülow burst into sobs as he embraced Minna, my wife, who had not been spared the insults of those next to her when they recognized her as the wife of the composer. Our trusty servant Therese, a Swabian girl, had been sneered at by a crazy hooligan, but when she realized that he understood German, she succeeded in quietening him for a time by calling him '*Schweinhund*' at the top of her voice.

Isolated moments of the performance were heard in silence, but there were interruptions in every scene of the opera. Twice, the performance was held up by fights in the auditorium lasting for a quarter of an hour or more. The greater part of the audience no doubt wanted genuinely to give *Tannhäuser* a fair hearing but, as Wagner himself realized, they were at a disadvantage. When all of the composer's supporters were utterly exhausted with applauding and calling for order, and it looked as if the performance might be resumed, the Jockey Club began again cheerfully playing the whistles and pipes they had brought into the theatre.

The philistines triumphed, and *Tannhäuser* was not heard again in Paris for thirty-four years. Princess Metternich, herself subjected to insults and ridicule at the first two performances, was heard to say to one of her French friends, 'I've had enough of your free France. In Vienna, where at least there is a genuine aristocracy, it would be unthinkable for a Prince Liechtenstein or Schwarzenberg to scream from his box for a ballet in *Fidelio*.'

It was not until November 1875, when Hans Richter conducted *Tannhäuser* in Vienna, that the work was performed in German with the changes made for Paris, and by this time Wagner had made several more alterations to his score. New York's first *Tannhäuser* was a production of the original Dresden version at the Stadt Theater on 4 April 1859, when it became the first opera by Wagner to be staged anywhere in the Americas. This seems to have been very much a German-community occasion: one critic wrote that 'objections were made . . . to the thoroughly German atmosphere pervading the whole affair. Boys went through the aisles with beer in stone mugs for the thirsty, and huge chunks of *Schweizerkäs* for the hungry.' The opera was not staged in London until 1875, when it reached Covent Garden in a production of which the critic Herman Klein wrote, 'Of the performance, the less said the better. It satisfied curiosity without affording a true idea of the opera. [Auguste] Vianesi knew little or nothing of Wagner's intentions as to the reading of the score, and only [Emma] Albani [who sang Elisabeth] and [Victor] Maurel [Wolfram] made any kind of permanent impression.'

Today, the sojourn of Tannhäuser, the medieval knight, with Venus, goddess of love, seems impossibly tame (though of course less so in what is loosely described as the Paris version), while his spiritual relationship with the pure Elisabeth is singularly unconvincing. It was the various set-pieces and arias, among them Elisabeth's '*Dich, teure Halle*' and Wolfram's song to the evening star, '*O du, mein holder Abendstern*', which were appreciated by Wagner's audiences, rather than the opera as a whole, and it is these separate numbers which are largely responsible for keeping *Tannhäuser* in the international repertory today.

Wagner never published a definitive performing edition of the work, which is usually staged nowadays in a 'Paris' version incorporating also those changes made after the 1861 Paris performances. Though the 1845 original is stylistically more unified, there can be no doubt that the infiltration of the mature Wagner into a work he had initially conceived as a young man makes the opera more interesting to modern audiences. *Tannhäuser* has, however, never attained the popularity of the earlier *Der fliegende Holländer* or Wagner's later masterpieces.

II

IN *My Life*, Wagner recalled something of the problems which attended the staging of *Tannhäuser*:

On the whole, I still built my hopes upon the general effect of the music alone, and was greatly encouraged by the rehearsals. [Ferdinand] Hiller [conductor and composer, and Wagner's confidant in Dresden], who had looked through the score and had already praised it, assured me that the instrumentation could not have been carried out with greater restraint. The characteristic and delicate sonority of the orchestra delighted me and strengthened me in my resolve to be extremely sparing in the use of my orchestral effects, in order to attain that abundance of combinations which I would need for my later works.

At rehearsals my wife alone missed the trumpets and trombones that had given such brightness and freshness to *Rienzi*. Although I laughed at this, I could not help feeling anxious when she confided to me how great had been her disappointment when, at a theatre rehearsal, she found the impression made by the music of the song contest really feeble. Speaking from the point of view of the public, who always want to be entertained or moved in some way or another, she had quite rightly called attention to an exceedingly questionable aspect of the performance. But I saw at once that the fault lay less with the conception than with the fact that I had not supervised the production of this scene with sufficient care.

In regard to the conception of this scene, I found myself on the horns of a dilemma, for I had to decide once and for all whether this song contest was to be a concert of arias or a competition in dramatic poetry. There are many people even now, who, despite having witnessed a perfectly successful performance of this scene, have not received the correct impression of its meaning. Their idea is that it belongs to the traditional operatic genre, which calls for a number of vocal styles to be juxtaposed or contrasted, and that these different songs are intended to amuse and interest the audience by means of their purely musical changes in rhythm and tempo, along the lines of a concert programme put together with an eye to variety.

This was not at all my idea. My real intention was, if possible, to force the listener, for the first time in the history of opera, to take an interest in a poetic idea, by making him follow all its necessary developments. For it was only by virtue of this interest that he could be made to understand the catastrophe, which in this instance was not to be brought about by any outside influence, but must be the outcome simply of the natural spiritual processes at work. Hence the need for great moderation and breadth in the conception of the music; first, in order that, according to my principle, it might prove helpful rather than the reverse to the understanding of the poetic lines; and second, in order that the increasing rhythmic character of the melody which marks the ardent growth of passion may not be interrupted too arbitrarily by unnecessary changes in modulation and rhythm.

Hence, too, the need for a very sparing use of orchestral instruments in the accompaniment, and an intentional suppression of all those purely musical effects which must be utilized, though gradually, only when the situation becomes so intense that one almost ceases to think, and can only feel the tragic nature of the crisis. No one could deny that I had contrived to produce the proper effect of this principle, the moment I played the music of the song contest on the piano. But in order to ensure my success in the future, I now had to confront the exceptional difficulty of making opera singers understand how to interpret their parts precisely in the way I desired.

In writing the libretto of *Tannhäuser*, Wagner drew upon more than one source. The historical Tannhäuser was a thirteenth-century German poet and minstrel who travelled widely, may have taken part in the Crusades, and who left a number of lyric poems and songs. He was first written about in a ballad, *Danhuser*, which appeared in 1515, nearly three hundred years after his lifetime, and which tells the story of the minstrel who succumbed to the enticements of Venus, goddess of love. Danhuser repents of his sins of the flesh, but is denied absolution by the Pope and so returns to the arms of Venus.

The song contest on the Wartburg played no part in the Tannhäuser legend. Wagner encountered it in *The Serapion Brethren*, a collection of stories by E. T. A. Hoffmann (1776–1822), a writer whose works were known to him as they were to every educated German of the time. Hoffmann, from whose tales Offenbach was to fashion his opera *Les Contes d'Hoffmann*, included in *The Serapion Brethren* a story entitled 'The Singers' Contest' in which six famous Minnesingers at the court of Thuringia compete in a song contest. The singer whose music sounds harsh and strange to the others is not Tannhäuser but one Heinrich von Ofterdingen, who has been aided by the magician Klingsor.

Hoffmann's story has its basis in a long fourteenth-century poem, 'The Contest of Song on the Wartburg', which Wagner no doubt also consulted. The composer was certainly acquainted with the *Deutsche Sagen* (German Sagas) of the brothers Jacob and Wilhelm Grimm, published in 1816–18, in which he would have found a version of the folk-tale of Tannhäuser and his sojourn with Venus. Another source which Wagner probably consulted is Ludwig Bechstein's *The Legends of Thuringia*, which includes versions of both the Tannhäuser and the song-contest stories. Wagner decided to combine the two legends in his libretto. In *A Communication to My Friends* (1851), he suggests that the idea to do so came from an old book of folk-tales in which he found a loose connection established between Tannhäuser and the Contest of Song:

What most irresistibly attracted me was the connection, however loose, between Tannhäuser and the Song Contest on the Wartburg, which I found established in that folk-book. With this second poetic subject too, I had already made an earlier acquaintance in a story by Hoffmann. However, as with Tieck's Tannhäuser, it had left me without the slightest urge to make theatrical use of it. I now decided to trace this Song Contest, all of whose characters suggested my homeland to me, to its simplest and most genuine source. This in turn led me to study the middle-high-German poem of the *Sängerkrieg*, through whose complexities I was guided by a friend, a German philologist, who happened to possess a copy. This poem, as is well known, is closely connected with a larger work, the story of Lohengrin. That I also studied, and thus at one stroke a whole new world of poetic material was made available to me; a world of which, in my previous search which had been mainly for ready-made material suitable for easy adaptation to the genre of opera, I had known absolutely nothing.

III

THE version of the opera described here is that which was staged in Paris in 1861. This, after all, represents the composer's last thoughts on *Tannhäuser*, although, had an occasion presented itself, Wagner would undoubtedly have continued to make changes. The original Dresden score of 1845 admittedly possesses a stylistic unity lacking in the later version, but it is the Paris *Tannhäuser* which provides the richer musical and dramatic experience, and which is to be preferred, although the Dresden version is still frequently encountered in the opera house.

The Overture to *Tannhäuser* begins with an *andante maestoso* statement of the slow march to which the pilgrims in Act III will sing their chorus. When it is repeated, the violins contribute an accompaniment of broken triplets, intended by Wagner to symbolize what he called 'the pulse of life'. This spiritual opening section is succeeded by an *allegro* depiction of the physical delights of the Venusberg, culminating in the theme of the song with which, in the opera, Tannhäuser will burst forth in praise of Venus.

The bacchanalian frenzy of the music grows in intensity, reaches a climax and then begins to subside into a blissfully contented detumescence. The curtain has risen upon the interior of the Venusberg, home of Venus, the goddess of love, a place which Wagner in a stage direction assures us is known to the world as the Horselberg, near Eisenach. In a grotto, youths, maidens, nymphs and satyrs are engaged in erotic disport. Venus herself reclines on a couch, with Tannhäuser resting by her side, his head in her lap.

A rosy mist descends upon the scene, isolating the figures of Tannhäuser (whom Wagner has saddled with a first name, Heinrich) and Venus, and then lifts momentarily to reveal a tableau of the rape of Europa. A chorus of invisible sirens issues a gentle invitation to love, which in the context of the Venusberg should always be understood as a euphemism for lust. The mist dissolves again, to reveal now a tableau of Leda and the swan, and the voices of the sirens retreat into the distance.

Satiated with the delights of love-making, Tannhäuser (tenor) has sunk into a state of post-coital melancholy. When Venus (soprano) asks what ails him, he replies that he has heard, as in a dream, the distant pealing of bells in the outside world, and that he yearns for that world from which he has been parted for too long a time. Venus chides Tannhäuser for wearying so quickly of her caresses. She reminds him of his good fortune in having won her favours, and commands him to take up his lyre and celebrate their love in song.

Tannhäuser launches enthusiastically into his song of love for Venus, '*Dir töne Lob*' (All praise be thine: Ex. 4), but as he sings his mood changes again

Ex.4

and he reminds himself that he is, after all, a mortal and, unlike the goddess of love, cannot devote his entire life to that particular sport. In the midst of joy, he realizes that he yearns for a little pain, and he begs Venus to release him. The goddess expresses her disappointment at the turn his song has taken, and Tannhäuser tries again, in a second stanza a semitone higher, to extol her virtues, only to find himself once again longing for woodland breezes, blue skies, green meadows, bird song and the sound of bells. Again he asks for his freedom.

The procedure is repeated. Once again, although Tannhäuser begins enthusiastically to praise Venus (a semitone higher again), he finds himself longing for earth and its pain. His song has remained unchanged between Dresden and Paris, but Venus has learned the musical language of *Tristan und Isolde*, which Wagner had just finished composing, and both her yearning and her scorn are expressed with a rich sensuousness which Tannhäuser must have found himself almost powerless to oppose. Oppose it he does, however, even though in the Paris version the goddess's role is greatly expanded and her musical argument made so overwhelmingly persuasive.

From anger, Venus moves to tender reproach, but Tannhäuser is adamant. 'Return to me if you are in need of salvation,' cries the goddess, to which he replies 'No, goddess of pleasure and delight. It is not with you that I shall find peace and repose. My salvation lies in Maria.' At mention of the Virgin Mary, Venus and the Venusberg suddenly disappear, and Tannhäuser finds himself in the outside world, in a green valley on which the sun shines brilliantly from a clear blue sky. In the foreground is a shrine to the Virgin. The tinkling of sheep bells can be heard, and a shepherd boy (soprano) sits on a high cliff, playing his pipe and singing a song of welcome to Holda, goddess of spring.

The young shepherd's pipe is represented by a cor anglais played off-stage. The melody of his song continues as a chorus of elderly pilgrims is heard approaching. As the pilgrims pass through the valley, singing of their sins and of their hope to find absolution in Rome, the shepherd boy calls a friendly greeting to them and asks them to pray for his poor soul. Tannhäuser, greatly moved, falls to his knees and utters a prayer. The shepherd boy follows his straying flock of sheep in the direction the pilgrims have taken, and, as the pilgrims' chorus and the tinkle of sheep bells fade away in the distance, the sound of nearby hunting horns is heard on all sides.

The Landgrave (Count Hermann of Thuringia) and a group of five minstrel-knights, or Minnesingers, now enter, clothed in hunting attire. To the five minstrels Wagner gives the names of historical characters. They are Wolfram von Eschenbach (baritone), Walter von der Vogelweide (tenor), Heinrich der Schreiber (tenor), Biterolf (bass) and Reinmar von Zweter (bass). Catching sight of Tannhäuser, who is still on his knees in prayer, the Landgrave (bass) wonders who he can be. As they draw nearer, the minstrels recognize their old colleague, Heinrich Tannhäuser. The Landgrave asks Tannhäuser if he can really be returning to the circle of friends from whom he had so arrogantly departed, while one or two of the minstrels suggest that perhaps he confronts them as a foe.

Wolfram is the first to welcome Tannhäuser back wholeheartedly, in generous melodic phrases in which the others then join. Tannhäuser will tell them only that he has been wandering in distant lands. He begs the knights to let him pass on, but they entreat him to stay with them. As the ensemble reaches its climax, the persuasive solo voice of Wolfram emerges from it with the words, 'Stay, for Elisabeth's sake.' The mention of Elisabeth seems to affect Tannhäuser, and, with the permission of the Landgrave, Wolfram reveals to the penitent knight in a lyrical arioso ('*Als du in kühnem Sänge uns bestrittest*': When you contested with us in blithe song) that he, Tannhäuser, is loved by the Landgrave's niece, Elisabeth, who since his absence has grown pale and has shunned all public meetings and song festivals.

A joyous ensemble develops, in which Tannhäuser contemplates the prospect of a new life, encouraged and supported by the pure love of Elisabeth (Ex. 5), and the Landgrave and minstrels express their delight at the return of their colleague. During the ensemble, the valley has filled with huntsmen. The Landgrave sounds his horn and is answered by loud blasts from all sides. An excited orchestral statement of Ex. 5 is heard as the curtain falls.

Act II takes place in the minstrels' hall of the Wartburg. Before the curtain has risen, an *allegro* orchestral introduction has described Elisabeth's

Ex.5

Allegro ♩ = 80

Ha, jetzt er-ken-ne ich sie wie - der die schö - ne Welt____

____ der ich ent-rückt!

happiness at the return of Tannhäuser, though it has also allowed itself a fleeting reference to the shadow that is soon to be cast over their future. When the curtain rises, Elisabeth (soprano) enters the Hall of Song, to which she sings an ecstatic greeting, *'Dich, teure Halle, grüss ich wieder'* (Dear hall, I greet thee again). It was in this place that she had often heard Tannhäuser singing his songs of courtly love. When Tannhäuser had left, joy too had departed from the hall. Now, Elisabeth assures the hall, 'he who revives both me and thee' has returned.

Elisabeth's aria is a magnificently spontaneous outburst of delight and eager anticipation, which ends with the orchestra repeating the joyous Ex. 5 from the conclusion of the preceding act. Wolfram and Tannhäuser now enter, and Tannhäuser throws himself at Elisabeth's feet. At first Elisabeth is confused, and attempts to leave, but Tannhäuser persuades her to remain. Elisabeth thanks him for having returned but, not surprisingly, also asks him where he has been. His only answer to this is that he has been in lands far away, that a deep forgetfulness has interposed to remove all recollection of his experiences from him, and that he can now remember only how he despaired of ever seeing her again.

Elisabeth wonders what brought him back, and Tannhäuser says it was a sublime miracle. In an ecstatic outpouring of innocent young love, Elisabeth exclaims that she praises this miracle from the depths of her heart, and describes how Tannhäuser's songs had always affected her so much more deeply than the pleasant singing of the other minstrels. Joy had fled from her heart at his departure. The virginal purity of Elisabeth's character is beautifully conveyed by Wagner in this charming passage. Tannhäuser tells her that it was the god of love who led him back to her, and he and Elisabeth join happily in a duet praising the hour of their reunion and the power that has brought it about.

At the conclusion of the duet both Tannhäuser and Wolfram, who has been standing to one side, withdraw, and the Landgrave enters. He is delighted to find his niece already there, and guesses at the feelings which have brought her back to the minstrels' hall. Elisabeth tenderly addresses him not only as uncle but also as 'kind father'. The Landgrave tells her that he has invited the nobles of the land, and that they are even now approaching. Their numbers are greater than usual, for they have heard that Elisabeth is to be the queen of the forthcoming festival of song.

The Landgrave's rather dull utterance, for which Wagner has reverted to the cumbersome recitative of his earliest operas, is followed by a splendid trumpet fanfare and by the arrival in procession of the knights and their ladies and attendant pages. As the stage slowly fills, to the accompaniment of Wagner's impressive processional music, the cumulative effect of the music and of the arrival of the guests who fill the hall can be quite exciting. After another trumpet fanfare, the now completely assembled guests sing a magnificent chorus in praise of the great hall of song and of the Landgrave, Count Hermann. The music builds to a splendid ceremonial climax.

The Landgrave addresses the assembly, again in ponderous recitative. He reminds the minstrels of their glorious past, and of the songs they sang to celebrate the coming of peace after the German people had fought off the attacks of the 'furious Guelphs'. He asks them now to welcome the reappearance of Tannhäuser in their midst. The knight's return appears to the Landgrave to be a great mystery, but perhaps the minstrels can throw some light upon it in the songs they are about to create. Their theme is to be the true essence of love. Whoever can define it most worthily in song will be rewarded by a prize which will be presented by Elisabeth. Although the Landgrave does not make it explicitly clear, it is doubtless inferred by the contestants that the hand in marriage of the fair Elisabeth herself is to be the prize.

The fanfares ring out again, the assembled company hails the Landgrave as a great protector of the arts, and the contest of song begins. Each minstrel places his name in a bowl carried by four noble pages. The bowl is presented to Elisabeth, who draws a name which she hands to them. The pages call out the first name: 'Wolfram von Eschenbach, begin!'

Wolfram's song, *'Blick' ich umher'* (As I gaze around), is a gentle expression of courtly love, couched in such flowery language that it is not easy to discern his meaning. Wolfram appears, however, to be saying that one star shines more brightly than all the other fair stars, and that he worships it with a holy and pure devotion from afar. This is his idea of the true essence of love. The knights and their ladies acclaim his sentiments, but Tannhäuser who, the orchestra at this point reminds us, has been thinking rather different thoughts, exclaims that the world would soon come to an end if Wolfram's pale and ineffectual yearnings were the true essence of love. He, Tannhäuser, would boldly approach the fount of delight, and refresh himself continually at its source. That, he tells Wolfram, is what real love is all about.

Tannhäuser's outburst is greeted with general consternation, and Biterolf responds to it angrily by inviting him to come outside and fight. He, Biterolf, would shed his last drop of blood to defend woman's honour, and he regards Tannhäuser's blasphemous words as beneath contempt. His attitude is endorsed by all, and Tannhäuser finds himself challenged by all the men present. Undeterred, and clearly in the grip of a self-destructive passion, Tannhäuser scornfully refers to Biterolf as a surly wolf who has obviously never experienced the real delights of love.

The knights have now all drawn their swords, and it is only the intervention of the Landgrave, who orders that the peace be kept, which saves Tannhäuser from being physically attacked. Wolfram attempts to save the situation by launching into a lyrical prayer to heaven to keep them all unpolluted and free from sin. His song is interrupted by Tannhäuser who, to the horror of all, bursts impulsively into his song from Act I in praise of the goddess of love, accompanying himself on his lyre. He ends by inviting all those poor creatures who have never known earthly love to join him in a visit to the mountain of Venus. A shocked ensemble calls for his obscenities to be punished immediately by death or banishment.

Tannhäuser is hardly aware of the physical danger which threatens him, for he is lost in rapturous thoughts of Venus. The knights advance upon him with their swords drawn, and are stopped only by a sudden command from Elisabeth, who steps forward to protect Tannhäuser. All are appalled to find the pure Elisabeth apparently about to speak up for the man they now regard as a pariah, but she defies their drawn swords. No wound from their weapons, she cries, could equal the death blow she has received from Tannhäuser's words. In a long and deeply felt arioso passage she sets about persuading the company that they would be committing a great sin if they denied the sinner, Tannhäuser, the chance of salvation through atonement. It is she who has been harmed by him, she insists, yet she, who loved him deeply, now prays for him.

Affected by her words, Tannhäuser gradually sinks to his knees, overcome with guilt and remorse, as the Landgrave and the entire assembly launch into an ensemble of the highest musical quality in praise of the angelic Elisabeth. Tannhäuser adds his voice in a prayer to heaven for mercy, and the ensemble builds up to an impressive climax, the soprano voice of Elisabeth soaring above it in phrases of desperate pleading that the soul of Tannhäuser may be redeemed.

The Landgrave, for whom Wagner appears to have reserved his duller, more workaday musical style, now passes sentence of banishment on Tannhäuser, but adds that a way to deliverance from eternal damnation is open to the disgraced knight. Huge numbers of pilgrims are making their way to Rome to seek absolution for their sins. The older pilgrims have already left, but the younger ones are still resting in the valley. The Landgrave suggests that Tannhäuser join them.

The minstrels, the knights and Elisabeth all add their voices to that of the Landgrave, exhorting Tannhäuser to prostrate himself before the Pope,

God's representative on earth, and to ask his blessing. It is made clear to Tannhäuser that, should redemption be denied him, he must never return on pain on death. The voices of the younger pilgrims are now heard singing in the distance, as they set forth on their journey. With a cry of 'To Rome', which is echoed by all, Tannhäuser rushes off to join the pilgrims as the curtain falls.

Act III is preceded by an orchestral introduction to which Wagner gave the title '*Tannhäusers Pilgerfahrt*' (Tannhäuser's Pilgrimage). At a dragging *andante* pace, it depicts the knight's pilgrimage by quoting both the chorus of pilgrims and the melody of Elisabeth's plea for Tannhäuser. The motif of pulsating life from the Overture introduces a new motif, that of heavenly grace, which will recur later in the act in Tannhäuser's narration.

The curtain rises on the valley of the Wartburg as in scene 2 of Act I, except that it is now autumn. The day is drawing to a close, and Elisabeth is discovered in prayer before the shrine of the Blessed Virgin. From a distance Wolfram observes her, and in melodic recitative tells himself that he was certain he would find her here, for she has prayed constantly for Tannhäuser, and is now anxiously awaiting his return among the pilgrims whose homecoming must surely be imminent now that the leaves are beginning to fall. Wolfram hopes, for Elisabeth's sake, that Tannhäuser will be among the pilgrims or that, if he is not, she will somehow be granted solace.

The distant sound of the pilgrims' chorus breaks in on Wolfram's musing. Elisabeth, too, hears it, for she exclaims 'They are returning home. You heavenly saints, reveal my task to me that I may fulfil it worthily.' The pilgrims, still singing, begin to cross the valley. Their chorus rises in volume, with pulsating strings emphasising their joy as they cry 'Alleluia', their sins having been forgiven. But as the last of them disappears, and their song fades in the distance, Elisabeth expresses her grief in one simple and poignant phrase: '*Er kehret nicht zurück*' (He has not returned).

When the last of the pilgrims has passed by, Elisabeth sinks to her knees before the shrine to the Virgin. Her aria, '*Allmächt'ge Jungfrau, hör mein Flehen!*' (Almighty Virgin, hear my prayer), in which she begs for release from life and yearns to be admitted into the blessed realm of the angels, is a somewhat prosaic piece of music. Its devotional mood is appropriate, and well sustained in an orchestral postlude, but the aria lacks any strongly defined character, and its woodwind accompaniment is monotonous.

As Elisabeth rises and turns to depart, Wolfram approaches and asks if he may accompany her. With a gesture, she gently refuses his offer. Wolfram watches her go, and then takes up his harp and sings his celebrated recitative ('*Wie Todesahnung, Dämm'rung deckt die Lände*': Like a presentiment of death, twilight covers the land) and aria ('*O du mein holder Abendstern*': Oh thou, my gracious evening star) in which he addresses the evening star, asking it to salute Elisabeth as her soul soars by on its way from earth to become a

99

heavenly angel. Wolfram's gentle aria is well-known to countless thousands who have never seen the opera, for its attractive tune, typical of the younger Wagner's melodic style, has made it a favourite concert item. An orchestral postlude sustains the rapt mood of the song, but is suddenly interrupted by a restless figure in the horns and bassoons as Tannhäuser enters, dressed in tattered rags.

At first Wolfram does not recognize his former companion, but Tannhäuser knows who he is. 'You are Wolfram, the very skilful minstrel,' he exclaims scornfully. Wolfram is surprised that Tannhäuser should have ventured back to the Landgrave's domain from which he had been banished, but Tannhäuser assures him he need have no fear. 'I do not seek to join you or your fellows,' he tells Wolfram. 'I seek someone to show me the way back to the Venusberg.' The horrified Wolfram asks if Tannhäuser did not go to Rome to seek absolution. Tannhäuser admits that he did, indeed, journey to Rome. When he realizes that Wolfram is sympathetic to his plight, he offers to reveal all that has happened. He seats himself wearily upon a rock, but when Wolfram attempts to join him, Tannhäuser warns him to keep his distance: 'Any place where I rest is accursed.'

Tannhäuser recounts his story in a lengthy narrative, '*Inbrunst im Herzen*' (With devotion in my heart). With such devotion in his heart as no penitent had ever felt before, he tells Wolfram, he had travelled to Rome with the other pilgrims. Throughout the journey, he had sought on every possible occasion to mortify his flesh. When the pilgrims took an easy route through meadows, he instead sought thorns and stones for his bare feet. When they refreshed themselves at a spring, he refrained from drinking, and walked on in the burning sun. In Rome, at the Holy See, he prostrated himself before the sanctuary. Bells pealed, heavenly anthems came floating down, thousands had grace bestowed upon them. When Tannhäuser approached the Pope, however, to beg forgiveness and absolution, the Holy Father replied, 'If you have participated in such wicked practices, and warmed yourself at the fires of hell, if you have sojourned in the Venusberg, then from this moment you are eternally damned. Just as this staff in my hand can never again blossom, so deliverance from the flames of hell shall never bloom for you.'

At these words, Tannhäuser had fainted. When he awakened, night had fallen. In the distance he could hear the singing of the other pilgrims, but the sound of their rejoicing now sickened him. He had fled from Rome with horror in his heart, his only desire now being to return to the warm breast of Venus where he had known such delight. As he sings of Venus, the Venusberg music is heard in the orchestra. Tannhäuser's frenzy increases, and so does Wolfram's horror as a vaporous mist gradually fills the darkening valley, glowing with a rosy light. Dancing shapes can be faintly distinguished. Wolfram identifies them as the forces of hell, but Tannhauser recognizes the court of Venus. The goddess herself can now be seen, reclining upon her couch. Tannhäuser's solo narration ends as a trio, as Venus calls seductively to him, Wolfram attempts to restrain him and Tannhäuser fights to free himself and rush to the embrace of the goddess of love.

Wolfram cries out in desperation that an angel who prayed for Tannhäuser on earth will soon intercede for him in heaven. As he mentions her name, 'Elisabeth', Venus utters a despairing cry, and she and her court disappear. A gleam of torches heralds the approach of the minstrels and knights, who sing of the maid whose soul has been united with the heavenly host. A procession now appears, comprising the older pilgrims and the minstrel-knights bearing Elisabeth's body on an open bier, followed by the Landgrave and his knights. Led by Wolfram to Elisabeth's bier, Tannhäuser utters a prayer, 'Holy Elisabeth, pray for me,' and falls dead. The younger pilgrims now arrive, bearing a staff from which fresh green leaves have blossomed. They sing of the miracle by which the Pope's barren staff was made to sprout leaves as a sign that Tannhäuser's soul has found redemption. To a fervent statement of the pilgrims' chorus, *fortissimo*, accompanied by its life-affirming triplet figure in the orchestra, the curtain falls.

BY the time *Tannhäuser* came to be produced at Bayreuth, in 1891, it had become one of Wagner's most popular operas. The composer having died eight years earlier without really having produced a definitive performing edition of the work, his widow Cosima had to decide whether to stage the Dresden or the Paris version, or perhaps one of the other versions prepared by Wagner himself (for the first Vienna production) or by someone else. That she was fully conscious of the difficulties involved is revealed in a letter Cosima Wagner later wrote to a Berlin publisher:

> If we were to make an operatic production (even in the best sense of the word), it was inevitable that the musical riches of the first scene would make not only the following scene but also the second and third acts appear pale and flat ... Whereas, if we could succeed in bringing to realization the characters with their tragic destiny and the life of the Middle Ages, the musical riches I spoke of would be seen as part of Venus's magical wiles and the simpler means would appear as the natural expression of the other way of life. The warmth in the welcoming of Tannhäuser (in Act I), the utmost simplicity and clarity in the enunciation of the words, the avoidance in positioning, expression, tempo etc., of everything that could remind one of a septet—this was our one endeavour.

On one level a tale of sacred and profane love, Wagner's *Tannhäuser* is also a tragic love story and even a dissertation on the decline of the romantic ideal—and a cry of despair at the standards and tastes of the composer's materialistic nineteenth century. In *A Communication to My Friends*, Wagner himself spoke of this, though in characteristically verbose language:

> If at last I turned impatiently away, and owed the strength of my repugnance to the independence already developed in my nature, both as artist and as man, so did that double revolt, of man and artist, inevitably take on the form of a yearning for appeasement in a higher, nobler element: an element which in its contrast to the only pleasures that the material present spreads in modern life and modern art, could but appear to me in the guise of a pure, chaste, virginal and unseizable, and unapproachable ideal of love. What, in fine, could this love yearning, the noblest thing my heart could feel—what other could it be than a longing for release from the present, for absorption into an element of endless love, a love denied to earth and reachable through the gates of death alone? And what, again, at bottom, could such a longing be, but the yearning of love; aye, of a real love seeded in the soil of fullest sentience—yet a love that could never come to fruition on the loathsome soil of modern sentience? How absurd, then, must those critics seem to me, who, drawing all their wit from modern wantonness, insist on reading into my *Tannhäuser* a specifically Christian and impotently pietistic drift! They recognize nothing but the fable of their own incompetence, in the story of a man whom they are utterly unable to comprehend.

The two worlds contrasted in *Tannhäuser*, the piety of the Middle Ages and the rebellious free thought of post-Renaissance man, both find sympathetic expression in Wagner's music. The eroticism of the Venusberg and the chaste utterance of Elisabeth are equally convincing, and it is at those moments when one is in conflict with the other, or at moments of transition from one to the other, that Wagner's creative genius shines forth most excitingly. The leitmotiv technique of the later operas, already adumbrated in *Der fliegende Holländer*, is used consciously and with confidence in *Tannhäuser*, especially in Tannhäuser's Act III narration of his pilgrimage to Rome, a clear precursor of the composer's later style with its declamatory vocal line above a symphonic accompaniment of strong melodic interest. Elsewhere in the opera, for instance in Wolfram's song to the evening star, Wagner retains the old Italian-style recitative and cavatina with simple accompaniment. The dullest passages are those for the Landgrave, in whom Wagner apparently could summon up little interest.

Today, *Tannhäuser* seems to be one of the more problematical of Wagner's operas. Originally a transitional work, bridging the stylistic gap between *Der fliegende Holländer* and *Lohengrin*, it is now itself a mixture of styles, 1845 blending none too smoothly with 1861 and several points between. Nevertheless *Tannhäuser* continues to hold the stage, for its theme of the contrast of carnal with spiritual love, although handled in a rather cumbersome manner by Wagner, is no less relevant today than it was in the nineteenth century or in medieval times.

SIX

Lohengrin

Romantic Opera in Three Acts

Dramatis personae
Henry the Fowler, King of Germany   (bass)
Lohengrin   (tenor)
Elsa von Brabant   (soprano)
Duke Gottfried, her Brother   (silent role)
Friedrich von Telramund, Count of Brabant   (baritone)
Ortrud, his Wife   (soprano)
The King's Herald   (bass)
Four Nobles of Brabant   (tenors and basses)
Four Pages   (sopranos and altos)

LIBRETTO by the composer

TIME: First half of the tenth century

PLACE: Antwerp

FIRST PERFORMED at the Hoftheater, Weimar, 28 August 1850, with Carl
Beck (Lohengrin), Rosa von Milde Agthe (Elsa), Hans Feodor von Milde
(Telramund) and Frau Fastlinger (Ortrud), conducted by Franz Liszt.

I

EVEN before the Dresden première of *Tannhäuser*, Wagner had begun to sketch the libretto of his next opera, *Lohengrin*, during a visit to the famous spa of Marienbad (now Marianske Lazne) in Bohemia, in the summer of 1845. (The subject of *Die Meistersinger von Nürnberg* came to him at the same time.) He had taken with him on holiday a copy of the old anonymous German epic *Lohengrin*, which so gripped his imagination as soon as he began to read it that he found himself excitedly drafting the synopsis of a libretto on the subject. '*Lohengrin*', Wagner wrote in *My Life*, 'stood suddenly revealed before me, complete in every detail of its dramatic construction.' He tried to put it out of his mind, having been advised by his doctor to rest, and turned instead to *Die Meistersinger*, as a cheerful subject and therefore not in the least likely to over-excite his nerves:

> I felt I must write it out in spite of the doctor's orders. I therefore proceeded to do this, and hoped that it might free me from the thrall of the idea of *Lohengrin*. I was mistaken, however, for no sooner had I got into my bath at noon than I felt an overpowering desire to write out *Lohengrin*, and this longing so overcame me that I could not wait the prescribed hour for the bath, but when a few minutes had elapsed, jumped out and, barely giving myself time to dress, ran home to write down what I had in my mind. I repeated this for several days until the complete sketch for *Lohengrin* was on paper.

This prose sketch, which Wagner completed on 3 August 1845, ran to nearly thirty pages when it was published in full for the first time in the Bayreuth Festival magazine in 1936.

In November, a month after the Dresden première of *Tannhäuser*, the composer Robert Schumann in a letter to Felix Mendelssohn described the Engelklub, a circle of artists and musicians in Dresden to which he belonged and which met weekly. 'To our surprise,' Schumann wrote, 'Wagner yesterday showed us his new opera text, *Lohengrin*. A double surprise for me, for I have been considering the same subject—or a very similar one about the Knights of the Round Table—for more than a year, and I must now consign it to oblivion.'

Wagner himself claimed that, when he read his libretto (which by this time he had turned into verse) to his colleagues in Dresden, Schumann failed to understand the musical form implicit in it, since there appeared to be no provision for individual musical numbers. 'I then had some fun in reading different parts to him in the form of arias and cavatinas,' Wagner wrote in *My Life*, 'after which he laughingly declared himself satisfied.'

The *Lohengrin* libretto assumed its final shape over the following months, and in 1846 Wagner busied himself with the composition of the opera, finishing it in sketch form in the summer while staying in the village of Graupe near Pillnitz. By the end of April 1848, *Lohengrin* had been completed in full score. Wagner was beginning to amass debts again, for he consistently and luxuriously lived beyond his means. In 1848, however, he also attracted trouble of a different kind by allying himself with the revolutionary movement of intellectuals and students.

When revolution broke out in the streets of Dresden in May 1849, it was quickly suppressed. Although in his autobiography Wagner minimizes his connection with the uprising, asserting that he had attended revolutionary meetings merely out of curiosity, he was sufficiently implicated for a warrant to be issued for his arrest. With Liszt's help, the Royal Kapellmeister fled to Switzerland, thence to Paris, and subsequently to Zurich, where Minna and her daughter joined him. The following year, while in Paris again, he embarked upon a scheme to flee to the isles of Greece and on to the Orient with one Jessie Laussot (née Taylor), a young English admirer. Unfortunately for Wagner, this came to the knowledge of Jessie Laussot's husband. His plans had to be abandoned, and the disappointed composer returned to Zurich and to the long-suffering Minna.

Wagner had already produced the first draft of a libretto for an opera which he intended to call *Siegfrieds Tod* (Siegfried's Death). In Zurich, he began to write essays on the theory of art, and also sketched out another libretto, *Wieland der Schmied* (Wieland the Smith), which he hoped to be commissioned to compose for Paris. Meanwhile, *Lohengrin* had been rejected by the Dresden Opera, although the finale to Act I was performed at a concert on 2 February 1847, to celebrate the three-hundredth anniversary of the founding of the court orchestra. Wagner now wrote to Liszt, sending him a copy of the score and asking for his help in getting *Lohengrin* produced. Although he had reservations concerning the work's dramatic effectiveness, Liszt agreed to stage it in Weimar in August. Wagner naturally wanted to attend the first performance but, fearing that he would be arrested, he decided against it. He did not, in fact, witness a performance of *Lohengrin* until 15 May 1861, when he attended a performance in Vienna.

At the beginning of August 1850, Liszt had written to Wagner about the preparations for the forthcoming première of *Lohengrin*:

We are quite full of the *ethereal* sounds of your *Lohengrin*, and I flatter myself that we shall succeed in putting it on as you intended. We are rehearsing for three or four hours a day, and by now we have got the solo parts and the quartet just about right. Tomorrow I shall start to rehearse with the individual wind instruments, of which we shall have the full complement required by your score.... In short, rest assured that everything which is humanly possible in Weimar in this year of grace 1850 will be done for your *Lohengrin* which, in spite of all the nonsense that is uttered, the false anxieties and the all-too-real incrustations, will—I promise you—be performed very respectably on the 28th of this month.

On 28 August 1850, *Lohengrin* was given its first performance at the Hoftheater in Weimar, conducted by Liszt. The critic of the Hamburg *Kleinemusikzeitung* wrote:

At last Wagner's opera *Lohengrin* has been produced in Weimar. The result, as was expected, was roughly the same as when *Rienzi* was performed in Berlin and Königsberg, in other words a gentle fiasco. . . . Wagner reveals himself in this work (not to mention his earlier ones) to be completely *unmusical*. He has given us not music but noise, and such an ugly noise that only a general cannonade on stage was missing to make it sound like the thunder of hell itself. After this experience, no doubt Herr Liszt will realize that the degraded taste of one individual is not enough to effect a degradation of the taste of the entire public. In fact we are amazed that Herr Liszt could dare to present the raw product of a false genius such as Wagner to such a cultivated public. In the town where Goethe, Schiller, Wieland and Herder held sway for so long, only the very finest of present artists should be permitted to have their works staged.

The Weimar première, given with a company of inadequate singers and a far too small orchestra, obviously did considerably less than justice to *Lohengrin*, which was at first considered a failure. Nevertheless, the opera was staged throughout Germany during the following decade, to be eventually hailed as the apotheosis of the German romantic opera. By then, however, its composer had left German romantic opera behind him, and was immersed in the creation of his new type of music drama.

It was not until 1 November 1871 that *Lohengrin* made its way to Italy, the first opera by Wagner to be heard there. It was performed in Bologna in an Italian translation, conducted by Giuseppe Verdi's erstwhile friend Angelo Mariani. Verdi attended a performance later in the month, armed with a vocal score on which he scribbled comments on the music and its performance. The following day, he wrote to a friend:

Impression mediocre. Music beautiful, when it is clear and there is thought in it. The action, like the text, moves slowly. Hence boredom. Beautiful instrumental effects. Too many held notes, which makes for heaviness. Mediocre performance. Much verve but no poetry or refinement. In the difficult passages, always wretched.

The first performance of *Lohengrin* in the United States was given in New York (in German) on 3 April 1871 at the Stadt Theater, with Theodor

Habelmann (Lohengrin), Louise Lichtmay (Elsa), Joseph Vierling (Telramund) and Marie Friderici (Ortrud), conducted by Adolf Neuendorff. London first heard the opera when it was performed at Covent Garden (at that time known as the Royal Italian Opera House) on 8 May 1875, in Italian, which was the customary language for opera in England at the time. The cast included Ernest Nicolini (Lohengrin), Emma Albani (Elsa), Victor Maurel (Telramund) and Anna d'Angeri Capponi (Ortrud), and the conductor was Auguste Vianesi. A reviewer in *The Era* the following day wrote:

> German critics tell us that in Wagner's operas it is not possible to judge the composer fairly without making ourselves fully acquainted with the story. Wagner is, they say, as much a poet as a composer, and one of his greatest merits is that the character of his music clearly indicates the character of the story. In order to increase the dramatic significance of the music, Wagner will not permit the action to be interrupted by separate melodies. All flows on in a continuous stream of sound, principals, chorus, and band all aiming at combined rather than isolated expression. There are instances, however, where the situations of the story compel the composer to treat them with individuality, and it is in some of these that Wagner's genius as a musician is most strikingly displayed.

II

LATER, in *A Communication to My Friends*, Wagner explained the significance to him of the Lohengrin myth:

> The medieval poem presented Lohengrin in a mystic twilight that filled me with suspicion and that haunting feeling of repugnance with which we look upon the carved and painted saints and martyrs on the highways, or in the churches, of Catholic lands. Only when the immediate impression of this reading had faded did the shape of Lohengrin rise repeatedly, and with growing power of attraction, before my soul; and this power gathered fresh force to itself from outside, chiefly by reason that I learned to know the myth of Lohengrin in its simpler traits, and alike its deeper meaning, as the genuine poem of the folk, such as it has been laid bare to us by the discoveries of the newer searchers into saga lore.
>
> After I had thus seen it as a noble poem of man's yearning and his longing—by no means merely seeded from the Christian's bent towards supernaturalism, but from the truest depths of universal human nature— this figure became ever more endeared to me, and ever stronger grew the urgency to adopt it and thus give utterance to my own internal longing; so that, at the time of completing my *Tannhäuser*, it positively became a dominating need, which thrust back each alien effort to withdraw myself from its despotic mastery.

This Lohengrin is no mere outcome of Christian meditation, but one of man's earliest poetic ideals; just as, for that matter, it is a fundamental error of our modern superficiality to consider the specific Christian legends as by any means original creations. Not one of the most affecting, not one of the most distinctive Christian myths belongs by right of generation to the Christian spirit, such as we commonly understand it: it has inherited them all from the purely human intuitions of earlier times, and merely moulded them to fit its own peculiar tenets. To purge them of this heterogeneous influence, and thus enable us to look straight into the pure humanity of the eternal poem: such . . . is the task which it must necessarily remain for the poet to complete.

Just as the main feature of the Flying Dutchman myth may be clearly traced to an earlier setting in the Hellenic Odyssey; just as this same Ulysses in his wrench from the arms of Calypso, in his flight from the charms of Circe, and in his yearning for the earthly wife of cherished home, embodied in the Hellenic prototype of a longing such as we find in Tannhäuser, immeasurably enhanced and widened in its meaning: so do we already meet in the Greek myth—nor is even this by any means its oldest form—the outlines of the myth of Lohengrin.

Who does not know the story of Zeus and Semele? The god loves a mortal woman, and for the sake of this love he approaches her in human shape; but the mortal learns that she does not know her lover in his true estate, and, urged by love's own ardour, demands that her spouse shall show himself to physical sense in the full substance of his being. Zeus knows that she can never grasp him, and that the unveiling of his godhead must destroy her. He himself suffers by this knowledge, beneath the stern compulsion to fulfil his loved one's dreaded wish. He signs his own death warrant when the fatal splendour of his godlike presence strikes Semele dead.

Could it have been some priestly fraud that shaped this myth? How insensate, to attempt to argue from the selfish state-religious, caste-like exploitation of the noblest human longing, back to the origin and the genuine meaning of ideals which blossomed from a human fancy that stamped man first as man! It was no god that sang the meeting of Zeus and Semele, but man, in his most human of yearnings. Who had taught man that a god could burn with love for an earthly woman? For certain, only man himself, who, however high the object of his yearning may soar above the limits of his earthly wont, can stamp it with the imprint of his human nature. From the highest sphere to which the might of his desire may bear him up, he finally can only long again for what is purely human, can only crave the taste of his own nature, as the one thing worth desiring.

What, then, is the innermost essence of this human nature, whereto the desire which reaches forth to farthest distance turns back at last, for its only possible appeasement? It is the necessity of love; and the essence of this love, in its truest utterance, is a longing for the utmost physical reality, for fruition in an object that can be grasped by all the senses, held fast with all the force of actual being. In this finite, physically sure embrace, must not the god dissolve and disappear? Is not the mortal, who had yearned for God, undone, annulled? Yet is not love, in its truest, highest essence, herein revealed? Marvel, you erudite critics, at the omnipotence of human minstrelsy, unfolded in the simple myths of the folk! Things that all your understanding can not so much as comprehend are there laid bare to human feeling, with such a physically perfect surety as no other means could bring to pass.

The ethereal sphere, from which the god is yearning to descend to men, had stretched itself, through Christian longing, to inconceivable bounds of space. To the Hellenes, it was still the cloud-locked realm of thunder and the thunderbolt, from which the lusty Zeus moved down, to mix with men in expert likeness. To the Christian, the blue firmament dissolved into an infinite sea of yearning ecstasy, in which the forms of all the gods were melted, until at last it was the lonely image of his own person, the yearning man, that alone was left to greet him from the ocean of his fantasy.

One primal, endlessly repeated trait runs through the sagas of those peoples who dwelt beside the sea or rivers which flowed into the sea: upon the blue mirror of the waters there approaches an unknown being, of the utmost grace and the purest virtue, who moves and wins all hearts by his irresistible charm. He is the embodied wish of the yearner who dreams of happiness in that far-off land he cannot sense. This unknown being vanishes across the ocean's waves as soon as he is questioned about his nature. Thus, so the story goes, there once came to the banks of the Scheldt, an unknown hero. There he rescued downtrodden innocence, and married a sweet maiden; but since she asked him who he was, and whence he came, he needs must seek the sea once more and leave his bride behind.

Why this saga, when I learned it in its simplest outlines, so irresistibly attracted me that, at the very time when I had but just completed *Tannhäuser*, I could concern myself with naught but it, was to be made clearer to me by the immediately succeeding incidents of my life.

The figure of Lohengrin makes its earliest appearance in Wolfram von Eschenbach's epic *Parzifal*, which dates from somewhere near the beginning of the thirteenth century. In the final section of the poem, Parzifal, now the custodian of the Holy Grail, retires to Montsalvat with his son Loherangrin, who in due course ventures forth to marry a princess of Brabant who had rejected all other suitors, declaring that she would consent to wed only a knight sent by God. Loherangrin warns her that he would have to leave if she were ever to ask his name. In this version of the story, Loherangrin and the princess marry and produce children. It is not until several years have passed that the princess asks the forbidden question, which leads to her husband's departure.

In another version of the story, *Der jüngere Titurel*, thought to have been written by Albert von Schaffenburg, Loherangrin marries Belaye, whose maid tells her that her husband's constancy can be secured if she cuts off a slice of his flesh and eats it. Though she refuses to do this, the story ends with the death of both Loherangrin and Belaye.

For the purpose of his opera, Wagner introduced the mythical figure of the knight whom he called Lohengrin into a historical situation involving Henry I of Saxony, who reigned from 919 to 936. Known as Henry the Fowler, supposedly because the messengers who came to announce his election as Saxon King found him hawking, Henry I was an early fighter for the cause of German unity, in which cause, presumably, he contrived to extend his authority westwards, over several territories in the Low Countries. In the year 924 he negotiated a nine years' truce with the Hungarians, who had been threatening Saxony. When the truce expired, Henry marched against the Hungarians and defeated them in 933.

Shortly before the end of the truce, Henry came to Antwerp, capital of Brabant (a territory which is now divided between Belgium and Holland), in order to persuade the nobles of Brabant to join him in battle against the Magyar hordes. It is against this historical background that the events in *Lohengrin* take place. The history remains in the background, Wagner's interest lying exclusively in the predicament of the strange outsider, saint or artist, who, in offering salvation, at the same time seeks it for himself. 'Lohengrin sought a woman who would believe in him,' the composer wrote in *A Communication to My Friends*,

a woman who would not ask who he was or whence he came, but would love him as he was, and because he was what he appeared to her to be. He sought a woman to whom he would not have to explain or justify himself, but who would love him unconditionally. For this reason he had to conceal his higher nature, for it was precisely the non-discovery, the non-revelation of this higher nature (higher because, to speak more accurately, it has been raised up) that was his sole guarantee that he was not admired or marvelled at, or humbly and uncomprehendingly adored, simply because of that quality. Admiration and adoration were what he did not seek. Only one thing could release him from his isolation and satisfy his yearning: love. To be loved and to be understood through love. All his highest thinking, his most conscious knowing, were filled with no other desire than to be a

A model of Max Bruckner's set for Act III of *Tristan und Isolde* at Bayreuth in 1886

Act I of *Tristan und Isolde* at Covent Garden, 1980, with Jon Vickers (Tristan), Donald McIntyre (Kurwenal), Berit Lindholm (Isolde) and Yvonne Minton (Brangäne)

The final scene of *Das Rheingold*, designed by Günther Schneider-Siemssen, at the Metropolitan Opera, New York, 1989

Design model by Josef Hoffmann for Act I of *Die Walküre* at Bayreuth in 1876

Design model by Josef Hoffmann for Act II of *Die Walküre* at its Bayreuth première in 1876

Siegfried at the Metropolitan Opera, New York: Günther Schneider-Siemssen's Act I set, 1989

above: Act II of *Siegfried* at
the Metropolitan Opera,
New York: Siegfried
Jerusalem in the title-role,
1990

right: Lauritz Melchior as
Siegfried at Bayreuth in
1927

complete, whole human being, swayed by and received with the warmth of human emotion, to be human entirely, not a god. In other words, an absolute artist. So he yearned for woman—the human heart. And so he descended from his blissful, barren solitude when he heard a cry for help arising from the midst of humanity, from this particular heart, from this woman. But he is unable to shake off the tell-tale aura of his higher nature. He cannot help but appear an object of wonder. The amazement of the commonality, the venom of envy throw their shadow even into the heart of the loving woman. Doubt and jealousy prove to him that he is not understood but only adored, and tear from him the confession of his divinity, with which he returns into his solitude, destroyed.

III

THOUGH Wagner made greater use of melodic motifs in *Lohengrin* than in any of his earlier operas, the number of them is still small compared to *Der Ring des Nibelungen*, in which he was most fully to develop his system of composition. The ethereally beautiful Prelude to *Lohengrin* is based entirely on one motif (Ex. 6), that of the Holy Grail, the chalice in which the blood of

Ex. 6 *Adagio*

pp

the crucified Christ is supposed to have been caught. First heard on divided violins, the solemn motif passes through the other instruments of the orchestra until, always at a slow, elegiac tempo, it reaches a climax on trumpets and trombones, and then as slowly fades away in the other-worldly harmonies in which it had first appeared. The composer himself described the Prelude in these terms:

> Out of the clear blue ether of the sky there appears to condense a wonderful yet at first hardly perceptible vision; and out of this there gradually emerges, ever more and more clearly, an angel host bearing in its midst the sacred Grail. As it approaches the earth, it exudes exquisite odours, like streams of gold, ravishing the senses of the beholder. The glory of the vision continues to grow until it seems as if the rapture must be shattered and dispersed by the very vehemence of its own expansion. The vision draws nearer, and a climax is reached when at last the Grail is revealed in all its glorious reality, radiating fiery beams and shaking the soul with emotion. The beholder sinks to his knees in adoring self-annihilation. The Grail

pours forth its light on him like a benediction, and consecrates him to its service. Then the flames gradually die away, and the angel host soars up again to the ethereal heights in tender joy, having once again purified the hearts of men by the sacred blessing of the Grail.

The Prelude fades into silence, and then the listener is brought back to earth by the more matter-of-fact orchestral bustle which accompanies the rise of the curtain on Act I, set in a meadow by the banks of the river Scheldt near Antwerp. King Henry (bass) sits in a ceremonial, throne-like chair, surrounded by his Saxon and Thuringian nobles and their retainers. Facing these visitors to their country are the nobility and a section of the populace of Brabant, among them Frederick von Telramund (baritone), with his wife, Ortrud (mezzo-soprano), at his side. A royal summons is sounded by four trumpeters, and the King's herald (bass) calls the nobles and freemen of Brabant to hear the words of King Henry. The Brabantians welcome the King to their land in peace, and Henry addresses them.

The burden of the King's address, delivered in lively recitative which is eloquently supported by the orchestra, is that, having negotiated a nine years' truce with the Hungarians, he had made use of the time to fortify a number of German towns and to train an army. The period of truce having now expired, the Hungarians had not only refused to pay tribute but had even begun to threaten German territory again. Now is the time, Henry tells the Brabantians, to defend the honour of all German-speaking territories, whether of the east or of the west. Troops must be raised wherever there is German soil.

The Saxons and Thuringians whom the King has brought with him add their voices in an exhortation to the Brabantians to rouse themselves for God and the German realm. Henry then resumes his speech. He has come to summon the men of Brabant to assemble under him at Mainz, but to his sorrow he has found the Brabantians leaderless and in a state of discord. He has heard tales of disorder and of bitter feuds. He appeals now to Frederick von Telramund, whom he knows to be a man of the highest virtue, to speak and reveal to him the cause of the turmoil and dissent.

Telramund steps forward and delivers a monologue in which he explains that, shortly before his death, the Duke of Brabant had asked him to be the guardian of the Duke's two children, Elsa and her young brother Gottfried. When the Duke died, Telramund had taken good care of the children, but one day, after Elsa had grown to be a young woman, she went into the forest with Gottfried, and returned without him. She claimed that the child had wandered away from her, and that she was unable to find him again. However, when Telramund questioned her closely, her pallor and her trembling convinced him that she had killed her brother.

Filled now with loathing of Elsa, Telramund had renounced the right to marry her which had been granted to him by her father, and had instead married Ortrud, daughter of Radbod, Prince of Friesland. Telramund now charges Elsa with the murder of her brother, and claims the land of Brabant for himself by virtue of his being next of kin to the late Duke. Moreover, his wife Ortrud is of the race which had formerly ruled in Brabant.

The assembled crowd comments in awestruck tones on the gravity of Telramund's accusation, and the King expresses his incredulity at the possibility of Elsa having committed so heinous a crime. Telramund explains that Elsa, whom he now admits had refused his hand in marriage, is an empty-headed creature who is always lost in dreams. He suggests that her motive in killing her brother was to become ruler of Brabant, and thus attain the power and authority to reject him, Telramund, and to take a secret lover.

Calling on heaven to grant him wisdom, the King orders Elsa to be brought before him for immediate trial. He constitutes the place a court of justice by solemnly hanging his shield on the oak-tree under whose shade his ceremonial chair has been placed, commanding that the shield not be removed until he has given severe but merciful judgement. All the men, Saxons, Thuringians and Brabantians, draw their swords, the visitors thrusting theirs into the earth while the Brabantians lay theirs flat on the ground before them, and all swear that their swords shall not return to their sheaths until judgement has been pronounced. 'Where you behold the King's shield,' calls the herald, 'there justice through judgement is to be found. Loud and clear I issue my summons: Elsa, appear now in this place.'

Accompanied by her ladies-in-waiting, Elsa (soprano) appears, wearing a simple white gown, and slowly makes her way to the King, to the accompaniment of her plaintive motif (Ex. 7) on oboe and cor anglais, as the

Ex.7

entire assembly softly comments on the beauty and innocence of her demeanour. The King asks her if she is Elsa of Brabant, and she inclines her head in affirmation. When he asks if she accepts him as her judge, Elsa turns her head towards the King, looks into his eyes, and then makes a gesture of trusting assent. She is asked if she is aware of the grave charge which has been brought against her, but she merely looks at Telramund and Ortrud, shudders, then sadly nods her head.

'How do you answer the charge?' the King asks, but she merely shakes her head. 'Do you then admit your guilt?' the King continues, at which Elsa speaks for the first time, but as though to herself. '*Mein arme Bruder*' (My poor brother), she murmurs. The men comment quietly on her strange behaviour, and the King urges her to confide her story to him. But instead, in an *andante* aria, '*Einsam in trüben Tagen*' (Alone in troubled days), Elsa recounts one of her dreams. In her anguish, she says, she had prayed to God, and then, falling into a sweet sleep, she had seen a pure and virtuous knight approaching in shining armour. Leaning on his sword, and carrying a golden horn at his side, he had brought her gentle consolation. It is he, she says, who will come forward now to defend her.

Elsa's aria begins gently, but becomes impassioned as she sings of the knight whom she has seen in her dream. King Henry, impressed by the maid's demeanour, warns Telramund to consider well before persisting in his accusation, but Telramund retorts that he is not taken in by Elsa's air of innocence. He is convinced, he says, that she has a lover, for has she not even now been prattling of him?

Telramund refuses to demean himself by calling a witness, and insists on having the truth of his accusation against Elsa determined by a contest of arms. When he asks which of the men of Brabant will venture to fight him, no one is prepared to do so. They will fight only on his behalf. Reminding the King that he had rendered him gallant service in a fight against the Danes, Telramund wins from Henry permission to vindicate his honour in knightly contest. 'God alone must decide this matter,' proclaims the King, echoed by the entire assembly.

Elsa and Telramund are both formally asked by King Henry if they are willing to have the truth decided by mortal combat, and both agree. When the King asks Elsa whom she will choose as her champion, Telramund mutters that the name of her lover is about to be revealed. But Elsa, as the music of her dream is heard in the orchestra, repeats that a knight sent by heaven will defend her, and adds that, if he so desires, he may then take her as his bride.

When the King announces that it is noon, and time to issue the challenge, the herald steps forward with the four trumpeters, who are positioned at the four points of the compass on the outside edge of the circle of judgement. The trumpeters sound their summons, and the herald calls on him who in heaven's name will do battle for Elsa of Brabant to stand forth. No one answers. Telramund observes that right is clearly on his side, but Elsa begs the King to have her knight summoned a second time. 'It may be that he dwells far away, and did not hear,' she suggests.

Trumpeters and herald repeat the summons, but again there is no reply. The assembly murmurs that perhaps this doleful silence is itself the judgement of God, but Elsa falls to her knees in fervent prayer that heaven send to her the knight who had already come to her, at the Almighty's behest, in her dream. The women add their voices to hers and, as though in answer, the motif of

Ex.8

Lohengrin (Ex. 8), which had earlier made its first appearance at the appropriate point in Elsa's aria, is now heard, as though from afar, on trumpets. In the distance, the figure of a knight now becomes visible in a boat on the river, drawn by a swan. The men nearest to the river describe the knight's appearance, the bright gleam of his armour and the golden chain by which the swan draws the boat.' It is a miracle, the like of which we have never before seen,' they exclaim, while the women praise God, protector of the weak.

As his boat reaches the bank, the knight is greeted by all except Ortrud and Telramund as a hero sent from heaven. The knight (Lohengrin, though he will not reveal his identity until Act III), in full armour with a helmet on his head, a shield on his back and a small golden horn at his side, steps ashore, and Telramund stares at him in speechless astonishment. Ortrud, who until now has stood haughtily remote from the proceedings, seems to be terror-stricken at the sight of the swan. Silence falls as Lohengrin (tenor) turns back to the boat to sing a tender farewell to the swan, whom he bids return to that place 'where alone lies our happiness'. The swan slowly turns and swims back up the river, still drawing the boat behind it. Lohengrin gazes sadly after the swan for a time as the assembled crowd softly expresses its awe and wonder, directed to do so 'in the softest of whispers'.

Approaching the King, Lohengrin makes obeisance to him. In answer to Henry's question as to whether, as the King supposes, he is sent by God, the knight replies merely that he has been sent to stand as champion for a maid falsely accused. Turning to Elsa, he asks if she will, without doubt or fear, entrust herself to his protection. Elsa enthusiastically greets him as her saviour, and offers to give herself wholly to him. 'If I am victorious in the combat,' Lohengrin continues, 'will you accept me as your husband?' Again Elsa unhesitatingly offers herself to him.

Lohengrin tells her that, if he is to marry her, to defend her country and her people, and never to be parted from her, there is one thing that she must solemnly promise: never to ask him, or seek to discover, his name, his lineage or whence he had come. The motif of the forbidden question is heard for the first time at these words (Ex. 9). (Twenty-five years later, Tchaikovsky was to

Ex.9

Nie   sollst du mich be-fra - gen

use it in a somewhat analagous situation in *Swan Lake*.) Elsa quickly and unthinkingly gives her word, but Lohengrin is at pains to impress upon her the high seriousness of her undertaking. He repeats the promise she must make, and she swears to honour his command. At this, Lohengrin declares tenderly, *'Elsa, ich liebe dich'* (Elsa, I love you).

When Lohengrin proclaims to the entire assembly that Elsa is free of all guilt, and that the judgement of heaven will prove Telramund's accusation false, the Brabantian nobles counsel their colleague to withdraw his charge, since the stranger is obviously protected by heaven. But Telramund, though shaken, is defiant. He has never, he says, stooped to lie, and he proudly accepts the knight's challenge.

On the King's command, three Saxon nobles step forward for Lohengrin, and three Brabantians for Telramund. They solemnly pace out a circular field of combat, and stand around its circumference with their spears thrust into the ground. The herald reminds everyone of the penalty for interfering in the fight: a freeman will lose his hand, and a serf his head. The males present repeat this, presumably to signify that they have understood. After the herald has cautioned the contestants, and they have made their formal reply, the King launches an impressive ensemble with his prayer that heaven will preside over the combat and that justice and truth will triumph. Elsa and Lohengrin express their confidence in the outcome, Telramund calls on God not to dishonour him, while Ortrud places her trust in her husband's strength.

At a signal from the herald, the trumpeters sound the call to combat. The King pulls his sword from the ground and with it strikes three times on his shield, which still hangs on the oak-tree. The combatants draw their swords, and fight. When Lohengrin strikes the decisive blow, his theme (Ex. 8) rises triumphantly from the orchestra. Holding his sword to his adversary's throat, Lohengrin proclaims that, through God's victory, Telramund's life is forfeit. He spares Telramund, however, suggesting that he devote his life to repentance.

The King now removes his shield from the oak-tree. He and the entire assembly hail Lohengrin as a hero, and Elsa begins the finale with a heartfelt cry of gratitude. As the ensemble develops, young Saxons raise Lohengrin on his shield, while Brabantians lift Elsa on the King's shield. The two are carried off amid general rejoicing, as Telramund falls unconscious at his wife's feet.

A sombre orchestral Prelude to Act II depicts the baleful and brooding character of Ortrud, the low notes of the cello moving slowly above a *tremolando* accompaniment played *pianissimo* and, twice interrupted by the motif of Lohengrin's warning (Ex. 9), on cor anglais. The curtain rises on the citadel of Antwerp, shortly before dawn. In the background the Palas, the knights' quarters, can be seen, brightly illuminated, but all else is covered in darkness. In the left foreground are the women's quarters, the Kemenate, and in the right foreground the gates of the minster. From the knights' quarters, the sound of festive music is heard.

On the steps of the minster Telramund and Ortrud, who have been condemned to banishment, are discovered sitting, both dressed in what appear to be the black robes of penitence or shame. Ortrud's gaze is fixed on the brightly lit windows of the knights' quarters, while Telramund stares moodily at the ground. Suddenly, Telramund stirs himself, exhorting Ortrud to flee with him before their presence is revealed by the approach of dawn. She replies, however, that she cannot leave, for she is bound to the spot by her determination to distil, from the sounds of their foes' revelry, a deadly poison to put an end to their joy and her shame.

Telramund bitterly accuses his wife of having caused him to lose his honour and his reputation. Because of her, his family's escutcheon is stained, his father's home accursed and he is shunned by all. Even robbers are offended by his sight. He wishes that he were dead, or that he had the strength of will to flee from her. When Ortrud scornfully asks why he is wasting his breath in wild lamenting, he replies that it is because he has lost the sword with which he would otherwise have struck her down.

Ortrud asks why her husband has lost faith in her. He reminds her that it was upon her false testimony that he had accused the innocent Elsa. Had not Ortrud assured him that she had actually seen Elsa drowning her brother in a pool? Had she not promised him that, if he renounced Elsa and married her, the descendent of Radbod's ancient race, they would rule jointly in Brabant? Ortrud denies that she has lied, and when Telramund claims that the vengeance of God upon them is proof of her villainy, she tells him that God is simply another name for his cowardice. If she were given the power, she would show Telramund how feeble is the God who protects Elsa's champion.

At this oblique reference to the old heathen gods whom his wife worships, Telramund shudders in fear. Bidding him move closer to her, Ortrud now begins to outline her plot to bring about Elsa's downfall. She tells him that, if the stranger were forced to reveal his name and race, all his power would instantly be lost. The only person able to wrest his secret from him is Elsa, so she must be induced to ask the forbidden question. Telramund wonders how this can be brought about, and Ortrud instructs him to arouse Elsa's suspicion of her defender by charging him with having resorted to sorcery to defeat Telramund in combat. Should this fail, Ortrud has another plan. Any person deriving his strength from a spell, she tells her husband, is deprived of his magic power as soon as he loses even the smallest part of his body. Had Telramund managed to cut off only a finger in the battle, the knight would have been at his mercy.

Telramund eagerly seizes the chance to redeem his honour, which he is only too ready to believe was taken from him by fraud. But he warns Ortrud that, if what she is now telling him should turn out to be further deceit, she will live to regret it. Ortrud advises him to place himself in her hands and learn the sweet bliss of vengeance. In a duet in which they sing in octaves throughout, they swear to be avenged on Elsa and her saintly knight, and warn those now lying asleep that disaster awaits them.

The malevolent atmosphere conjured up by Ortrud and Telramund lingers momentarily in a sinister phrase in the bass clarinet, only to be dispelled by a serene melody which anticipates the wedding music to be heard later in the act. This melody accompanies the approach of Elsa, who now appears on the balcony, wearing a white robe. Coming forward to the balustrade, she sings an aria, '*Euch Lüften, die mein Klagen so traurig oft erfüllt*' (You breezes, that my lamenting so often sadly filled), in which she tells the evening breeze of her newly found happiness. As she sings, Ortrud and Telramund, still crouching below in the darkness on the steps of the minster, utter *sotto voce* imprecations. Ortrud orders Telramund to be gone, and concern himself with the hero, leaving her to deal with Elsa.

The serene mood of Elsa's communing with nature is interrupted by a warning chord on oboe and horns, and Ortrud's cry of 'Elsa!' Wondering who it is who calls her name in so mournful and sinister a fashion, Elsa peers down into the darkness. Ortrud now makes herself known. Can Elsa have forgotten, she asks plaintively, the voice of the wretched woman whom she has consigned to the deepest misery?

'What are you doing here, you unhappy woman?' asks Elsa, to which Ortrud replies that she is indeed unhappy. She had lived quietly in the remoteness of the forest, bewailing the ill fate which had overtaken her race, but doing nothing to harm Elsa in any way. Why should Elsa envy her for having married the man whom she, Elsa, had scornfully rejected? Was it her fault that, misled by some fatal delusion, Telramund had made a false accusation against Elsa? He is now filled with remorse, and condemned to a fearful punishment.

Ortrud bewails the fact that Elsa, now that she has achieved happiness after a brief period of undeserved suffering, can calmly turn away from her, ignoring her suffering. Elsa, of course, is deeply affected by Ortrud's hypocritical complaint. 'How little would I deserve thy blessing, almighty God,' she exclaims, 'if I were to turn away from the miserable woman kneeling before me in the dust.' She cries to Ortrud to wait for her. She will herself come down and take Ortrud in to the Kemenate.

As Elsa hurries inside, Ortrud springs to her feet in fierce exaltation, and in a magnificent outburst, '*Entweihte Götter!*' (Dishonoured gods!), calls on her heathen gods to aid her vengeance and confound the vile beliefs of the apostates. She invokes Wotan and Freia, asking them to bless her with guile and deceit so that her revenge may be sweet. When Elsa and two maidservants with candles emerge from the lower door of the Kemenate, Ortrud abruptly reverts to her former cringing tone, and humbly throws herself at Elsa's feet.

Completely deceived by Ortrud, Elsa hastens to assure her that she is forgiven, and even begs Ortrud in turn to forgive her, Elsa, for what she has been made to suffer. Elsa assures Ortrud that she will also entreat the knight whom she is to marry on the morrow to show mercy to Telramund. She instructs Ortrud to appear next day in her finest garments and accompany her to the minster to see her become the bride of her rescuer. Ortrud humbly thanks Elsa, in whose debt she says she will live forever. She herself possesses only one power, which no decree of law could take from her, but perhaps she could use it now to protect Elsa's welfare.

When Elsa asks what she means, Ortrud warns her not to place too blind a trust in her present happiness. She offers to look into Elsa's future, in order to ward off misfortune. The orchestra at this point makes Ortrud's malevolence clear, though not to Elsa. Has Elsa never considered, asks Ortrud, that the knight who arrived so mysteriously to aid her might eventually leave her just as mysteriously?

This first attempt to destroy Elsa's faith in her saviour is unsuccessful. In her reply, Elsa merely expresses her pity for Ortrud, who, she says, can never have known the happiness that only faith can give. She invites Ortrud to come inside with her and to be converted to the true faith. Muttering to herself that she will find a way to make Elsa's pride work to her disadvantage, Ortrud allows herself to be led inside by Elsa and the maidservants. The orchestral comment which now develops from Elsa's confident phrases to accompany their exit is of a rare serenity and compassion.

As the door closes behind the women, Telramund steps forward from the background, where he has been lurking. 'Thus evil enters this house,' he exclaims. 'Accomplish, wife, what your cunning has devised. I have no power to hinder your plans. The evil began with my defeat. Now it is time for those who defeated me to be themselves overthrown. I see but one goal clearly before me—to destroy him who destroyed my honour.' Telramund retreats into the darkness again.

Day gradually dawns, a reveille is blown from the tower by two watchmen, and an answer is heard from a distant tower. The stage begins to fill with retainers, Brabantine nobles and soldiers, who sing excitedly in a somewhat conventional double chorus of the rich promise of the coming day. The herald appears from the Palas, preceded by the four royal trumpeters. A fanfare is sounded, and the herald proclaims the banishment of Friedrich von Telramund for having dared to do battle against the will of God. All who harbour or consort with Telramund are to suffer the same punishment.

The men present burst into a chorus of denunciation, cursing Telramund and vowing to shun him and his evil ways, but are called to order by another fanfare. The herald now announces the King's decree that the unknown knight sent from God is to rule over Brabant. However, since he refuses the title of Duke, he is to be known as Protector of Brabant. The male chorus enthusiastically vows to serve the Protector loyally, and the herald resumes his speech. Today the wedding of Elsa and the knight is to be celebrated, but tomorrow all are to come prepared to be led off to battle against the enemies of Brabant and of the King. The assembled nobles and soldiers respond to this news even more enthusiastically. They sing of their delight at the prospect of fighting under their Protector, as the herald and trumpeters return to the Palas.

While the populace surges about joyously, four knights, former adherents of Telramund, move together to the foreground. They express their discontent at being led off to fight against a foe who has never been a threat to Brabant. Who, they ask, will dare to oppose this new ruler? 'I will,' declares Telramund, who suddenly appears among them. He assures the four knights that he intends to accuse the Protector of sorcery. His supporters hurry Telramund away before he can be recognized by the crowd. Four pages now enter through the door of the Kemenate, announcing the arrival of Elsa von Brabant on her way to the minster, and clearing a way for her through the crowd.

A procession of women in splendid attire advances slowly from the door of the Kemenate and makes its way to the steps of the minster. The orchestra plays a solemn melody as Elsa appears in the procession, and the nobles and soldiers sing a chorus in her praise, at first softly, and then with growing fervour until a *fortissimo* climax is reached. At this point, as Elsa is about to set foot on the first of the minster steps, Ortrud, who has hitherto followed at the end of the procession, now rushes forward violently, advancing towards Elsa and confronting her on the steps.

'Stand back, Elsa!' Ortrud cries. 'No longer will I endure it that I should follow you like a servant. Precedence is mine, and you should humbly bow before me.' All are amazed, including Elsa, who asks what has caused this sudden change. 'Just because I forgot my position for an hour or so, do you think I shall forever cringe before you?' Ortrud continues. 'I intend to have my revenge for what I have suffered. I demand what is mine by right.'

Elsa finally realizes that she has been deceived by Ortrud. She wonders how a woman condemned by God can now behave so arrogantly. Ortrud replies that, although false judgement has condemned her husband, he is nevertheless the bearer of an honoured name, a man renowned for his virtue and his bravery. What, she asks, is known about Elsa's husband, whom not even the bride herself can call by his name.

Ignoring the shocked and angry comments of the bystanders, Ortrud continues her tirade. Can Elsa swear to the lineage or the nobility of the man she is about to marry? Does she know where he has come from, or where he will go when he leaves her? Of course not. The crafty knight has persuaded her that it would bring disaster upon them if she were to question him.

The crowd begins to wonder if she is speaking the truth, or whether her words are outrageous slander. Elsa, however, has no doubts. In a state of exaltation, she exclaims that her saviour's nature is so pure and noble, so full of virtue, that one would have to be completely base to doubt his mission. Did he not, with God's help, defeat Telramund in conflict? She calls on the assembled crowd to decide which of the two men is the virtuous one.

All raise their voices in support of Elsa's knight, but Ortrud is not silenced. 'Your hero's innocence', she tells Elsa, 'would soon be besmirched if he were forced to reveal the magic craft by which he wielded his power. If you do not dare to question him, we shall all quite rightly believe that it is because you yourself have doubts about him.' As Elsa's women rush forward to defend her from Ortrud's fury, the door of the Palas is opened, the royal trumpeters sound a fanfare, and the King appears, accompanied by Lohengrin and the Saxon nobles.

The Brabantine nobles acclaim the King and their new Protector. When the King demands to know why the procession to the minster has been interrupted, Elsa addresses the knight as her lord and protector, explaining to him how she had taken pity on Ortrud only to have the woman taunt her now for her faith in him. Lohengrin addresses Ortrud sternly, ordering her to keep away from Elsa. 'Tell me, Elsa,' he continues, turning to her, 'has her poison succeeded in entering your heart?' Elsa's reply is to hide her face against his breast, weeping. 'Come,' he says to her tenderly, 'let these tears turn within the church to tears of joy.'

Lohengrin turns with Elsa and the King at the head of the procession towards the minster. As they are about to enter, Telramund suddenly appears on the minster steps. The women and the pages, as they recognize him, shrink back in horror. Ignoring the King's command that he remove himself, Telramund angrily insists that he has been wronged, that the judgement of God has been profaned and cheated, and that they have all been deluded by the craft of a sorcerer.

The question which Telramund asserts the King should have put to the stranger before allowing him to defend Elsa is the one which Telramund himself now insists on putting to him. Before everyone, he demands to know the knight's name, rank and lineage. Would an honourable knight have arrived, drawn down the river by a wild swan, he asks? Let the stranger answer him, or be revealed as an impostor.

The King and the knights murmur that Telramund's is a weighty charge, and the assembled company wonders how the stranger will answer it. Lohengrin, however, says merely that he scorns to satisfy the doubts of an evil man. Telramund now turns to King Henry and invokes his aid. Will this stranger, he asks, also call the King degraded and refuse to answer him? Giving the King no chance to reply to Telramund, Lohengrin says he would deny an answer to the King and the entire assembly. They have no need to doubt, for they have witnessed the worth of his deed. There is but one person whom he would be forced to answer, and that is Elsa. He turns to her, as the orchestra makes a reference to Ortrud and then to Lohengrin's warning to Elsa. Observing that she is shaking with emotion, he prays that doubt may not enter her soul.

Elsa's agitated demeanour has been noticed by all. An impressive ensemble develops in which all express their feelings, Elsa telling herself that, if she were to learn the truth about her hero, she would guard his secret faithfully, though she cannot help wondering about him. At the conclusion of the ensemble the King vigorously upholds the Protector's right to ignore Telramund, and the assembled nobles echo his words, professing their faith in the nobility of the stranger's name, even though they do not know what it is.

While Lohengrin is busy shaking the outstretched hands of the knights, Telramund makes his way to Elsa and softly assures her that he knows a way of putting her doubts at rest. She attempts to repulse him, but he tells her that, if he were to wound the smallest part of her knight, just a fingertip, his secret would be made known to her and he would be faithful and never leave her. He, Telramund, will be close to her on her wedding night, She has only to call, and it will be done quickly.

Suddenly, Lohengrin notices Telramund with Elsa. Angrily he orders Telramund and Ortrud to keep away from her for ever. 'In your hands', he tells Elsa, 'and in your trust lies the guarantee of all our happiness. Do you still doubt me? Do you wish to question me?' Overcome with shame, Elsa assures him that her love has banished all doubt. 'Now let us go before God,' her bridegroom says as he leads her to the King, and the procession continues. A huge choral and orchestral ensemble builds up again, with the bells and the organ of the minster adding to the festive sound. The King conducts Elsa and Lohengrin to the top of the steps, and the bridal pair embrace. Elsa looks back and sees Ortrud raising her arm as though in triumph. Trumpets and trombones sound the motive of warning, but it is overwhelmed by a final ceremonial fanfare as Elsa and her bridegroom enter the minster. The curtain falls.

The orchestral Prelude to Act III of *Lohengrin*, so familiar in concert performance, is a brilliant piece (Ex. 10) in a very lively tempo, obviously intended to depict the wedding festivities of Elsa and Lohengrin. A quieter middle section (Ex. 11) is followed by a return of the opening themes, Ex. 10, and the brutally militaristic Ex. 12.

The curtain rises on the bridal chamber, which contains a richly decorated

bed at the back of the room and a low couch set against an open bay-window. Through two doors, processions enter: one of women escorting Elsa and the other consisting of the King and nobles, conducting Lohengrin. As the King presents the bride to her husband, the chorus sings the stately bridal song which church organists were later to commandeer for use at weddings. The King embraces and blesses the newly married pair, and then departs with the others, leaving Elsa and her husband alone.

A tender love duet, '*Das süsse Lied verhallt*' (The sweet song dies away), is begun by Lohengrin. Elsa assures him of her love, but when he breathes her name lovingly she observes that, although her name sounds sweetly on his lips, she can never know the sound of his name. He changes the subject, drawing her attention to the fragrant scents of the night, and reminding her that, just as those scents bewitch his senses, so did her innocence enchant him, although she was suspected of heinous crimes. Elsa, however, is unable to restrain herself. She begs him to confide in her, so that she may prove how worthy she is of his trust by never revealing his secret to another soul.

Lohengrin is moved to protest that he gave up much for her sake, that he feels amply rewarded by her love, but that she must not question him. Elsa now begins to feel jealous. 'The life you forsook for me', she complains, 'was filled with perfect joy, and now you yearn to return to such bliss. One day you will regret your love, and you will leave me.' Ortrud's motif invades the orchestral texture as Elsa expresses her fear that, just as he had come to her by magic, so he may be taken from her by magic. In her imagination she envisages the swan returning to take him. Now completely carried away, and deaf to his warnings, Elsa asks the forbidden questions. 'What is your name?' 'Whence have you come?' 'What is your lineage?'

As soon as she has uttered the questions, Elsa notices Telramund and his four companions, who break into the room through a rear door with drawn swords. Shouting a warning to her husband, Elsa hands him his sword. Grasping it, Lohengrin turns and strikes Telramund dead with one blow. Telramund's four companions drop their swords in terror and fall to their knees before Lohengrin, while Elsa slowly sinks, unconscious, to the ground. 'Alas,' cries her husband, as he picks her up and places her on the couch, 'now all our happiness is past.' He commands the knights to carry the dead Telramund to the King's seat of judgement. When they have gone, he strikes a bell summoning four serving-women, whom he orders to bring Elsa before the King. There he will answer her questions. All the appropriate themes are heard in the orchestra as the curtain falls.

A lively orchestral introduction, its martial tone announced by trumpet calls, precedes the rise of the curtain on the final scene, the meadow on the banks of the Scheldt where Act I had taken place. It is dawn: day breaks as the action progresses. The Brabantine nobles assemble as the music continues, with frequent trumpet fanfares emphasizing that the occasion is a call to battle. When King Henry enters with his Saxon forces, he is acclaimed by the assembled troops, and responds with a speech inciting them to patriotic fervour. 'For German land, the German sword: thus may our Kingdom's strength be protected,' they reply enthusiastically.

When the King asks the whereabouts of the Protector, he whom God had sent for the glory and greatness of Brabant, he is answered by the arrival of the four Brabantine nobles bearing Telramund's covered body on a bier. The bearers are recognized as Telramund's followers, but all begin to wonder whose corpse lies on the bier. The sorrowful entrance of Elsa, followed by a train of ladies-in-waiting, only serves to increase their bewilderment, as the orchestra sounds the motifs of the warning and of Ortrud. 'Why are you so sad?' the King asks Elsa as he conducts her to a seat opposite the oak-tree beneath which his ceremonial chair has been placed. 'Is it grief at parting from your husband?'

Elsa is unable to answer, but voices now announce the hero of Brabant, who enters solemnly, dressed in the armour he wore on his first appearance. He is greeted eagerly by the King and the nobles, who expect him to lead them into battle, but he dismays them by announcing that he has come, not to help them defeat their foes, but as a plaintiff. Uncovering Telramund's body, he says, 'This man attacked me by night. Say if I was right to strike him dead.' When he is unanimously acquitted of guilt, he goes on to accuse Elsa of having been misled into betraying him. All had heard her promise never to ask him who he was. That promise she had broken, so he must now disclose his name and rank.

Lohengrin recounts his story in the narrative aria '*In fernem Land*' (In a far-off land). He tells of the castle of Montsalvat, within which is the holiest of treasures: a vessel blessed with miraculous powers, brought down from heaven by an angelic host and entrusted to the care of men of the utmost purity. It is called the Grail, and the knights who are in its service are armed with supernatural might. When one of them is sent by the Grail into distant lands to champion the innocent, he is protected by its holy powers only while his identity is unknown. If a knight of the Grail is recognized by the profane world, he must leave and return to Montsalvat. 'Hear now', he concludes, 'how I answer the forbidden question. I was sent here to you by the Grail. My father, Parsifal, wears its crown. I am his knight. My name is Lohengrin.'

The King and everyone present but Elsa react with reverence to Lohengrin's disclosure. The unhappy bride, however, is filled with horror and remorse. The swan is now seen approaching down the river. This fills Elsa with even greater despair, as Lohengrin observes that the Grail has sent for its loitering knight. He goes to the river bank, and bends down to the swan, gazing at it sadly. 'My beloved swan,' he sings, 'how gladly would I have spared you this last, sad journey. Within a year, when your term of service had come to an end, I would have seen you again, freed by the power of the Grail.'

He turns to Elsa in an outburst of grief. 'Oh, Elsa,' he cries, 'had I but spent a year in happiness by your side, then your brother, whom you believed dead, would have been returned to you.' Should Gottfried return, however, after Lohengrin's departure, Elsa is to give him the horn, the sword and the ring which the holy knight now gives to her. The horn will bring help to him if he is threatened, the sword will grant him victory in battle, while the ring will serve to remind him of Lohengrin who once freed his sister from shame and distress. 'Farewell, my sweetest wife,' he ends. 'The Grail will chide me if I stay longer.'

Lohengrin turns to go, accompanied by the lamentations of the King and the entire assembly, when suddenly Ortrud emerges from the crowd. 'Go home, proud hero,' she cries, 'and let me tell your foolish bride who it is that draws your boat. I know by the chain around his neck that this is her brother, the heir of Brabant, whom I had bewitched.' She turns to Elsa. 'I thank you for driving the knight away,' she exclaims venomously. 'Had he stayed longer, he would have freed your brother.' All turn on Ortrud in fury, but she defies them. 'This', she cries, 'is how the gods take their revenge when you turn away from them.'

Having listened intently to her, Lohengrin solemnly kneels in silent prayer. All eyes are fixed on him in breathless anticipation. The white dove of the

Grail descends, hovering over the boat, and Lohengrin springs up with a look of gratitude. He unfastens the chain from the swan, whereupon it immediately plunges beneath the water. In its place there emerges a handsome youth dressed in gleaming silver, whom Lohengrin helps up on to the bank. 'Behold', he announces, 'the Duke of Brabant. Let him be proclaimed your leader.'

At the sight of Gottfried, Ortrud sinks to the ground with a shriek. Lohengrin quickly springs into the boat, which the dove has seized by its chain and now draws away. Elsa gazes joyously at her brother Gottfried, who comes forward and makes obeisance to the King. All watch in delight, and the Brabantine nobles bow to him in homage. Gottfried and Elsa embrace joyously, but then Elsa gazes after Lohengrin, whose boat is still just visible. 'My husband!' she cries, and sinks lifeless to the ground in her brother's arms, as the orchestra sounds the theme of the Grail with which the opera had begun, and the curtain falls.

LOHENGRIN stands at the cross-roads. Romantic in its almost Pre-Raphaelite purity and its static, two-dimensional characterization, it also contrives to anticipate the direction Wagner was to take in his next work, *Tristan und Isolde*, by virtue of its delicate balance, though not yet complete fusion, of music and drama. The music was already being made subservient to the drama whenever Wagner felt a tension between the two. An important instance of this can be found in the composer's letter to Liszt of 2 July 1850, only a few weeks before the opera's première:

> Give my opera as it is, without cuts. Just one cut I myself prescribe: I want you to take out the second part of Lohengrin's Narration in the big final scene of the third act. After Lohengrin's words, '*Sein Ritter ich, bin Lohengrin genannt*', fifty-six bars are to be omitted, down to '*Wo ihr mit Gott mich alle Länden saht.*' I have many times performed the entire work to myself, and I am now convinced that this second section of the Narration can have only a chilling effect. The passage must also be omitted from the libretto.

It will be recalled that the elements of the supernatural and of redemption through love, which were now to remain constant preoccupations throughout the composer's life, had already been present in his first completed opera, *Die Feen*, and had reappeared in more mature form in both *Der fliegende Holländer* and *Tannhäuser*. With the exception of that magnificent hymn to national pride and artistic compromise, *Die Meistersinger von Nürnberg*, which was still some years in the future, these were to be, in one form or another, the subjects of every subsequent opera and music drama that

Wagner composed. The themes were interconnected: love triumphed over evil, but spiritual love triumphed over temporal, earthly passions. The conflict between the world of the flesh and the world of the spirit was Wagner's basic subject.

Those to whom the word 'spiritual' presents problems can substitute 'unconscious' or, if psychological terms are unacceptable, 'aesthetic'. For Wagner himself the terms were interchangeable. 'Elsa', he wrote, 'is the unconscious, the unvolitional, into which Lohengrin's conscious, volitional being yearns to be redeemed: but that yearning is itself the unconscious, unvolitional in Lohengrin, through which he feels himself akin in being to Elsa.'

Elsewhere, Wagner sees Lohengrin as saint and redeemer. However, the most useful key to the understanding of Lohengrin's character is the suggestion that he represents Wagner the misunderstood genius, just as Vanderdecken, the Flying Dutchman, represented Wagner the betrayed idealist, and Wotan was to represent Wagner the unheeded prophet. The tension between inner and outer world, sacred and profane, eternal and temporal, is also that which existed between Wagner the artist and his audience. It is upon this tension that, to a large extent, the shaky philosophical structure of Wagner's theories of music drama are constructed. Inevitably, the composer was for a time led seriously to contemplate Christ as an operatic subject: Wagner as crucified Messiah. He actually sketched out a libretto which he called 'Jesus of Nazareth'.

It is not to be thought that his identification with his heroes was necessarily a conscious act on Wagner's part. Writing to a friend in 1856, the composer says that the period in which he worked in response to his intuitions began with *Der fliegende Holländer*, and asserts that, if in *Tannhäuser* or *Lohengrin* there is any underlying poetic theme, it must be looked for in the supreme tragedy of renunciation, the abnegation of the will 'which is shown there as necessary and unavoidable, and alone capable of achieving redemption'. One does not have to read very far between these Schopenhauerian lines to realize that Wagner is talking about art as much as philosophy.

In *Lohengrin*, by asking the forbidden questions, 'Who are you? Where do you come from?', Elsa does indeed lose her saviour, but with those same questions she regains her brother, who is finally more real to her than the magical knight precisely because his only existence is in the real world. The visible world has its legitimate delights, and Wagner is not, after all, the only artistic genius. This is what, despite its author, the libretto of *Lohengrin* appears at that point to be saying.

The libretto, however, is not simply a peg upon which to hang the music. Although its philosophical meaning and validity may be open to question, it works magnificently in purely dramatic terms. Upon a two-dimensional, medieval fear of the unknown world, Wagner has superimposed a drama which is modern in its psychology and unerring in its poetic instinct. Thus he retains the best not of two apparent worlds but of three: the spiritual, the psychological and the aesthetic. In a sense, they are one, or rather they are three ways of looking at the same world. It is the interplay between these three views of the world, in Wagner's music and his words, which makes *Lohengrin* a great opera.

SEVEN

Tristan und Isolde

(Tristan and Isolde)

Opera in Three Acts

Dramatis personae
Tristan, a Cornish Knight, Nephew to King Marke   (tenor)
King Marke of Cornwall   (bass)
Isolde, an Irish Princess   (soprano)
Kurwenal, Tristan's Retainer   (baritone)
Melot, a Knight at the Court of King Marke   (tenor)
Brangäne, Isolde's Attendant   (soprano)
A Shepherd   (tenor)
A Helmsman   (baritone)
A Sailor   (tenor)

LIBRETTO by the composer

TIME: The legendary past

PLACE: The Irish Sea; Cornwall; Brittany

FIRST PERFORMED: at the Hofoper, Munich, 10 June 1865, with Ludwig Schnorr von Carolsfeld (Tristan), Malvina Schnorr von Carolsfeld (Isolde), Anne Deinet (Brangäne), Anton Mitterwurzer (Kurwenal) and Ludwig Zottmayer (King Marke), conducted by Hans von Bülow.

I

IN the fourteen years between 1836, when *Das Liebesverbot* became the first opera by Wagner to be performed, and 1850, when *Lohengrin* was given its première, three other Wagner operas had been staged. But after 1850, fifteen years were to elapse before his next opera, *Tristan und Isolde*, made its appearance at the Hofoper, Munich, in 1865. This, however, does not mean that, as a composer, Wagner was idle for an extended period. Although he continued to write long and digressive articles on a number of diverse subjects, at any given moment he was almost certainly planning or working on more than one operatic project. He did, however, in the two years immediately following his flight from Germany in 1849, write four lengthy polemical articles which represent his mature thoughts on music, especially opera, and its relation to society. These were 'Art and Revolution', 'The Art-work of the Future', 'Judaism in Music' and 'Opera and Drama'.

In 'Art and Revolution' he wrote reverently of the drama of ancient Greece, and claimed that only by political revolution could German society raise itself beyond a narrow materialism and hope to produce works of art worthy to be set beside those of the Greeks. 'The Art-Work of the Future' asserted that, after the decline of classical Greece, the individual art-forms went their separate ways. Opera, wrote Wagner, was the total art-work (or *Gesamtkunstwerk*) of the future in which the various arts would once again be united.

'Judaism in Music' is a scurrilous pamphlet which Wagner took the precaution of publishing under the pseudonym of K. Freigedank (which translates as K. Free-thought!). The product of a mind contorted with hatred and envy, it merits little consideration except as a reflection of Wagner's character. The essay begins by describing itself as an attempt to 'explain people's instinctive dislike of Jewishness', which it takes for granted. It consists in the main of an irrational diatribe against Jews, whom Wagner insists must be eliminated from German society, and ends by gleefully prophesying the decline and fall of the Jewish race. The following paragraph is typical:

We have no need to prove that modern art has been taken over by the Jews; this is a fact that leaps to the eye unbidden. And we should have to cover too great a field were we to undertake an explanation with reference to the history of our art. But if emancipation from Judaism seems to us a prime necessity, we must test our strength for this war of liberation. We shall not gain this strength merely by an abstract definition of the situation, but by an intimate knowledge of the nature of our deep-seated, involuntary feeling of repugnance for Jewish nature. By this unconquerable feeling, what we hate in the Jewish character must be revealed to us, and when we know it we can take measures against it. By revealing him clearly, we may hope to wipe the demon from the field, where he has been able to thrive only under the protective cover of darkness, a darkness that we good-natured Humanists ourselves have offered him to make his appearance less disgusting.

The last of these essays, 'Opera and Drama', is the longest and the most important in any consideration of Wagnerian music drama. In it, Wagner postulates the new kind of opera which, after *Lohengrin*, he himself was to devote his energies to creating. The orchestral motifs used to such impressive effect in *Lohengrin* would be extended to permeate the entire texture of the opera. The drama, presented on a conscious level by the words (which Wagner himself, of course, would continue to write), would be pursued on a deeper, unconscious level in the orchestra. Musical form, as such, would be irrelevant; would, indeed, cease to exist:

In opera, hitherto, the composer has not even attempted to devise a united form for the whole art-work. Each separate vocal piece was a form filled out for itself, and merely hung together with the other tone pieces of the opera through a similarity of outward structure—not at all through any true conditioning by an inner content. The disconnected was so peculiarly the character of operatic music. Only the separate tone piece had a form coherent in itself; and this was derived from the delights of absolute music, maintained by custom, and imposed upon the poet as an iron yoke. The connecting principle, within these forms, consisted in a ready-made theme making place for a second, a middle theme, and then repeating itself according to the dictates of musical caprice . . .

If we consider the present attitude assumed by poet and composer towards each other, and if we find it ordered by the same maxims of self-restriction and egoistic severance as those which govern all the factors of our modern social state, then we cannot but feel that, in an unworthy public system where every man is bent on shining for himself alone, none but the individual can take into himself the spirit of community, and cherish and develop it according to his powers, however inadequate they may be. It is not to two people that the thought of jointly making possible the perfected musical drama can occur . . . only the solitary one, in the thick of his endeavour, can transmute the bitterness of such a self-avowal into an intoxicating joy which drives him on, with all the courage of a drunkard, to undertake the making possible of the impossible; for he alone is thrust forward by two artistic forces which he cannot withstand—by forces which he willingly allows to persuade him to offer his entire being.

Early in 1848 while he was still finishing *Lohengrin*, Wagner had begun to make plans for an opera, or music drama as he now preferred to call his works for the stage, based on the old Nordic myth of the Nibelungen. By the autumn he had produced an essay, a scenario ('The Nibelungen Myth as Sketch for a Drama') and a play in verse, *Siegfrieds Tod* (Siegfried's Death), based on the final portion of the myth. (Eventually this was to become the opera *Götterdämmerung*.)

In the spring of 1851, in answer to one of Wagner's appeals for money, Liszt offered him a commission to compose an opera for the sum of 1500 marks, using *Siegfrieds Tod* as its libretto. Wagner's reply was to propose another opera, *Der junge Siegfried* (Young Siegfried), to act as a prelude to *Siegfrieds Tod* which he would compose later. In June, he wrote the libretto for *Der junge Siegfried* and began to plan the opera. But when Frau Julie Ritter, an elderly widow in Dresden who was one of his admirers (even though she had been the confidante of Jessie Laussot, the wealthy young Englishwoman with whom Wagner had hoped to elope), offered him an annuity of 2,400 marks, Wagner took the opportunity to repay the advance he had received from Liszt for *Der junge Siegfried* and to plan to set the entire Nibelungen myth to music. He prefaced *Der junge Siegfried* with the libretto for another opera, *Die Walküre* (The Valkyrie), and in turn prefaced that with *Das Rheingold* (The Rhinegold).

Wagner's intention in 1851 was to devote himself to the composition of the four operas in their correct chronological order, a task which he expected would occupy him for at least three years. In fact, however, two years were to pass before he was able to begin composing what was to become his great tetralogy, *Der Ring des Nibelungen* (The Nibelung's Ring). He and Minna were now living in Zurich, where, early in 1852, he conducted three concerts in order to augment his income, and superintended a production of *Der fliegende Holländer*.

Among the friends Wagner had made in Zurich were Otto Wesendonk, a wealthy silk merchant, and his wife Mathilde. Acting true to his nature, the composer borrowed money from Otto and fell in love with Mathilde. The four Nibelung libretti were completed by the end of 1852, but it was not until a visit to Italy the following year that Wagner began work on the music. Returning one day to his room in Spezia after a walk in the country, he lay down exhausted and, in a kind of half-sleep, found himself 'sinking in swiftly flowing water. The rushing sound', he wrote later, 'formed itself in my brain into a musical sound, the chord of E flat major, which continually re-echoed in broken forms.' This was the beginning of the prelude to *Das Rheingold*.

On his eventual return to Zurich, Wagner worked on *Das Rheingold*, whose full score he had completed by the end of September in the following year. By this time, he had already begun the composition of *Die Walküre*, interrupting the task to accept an invitation from the Philharmonic Society to conduct eight concerts in London between March and June 1855. Although he was gratified to be received, during the interval of the penultimate concert, by Queen Victoria who requested a repetition of the Overture to *Tannhäuser*, Wagner's London visit was financially disappointing, and the English music critics were uncomplimentary. Denouncing them as a gang of Jews, the composer returned to Switzerland.

In 1854, inspired by his feelings for Mathilde Wesendonk, Wagner had conceived the idea of writing *Tristan und Isolde*. In April 1857, shortly after moving into a small house adjoining Wesendonk's mansion, which the silk merchant leased to him at a low rental, Wagner began to compose *Tristan*. During the course of its composition, he also wrote five songs, to poems by Mathilde Wesendonk, into two of which, '*Träume*' (Dreams) and '*Im Treibhaus*' (In the hothouse), he wove themes from the opera. '*Träume*' is thematically related to the love music of Act II, while '*Im Treibhaus*' quotes from the Prelude to Act III.

The personal relationship of the Wagners and the Wesendonks soon deteriorated. The two wives quarrelled openly and, when Minna intercepted a note which Richard had sent to Mathilde with a sketch of the Prelude to *Tristan*, a series of unpleasant scenes ensued. Wagner's behaviour to Otto Wesendonk, his benefactor, was hardly calculated to improve matters: when the composer and Mathilde were communing artistically, Wagner even began to object to Wesendonk's presence in his own drawing-room.

The foursome broke up when Minna was sent to Dresden to intercede for a pardon for her husband and Wesendonk took Mathilde on a visit to Italy. Before she left, Minna wrote to Mathilde, 'I must tell you with a bleeding heart that you have succeeded in separating my husband from me after nearly twenty-two years of marriage. May this noble deed contribute to your peace of mind, and to your happiness.' The harrassed composer, deprived of his benefactor, his muse–mistress, and his domestic helpmate all at once, gloomily made his way alone to Venice to work on *Tristan und Isolde*. He was short of money, had recourse to pawnbrokers, and wrote desperately to Liszt that 'Wagner does not give a curse for any of you, or your theatres, or even his own operas. He needs money, that is all.' He also wrote to the Saxon Minister of Justice for permission to return to Saxony. The reply was discouraging, Saxony put pressure on Austria to expel him, and in due course he was requested by the authorities to leave Venice, which was at that time under Austrian rule.

During his stay of seven months in Venice, Wagner had managed to complete the second act of *Tristan und Isolde*. He finished the third act in Lucerne, his place of retreat after his enforced departure from Italy. The Wesendonks had by this time returned to Zurich, and when Wagner paid them a visit he apparently found that Otto was prepared not only to resume relations with him but also to help him again financially. Wagner felt it necessary that he should settle in Paris, where he would be in close proximity to the major musical organizations, and Wesendonk agreed to purchase from him the copyright in both *Das Rheingold* and *Die Walküre* for the sum of 12,000 francs, the amount Wagner required to set himself up in Paris. He also required the presence of Minna, and wrote to her in Dresden, where she was now under the care of a physician who was treating her for a heart condition and for general nervous exhaustion. Wagner urged her physician to make it clear to Minna that her health would never allow her to sleep with her husband again: it was not as a wife that he needed her, but as a housekeeper. In November 1859 Minna arrived in Paris with dog and parrot, and the Wagners set up house yet again.

Having taken a three-year lease of a villa near the Champs Elysées, Wagner had spent much of the money he had received from Wesendonk in improving and decorating it. Now he set about promoting himself in Paris as a composer. His first steps were to hire a theatre in which to give concerts of his music, and to attempt to persuade the Paris Opéra to produce *Tannhäuser*. In due course the concerts were presented, and the opera (as related in Chapter 5) was staged in March 1861.

The following month, Wagner left Paris for Karlsruhe to try to arrange for *Tristan und Isolde* to be staged there. Apparently successful in this, he moved on to Vienna in May, to choose singers for the Karlsruhe production. Here he heard *Lohengrin* for the first time, in a fine performance at the Vienna Opera which moved him to tears. He decided that it would be better to have *Tristan* produced in Vienna than in Karlsruhe, but as a result the opera was staged in neither place. After a visit to the Wesendonks in Venice, where he was persuaded by Mathilde to begin work on *Die Meistersinger von Nürnberg*, Wagner proceeded to Paris, where he started on the libretto, and thence to Mainz to arrange for the eventual publication of *Die Meistersinger*, and to Biebrich, near Mainz, which became his temporary headquarters. Here Minna, who had gone back to Dresden, arrived in a state of mental and physical near-collapse, demanding that her husband return to Dresden with her.

When Wagner visited her for four days in Dresden some months later, he and Minna had come to the parting of the ways. Realizing that their life together was an impossibility, he attempted to ensure that she would be provided for, and never saw her again. By the time Minna died, in January 1866, Wagner had become emotionally involved with Cosima von Bülow, illegitimate daughter of Liszt and wife of the conductor Hans von Bülow, who was a Wagner disciple and friend, and an ardent apologist for the Master's music and theories. Wagner had spent three years leading the nomadic life of a travelling musician, giving concerts of his own and other composers' works in Prague, St Petersburg, Moscow and Berlin, and during that time had lived briefly with other mistresses before he and Cosima, as he expressed it, 'sealed our vow to belong to each other alone'.

Now, however, another person forced an entry into Wagner's emotional life: none other than the eighteen-year-old King Ludwig II of Bavaria. On 3 May 1864, in Stuttgart, whither the composer had fled to avoid creditors and an Austrian warrant for his arrest for debt, the secretary of King Ludwig brought to Wagner the curious news that Ludwig was passionately interested in him and his music and wished to constitute himself the composer's protector. Wagner immediately travelled to the Bavarian capital of Munich, and became the close friend of the young homosexual monarch, who was already well advanced towards the insanity in which he was to end his days. The composer's entourage, consisting of Bülow and Cosima, turned the usual Wagner triangle into a rectangle. Wagner received Ludwig's bounty and also his devotion, expressed by the young King in highly romantic terms:

> The mean cares of everyday life I will banish from you forever. I will procure for you the peace you have longed for in order that you may be free to spread the mighty wings of your genius in the pure air of rapturous art. O, how I have looked forward to the time when I could do this! I hardly dared indulge myself in the hope of so quickly being able to prove my love to you.

Wagner soon persuaded the King to agree to build him a theatre of his own. To Ludwig, who was to scatter fairy-tale castles around his kingdom, a mere theatre presented no great difficulty, and the Dresden architect Gottfried Semper was summoned to prepare plans. In November 1864, the young King wrote to his beloved composer:

> I have decided to have a large masonry theatre constructed, so that the performance of *Der Ring des Nibelungen* shall be perfect. This unique work must be presented in a theatre worthy of it. May your efforts to find capable dramatic singers meet with glorious success! I shall expect to discuss with you in person the details of this theatre, to ensure that your requirements as stated in the preface to the poem of *Der Ring des Nibelungen* shall be carried out. I proclaim: 'In the beginning let there be the *deed*!'

Trouble, however, was brewing for Wagner, for his relationship with the young King was creating a scandal at the Bavarian court. Ludwig I, the previous King, had been thought disreputable because he had a mistress, the entertainer Lola Montez, and now the nickname of 'Lolette' was conferred upon Wagner, who began to acquire in Munich the reputation of being an active homosexual. Ludwig had given Wagner an opulent apartment, and the composer summoned Bertha, a Viennese milliner, to Munich to transform it into what a Wagner biographer has called 'a whorish fantasy of silks, satins, velvets and laces'.

In April 1865, Cosima gave birth to Wagner's child, Isolde, whom Bülow accepted as his own. Later that month, Wagner wrote to Friedrich Uhl, a friend in Vienna, inviting him to attend the first performance of *Tristan und Isolde*:

> The first performances of *Tristan und Isolde*, of which it is almost certain that there will be three, will be exceptional and exemplary in every way. Above all, the two particularly difficult principal roles are to be performed by my dear friends, Ludwig and Malvina Schnorr von Carolsfeld, who have been engaged especially. With them there will be my old comrade-in-arms in the battle of art, Anton Mitterwurzer, as Kurwenal, incomparably staunch and true. As far as circumstances will allow, trouble has been taken and no expense spared to get the best available singers for the other roles. Every member of the cast is sincerely well disposed towards me . . . The superb Court Orchestra, the exemplary creation of Franz Lachner, is at our disposal almost every day for rehearsals. We are concerned only with the highest artistic standards and with correctness in delivery, and the large number of rehearsals give us all the time we need to achieve them without strain.
>
> Since the production as a whole will benefit if I am in a position to give it overall supervision, I have my dear friend Hans von Bülow to conduct the orchestra—the very man who also accomplished the impossible, making a piano reduction of this score that can actually be played, although nobody yet understands how he contrived to do so. He knows this score, which still completely mystifies so many musicians, so well that he has every tiny portion of it by ear, and has absorbed every last nuance of my intentions. With him, a second self, at my side, I can attend to every detail of the musical performance and of the staging, in the tranquil, relaxed, artistic atmosphere which only the sympathetic collaboration of artists who are also true friends can evoke.
>
> These performances . . . are to be regarded as festivals, to which I can invite the friends of my art from near and far. They will therefore be far removed from the atmosphere of ordinary theatrical performances and will depart from the normal relationship obtaining between theatre and public in our time. It is my gracious patron's wish that these epoch-making performances shall not be offered to common curiosity, but solely to those who have a more serious interest in my art. I am empowered, therefore, to extend an invitation to every distant region where there are hearts won over by my work.
>
> The performances will probably take place in the second half of May, and as soon as the dates are known with reasonable certitude they will be announced in good time in the newspapers with the widest circulations. We

assume that anyone who is prepared to travel to Munich specially for this purpose will not wish to combine the journey with any other superficial end, but will be demonstrating his serious interest in the success of a significant and noble artistic undertaking. Anyone who, with this understanding, makes his interest known to the Court and National Theatre in Munich, can be assured of a place being reserved for him in the theatre for the performance of his choice. The same invitation, in purpose and expression, will be sent to both foreign and native friends of my art.

In the event of sneers that these measures appear to be designed to ensure particularly well disposed audiences, whom it will not take any very great art to please, we shall calmly reply that on this occasion we are not concerned with the extraordinary modern theatrical game of chance, of pleasing or not pleasing an audience, but solely with whether the artistic challenges that I have set in this work can be met, how they are to be met, and whether it is worth the trouble of meeting them . . .

On the day in early spring 1865 that *Tristan und Isolde* was to have had its première in Munich by command of the King, Wagner received the news that Minna lay fatally ill. He also received a love-letter from Ludwig, who seemed to have cast himself as Isolde to Wagner's Tristan. In addition, Malvina Schnorr von Carolsfeld, who was to sing Isolde, developed a sudden attack of catarrh and lost her voice. To cap it all, at the instigation of Ludwig's ministers, who had begun to plot the composer's downfall, police officers entered Wagner's apartment with a warrant to attach his possessions for debt.

Cosima was hastily despatched to the royal treasury, and returned with 2,400 florins. The première of the opera was postponed. *Tristan und Isolde* finally reached the stage on 10 June. Many of Wagner's former friends and admirers stayed away from this first performance, preferring not to expose themselves to the monster of vanity they considered he had become. Of those who did witness the première, which was conducted by Hans von Bülow, few recognized the stature of one of the great masterpieces of romanticism, except perhaps the half-mad Ludwig, who proclaimed it his favourite opera, and who wrote to Wagner immediately after the première, quoting the words of Isolde's '*Liebestod*':

Only one! Hallowed One!
What rapture!—*Perfect*. Overwhelmed by delight! . . . To drown . . .
to sink—unconscious—highest bliss—*Divine* work!
Eternally true,
till death and beyond!

Except on the part of Ludwig, reaction to *Tristan und Isolde* was respectful, and indeed somewhat puzzled, rather than enthusiastic. A parody, *Tristanderl und Süssholde*, had been produced at a suburban theatre in Munich two weeks before the opera's première, but nine years were to elapse before *Tristan und Isolde* was staged outside Munich. It reached Weimar in 1874, and Berlin two years later. London first heard the opera when it was conducted by Hans Richter at the Theatre Royal, Drury Lane, in 1882, with Rosa Sucher as Isolde and Hermann Winkelmann as Tristan. The London critics were divided, Herman Klein writing in the *Sunday Times*, 'My first reaction on regaining my mental equilibrium was to solemnly vow that I would never write another word in disparagement of Richard Wagner or his music as long as I lived,' while the critic of *The Era* could not refrain

> from making a protest against the worship of animal passion which is so striking a feature in the later works of Wagner . . . The passion is unholy in itself and its representation is impure, and for those reasons we rejoice in believing that such works will not become popular. If they did we are certain their tendency would be mischievous, and there is, therefore, some cause for congratulation in the fact that Wagner's music, in spite of all its wondrous skill and power, repels a greater number than it fascinates.

The first American performance of *Tristan und Isolde*, at the Metropolitan Opera House in 1886, was conducted by Anton Seidl, with Albert Niemann and Lilli Lehmann in the title-roles. This time, the opera was an immense success.

II

THE origins of the Tristan and Isolde legend are lost in antiquity: the story as found in the German Minnesinger Gottfried von Strassburg's thirteenth-century romance contains elements from a number of disparate sources, some Celtic, some French, though it is now generally thought that the legend must originally have come from Wales or Cornwall. Wagner had no doubt first come across the story in the course of his studies of medieval literature, and he had subsequently read Gottfried von Strassburg's poem in a modern German version published in 1847. The seeds of his Tristan were sown well before he met Mathilde Wesendonk; his feeling for Mathilde merely provided a convenient excuse for turning aside from *Der Ring des Nibelungen* at the moment when, for the creative impulse's more complex reasons, the need to compose his great apotheosis of romanticism welled up within him.

In a letter to Liszt, in December 1854, Wagner had written, 'Since never in my whole life have I tasted the real happiness of love, I mean to raise a monument to that most beautiful of dreams in which, from beginning to end, this love shall really sate itself to the full for once. I have in my mind a plan for a *Tristan und Isolde*, the simplest but most full-blooded musical conception.'

As always, the composer needed the poet, and in Wagner composer and poet necessarily continued to be one. He drafted his *Tristan* libretto before allowing musical ideas to come to the surface, but the words he wrote for himself to set to music eventually were not only written for a composer, they were written *by* a composer: the musico-dramatic process had begun the moment the first words of the libretto were conceived. As Wagner once wrote to a friend, 'I can conceive a subject only when it comes to me in such a form that I myself cannot distinguish between the contribution of the poet and that of the musician in me; and its completion in word and tone is simply the ultimate realization of something that had originally presented itself to me only in vague outlines.'

In *Tristan und Isolde*, external action is minimal, the drama being carried on internally in the emotions of the protagonists. Wagner's own outline emphasizes this:

The loyal vassal, on behalf of his king, woos Isolde, the woman whom he will not admit to himself he loves, who goes with him as his sovereign's bride because she is powerless herself to do anything but follow the wooer. The goddess of love, jealous for her rights that are thus suppressed, takes her revenge. She arranges, through an ingenious error, for the young couple to drink the love potion that Isolde's mother has prudently sent along, according to the custom of the time, for the man with whom her daughter is to make a political marriage.

Thanks to the potion, the passion of Tristan and Isolde suddenly flares up and they have to confess mutually that they belong only to each other. And now there are no bounds to the longing, the desire, the bliss and the anguish of love. The world, power, fame, glory, honour, chivalry, loyalty, friendship are all swept away like chaff, an empty dream. Only one thing is left alive: yearning, yearning, insatiable desire, ever reborn—languishing and thirsting; the sole release—death, dying, extinction, never more to awaken!

Here, in music's own most unrestricted element, the musician who chose this theme to introduce his drama of love could have but one care—how to restrain himself, since it would be impossible to exhaust the theme. So in one long breath he allowed that unslaked longing to swell from its first avowal with the gentlest tremor of attraction, through half-heaved sighs, through hopes and fears, laments and wishes, joy and torment, to the mightiest onset, the most resolute attempt to find a path into the sea of the delight of endless love.

In vain, however. Its power spent, the heart sinks back and yearns with desire again, desire without attainment. For each fruition sows the seeds of fresh desire, till in its final lassitude the eye beholds a glimmer of the highest bliss. It is the bliss of renouncing life, of being no more, of a last redemption into that wondrous realm from which we stray the furthest when we strive to enter it by force. Shall we call it death? Or is it not the wondrous world of night, whence—so the story goes—an ivy and a vine sprang up in locked embrace over the grave of Tristan and Isolde?

III

Tristan und Isolde is like no other opera by Wagner, or anyone else, in its concentration upon the inner lives of its protagonists. It is an opera about love or, to be more precise, about desire and romantic yearning. The love of Tristan and Isolde is really not in any way akin to the love of Romeo and Juliet, or Heloïse and Abélard. Indeed, Tristan and Isolde themselves are, in a way, abstractions whom Wagner needed in order to embody, on the opera stage, his ideas about a yearning which is as much for death as for love.

This is an opera which is usually, and correctly, described as symphonic, and one might perhaps be forgiven for wondering why, in fact, Wagner did not compose it as a symphony rather than as a work for the theatre. If such a question can be answered at all, the answer presumably is that Wagner was a man of the theatre, and that it therefore came naturally to him to attempt to widen the scope of his chosen *métier*, the theatre, to include material of a kind it was not used to dealing with, instead of turning to the concert hall.

Although they are revealed in Isolde's narration during Act I, it is helpful for the listener to be aware, before the rise of the curtain, of certain preceding events. Tristan, the nephew of King Marke of Cornwall, had killed, in a duel, Morold, the lover of the Irish princess Isolde. Grievously wounded in the duel, Tristan had asked to be placed in a boat with his weapons and to be cast adrift on the sea to die. When his boat was thrown up by the tide on the Irish shore, Tristan was nursed back to health by Isolde, who was at first unaware of his identity. When she discovered who he was, her first impulse was to kill him while he was in her power, but instead she allowed him to convalesce and in due course to return to Cornwall unharmed. Later, Tristan was sent by King Marke to make peace with Ireland, and to demand the hand of Isolde in marriage with Marke, by way of sealing the treaty. Isolde was forced to consent, and she is now being carried back to Cornwall by Tristan, as the future bride of his uncle.

As much of the external world as can be omitted from his telling of the story is ruthlessly excised by Wagner. Those characters and incidents that are allowed to remain are there mainly to give an audience something to look at while the drama is being unfolded in the orchestra. This is immediately clear from the opening bars of the Prelude, which is not really a prelude to what is to happen but a first statement of Wagner's theme.

Tristan und Isolde

More than forty leading motifs can be easily identified in *Tristan und Isolde*. It was not, of course, Wagner's intention that they should be consciously identified, rather that they should work on the subconscious feelings of his hearers. He is not the only great artist to address his audience simultaneously on two levels, but he is the first composer consciously to have known that he was doing so. Wagner did not do anything so crass as to label his motifs, and he would doubtless have been contemptuous of arguments as to whether the two-part motif at the beginning of the Prelude (Ex. 13) should be thought to denote first Tristan (the initial phrase, descending chromatically) and then Isolde (an answering phrase, ascending chromatically), or whether both parts represent romantic yearning or, to be prosaic, the love-potion which, in Act I, is used to induce it.

Ex.13

The Prelude is a slow, sensuous, bitter-sweet evocation of romantic desire, which introduces several of the motifs embedded within the score of the opera. It sets the mood, one of being 'half in love with easeful death', which persists underneath the work's occasional spurts of action until it finds its final glorious release at the end in Isolde's '*Liebestod*'. Dare one hint, however, that perhaps, even as early in the opera as here in the Prelude, Wagner's besetting sin of prolixity, in which he indulged himself increasingly in his later works, is already evident? As the Prelude, which is perhaps just a trifle over-long, sinks to its conclusion, the curtain rises on Act I, which is set on the deck of Tristan's ship at sea, crossing from Ireland to the northern coast of Cornwall. A pavilion, enclosed by walls of rich tapestry, has been erected on the deck. Within it are Isolde (soprano) and her attendant, Brangäne (soprano). From above, as though from the mast-head, can be heard the unaccompanied voice of a young sailor (tenor), singing a sad farewell to the Irish maiden he has left behind.

The sailor's song appears to Isolde to be taunting her. She asks Brangäne where they are, and when she is told that by evening they will have reached Cornwall's green shores, she bursts into an excited appeal to the elements to wreck the arrogant ship and all who sail in it. She calls for air, and Brangäne draws back the wall of tapestry, revealing the entire length of the vessel, with Tristan (tenor) on deck, gazing sadly across the sea, his faithful friend and retainer Kurwenal (baritone) by his side.

The plaintive song of the young sailor is heard again, but the sight of Tristan distracts Isolde's attention from it, and she now launches into an angry denunciation of 'that varlet . . . that hero who hides his gaze from mine, and casts his eyes down in shame and embarrassment'. She commands Brangäne to summon Tristan to come to her. When he sees Brangäne approaching, Kurwenal mutters laconically, 'Beware, Tristan! Message from Isolde.' Three times Brangäne is forced to deliver Isolde's summons, each time receiving a temporizing reply, the last of which is to the effect that, if he were to leave the helm now, Tristan would be unable to steer the ship safely home. When Brangäne persists, Kurwenal answers more roughly than Tristan. 'Remind the lady Isolde', he tells Brangäne, 'that Sir Tristan is a lord of all the world. . . . Sir Morold crossed the sea to us to exact tribute from Cornwall, but his head now hangs in Ireland as a tribute to England. This is how our hero Tristan pays tribute.' His words are echoed with gleeful enthusiasm by the ship's crew.

Scolded by Tristan, Kurwenal descends into the ship's cabin. Brangäne returns in agitation to Isolde, closing the curtains behind her to shut out the sound of the crew's singing. Isolde reacts indignantly to Tristan's answer, and in a lengthy solo, known as Isolde's Narration (*'Wie lachend sie mir Lieder singen'*: As they laughingly sing their songs to me), she tells Brangäne of the events which have led to the present situation.

Isolde sings of the arrival of Tristan in a small, frail vessel; of how she used her magic skills in healing to bring him back to health; of how 'Tantris', as he anagramatically called himself, was soon recognized by her as Tristan, due to a notch in his sword which exactly matched a splinter taken from the head of Morold. She had been about to strike Tristan dead with Morold's sword when his glance touched her heart and she let the sword fall. She healed Tristan's wounds, and allowed him to return home to Cornwall, so that she would no more be troubled by his gaze.

Now, however, Tristan has returned under his own name, demanding Ireland's heiress as bride 'for Cornwall's weary king'. He whom she had treated so tenderly has now exposed her to shame by claiming her on his uncle's behalf, and has compounded the felony by studiously avoiding her during the voyage from Ireland to Cornwall. Isolde's Narration, the only passage of exposition throughout *Tristan und Isolde*, and a splendid, though sole, opportunity for the dramatic soprano singing Isolde to enliven the external aspects of Wagner's deliberately thin plot, builds to a marvellous climax in which she curses Tristan and utters an agonized plea for death for them both. It is obvious that Isolde harbours strong feelings for Tristan, whether of hatred or of love. As so often in life, apparent opposites are seen to be mirror-images.

Brangäne endeavours to soothe Isolde by pointing out that Tristan could

144

have done her no greater honour than to claim her as the bride of the King of Cornwall, a man of exalted race and gentle manner, a man faithfully served by Tristan, the noblest of heroes. In her response to this, Isolde reveals that she is really already in love with Tristan. 'How could I endure the torture', she asks, 'of being unloved, and seeing the noblest man close beside me?'

Her handmaiden's answer to this is that, if there were any man who did not love Isolde, he could be made to do so by the magic potion which Isolde's mother has entrusted to Brangäne's care. This potion was to be given to Isolde to administer to King Marke on their wedding-day. Brangäne produces a small casket containing various phials: balsam for wounds, antidotes for poisons, and what she calls the noblest draught of all, the love-potion. 'You are mistaken,' Isolde tells her. 'I know one better suited to my purpose.' She points to the phial containing what Brangäne identifies as a draught of death.

They are interrupted suddenly by a shout from the sailors taking in the mainsail, and the entrance of Kurwenal to announce that they are nearing land. Tristan has sent him to request Isolde to prepare herself for her reception by King Marke. Isolde replies that, if she is to stand by Tristan's side before the king, custom and courtesy require that the hero first present himself to her to beg her forgiveness for his treatment of her. When Kurwenal has left to deliver this message, Isolde instructs Brangäne to prepare 'the drink of atonement', indicating the phial of poison, and adding that she intends it for Tristan, her betrayer.

While a horrified Brangäne attempts to expostulate, Tristan is announced, and enters to ask what Isolde requires of him. She upbraids him for having shunned her during the voyage. To his reply that he was merely showing respect, her response is that his attitude had been scornful. He pleads etiquette. In his country, custom dictates that he who accompanies the bride home must keep his distance from her. Isolde reminds Tristan of another custom: to make atonement to a foe whom one wishes to turn into a friend. Tristan replies that peace has already been made, but Isolde insists that it was not made between them personally. She had sworn to avenge the death of Morold, and she has yet to discharge her oath.

If Morold was so dear to her, Tristan tells Isolde, she has only now to take the sword he offers her and kill the enemy who stands before her. 'What would King Marke say', Isolde asks with some bitterness, 'if I were to slay the finest of his knights?' No, she wants only to end the feud with a cup of atonement. The cry of the sailors is heard again, as Isolde awaits Tristan's answer. The music, as much as Tristan's obscure, telegraphic words, indicate that he is aware that he is being offered poison. 'Well do I know Ireland's queen, and her magic arts,' he tells Isolde. 'The balsam she once gave me I took, just as now I take this cup which will heal me completely. Pay careful heed to the oath I swear to you. A troth to Tristan's honour, and defiance to

Tristan's torment. Heart's deception, dream of presentiment. The sole balm for endless grief, oblivion's kind draught, I drink you now without wavering.'

As Tristan drinks from the goblet which Brangäne has offered him, Isolde snatches it from his hands with a cry of 'Do you betray me still? Half is mine. Traitor, I drink to you! Tristan!' But, before offering the goblet to Tristan, Brangäne had substituted the love-potion for the fatal poison which Isolde had intended to use. Tristan and Isolde stand, gazing at each other as the orchestra speaks of the awakening of love. Slowly they melt into each other's arms. 'Faithless dear one,' Isolde cries. 'Most blessed of women,' replies Tristan.

Clasped in an embrace, the lovers are oblivious to the voices of the sailors hailing King Marke, whose boat is drawing near. Rapturously, they sing words of love to each other, and it is with the greatest difficulty that Brangäne manages to separate them. 'Who draws near?' asks Tristan confusedly. When Kurwenal replies, 'The King,' Tristan asks 'What King?' He and Isolde attempt to take in what is happening around them, as King Marke steps on board and the curtain quickly falls, with Isolde's love motif (Ex. 13) ringing out above, and only at the last moment drowned by, the cries of welcome and the noises of the outside world.

Act II, which takes place at night in the garden of King Marke's royal castle in Cornwall, begins with an orchestral introduction which introduces the motif of day, the day of the hated mundane outside world as opposed to the world of night and of love which Tristan and Isolde have entered. Making its first appearance at the very beginning of the Act II prelude, the day motif is followed, in the ninth bar of the prelude, by another motif, that of the lovers' impatience. Other motifs are also woven into the texture of this fine orchestral tone-poem.

When the curtain rises, a garden with tall trees is revealed in the fading daylight. To one side, with steps leading up to it, is Isolde's chamber. A burning torch stands at the open door as a signal, warning Tristan not to approach until it is extinguished. Hunting-horns are heard in the distance as Brangäne, on the steps, watches the retreat of the hunting-party. Isolde emerges from her chamber to await the arrival of Tristan once night has fallen. Brangäne warns her mistress that her lover's passion for her had been noticed on board the ship by at least one member of the welcoming party, Melot, whose eyes had been fixed craftily upon Tristan.

Isolde will not listen to her. Melot is Tristan's greatest friend, a man with whom he spends all his time whenever he is forced to be absent from her side. It was Melot, Isolde tells Brangäne, who had organized the nocturnal hunt in order to facilitate her assignation with Tristan. Unconvinced, Brangäne suggests that Melot is intent on hunting a nobler quarry than Isolde imagines, and begs her mistress not to extinguish the warning torch. She blames herself for having substituted a love-potion for the poison which Isolde had intended to administer to Tristan. But Isolde scornfully denies that Brangäne's act was in any way significant. 'The work of death which I had presumptuously taken into my hands', she cries, 'was snatched from me by the goddess of love. Now, wherever love leads me, I shall follow.'

As the evening sky now darkens, Isolde discerns the figure of Tristan approaching, and despite Brangäne's warning she takes the torch from the doorway and extinguishes it. Brangäne retreats to keep watch for the return of Marke and his hunting-party. To the sound of the impatience motif, Tristan now rushes in, and the lovers clasp each other in a transport of delight, as the orchestra ardently sings of their ecstatic passion.

A rapturous love duet begins as Tristan and Isolde exchange short, urgent phrases to music dominated by the day motif. This earlier part of the lengthy duet is hectic and, musically, not particularly distinguished. It is from these pages that the popular description of Wagner's love music as erotic screaming must have arisen. But the tempo slows as the lovers sink into each other's arms, the night motif now permeating their softly whispered confessions. '*O sink hernieder, Nacht der Liebe*' (O sink down upon us, night of love), they sing, becoming increasingly oblivious to their surroundings. This beautiful central section of the duet is the very essence of musical romanticism. From the turret nearby, Brangäne's voice now floats down as she keeps watch ('*Einsam wachend in der Nacht*': Alone I watch in the night), warning the lovers that the night will soon end. Brangäne's long phrases add their own beauty to the atmosphere of night and love, almost belying her words of warning.

Still lost in each other, Tristan and Isolde pay no attention to Brangäne. To the '*Liebestod*' (Love–death) motif (Ex. 14), over a throbbing accompaniment

Ex.14

('*So stürben wir, um ungetrennt*': Thus might we die, undivided), they yearn for death to unite them. Brangäne repeats her warning more urgently, but is again unheeded. The lovers are still completely oblivious to the outside world, locked in an embrace, when Kurwenal rushes in with drawn sword, crying 'Save yourself, Tristan,' closely followed by the hunting-party headed by King Marke (bass) and Tristan's friend Melot (tenor). At the same time, Brangäne descends from the tower and rushes protectively towards Isolde who, in shame, has averted her face from the newcomers, while Tristan has instinctively shielded her with his cloak. 'Were my accusations not justified?'

Melot asks Marke, who is deeply distressed at finding himself betrayed by Tristan, whom he refers to as the truest of friends and the staunchest of men. Tristan's only response is to call Marke and his followers daylight phantoms, and bid them be gone.

Violently affected, in a musically undistinguished monologue which is stretched out to almost ten minutes, and seems longer, Marke expresses his distress at the great wrong Tristan has done him. '*Mir dies? Dies, Tristan, mir?*' (This to me? To me, Tristan, this?), he begins. Where are honour and true breeding, he asks, if Tristan, the defender of all honour, has lost them? He recalls that he had loved and cherished Tristan as a son, and recounts the events leading up to the hero's voyage to Ireland to bring Isolde back as Marke's queen. He wonders why this suffering has been brought upon him, and ends by philosophically questioning its secret cause.

Tristan, completely engrossed in his love for Isolde, cannot bring himself to deal with Marke's mundane complaints. 'O King,' he replies to Marke, 'I cannot answer your question. What you ask, you can never hope to know.' Seeing his own death as imminent, Tristan turns to Isolde, asking her if she will follow him to that land where the sun never shines, the wondrous realm of night from which he first emerged, his mother having died in giving birth to him, and to which he is about to return. Isolde's reply is that, just as she followed him unwillingly to Cornwall, so will she now with loyalty and love follow him to his own true country.

As Tristan bends slowly to kiss Isolde's forehead, Melot suddenly leaps forward, his sword drawn. Tristan remarks sorrowfully that, until Melot, too, had fallen victim to Isolde's beauty, he had been a friend who truly loved Tristan. He and Melot fight, but Tristan makes no attempt to defend himself. As Melot stretches forth his sword, Tristan lets his guard fall, and sinks, wounded, into the arms of Kurwenal. Isolde throws herself upon Tristan's breast, Marke restrains Melot, and the curtain quickly falls.

Act III opens with a sad, desolate orchestral introduction based on Isolde's motif. When the curtain rises, the overgrown garden of Tristan's dilapidated castle in Brittany is revealed. On one side are high castellated buildings, on the other a low wall with a watch-tower and, at the back, the castle gates. The castle is situated on a rocky promontory overlooking the sea, which can be seen in the distance, stretching to the horizon. In the foreground, Tristan lies sleeping on a couch under the shade of a huge lime-tree. Kurwenal sits beside him, bending over his master in grief and anxiously listening to his breathing. From the near distance there comes the sound of a shepherd's horn (actually a cor anglais) playing a mournful tune which quickens somewhat before dying out sadly.

The shepherd (tenor) looks over the wall, and asks Kurwenal how the young master is faring. Kurwenal replies that he is still unconscious, and that only the arrival of a certain lady can heal his wounds. Has the shepherd not yet seen any ship upon the horizon? The shepherd promises to change his tune from a sad to a merry one as soon as he sights a ship. He retreats and begins his mournful tune again, the sound of which awakens Tristan, who at first does not know where he is or what has happened to him. Kurwenal describes how he had borne the wounded Tristan on his broad shoulders to a ship which had carried him from Cornwall to his castle at Kareol, in Brittany. 'Here in your native land,' he assures Tristan, 'surrounded by your pastures, and with the sun shining down upon you, you will soon recover.'

Tristan thinks otherwise. He begins feverishly to recall Isolde and their love, and fears that he will die before she can arrive. Kurwenal assures him that he will see Isolde that very day, if she is still alive, at which Tristan revives somewhat. He expresses his gratitude to Kurwenal, who has always served him so faithfully, loving those whom Tristan loved, and hating his enemies. 'Never your own man, you suffer with me when I suffer,' he tells Kurwenal, but adds that what he, Tristan, suffers now is something that Kurwenal can never share. He begs him to go and watch for Isolde's ship, and continues to rave of Isolde, their first meeting when she healed his wound, and the poison she gave him on the ship bearing them to Cornwall, a poison which infected him only with the pain of yearning, a poison which, with shrewd, mystical self-knowledge, he accuses himself of having brewed 'from father's grief and mother's sorrow, from the tears of love throughout the ages'.

Though Tristan imagines Isolde's ship to be near, and keeps asking Kurwenal if he can see it, the shepherd's doleful tune makes it clear that there is no ship on the horizon. When Tristan sinks back, exhausted, Kurwenal fears that he has died. But suddenly the cor anglais changes its tune to a merry one. Kurwenal springs up joyously and rushes to the watch-tower. 'Oh rapture,' he exclaims to Tristan. 'The ship! I see it coming from the north.' He describes the approach of the vessel, to Tristan's mounting excitement. 'The ship is now in port,' Kurwenal tells him, 'and Isolde has leapt to the shore.' He rushes off to meet her and escort her to his master.

The entire act until now has been a rich repository of musical motifs woven into the texture of the score in a variety of ways. Now, as Kurwenal departs to greet Isolde, Tristan bursts into an ecstasy of delirious anticipation and his music erupts with him into a kind of madness. 'O, this sun, this day,' he cries. 'O the bliss of this most sunny of days.' He manages to rise from his couch, and tears the bandage from his wound. 'Once with a bleeding wound I fought against Morold,' he exclaims, 'and today with a bleeding wound I will capture Isolde. Flow joyfully, my blood. She who will close my wound forever is approaching to save me. Forsaking the world, I hasten to her in joy.'

Isolde's voice, nearby, is heard calling 'Tristan! Beloved!' The orchestra now recalls, ironically, that earlier occasion, in Act II, when the lovers had

149

hastened to each other's arms. As Isolde enters, Tristan staggers towards her. In his feverish confusion he imagines her cry to be the extinguishing of the warning torch of that earlier evening. 'What, do I hear the light? The torch, ha, the torch is put out. To her! To her!' he exclaims. With a cry of 'Tristan!', Isolde clasps him in her arms, and with her name on his lips he sinks to the ground, lifeless.

At first Isolde deludes herself into hoping that Tristan has merely fainted. Holding him in her arms, she tells him that she has come to die with him. Surely he will not cheat her of this last brief hour of earthly happiness? 'Where is your wound?' she asks. 'Let me heal it, so that we may share the night in bliss.' But at last she realizes that he has gone from her. 'Stubborn man, do you punish me so harshly? Have you no pity for my grief?' With a final appeal to him to awaken once more, if only for a moment, Isolde sinks, unconscious, upon Tristan's body.

Kurwenal, who had re-entered with Isolde, has remained by the castle gate in speechless horror, gazing motionless on Tristan. From outside can now be heard voices and the clash of weapons. The shepherd clambers over the wall to tell Kurwenal that a second ship has landed. Kurwenal, looking down to the shore, recognizes Marke with Melot and a party of knights and squires. The steersman rushes in, crying that Marke and his followers have set upon the crew of the ship which carried Isolde, whom they outnumber, and that resistance is useless. Determined to defend his dead master and Isolde with his own life, Kurwenal hastens to leave, but is stopped by the arrival of Brangäne, whom he curses as a traitress. He stabs and kills Melot as he appears at the gate with armed men, and attempts to stop Marke and his followers from entering, but soon falls mortally wounded. 'Tristan, dear master,' Kurwenal exclaims as he crawls to Tristan's side to die, 'do not chide your faithful follower for coming with you.'

But, as Brangäne now attempts to tell Isolde, who remains oblivious to their presence, Marke has come not to be revenged but to forgive. Brangäne had confessed to him that she had administered a love potion to Tristan and Isolde, and Marke had followed Isolde only in order to bestow her in marriage on the man whom she loved. 'Why', asks Marke rhetorically, 'must he who brings peace be met with such fierce malevolence?'

Brangäne again tries to attract her mistress's attention, but Isolde has by now progressed beyond the external world. Lost in rapt contemplation of Tristan's body, she begins to sing softly, to the melody of Ex. 14, her 'Liebestod', a song of mystical reunion with her beloved Tristan. The words are, in themselves, almost devoid of meaning, but they carry the ecstatic music to a great climax of cosmic joy as Isolde finally sinks upon Tristan's breast, transfigured by death to a higher state of immortal love. Marke invokes a benediction upon the dead as the curtain slowly falls.

CLEARLY, *Tristan und Isolde* was written out of Wagner's love for Mathilde Wesendonk. It was also written under the influence of the philosopher Schopenhauer, whose principal work, *Die Welt als Wille und Vorstellung* (The World as Will and Idea), Wagner had read in 1854. From Schopenhauer's belief that, in the world, there is so great a gap between the ideal and the real that suffering is a natural condition of mankind grew Wagner's theoretical interest in renunciation of the worldly. But he, the most worldly of men, could embrace this belief only by turning from the outside world to the world of feeling, by renouncing day and its falseness and turning to night and love. The juxtaposition of hated day and longed-for night, the idea of day as mundane life and night as death-in-love, which permeates his libretto of *Tristan und Isolde*, is a specifically Wagnerian concept, playing no part in the old Celtic myth or in the *Tristan* epic written by Gottfried von Strassburg in the thirteenth century.

Curiously, Wagner's original intention had been to write *Tristan und Isolde* in the style of Italian opera, as he expected that this would earn him the most money. He even began negotiations to provide such an opera for performance in Rio de Janeiro. It was only after his meeting with Mathilde Wesendonk in 1852 that the opera began to take shape in his mind in the form in which it was finally to emerge. When he began to compose *Tristan*, all thoughts of deliberately copying the style of contemporary Italian opera were forgotten. The music, coming from deep within him, addresses itself to deep responses in its hearers, to intuition, to the subconscious. It is music which is as susceptible to analysis as that of the composer's earlier operas, but to analyse *Tristan und Isolde*'s leading themes, its harmonies, its chromaticism, is more than usually irrelevant to an understanding of the work itself.

Nevertheless, though one may be reluctant to theorize about *Tristan und Isolde*, it is in this opera that Wagner's theories of drama find their most felicitous expression. In *Tannhäuser* and *Lohengrin* a division of the music into separate numbers can still be quite easily discerned: it is in *Tristan* that the drama flows smoothly through uninterrupted music which appears to grow, indeed to generate spontaneously, from the seed of the Prelude. The score's heavily sensuous chromaticism and the ecstatic richness of its orchestration combine to give the opera a curious psychological strength. In *Tristan und Isolde* Wagner has discovered for the first time how to reach simultaneously his audience's conscious and subconscious responses.

It should be emphasized, however, that this masterpiece of music drama was composed to a libretto which is occasionally even less well written than Wagner's earlier libretti. In his review of the opera, the Viennese anti-Wagnerian critic Eduard Hanslick singled out the following passage, sung by Tristan in Act I as he drinks the love-potion:

Tristans Ehre—höchste Treu':
Tristans Elend—kühnster Trotz.
Trug des Herzens, Traum der Ahnung:
Ew'ger Trauer einz'ger Trost,
Vergessens güt'ger Trank,
Dich trink' ich sonder Wank!

(Tristan's honour—highest loyalty:
Tristan's anguish—keenest defiance.
Heart's deceit, wishful dreaming:
Endless mourning the only consolation,
Oblivion's kindly draught,
I drink thee unquestioningly.)

Hanslick asked, 'Are there really connoisseurs who find this sort of thing poetic, profound, or even German?' It is a fair question, though the only answer to it may be an evasion: whether poetic, profound, or whether bombastic mediocrity, this is what Wagner the composer required from Wagner the librettist in order to create one of the most remarkable operas ever written; remarkable not only for its extraordinary evocation of the very essence of romanticism but also for its composer's ability to make a very little melody go a very long way.

EIGHT

Die Meistersinger von Nürnberg

(The Mastersingers of Nuremberg)

Opera in Three Acts

Dramatis personae
Hans Sachs, Shoemaker   (bass-baritone)
Veit Pogner, Goldsmith   (bass)
Kunz Vogelgesang, Furrier   (tenor)
Konrad Nachtigall, Tinsmith   (bass)
Sixtus Beckmesser, Town Clerk   (baritone)
Fritz Kothner, Baker   (bass)
Balthasar Zorn, Pewterer   (tenor)
Ulrich Eisslinger, Grocer   (tenor)
Augustin Moser, Tailor   (tenor)
Hermann Ortel, Soapmaker   (bass)
Hans Schwarz, Weaver   (bass)
Hans Foltz, Coppersmith   (bass)
Walther von Stolzing, a Young Knight from Franconia   (tenor)
David, Hans Sachs's Apprentice   (tenor)
Eva, Pogner's Daughter   (soprano)
Magdalene, Eva's Nurse   (mezzo-soprano)
A Night-watchman   (bass)

LIBRETTO by the composer

TIME: The middle of the sixteenth century

PLACE: Nuremberg

FIRST PERFORMED at the Hofoper, Munich, 21 June 1868, with Mathilde Mallinger (Eva), Sophie Dietz (Magdalene), Franz Betz (Hans Sachs), Gustav Hölzel (Beckmesser), Franz Nachbaur (Walther), and Karl Schlosser (David), conducted by Hans von Bülow.

I

THREE weeks after the final performance of *Tristan und Isolde* in Munich, Ludwig Schnorr von Carolsfeld, who had sung Tristan, died of rheumatic fever. It was thought that the physical strain of the role probably contributed to his collapse. Despite the success of the opera, Wagner's position in Munich was becoming increasingly untenable, as King Ludwig's ministers cleverly succeeded in attributing to the composer's influence over the King all those aspects of Ludwig's behaviour which offended public opinion.

On 7 December 1865, no longer able to resist the pressure being put upon him by his ministers and by the police, who claimed that they could not be responsible for the composer's safety, Ludwig asked his beloved hero to leave the kingdom of Bavaria, at least for a few months. 'Though sundered, who can separate us?' he quoted from the libretto of *Götterdämmerung*, as he bade Wagner farewell. Wagner, of course, was more concerned at the loss of the rich life which Ludwig had made possible than at the loss of the young King's no doubt suffocating emotional friendship. He was also less concerned at losing Ludwig than at losing Bülow's wife, Cosima, who would not be able to travel openly with him. He left Munich with a heavy heart.

Wagner's relationship with the young King of Bavaria was on the way to becoming an international scandal. Some weeks before the *Tristan und Isolde* première, the Austrian Ambassador had compiled a report on the situation:

There are regrettably a host of rumours in general circulation which do little to arouse confidence in the new government. The hero-worship which the king reveals for Richard Wagner has made the worst impression of all on the public. I pass over the 80,000 gulden which His Majesty has already offered up to the whims of this artist, as being of little consequence, likewise the various scandals which have accompanied the preparations for the première of his opera *Tristan und Isolde*, and which have filled all the newspapers for weeks. But what comment can one make on the reports that Wagner is showing people letters from the king, in which he is addressed as 'Du', and praised in the most extravagant terms? . . . That Wagner was invited to Schloss Berg two days ago on his birthday, was received by the king with a bouquet of flowers, and the servants received extraordinary gratuities to mark the joyful occasion?

On 10 December 1865, the day of Wagner's departure from Munich, the newspaper *Der Volksbote* commented that

The news that Richard Wagner has been ordered to leave Bavaria ran through the city the day before yesterday like wildfire, which is enough in itself to show the extent and the depth of the agitation that the man has aroused by his behaviour. Expressions of the liveliest satisfaction have been voiced everywhere, which are by no means mere *Schadenfreude*, as claimed in an Augsburg newspaper, but patriotic joy, which only increases as gradually more and more is learned of how, in spite of all the previous denials, Wagner has tried to exploit our youthful monarch's favour, even going so far as attempting to influence him in matters of state.

Wagner left Munich accompanied by his servant and his dog. Travelling to Switzerland, he rented a house near Geneva where he worked on the composition of *Die Meistersinger von Nürnberg*. The following spring, he moved to a country house named Triebschen, near Lucerne, a white house on a little peninsula overlooking the lake, where he was to live for the next six years. The rent was paid by Ludwig, who sent Wagner this telegram some weeks after he had moved in:

Ever increasing longing for the Dear One. The horizon grows ever darker, the crude sunlight of peaceful day torments me unspeakably. I beg my friend for a speedy answer to the following questions: If the Dear One so wishes and wills, I will joyfully renounce the crown and its barren splendour, and come to him, never to part from him again. And when he sits at the mysterious loom, weaving his wondrous works, let it be my care to shield him from the world, the thief of peace and calm. I must repeat, I cannot endure any longer to remain separate and alone. But to be united and with him, withdrawn from earthly existence, is the only means of preserving me from despair and death. This is not a passing impulse, it is the dreadfully painful truth! I long for your answer. Ludwig.

What Ludwig did not know was that Cosima von Bülow was now living with Wagner. The composer had invited Bülow, Cosima and their children to visit him at Triebschen, and Bülow had sent Cosima and the children on ahead. After their departure, Bülow opened a letter from Wagner addressed to Cosima, thinking that it might contain news that he should telegraph to her, and discovered it to be an ardent love-letter. He hastened to Triebschen in an attempt to persuade his wife to return to him, but eventually retired to spend the winter months in Basle, leaving the children with Wagner and Cosima.

King Ludwig had paid an unexpected visit to Triebschen on 22 May 1866, Wagner's birthday, but was unsuccessful in persuading the composer to return to him. Wagner and Cosima remained in their idyllic Swiss retreat in what, for the composer, was an unusual state of domestic bliss. Here Wagner completed the composition of *Die Meistersinger* and began to dictate his memoirs to Cosima. On 17 February 1867 their second child was born, and named Eva after the heroine of *Die Meistersinger*. Wagner worked on the orchestration of the opera during the spring and summer of 1867, and early in the following year rehearsals began in Munich for its première.

The victory of Prussia over the South German states and Austria in the Austro–Prussian war had brought about the downfall of those advisers of Ludwig who were most dangerous to Wagner, so the composer was able to return to Munich to supervise the production of his opera, which was conducted by the long-suffering Hans von Bülow. The première on 21 June 1868 was an absolute triumph, the only unfortunate incident occurring when Wagner, who had sat consort-like beside King Ludwig in the royal box, stepped forward to acknowledge the applause. Bourgeois feeling in Munich was again outraged.

II

IN *My Life*, Wagner left a partial account of the composition of *Die Meistersinger*, which he had begun while travelling from Venice to Vienna in 1861:

I had spent four dreary days [in Venice], and now started by train on my dull journey to Vienna, following the roundabout overland route. It was during this journey that the music of *Die Meistersinger* first dawned on my mind, in which I still retained the libretto as I had originally conceived it. With the utmost distinctness I at once composed the principal part of the Overture in C major.

Under the influence of these last impressions I arrived in Vienna in a very cheerful frame of mind. I at once announced my return to Cornelius [Peter Cornelius, the German composer with whom Wagner had become friendly]. . . . The communication of my plan for the immediate composition of *Die Meistersinger* made him almost frantic with delight, and until my departure from Vienna he remained in a state of delirious excitement.

I urged my friend to procure me material for mastering the subject of *Die Meistersinger*. My first idea was to make a thorough study of Grimm's controversy on the *Song of the Mastersingers*, and the next question was how to get hold of old Wagenseil's *Nuremberg Chronicle*. Cornelius accompanied me to the Imperial Library, but in order to obtain a loan of this book, which we were fortunate enough to find, my friend was obliged to visit Baron Münch-Bellinghausen, a visit which he described to me as very disagreeable. I remained at my hotel [the Kaiserin Elizabeth], eagerly making extracts of portions of the *Chronicle*, which to the astonishment of the ignorant I appropriated for my libretto.

Wagner left Vienna in December, and proceeded to Paris, where he stayed at the Hotel Voltaire and worked on his libretto:

The cause of the almost cheerful complacency with which I managed to regard my adverse [financial] situation in Paris, and which enabled me afterwards to look back on it as a pleasant memory, was that my libretto of *Die Meistersinger* daily increased its swelling volume of rhyme. How could I help being filled with facetious thoughts when, on raising my eyes from the paper, after meditating upon the quaint verses and sayings of my Nuremberg Mastersingers, I gazed from the third-floor window of my hotel on the tremendous crowds passing along the quays and over the numerous bridges, and enjoyed a prospect embracing the Tuileries, the Louvre, and even the Hôtel de Ville! . . .

Throughout the month of January I continued working on the *Meistersinger* libretto, and completed it in exactly thirty days. The melody for the fragment of Sachs's poem on the Reformation, with which I make my characters in the last act greet their beloved master, occurred to me on the way to the Taverne Anglaise, whilst strolling through the galleries of the Palais Royal. There I found Truinet [Charles Truinet, who under the anagrammatic pseudonym of Nuitter was a well-known librettist and translator] already waiting for me, and asked him to give me a scrap of paper and a pencil to jot down my melody, which I quietly hummed over to him at the time. I usually accompanied him and his father along the boulevards to his flat in the Faubourg St Honoré, and on that evening he could do nothing but exclaim, '*Mais, quelle gaieté d'esprit, cher maître!*'

Die Meistersinger, of course, had been in Wagner's mind for many years before he began to compose a note of it, or even make the definitive sketch for its libretto. It was in the summer of 1845, while he was taking the cure in Marienbad, having just completed the composition of *Tannhäuser*, that he first became interested in the medieval tradesmen's guilds:

Owing to some comments I had read in Gervinus's *History of German Literature*, both the Mastersingers of Nuremberg and Hans Sachs had acquired quite a vital charm for me. The Marker alone, and the part he takes in the 'master-singing', were particularly pleasing to me, and on one of my lonely walks, without knowing anything in particular about Hans Sachs and his poetic contemporaries, I thought out an amusing scene, in which the cobbler—as a popular artisan-poet—with the hammer on his last, gives the Marker a practical lesson by making him sing, thereby taking revenge on him for his conventional misdeeds.

To me the force of the whole scene was concentrated in the two following points: on the one hand the Marker, with his slate covered with chalk-marks, and on the other hand Sachs holding up the soles covered with his chalk-marks, each intimating to the other that the singing had been a failure. To this picture, by way of concluding the second act, I added a scene consisting of a narrow, crooked little street in Nuremberg, with the people all running about in great excitement, and ultimately engaging in a street brawl. Thus, suddenly, the whole of my comedy about the Mastersingers took shape so vividly before me that, inasmuch as it was a particularly cheerful subject, and not in the least likely to over-excite my nerves, I felt I must write it out in spite of the doctor's orders. I therefore proceeded to do this, and hoped it might free me from the thrall of the idea of *Lohengrin*.

It did not, and Wagner turned aside from his comedy to sketch the libretto of *Lohengrin*, which was to be his next opera. He did not return to *Die Meistersinger von Nürnberg* until sixteen years later, in Vienna, when he made his second sketch for a libretto on the subject. On this occasion he consulted Jakob Grimm's *Über den altdeutschen Meistergesang* (On the Old German Mastersong: 1811) and Wagenseil's *Nuremberg Chronicle*, a history of Nuremberg published in 1697 which contains an account of the 'Origins, Practice, Utility and Rules of the Gracious Art of the Mastersingers'. From Wagenseil, Wagner took the names of several Nuremberg Mastersingers, though in his opera he invented trades for them. Eisslinger, for example, was not a grocer but a timber-merchant. Nor was the historical Beckmesser the talentless pedant that Wagner makes him out to be.

With the exceptions of Sachs and Pogner, the Mastersingers of Wagner's opera are little more than figures of fun, only one step up from Bottom the Weaver and his fellow amateur actors in Shakespeare's *A Midsummer Night's Dream*. But, as Ernest Newman pointed out in *Wagner Nights*, the Mastersingers

> had done much good work throughout the generations, and their rules and faults and definitions were simply the codified results of long experience; it goes without saying, indeed, that no Guild of mere pedantic dunderheads could have earned and kept the respect of intelligent people all over Germany for so long a stretch of time. Their intentions, seen at their best, were a combination of those of, say, the French Academy, the prosodist, the grammarian, the musical Conservatoire, and the adjudicators at a competition festival.

The historical Mastersingers had their origin in Germany in the early fourteenth century, when a passion for poetry, or at least for versifying, took hold of the working classes. Tradesmen of all kinds, blacksmiths, weavers, carpenters and so on, formed themselves into Guilds of Mastersingers, and held regular meetings at which they discussed and criticized one another's poetic creations. Strict rules were introduced, and apprentices studied not only the craft of their particular trade with their masters but also the art or craft of writing and singing songs.

A Guild of Mastersingers is known to have existed at Mainz as early as 1311, but it was in sixteenth-century Nuremberg that the Mastersingers reached the highest peak of their popularity, led by the cobbler–poet Hans Sachs, who was born in 1494 and who died in 1576. Sachs wrote six thousand poems and composed more than four thousand songs. He became a Mastersinger in the Nuremberg song school, and also a master cobbler, while in his early twenties, and in 1554 at the age of sixty he became head of the Nuremberg Mastersingers. After his death, he was virtually forgotten until rediscovered by Goethe.

It is probable that Wagner had seen or read a now forgotten play, *Hans Sachs* by Johann Ludwig Deinhardstein, which was produced in Germany in 1827, and that from it he derived the idea of showing Hans Sachs in love and quarrelling with his fellow-poets over the rules of poesy. (He certainly knew the opera, *Hans Sachs*, which Lortzing based on the play, and which was staged in Leipzig in 1840, Berlin in 1841 and Prague in 1842.) Wagner's plot has no connection with Deinhardstein's, however, nor is his Sachs the young gallant of the play, but an artisan in late middle age.

The character of Beckmesser, the pompously pedantic Town Clerk of Nuremberg who aspires to marry Eva but whose chicanery is exposed by Sachs, is sometimes said to have been a satirical portrait of the Viennese music critic Eduard Hanslick, whose conservative musical tastes had led him to write unfavourably of Wagner. However, the truth of the matter is rather more complex. Wagner and Hanslick had first met in Marienbad in the summer of 1845, when the thirty-two-year-old composer, delighted to discover that Hanslick was familiar with the piano scores of *Rienzi* and *Der fliegende Holländer*, invited the twenty-year-old student to attend the forthcoming première of *Tannhäuser* in Dresden. Hanslick's subsequent essay on the opera, published the following year in the *Wiener Theaterzeitung*, was a balanced and fair piece of criticism. Though he did not praise the work unreservedly, he described Wagner as the leading opera composer of the day.

By 1858, when Wagner's next opera, *Lohengrin*, was staged in Vienna, Hanslick had become that city's leading music critic. In his view, *Lohengrin* was likely to lead the art of opera down an unpromising bypath. He also found Wagner's polemical writings distasteful, correctly observing that the composer tended to claim as a universal principle that which suited his own particular talents. Or, as Nietzsche put it, those faculties which Wagner lacked he would ban as inimical to the art of music drama. With especial reference to *Lohengrin*, Hanslick wrote:

Let us put the purely musical element aside for the moment and ask merely if Wagner has really achieved anything new and unprecedented in the way of dramatic truthfulness—as is claimed for him by his vindicators—or if he has even equalled what the aforementioned masters have already achieved. The latter knew and respected the demands of the poet, but at the same time they were musicians—and inventors. They had the gift which Wagner disdains—because he doesn't have it: the gift of melody, of independent, self-sufficient, beautiful musical thought. It is a great error to represent melody as the enemy of all dramatic characterization; an error that can be committed only by one who is, by nature, without melody and who must be content with the lesser profits yielded by clever effects. The truth is rather that in the formal musical thought, in the melody itself, there resides a dramatic force which emotional declamation and all the instrumental wizardry in the world can never equal.

There is more than a little truth in this, but of course it hardly endeared Wagner to Hanslick. Indeed, it induced in the composer an absolute loathing of the critic, who, for his part, always attempted to deal fairly with Wagner's merits and defects as he perceived them. When Wagner produced his definitive version of the libretto of *Die Meistersinger* in Vienna in 1862, he first gave the character whom we now know as Beckmesser the name of 'Veit Hanslich', and maliciously invited Eduard Hanslick to hear him read the libretto at the house of Dr Joseph Standhartner, a Wagner enthusiast and the Empress Elizabeth's physician. Hanslick attended the reading but, finding himself mocked as a humourless and dishonest pedant, fled from the room, no doubt to Wagner's amused satisfaction.

III

HANSLICK'S final thoughts on *Die Meistersinger* are to be found in the essay which he published after the Vienna production of the opera in 1870, a shortened version of which follows:

The management of the Vienna Court Opera came in for some criticism in Wagner's famous essay on Jews, where he stated that the management had revealed by its tricks 'that it strove not only to avoid a performance of *Die Meistersinger* but also to prevent its performance in other theatres'. The Vienna Court Opera answered this incredible accusation in 1870 with a brilliant production of the opera. The public met *Die Meistersinger* more than half-way, with that close attention which every new Wagner opera has a right to expect.

Friends and foes are well aware that a new opera by Wagner means something extraordinary, something to occupy the imagination and the intellect in all respects. *Die Meistersinger* is, indeed, a remarkable creation, uniquely consistent in method, extremely earnest, novel in structure, rich in imaginative and even brilliant characteristics, often tiring and exasperating, but always unusual. It is of compelling interest, if only as a phenomenon; whether one is pleased or repelled depends upon one's conception of musical and dramatic beauty. Its virtues cannot be denied— nor its faults; there are scenes which rank among Wagner's most fortunate musical inspirations, surrounded by long, unrewarding stretches of dull or disagreeable music. And as a theatrical spectacle alone it is worth seeing.

If we give the synopsis, as can be done in a few words, it will be difficult to understand how an opera longer than *Le Prophète* or *Les Huguenots* [both by Meyerbeer] could be made of it. Its greatest fault is in the over-elaboration of a small, meagre plot which, with neither intricacies nor intrigue, is continually at a standstill and would normally offer barely enough material for a modest two-act operetta. One can hardly give an apt description of the tenacious verbosity of the dialogue, with all the domestic altercations and dry instruction. Everything is composed in the same monotonous manner and in a slow tempo, Wagner having made the momentous discovery in his latest pamphlet, 'German Art and Politics', that the *andante* is the specifically 'German' tempo!

Let us sketch, as well as possible in a few lines, the dramatic and musical synopsis. The overture is hardly calculated to win the listener. All the leitmotives of the opera are dumped consecutively into a chromatic flood and finally tossed about in a kind of tonal typhoon. It is a contrived piece, brutal in effect and painfully artificial. It leads immediately into the first scene, the interior of St Catherine's Church in Nuremberg. The congregation sings a hymn. Between verses the orchestra depicts the tender emotions of a young knight who, standing in the foreground, follows a burgher's young daughter with his eyes. The service ends; the knight, Walther von Stolzing, rushes to the unknown beautiful maiden: 'Fair maiden, say, are you betrothed?' With the electrical swiftness and energy characteristic of all love affairs in Wagner's operas, Eva Pogner replies: 'To you, or else no one!' The wooer must only meet the terms stipulated by her father: namely, win the Mastersingers' prize. Eva leaves, accompanied by her nurse, Magdalene. Walther remains behind in the church, where arrangements are being made for the meeting of the Mastersingers. A fussy apprentice, David, with devastating thoroughness, instructs the knight in the rules and regulations of the 'Singers' Court', and the poetic rules and regulations of the *tabulatura*, enumerating forty or fifty different 'tones and tunes'. It sounds like an extract from a volume by Wagenseil set to music.... [Hanslick then proceeds to discuss the opera, scene by scene.]

For a comic opera—and that is what *Die Meistersinger* is, according to its exposition and its two pronounced buffo roles—Wagner's talent seems inadequate, particularly with respect to humour. The conversational tone which dominates the first two acts is never easy and fluent. Quite the contrary, it is expressed through an awkward, contrived, continuously restless music, with a noisy and complex instrumentation. The most trivial questions and answers, commonly expressed in normal tones, are shouted above the tumult of the orchestra. To this false colouring is added a false design by a declamatory style characterized by leaps contradictory to all rules of diction. In comedy Wagner's music is even less successful; it is stilted, profuse, even repulsive. With the horrible dissonances in which the 'comical' Beckmesser scolds or complains, one could accompany the most hair-raising scenes of a thriller. When David speaks of 'bread and water' the orchestra sounds like gallows and rack. If peaceful citizens and artisans express their disapproval of a poem in such irate tones as in the first and last acts of *Die Meistersinger*, what resources are left to the composer who would treat the French Revolution? Not to speak of the unfunny and vulgar riot finale of the second act. . . .

In *Die Meistersinger* Wagner has remained true to the musical reforms dominating the larger part of *Lohengrin* and the whole of *Tristan und Isolde*. This consistency lends the work an imposing sense of security and conviction. Wagner knows what he wants; every note of the score speaks of intentions fully realized. Nothing is left to chance, but neither is there anything of those intriguing coincidences which lend an ultimate charm to the creations of fantasy and nature. One must respect the consistency with which he sticks to his peculiar principle; but no more than any of his other operas has *Die Meistersinger* converted me to it. It consists of the intentional dissolution of every fixed form into a shapeless, sensually intoxicating resonance; the replacement of independent, articulate melody by vague melodization. One may confidently use Wagner's dry technical expression, 'infinite melody', since everyone knows by now what is meant. The 'infinite melody' is the dominant, musically undermining power in *Die Meistersinger*, as in *Tristan und Isolde*. A small motive begins, and, before it can develop into an actual melody or theme, it gets twisted, pinched, set higher or lower by continual modulation and enharmonization, enlarged and reduced, repeated or echoed, now by this instrument, now by another. Anxiously omitting every conclusive cadence, this boneless tonal mollusc floats on towards the immeasurable, renewing itself from its own substance. Afraid of the 'profanity' of perfect or deceptive cadences, Wagner falls prey to another, and certainly not superior, pedantry: he becomes monotonous through the continual use of dissonant chords when the ear expects a concluding triad.

What a surprisingly agreeable effect is created by the two fully resounding C major chords which precede Walther's Prize Song in the third act, if only because the listener has been longing for three hours for just such a simple, healthy triad! If one surveys larger parts of the opera, one will observe everywhere the same monotony, together with a continuous nervous unrest and interruption in detail. Only in those few spots where the text offers a lyrical resting place (Walther's songs, Hans Sachs's second-act monologue) is the singing concentrated for a while in an independent melody. Throughout the whole dramatic sequence, in the monologues, dialogues, and ensembles, the thread of melody runs, not in the voices, but in the orchestra, where it is 'infinitely' unwound as in a spinning mill. This melody-spinning orchestral accompaniment actually forms the integral and independent tone picture. The voice accommodates itself to this accompaniment by weaving its half-declamatory, half-melodic phrases into it.

It is obvious that his method of composition is diametrically opposed to that used by all the older masters. Vocal melody was ever their first and decisive consideration; the accompaniment (free of complexity) was subordinate. To a given melody one could usually approximately anticipate the accompaniment, or at least an accompaniment; the accompaniment alone, however, was dependent. In *Die Meistersinger* the vocal part alone is not only non-independent, it is non-existent! The accompaniment is everything, an independent symphonic creation, an orchestral fantasy with an accompanying vocal part. Given the text and the orchestral accompaniment, a good musician, well versed in Wagner's music, would be able to insert suitable vocal parts in the empty space, just as a sculptor can restore the missing hand of a statue. But one could as little restore the lost orchestral accompaniment to Hans Sachs's or Eva's vocal parts as create the whole statue with only the single hand to go by. The natural relationship has been reversed: the orchestra is the singer, bearing the guiding thoughts; the singers are merely complementary.

Far from pointing up character, this method tends rather to level and generalize. Thus, in order to achieve characterization, and to establish an aural anchor in the ocean of melodic infinity, Wagner employs the so-called memory or 'leitmotives', i.e. themes which recur in the orchestra when a certain person appears on the scene, or when a certain event is mentioned. The Masters' Guild has its own marchlike theme; the apprentice David has fussy figures in sixteenth notes, and Walther and Beckmesser each have their theme—musical uniforms, so to speak, with which one can recognize people in darkness or twilight. These reminders accompany both persons and things. When someone speaks of the Feast of St John or of the song contest, the Pogner motive from the first act is heard. Walther's motive accompanies not only his person but also every allusion to him, to Eva's love, to true poetry in contrast to the Guild poetry, etc. Since the facts to which the motives refer constitute more or less the whole plot, and since, moreover, the motives are the most fortunate melodic

163

inspirations of the entire opera, we hear them all evening, singly or together, now from one instrument, now from another, in lighter or darker colour.

The listener at first enjoys these little melodies. They occupy his mind, if nothing else. But the more they pitch and toss, the more uncomfortable he feels. For the musician, able and inclined to enjoy essentially technical details and to forget for a time the disagreeable impression of the whole, the orchestral accompaniment has an indisputably compelling charm. Of all the many instruments working at the same time, each is actually playing solo. The skill with which Wagner fits the different leitmotives into the orchestra, modulates them, weaves two or three of them together, is unquestionably admirable. It is only a pity that this 'dramatic polyphony', as one could describe it in contrast to musical polyphony, is but a product of cerebration. The magic power of the 'unconscious', which should play the first role in the conception of every work of art, recoils from such absolutism of the intellect.

The performance will remain a memorable artistic experience for every music lover who heard it, although the opera is not one of those whose beauty is a lifelong source of pleasure and elevation. It is hardly to be regarded as a creation of profound originality or lasting truth and beauty, but rather as a lively experiment, astonishing in the tenacious energy of its execution and its indisputable novelty. In a word, it belongs among the more interesting musical abnormalities. If such abnormalities should become the rule it would mean the end of music, but as an exception they are more stimulating than a dozen run-of-the-mill operas by numerous 'correct' composers in Germany, who are honoured by a half too much when one calls them half-talents.

Though Hanslick's concept of melody is determinedly pre-Romantic, much of his comment on *Die Meistersinger* is both pertinent and penetrating. Needless to say, it brought him the increased animosity of Wagner, who published an 'open letter' to one of his patronesses in which he revealed Hanslick's Jewish ancestry, to which he ascribed the critic's opposition to his music.

IV

THE C major Prelude, which Wagner had initially, and perhaps more accurately, described as an Overture, opens with the stately, somewhat pompous theme of the Mastersingers (Ex. 15), which is succeeded by other motifs from the opera, some relating to the Guilds, and others to Walther and his love for Eva. The themes are combined, juxtaposed and set against each other in a rich orchestral tapestry in Wagner's most extrovert manner, until

Ex.15

the Prelude reaches an exciting conclusion whose final emphatic chord is drowned by the chorale being sung by a church congregation as the curtain rises on the interior of St Catherine's Church, Nuremberg. It is the day before Midsummer's Day (*Johannestag*, the name-day of St John the Baptist), and the afternoon service is just ending.

The stage picture, as described in Wagner's libretto, represents an oblique view of the interior of the church. The last few rows of seats in the nave are visible. In front is the open space of the choir, which will later be separated from the nave by a black curtain when it is used for the meeting of the Mastersingers. In the back row of pews, Eva Pogner (soprano) sits with her nurse or companion, Magdalene (mezzo-soprano). A young knight, Walther von Stolzing (tenor) stands at the side, leaning against a column, his eyes fixed on Eva, who frequently during the congregation's singing of the chorale turns around to look at him. His covert flirtation is represented by tender interjections from the orchestra which punctuate the organ-accompanied choral phrases.

The chorale ends, and the congregation rises, the orchestra sharing Walther's excitement as Eva, followed by Magdalene, walks towards him. He forces his way to her side, through the emerging crowd, and Eva sends Magdalene back to their pew to search for a handkerchief while she exchanges a quick word with the young stranger. Walther is attempting to stammer a declaration of love to Eva, when Magdelene returns and is immediately sent away again, this time to look for a brooch which Eva claims to have lost. When Magdelene goes back to the pew for a third time, having left her Bible behind, Walther continues his tongue-tied attempts to make his feelings known, and eventually summons up the courage to ask Eva if she is betrothed.

Though Wagner's ill-written dialogue obscures the fact, this is not the first meeting of Walther and Eva. We are to understand that the knight, who is visiting Nuremberg from Franconia, had been received in the house of Pogner, the goldsmith, the previous evening. There he had met Pogner's daughter, Eva, and instantly fallen in love with her. Eva now explains to Walther that her father has decided she will be given as wife to the man who wins the song contest to be held the following day, but that she will marry no one but him. Walther immediately determines to become a member of the Mastersingers' Guild, enter the contest and win the hand of Eva.

During this conversation, a number of apprentices, led by Hans Sachs's apprentice David (tenor), have been curtaining off the nave and bringing in chairs to prepare the space in front of the choir for a meeting of the Mastersingers. Magdalene asks David to teach Walther the rules of the Guild of Mastersingers and, after Eva and Walther have arranged to meet later that evening, the two young women depart. (Magdalene and David are supposed to be sweethearts, though she is obviously much older than he: Walther refers to her in Act II as '*die Alte*', the old woman.)

While the other apprentices are bustling about, David attempts to tell Walther something of the rules. There are various stages, such as 'Schulfreund' (School-friend) and 'Schuler' (Scholar) to be gone through before one can become a Singer, and one's song must have the correct number of sections. The tones or phrases all have their individual names, and David horrifies Walther by enumerating a few of them: short, long, overlong, writing-paper, black ink, red, blue, green, hawthorn blossom, straw-blade, fennel, tender, sweet, rose, short-lived love, forgotten, rosemary, wall-flower, rainbow, nightingale, pewter, cinnamon stick, fresh oranges, green lime-blossom, frogs, calves, goldfinch, departed glutton, lark, snail, barker, tawny lion-skin, true pelican, brightly gleaming thread.

The list is apparently never going to end, and Walther interrupts, only to be told that these are merely the names of the tones. One must learn to sing every one of them, David reminds him, and proceeds to list the numerous ways in which one can fail to sing correctly. The other apprentices attempt to call David back to his tasks, but at Walther's request the youth explains how one becomes a Master. Only the poet who can fashion a new melody from the tones, he informs Walther, can be recognized as a Master.

While David has been busy instructing Walther, the apprentices have erected the wrong kind of structure, that used for the song-school. But today, David irritably points out, is only a trial session. They must replace the larger structure by a smaller platform. The apprentices dutifully bring out the appropriate pieces of furniture, including a curtained-off seat for the Marker. This, David tells Walther, is the individal who will judge the applicant. He will allow seven mistakes or faults, which he will mark on his slate, but anyone committing a larger number of faults will be instantly disqualified. A bemused Walther decides, nevertheless, to undertake the trial immediately, in the hope of evading all the intermediate stages and being accepted straightaway as a Mastersinger.

More themes have been introduced during this scene between Walther and David, among them one which will be associated throughout the opera with the carefree enthusiasm of the apprentices. The scene itself is rather too long for its content and purpose, but this is a fault which will recur in *Die Meistersinger*, for Wagner's idea of comedy is more than a trifle heavy-handed, and the gaps between passages of real melodic and dramatic interest are lengthier than they should be.

The apprentices scatter as the first two Mastersingers enter, conversing. They are the goldsmith Veit Pogner (bass), Eva's father, and Sixtus Beckmesser (baritone), the Town Clerk. Beckmesser is attempting to importune Pogner to intercede on his behalf with Eva, for he hopes to win the song contest and the maid's hand in marriage, and is annoyed that the final decision is to rest with Eva herself. Walther now greets Pogner, who is somewhat surprised to find the young knight here in the song-school. When Walther tells him that he wishes to become a Mastersinger, Pogner introduces him to two more members of the Guild who have just entered: Kunz Vogelgesang, a furrier, and Konrad Nachtigall, a tinsmith. Other Masters now arrive. Beckmesser, who has been muttering anxiously to himself about his chances with the contest and with Eva, suddenly catches sight of Walther, and exclaims in an aside, 'Who is that man? I don't like him. What does he want here?'

Pogner informs Walther that he will have to undergo a trial if he wishes to be allowed to compete in the song contest, but he agrees to propose the young knight. The Masters have now all assembled, the last to arrive being Nuremberg's famous poet, the shoemaker Hans Sachs (bass-baritone). The baker Fritz Kothner (bass) conducts a roll-call to which all respond except one, Niklaus Vogel, whose apprentice answers that his master is absent through illness. The Mastersingers all sit, and Pogner, in a long address, announces formally that, on the morrow, which is St John's Day, the town's midsummer festival will be held as usual in the meadow by the river. Prizes will be given to the winners of various competitions, but he, Pogner, whom God has made a wealthy man, wishes to give a more valuable prize than usual to the winner of the song contest. Vexed that the bourgeoisie has the reputation of being mean and interested only in usury and making money, Pogner is determined to demonstrate his selfless love of art by giving to the winner of the contest his only child Eva in marriage, together with all his worldly goods. Pogner's solo, '*Das schöne Fest, Johannestag*' (The beautiful festival, St John's Day) is cleverly and economically constructed from no greater wealth of melodic material than its opening phrase.

Although Pogner's announcement is already known by Beckmesser (and by Walther, to whom Eva has revealed it), it is new to the majority of the Mastersingers, who greet it with delight and enthusiasm. 'Many a man would gladly give up his wife,' Sachs genially observes. But when Pogner makes it clear that, since she is to be the prize, Eva will also be one of the judges, with the casting vote, Beckmesser objects. Pogner explains that, if Eva refuses the man to whom she is awarded as prize, she must remain single for life. At this, Sachs is moved to protest. In his view, the entire populace should be allowed to judge, for it is more than likely that their vote will accord with Eva's. But

Sachs is overruled, and the Masters agree to the proposal as first put forward by Pogner. Kothner notes that only bachelors will be able to enter the contest, and Beckmesser comments that, since widowers will also be eligible, perhaps Sachs will compete. Sachs offends him by replying that the winner will have to be a much younger man than either himself or Beckmesser if he is to prove acceptable to Eva.

Pogner now announces that the knight Walther von Stolzing seeks to become a Mastersinger, and Walther steps forward. Some of the Masters are not sure that they want to admit a nobleman to their Guild, but Sachs reminds them that their rules do not admit of class distinction. Art is the only deciding qualification. Kothner asks Walther to tell them with whom he has studied, and Walther replies in a lyrical aria, '*Am stillen Herd in Winterszeit*' (At the quiet heath in winter time), in which he claims that he learned the art of poetry by reading an old book by Walther von der Vogelweide, a poet who had flourished three centuries earlier. In the summer, he learned about song from the birds in the forest, and from these lessons in poetry and singing he now fashions his own song.

Between stanzas of his song, Walther is interrupted by the Masters, who are clearly perplexed at the novelty of his musical language, even though his trial has not yet officially begun. '*Am stillen Herd*' is an attractive aria, but it is only Sachs who is open-minded enough to perceive it as such. After the second stanza, Kothner is ready to reject Walther on the ground that he has not had proper tuition. But, as Sachs observes, 'If he is a true artist, what does it matter who taught him?' Walther is allowed to continue, and to finish his aria with what the Mastersingers call an *Abgesang*, or 'Aftersong', which introduces a new theme but concludes with the melody of the first two stanzas. (This is to be the form, in Act III, of the song with which Walther wins his prize.)

Walther is allowed to proceed to trial. Asked if he has chosen a sacred theme, he replies that it is something sacred to him, for it is the banner of love that he intends to wave. 'We call that profane,' Kothner comments, as he invites Beckmesser to enter the Marker's curtained-off box. Beckmesser, before seating himself in the box with a feigned reluctance, reminds the contestant that he will be allowed seven faults, each of which will be noted on the Marker's slate. If he accumulates more than seven chalk-marks, he will have failed. For Walther's further edification, the Table of Rules is recited by Kothner, from a board held in front of him by apprentices:

Each unit of a Mastersong shall reveal a proper balance of its various sections, against which no one may offend. A section consists of two stanzas which should share the same melody. The stanza is a group of a given number of lines, with the rhyme at the end of the line. This is followed by the Aftersong which is also to be a certain number of lines in length and is to have its own particular melody, which is not to be found in the stanzas. Each Mastersong should have several units so constructed, and whoever composes a new song which does not coincide for more than four syllables with an existing Mastersong, shall be awarded a Master's prize.

When he has finished his recitation of the Tables of Rules, in which each vocal phrase has culminated in a flourish of coloratura which is then imitated by the orchestra, Kothner instructs Walther to seat himself in the Singer's Chair. 'Here, in this chair?' asks Walther in disbelief. Informed that it is the custom, he murmurs an aside, 'This I do for you, beloved,' and sits. 'The singer sits,' Kothner announces very loudly, for the benefit of the Marker, and from within his booth Beckmesser calls, '*Fanget an!*' (Begin!)'

Taking his inspiration from this unlikely source, Walther starts to sing: '"*Fanget an!*" *So rief der Lenz in den Wald*' ('Begin!' Thus spring cried to the forest). He sings ardently of the rejuvenation of nature in spring, and attempts to ignore the sounds of chalk scratching upon slate which emanate from the Marker's box. 'Consumed with jealousy and grief, gloomy old winter tries to impede the joyful song of spring,' he declaims, obviously casting the Mastersingers in the role of winter and himself as the harbinger of spring. At the climax of his song he so far forgets himself as to commit the grievous fault of rising from his chair as he sings in praise of romantic love. He is suddenly interrupted by Beckmesser, who draws his curtain aside to ask, 'Have you finished?' Walther complains that he has by no means finished, for he has yet to sing the praises of his beloved, but Beckmesser points out that there is no more room on the slate to list any further errors.

The Masters cannot refrain from laughter, and Beckmesser goes on to denounce Walther's song as a mere collection of mistakes from beginning to end. The verdict of all except Sachs is that what they have heard was completely without melody, could hardly be called singing, and in short was nothing but an ear-splitting din. When Sachs attempts to commend the novelty of Walther's composition and suggests that they should forget their old rules and try to understand the young knight's new ways, Beckmesser argues that Sachs is opening the doors to artistic anarchy. Sachs accuses Beckmesser of attempting to discredit a newcomer whom he considers to be a rival, and Beckmesser responds by wishing that Sachs would concentrate more on his cobbling.

At Sachs's instigation, Walther resumes his song, 'if only in order to annoy the Marker', but his lyrical phrases can hardly be heard, for all begin to voice their opinions. A noisy and argumentative *parlando* ensemble ensues, at the climax of which the apprentices dance merrily in a ring around the Marker's box. The Masters vote to reject Walther, who departs with a gesture of contempt. The others all leave, but Sachs remains for a moment, gazing pensively at the chair vacated by Walther as the oboe recalls a passage from the knight's song. When the chair is removed by the apprentices, Sachs shrugs his shoulders in humorous dismissal of the situation, and turns to go, as the orchestra's bassoons enjoy themselves satirizing the pompous dignity of the Masters and the curtain falls.

After a brief, light-hearted orchestral introduction in a moderate tempo, based on the Midsummer's Day motif, the curtain rises on Act II to reveal a Nuremberg street scene later on the same day. Between two houses, a narrow alley winds towards the back of the stage. The grander house on the right is Pogner's, and the simpler house on the left that of Hans Sachs. In front of Pogner's house a lime-tree grows, and in front of Sachs's an elder. It is a pleasant summer evening, towards nightfall. David is engaged in closing the shutters of Sachs's house, and the other apprentices can be seen doing the same for houses further down the alley. As they work, the apprentices sing and dance in joyful anticipation of St John's Day on the morrow.

Magdalene emerges from Pogner's house. She has brought a basket of delicacies for David, but before giving it to him she asks how the knight fared at the song trial. When David informs her that Walther has failed, Magdalene snatches the basket away from his outstretched hand, and hastens back into the house. His fellow-apprentices, having observed what they take to be a sweethearts' quarrel, mock David, and his master Sachs as well. 'St John's Day,' they sing, as they dance around their colleague. 'Every man woos where he wishes. . . . The old man woos the young maid, and the young man woos an old maid.' David is about to begin a fight with the other apprentices, when Hans Sachs arrives from the alley and steps between them. The apprentices scatter, and Sachs in ill temper refuses David a singing lesson, ordering him instead to put a pair of shoes on the last. Both of them enter Sachs's house through a side door which leads directly to the shoemaker's workshop.

Pogner and Eva now enter, as though returning from an evening stroll. Pogner contemplates paying a visit on Sachs, but decides against it. He and Eva sit on the stone seat under the lime-tree. Both father and daughter are troubled in spirit; he because he is not sure if he has acted wisely in offering his daughter as prize, and she because she does not yet know how Walther fared with the Mastersingers earlier that day, and is too nervous to ask her father. Above a new orchestral motif, that of the city of Nuremberg itself, Pogner asks Eva if she does not eagerly anticipate the happy morrow when she will crown the Mastersinger who wins the song contest. 'Dear father, must it be a Master?' Eva asks, at which Pogner emphasizes that it must indeed be a Master, but one of her choice.

When her father goes into the house to prepare for supper, Eva learns from Magdalene the bad news concerning Walther. Her impulse is to consult her old friend Hans Sachs, but Magdalene advises her to wait until after supper, for her father would notice her absence if she were to be late for the meal. Magdalene also has a message which she will give to Eva later. 'Is it from the knight?' Eva asks. When told it is from Beckmesser, she mutters contemptuously 'That should be good,' and precedes Magdalene into the house.

Sachs re-enters his workshop and turns to David, who is still at his workbench. Addressing him gruffly, he sends the lad off to bed, and then sits at his bench, arranging his tools and preparing to work on a pair of shoes which he is making for Beckmesser. But he soon leaves off as there steals into the orchestra a lyrical reminiscence of Walther's song. Softly he begins to sing a reflective monologue, '*Was duftet doch der Flieder so mild, so stark und voll*' (The scent of the elder-tree is so mild, yet strong and full). This soliloquy, of great poetic beauty, is based on a yearning spring motif (Ex. 16), heard at first in the orchestra but later sung by Sachs to the words '*Lenzes Gebot, die süsse Noth*' (Spring's command, the sweet necessity).

It is really the mysterious nature of art upon which Sachs meditates: he cannot get the young knight's song out of his mind, even though it broke all those rules which he himself upholds. At one moment he tells himself that he would do better to stick to his last and give up all thoughts of poetry. At this, the orchestra bursts into the noisy cobbling music which will be heard again later in the act when Sachs makes use of a work-song to thwart Beckmesser. Now, however, it is dispelled after a few bars as a mood of lyrical reflection overtakes the shoemaker again. Finally, he decides to put all thoughts of Walther and his art aside for the time being, contenting himself with observing that, though the knight may have upset the other Masters, he certainly pleased Hans Sachs.

Eva emerges from her house, and walks shyly across the alley to Sachs's workshop. She longs to ask Sachs about Walther and the trial, but does not know how to go about it. She and he talk of the next day's contest, and Sachs tells Eva that he must finish Beckmesser's new shoes before morning, for the Town Clerk plans to wear them in the song contest. 'Use plenty of pitch, so that he will stick to it and leave me in peace' is Eva's only comment on this, but when Sachs observes that there are, after all, not very many eligible bachelors about, she asks demurely, 'Might not a widower be successful?' Sachs gently tells her that he would be too old for her, at which Eva accuses him of being fickle. She had thought, she says, that he was fond of her, and that he might one day take her into his house as both wife and child.

Eventually, Sachs reveals that Walther failed the test, and that there is no chance of his becoming a Master. In order to test the strength of Eva's feeling for the knight, Sachs tells her that he wishes the high and mighty young nobleman would leave the honest artisans of Nuremberg to practice their art in peace, and allow fortune to smile on him somewhere else. 'Yes,' Eva replies angrily, 'it shall smile on him somewhere far away from you nasty, jealous men,' and she crosses to her own front door as she hears Magdalene calling her.

Having found out what he wanted to know, that Eva loves Walther, Sachs murmurs to himself that he must find a way to help them. He closes the upper half of his workshop door, but continues to work at his bench, from where he can overhear any conversation taking place outside. When Magdalene tells Eva that Beckmesser intends to serenade her later that evening with the song he is going to sing in the contest, Eva asks her friend to sit at the window in her place, which Magdalene is very happy to do, hoping thereby to arouse feelings of jealousy in David, who sleeps on that side of Sachs's house which overlooks the alley.

Eva is about to go indoors with Magdalene when she sees Walther approaching. The young lovers greet each other passionately, but Walther is in a state of despair, for he realizes he is about to lose Eva to one of the Mastersingers, whose pedantry he despises. Furiously denouncing them, he becomes almost delirious in his rage, imagining he sees Masters in every corner, crowding together to mock him and demanding Eva as their bride. At the height of his frenzy, the sound of a cow-horn is heard, and Walther claps his hand to his sword, staring wildly about him. The noisy orchestra suddenly quietens to a romantic phrase depicting Midsummer's Eve, as Eva assures the knight that it was only the night-watchman's horn, advising Walther to hide behind the lime-tree until the watchman has passed by. Before she goes into the house with Magdalene, Eva promises Walther that she will elope with him later, and runs into the house to change clothes with Magdalene. As she goes, the night-watchman can be seen walking along the alley, singing his traditional warning: 'Hear, people, what I say. The clock has struck ten. Guard your fire and your light so that no one comes to harm. Praise the Lord God!'

Eva returns wearing Magdalene's dress, and she and Walther have begun to plan their escape route when Sachs, who has been listening to them, places his lantern so that it sheds a strong beam of light across the alley, making it impossible for the young lovers to flee. On the arrival of Beckmesser, who begins to tune his lute preparatory to serenading Eva, Sachs brings his work-bench outdoors and embarks upon a noisy song in three stanzas. Its words, ostensibly about Adam and Eve, contain a hidden cautionary message to Eva, who, with Walther, has now retreated to a seat behind the lime-tree. Sachs's song, which is punctuated by the exasperated complaints of Beckmesser and the *sotto voce* comments of Walther and Eva, is a jovial piece in popular style.

Beckmesser is, of course, furious at this disturbance, but is forced to agree to Sachs's suggestion that he should sing while Sachs acts as Marker, tapping on the shoes which he is making to indicate any faults in Beckmesser's song. The Town Clerk retunes his lute and begins his plaintive song, with the stresses all in the wrong places. Sachs taps away at the soles of the shoes, and manages to finish his task well before Beckmesser has completed his song. By now the neighbours have been awakened by all this noise, and David, looking out from his window, thinks he sees his beloved Magdalene being serenaded by a stranger. In a jealous rage, he leaps from the window upon Beckmesser and begins to cudgel him, while various neighbours, among them some of the Mastersingers, as well as a number of apprentices, all converge upon the alley and join in the fight.

In the confusion of the ensuing tumult, Eva and Walther attempt to make their escape, but Sachs separates them and drags Walther into his house. The night-watchman's horn is heard again, causing the crowd quickly to disperse. Pogner, who has come out on to the steps of his house, pulls Eva inside; Sachs drags David off the unfortunate Beckmesser, whom he is still pummelling, and kicks his apprentice into the workshop. Beckmesser limps away down the alley, and by the time the night-watchman appears upon the scene all is quiet. In a somewhat tremulous voice, the watchman repeats his hourly announcement and then walks slowly up the now deserted alley, disappearing around the corner as the curtain descends to the sound of a tranquil theme in the orchestra.

There are two scenes to Act III, the first of which is preceded by a sombre orchestral Prelude depicting Sachs's mood as Midsummer's Day dawns. The curtain rises on the cobbler's workshop. At the back is the half-open door to the street, to the right a door to an inner room of the house, and to the left a window through which the morning sun streams in. Sachs is seated in an armchair by the window, reading. David returns from having delivered Beckmesser's shoes to him, and attempts to apologize to his master for his behaviour of the previous night, but Sachs at first pays no heed to him. Eventually, however, David is allowed to sing his Midsummer's Day verses. With the events of the previous night still on his mind, he begins to sing the melody of Beckmesser's dreadful song, and is sharply called to order by Sachs.

The apprentice then proceeds to perform a song about John the Baptist, to Sachs's satisfaction. Its words remind the young apprentice that St Johannes has the same name as his master, Hans being its familiar form. Realizing that St John's Day is therefore also Hans Sachs's name-day, David attempts to present Sachs with a basket of flowers which Magdalene had given to him earlier. He even finds the courage to suggest that his master should compete that day for the hand of Eva, for he would be certain to defeat Beckmesser. Sachs gently evades the subject, and sends David inside to dress for the festival, warning him not to disturb Walther, who has apparently spent the night at Sachs's house.

The orchestra repeats the brooding theme with which the Act III Prelude had begun, as Sachs, left alone, muses on the state of the world in his great monologue, '*Wahn! Wahn! Überall Wahn!*' (Madness! Madness! Everywhere madness!) This soliloquy, weightily impressive in itself, is an aesthetic error in its intrusion of a tragic view of the world into what its composer intended to be a comedy about the course of true love in medieval Nuremberg. Wagner has been unable to resist the temptation to place himself on the stage for a few minutes, in his most Schopenhauer-like mood. He sees madness everywhere in the world around him. 'Wherever I seek in city and world chronicles', Sachs–Wagner tells himself, 'to find the reason why people torment and kill one another . . . I find only this same old madness.' He cannot understand why, in his beloved Nuremberg, its peaceful citizens should suddenly erupt in violence, conveniently forgetting that he began it by taunting Beckmesser and arousing the entire street with his noisy method of criticizing the town clerk's song. Sachs ends his deliberations on a positive note, however, resolving to harness this madness or creative frenzy in order to achieve a noble aim: the union of Walther and Eva.

Walther now enters from the inner room. He tells Sachs that he has slept little, but soundly, and has had a most beautiful dream of love, at which Sachs points out to him that it is precisely the poet's task to interpret and record his dreams. In the ensuing scene, he instructs Walther in the Mastersingers' rules, doing his best to instil in the somewhat distrustful young knight a spirit of artistic compromise. Slowly and patiently, Sachs guides Walther through the composition of the song, a graceful and ardent melody which he will sing in the contest, coaching him in the shaping of its form. Two stanzas are thus created, but when Sachs attempts to play midwife to a third, Walther becomes impatient. Sachs is wise enough to realize that, when the time comes, Walther will find the inspiration to complete the song, which Sachs has been writing down as it came into being. The knight's servant, Sachs tells him, has found his way to Nuremberg and delivered to the shoemaker's house Walther's resplendent formal wear. (We are not to question how or why this has happened; nor, for that matter, how Walther is able to take part in a contest which he has already been disqualified from entering.) Sachs ushers Walther into the inner room, where they will both adorn themselves for the festival.

Beckmesser, elaborately but tastelessly attired, has been approaching the house. Peeping into Sachs's workshop and finding it empty, he enters, still limping somewhat. His eyes fall on the song which Sachs has copied, and which is lying on the work-bench. Assuming it to be a song composed by Sachs himself, he thrusts it into his pocket, and when Sachs enters, now in festive attire, Beckmesser accuses the shoemaker of having interrupted his singing the previous evening, and even of having had him set upon by ruffians, in order to be rid of a dangerous rival. Sachs, he is convinced, intends to enter the contest and win Eva for himself. When Sachs denies this, Beckmesser produces the song he had pocketed. To his astonishment, Sachs merely replies, 'I have never yet taken what I found on other people's tables. So that people will not think ill of you for having done so, I make you a present of it.'

Overjoyed to have a song apparently by Sachs, but understandably suspicious of such generous behaviour, Beckmesser asks Sachs to swear that he will never tell anyone that he had composed the song. Sachs is happy to give this assurance, and Beckmesser limps happily away with his newly acquired treasure. Watching him leave, Sachs observes that he has never before encountered anyone so malicious. That Beckmesser has stolen the song fits in well with his plans. This amusing scene between Sachs and Beckmesser is lightly written for the voices and wittily scored. If only the entire opera had been sustained at this level, and with such graceful humour, what a delightful comedy it could have made.

The remainder of the first scene of Act III is equally fine. A somewhat distraught Eva now enters, on the pretext that the shoes which Sachs has made for her do not fit properly. It is clear, however, that her real concern is for Walther. When he appears from within the house, in glittering knightly apparel, the orchestra bursts into the romantic Midsummer's Eve motif. Inspired by the sight of his beloved, Walther improvises the final verse of his song. 'Listen, my child,' says Sachs to Eva. 'That is a Master Song.' An overjoyed Eva rests her head on Sachs's breast, and in a rapturous outburst, beginning '*O Sachs, mein Freund*' (Oh Sachs, my friend), confesses that he would have been her choice as husband had not Walther swept her off her feet. Sachs replies tenderly that he knows only too well the sad tale of Tristan and Isolde, and has no desire to play the role of King Marke.

David and Magdalene now arrive, she from the street and he from within the house. Sachs announces that the new song must be given a name, and be christened in the presence of two witnesses. Since an apprentice cannot act as a witness, he formally promotes David, with a cuff on the ear, to the rank of journeyman, and names the song '*Die selige Morgentraum-Deutweise*' (the blissful morning-dream interpretation melody). A serene quintet, '*Selig wie die Sonne meines Glückes lacht*' (Blissfully as the sun of my happiness laughs), is launched by Eva. Each of the characters sings of the particular joy this day brings, though Sachs's joy is tinged with an autumnal sadness, for he realizes he is losing Eva for ever.

As the scene now changes to an open meadow by the banks of the Pegnitz river, with the town of Nuremberg in the background, the orchestra develops the Nuremberg motif, followed by those of the Mastersingers (Ex. 15) and Midsummer's Day. Boats continually disgorge fresh parties of citizens from the river to the meadow, which is dotted with fairground tents offering various kinds of refreshments. In the foreground, to one side, a raised stand with benches awaits the arrival of the important personages of the festival: the Mastersingers. Various guilds now arrive, and march past with their banners: first the shoemakers, then the tailors and the bakers. The apprentices dance gaily, and are dispersed only by the arrival, in great pomp, of the Mastersingers. Finally, the apprentices call for silence, and Sachs steps forward to address the assembled crowd.

Before he can speak, the entire assembly joins in singing a song whose words are by the historical Hans Sachs, acclaiming Martin Luther and the Reformation: '*Wach' auf, es nahet gen dem Tag*' (Awake, the dawn of day draws near). The mighty chorus thunders to its close, and Sachs delivers his opening address, his voice at first trembling with emotion but later gaining in firmness. Beckmesser, in a state of high anxiety because he has been unable to understand properly the song he took from Sachs, is the first competitor to be called. Of course, he makes a complete mess of the song, and before he has finished the crowd bursts into derisive laughter. In a fury, Beckmesser declares that the wretched song was composed not by him but by Sachs, and makes a hasty exit.

Asked to explain, Sachs says he would never dare to boast of having composed so beautiful a song. Beckmesser's performance was a distortion, but whoever was able to perform it correctly would surely reveal himself to be the creator of the song and worthy to be a Mastersinger. He calls on whoever knows this to be true to come forward and give witness. Walther advances from the crowd. His appearance and bearing make a favourable impression on the citizens, and all listen in complete silence as he begins his Prize Song, '*Morgenlich leuchtend im rosigen Schein*' (Shining in the roseate light of morning). Murmurs of approbation, from the Masters as well as the crowd, are heard between the stanzas, and Walther concludes his song in a state of the highest exaltation. 'Take the wreath,' exclaim the Mastersingers as one man. 'Your song has won you the Masters' prize.'

Eva places a wreath of myrtle and laurel on Walther's brow, but when Pogner attempts to adorn him with the gold chain of the Guild of Masters, Walther rejects it vehemently. At this, Sachs steps towards the young knight, advising him not to scorn the Masters, for they are the only guardians of true German art. In a jingoistic sermon in which he warns of the dangers of foreign influence, he lauds '*die heil'ge deutsche Kunst*' (holy German art). Walther is suitably chastened, the crowd patriotically takes up Sachs's call to 'honour your German masters,' Eva removes the wreath from Walther's head and

Act II of *Götterdämmerung* at the Metropolitan Opera, New York, designed by
Günther Schneider-Siemssen, 1989

The final scene of the 1989 production of *Götterdämmerung* at the Metropolitan
Opera

above: Peter Hofmann in Act II of *Parsifal* at the Metropolitan Opera, New York, in 1986

right: Emil Scaria (Gurnemanz), Amalie Materna (Kundry) and Hermann Winkelmann (Parsifal) in the première of *Parsifal* at Bayreuth in 1882

opposite: Peter Hofmann as Parsifal and Kathryn Harries as Kundry in *Parsifal*, Metropolitan Opera, 1986

Paul von Joukowsky's set for Acts I and III of *Parsifal* at Bayreuth in 1882

The auditorium of the Festival Theatre, Bayreuth, in 1882, with the stage set for *Parsifal*

places it upon Sachs's, while Sachs takes the chain from Pogner and places it around the neck of the now unresisting knight. Pogner kneels in homage to Sachs, all acclaim the cobbler as their leader, and the opera ends with a general cry of '*Heil! Sachs! Nürnbergs teurem Sachs*' (Hail! Sachs! Nuremberg's dear Sachs!)

The blatant appeal to German nationalism of Sachs's outburst is a stunning example of Wagner the politician dominating Wagner the artist, for it has no rightful place, aesthetically, in the opera. At the time of the première of *Die Meistersinger*, it must have sounded like a clear invitation to launch a racial war against Germany's neighbours. Not only is '*heil'ge deutsche Kunst*' upheld as the great ideal, but the means of achieving and maintaining it are spelt out as clearly as Wagner elsewhere in his writings spelt out how to get rid of the Jews. The people—to whose judgment, as the libretto makes clear, art must in the end bow—are exhorted to obliterate the influence of French culture with its ephemeral and un-Germanic values: a project which was eventually to be implemented by Hitler, who also took action on one or two of Wagner's other hints. Sachs's address to the crowd aroused that first Munich audience to a frenzy of enthusiasm, and led a Bayreuth audience in the 1930s to rise to its feet and stand with hands raised in the Nazi salute until the end of the opera.

There can be no denying that the music of Hans Sachs's great address is of an extraordinary emotive force, of the kind that was peculiarly Wagner's own. The question that it poses is whether the nasty taste of the words is redeemed by the power of the music, or whether the music's qualities merely render more dangerously effective a message which, deprived of its music and left in Wagner's raw words, would surely have less appeal, for words speak primarily to the intellect and music to the emotions. It is a question which has never been satisfactorily answered, and one which is far removed from the comparatively simple matter of having to accept that artistic genius does not necessarily reside only in the breasts of those of the most impeccable moral purity.

GIVEN that its composer insisted on describing it as a comedy, *Die Meistersinger* is a monstrously long opera, its third act alone lasting nearly two hours in performance. But then it is by no means the kind of work which Wagner claimed it to be. A sense of artistic discretion, which was never one of his strongest attributes, is considerably less evident here than in *Der fliegende Holländer* or even *Tristan und Isolde*. One could say that Wagner the composer has set to music the hidden libretto of *Die Meisteringer* that exists between the lines of the printed one: a hymn to artistic compromise with, in its final scene, an irrelevant aside appealing to the baser aspects of nationalistic feeling. Walther von Stolzing begins as an artist answerable only to himself and his art. He is taught by the wise, kindly Sachs how to curry the favour of his audience and thus win the hand of Eva by compromise, by giving the people what they want. Act I's '*Am stillen Herd*' is the finer song, but it is Act III's '*Morgenlich leuchtend*' that wins the prize.

NINE

Der Ring des Nibelungen
(The Nibelung's Ring)

A stage-festival-play for three days and a preliminary evening
(1. *Das Rheingold.* 2. *Die Walküre.* 3. *Siegfried.* 4. *Götterdämmerung.*)

Das Rheingold

(The Rhinegold)

Prologue in One Act to Der Ring des Nibelungen

Dramatis personae
Wotan   (baritone)
Donner   (bass)
Froh   (tenor)
Loge   (tenor)
Alberich   (bass-baritone)
Mime   (tenor)
Fasolt   (bass)
Fafner   (bass)
Fricka   (mezzo-soprano)
Freia   (soprano)
Erda   (contralto)
Woglinde   (soprano)
Wellgunde   (soprano)
Flosshilde   (contralto)

LIBRETTO by the composer

TIME: Legendary

PLACE: The Rhine, and surrounding country

FIRST PERFORMED at the Hofoper, Munich, 22 September 1869, with August Kindermann (Wotan), Heinrich Vogl (Loge), Karl Fischer (Alberich), Karl Schlosser (Mime), Sophie Stehle (Fricka), Henriette Müller (Freia) and Therese Seehofer (Erda), conducted by Franz Wüllner.

First performed as part of the complete *Ring* cycle, at the Festspielhaus, Bayreuth, 13 August 1876, with Franz Betz (Wotan), Heinrich Vogl (Loge), Karl Hill (Alberich), Karl Schlosser (Mime), Friederike Grün (Fricka), Marie Haupt (Freia) and Luise Jaïde (Erda), conducted by Hans Richter.

I

IT was as early as 1848, when he was in his mid-thirties, that Wagner first put on paper his ideas for the project which was to come to fruition in 1876 at Bayreuth as *Der Ring des Nibelungen* (The Nibelung's Ring). The prose sketch which he wrote in October 1848 is a retelling of the old Nibelung myth, with some material drawn from the medieval German epic *Das Nibelungenlied*, and some from the older Scandinavian Edda, mythological stories of the Norse gods and heroes.

Wagner's intention at this stage seems to have been to use the earlier parts of the story as prehistory in synopsis form, and to compose an opera about the last days of Siegfried, *Siegfrieds Tod* (The Death of Siegfried). He wrote a verse libretto for *Siegfrieds Tod*, but found, when he began to compose the music in 1850, that he needed to start at an earlier point in the narrative. He therefore broke off from working on the music, and in 1851 wrote a second libretto on the subject of the young Siegfried (*Der junge Siegfried*). This in turn led him to the realization that he would have to begin at the very beginning, and so the libretti of, first, *Die Walküre* (The Valkyrie) and then *Das Rheingold* (The Rhinegold) were written in 1852.

Though the libretti of what was now to be a tetralogy, or series of four related works, had been written in reverse order, the operas themselves were composed in the correct chronological sequence. *Das Rheingold* occupied Wagner in 1853–4, and *Die Walküre* from 1854 to March 1856. He began *Siegfried* (formerly *Der junge Siegfried*) in 1856, but put it aside to work on *Tristan und Isolde* for two years and *Die Meistersinger* for five. He returned to *Siegfried* in 1864, completing it in 1871. The last work of the tetralogy, its title no longer *Siegfrieds Tod* but *Götterdämmerung* (Twilight of the Gods), was composed between 1871 and 1874.

After the première of *Die Meistersinger* in June 1868, Wagner and Cosima were to live together for the rest of their lives. Cosima's husband, Hans von Bülow, having filed a petition for divorce, fled to Italy after conducting the première of *Die Meistersinger*, and thereafter severed all connections with Wagner. In June 1869, Cosima, who had already borne the composer two daughters, Isolde and Eva, gave birth to a third child, a son whom they named Siegfried, Wagner having completed a first draft of the third act of *Siegfried* the day before the child was born.

He had finished writing the music of *Das Rheingold* a good fifteen years earlier, and that of *Die Walküre* thirteen years earlier. He now returned to *Götterdämmerung*, the last section of his tetralogy, whose libretto had been the first to be written. Its composition occupied him for the next three years, during which period he also wrote a number of polemical articles and an essay on Beethoven, and finally completed his autobiography. On 25 August 1870, he married Cosima, who had been divorced from Bülow the previous month. Later that year, he composed the instrumental *Siegfried Idyll*, from musical material related to the final act of *Siegfried*, as a Christmas present for Cosima. The piece was played for the first time on the staircase of their villa, Triebschen, on Christmas morning, which was also Cosima's birthday.

Among Wagner's journalistic essays were a series of fifteen articles contributed anonymously to the *Süddeutsche Presse*, called 'German Arts and German Politics', expanding on the views which had been expressed by Hans Sachs in the last act of *Die Meistersinger*. In these articles, the shallow and degenerate French were contrasted with the vigorous and virtuous German race and its God-given mission to civilize the world. In one of the pieces, Wagner eulogized the murderer of the playwright Kotzebue, one Karl Sand, an insane disciple of the proto-Nazi Friedrich Ludwig Jahn. That such scurrilous articles could appear in an official newspaper began to worry King Ludwig. After the article in which Wagner wrote enthusiastically of Jahn's theory propagating the creation of a new nobility to be based on duty to the state, Ludwig finally heeded the advice of his ministers and ordered the publication of the articles to cease.

When Wagner then decided to reissue his notorious essay 'Judaism in Music', even Cosima thought it indiscreet of him. But he was becoming increasingly obsessed with what he saw as the Jewish problem. As at least one of Wagner's twentieth-century biographers has observed, the composer's reputation as an anti-Semite was so great that racial gibes were suspected even where they were probably not intended. For instance, at the Viennese première of *Die Meistersinger* in February 1870, Beckmesser's ludicrous attempt to serenade Eva was hissed because it was believed to be a parody of synagogue chant: there were cries from the audience of 'We won't listen to it.' Wagner professed to consider this incident a Jewish insult to the authority of the Emperor Franz Josef.

In 1868 Wagner had met the young student-philosopher Friedrich Nietzsche, who at the age of twenty-four was barely a year older than King

Ludwig. As his influence over Ludwig waned, the composer began to concentrate instead on Nietzsche, whom he invited to Triebschen. The future author of *Thus Spake Zarathustra, Beyond Good and Evil* and *The Will to Power* was, therefore, early in his life privileged to observe at close range the will to power in action. Although Nietzsche, who in 1869 had become a professor of classical philology at the University of Basel, was still relatively unknown, Wagner tended to drop his name as though it had a resounding ring to it. Craving academic respectability, of which his theories were sorely in need, the composer referred to young Nietzsche and his colleague Erwin Rohde as 'my friends, the two university professors'.

It was King Ludwig's desire that the *Ring* operas should be given their premières separately, as soon as each was composed. Although he at first favoured this suggestion, Wagner subsequently turned against the idea, not so much for aesthetic as for domestic reasons. Early in 1869, he had not yet married Cosima, and it was therefore impossible for him to return to Munich for any length of time without causing a scandal. But Ludwig was determined that *Das Rheingold* would have its première in Munich at the earliest possible opportunity.

The events leading up to the première were decidedly bizarre, due to Wagner's determination to regain power and influence for himself in Munich by sabotaging the performance. The conductor was to be Bülow's successor in Munich, the young and, as yet, relatively inexperienced Hans Richter. By ordering Richter to resign, on the grounds that the production of the opera had been badly organized and would discredit Wagner, the composer hoped and expected that Ludwig would then dismiss the theatre's administrator, Baron von Perfall, and install Richter in his place. Wagner would then be able to rule through his puppet, the young conductor.

Unfortunately for Wagner, his plan misfired. There were mishaps at the dress rehearsal, and Richter duly offered his indignant resignation, but the chief mechanist remedied the scenic mistakes without difficulty, and King Ludwig was furious when he realized he was being made the dupe of his ex-hero. Richter was suspended, a new conductor was found, and the première was postponed for a month. Ludwig departed for one of his castles, remarking '*J'en ai assez*' (I've had enough), but not before writing angrily to his Court Counsellor:

The way Wagner and the theatrical rabble are behaving is really criminal and completely shameless. It amounts to open defiance of my orders, and I cannot allow it. Richter must definitely not be allowed to conduct again, and is to be dismissed forthwith. That is final. The theatre personnel are to obey my orders and not Wagner's whims. As I anticipated, several newspapers have insinuated that I have cancelled the performances. It is very easy to spread false rumours, and it is my wish that you should announce the true situation immediately, and summon every resource necessary to enable the première to take place. For, if Wagner's loathsome intrigues were to succeed, the whole mob would grow more impudent and shameless, and would finally become uncontrollable. The evil must therefore be eradicated, root and branch. Richter must go, and Betz and the others must be brought to heel. I have never in my life experienced such effrontery. [Franz Betz, who had created the role of Hans Sachs in *Die Meistersinger*, was the baritone who was to have sung Wotan. He eventually did perform the role in the first complete Ring seven years later.]

When Wagner arrived in Munich, he found to his astonishment that he was refused admission to the *Rheingold* rehearsals. There was nothing for him to do but return to Triebschen, whence he wrote hysterically to Franz Wüllner, the conductor who had been engaged to replace Richter:

Keep your hands off my score! Take my advice, sir, or go to the devil! Go and beat time for choral societies and glee clubs, or if you must conduct operas at all costs, get hold of those your friend Perfall has written! And tell that fine gentleman that, if he fails to admit frankly to the king that he is incapable of staging my work, I will light under him a fire which all the gutter journalists he pays with what he filches from the *Rheingold* budget will be unable to extinguish. You gentlemen are going to have to take a lot of lessons from a man like me, before you realize that you are incapable of understanding anything.

The première of *Das Rheingold* under Wüllner took place in Munich, successfully, on 22 September 1869, and Wagner received news of it in Triebschen with dismay. He and his circle of friends were to maintain that the Munich performances of *Das Rheingold* (and of *Die Walküre* the following year) were poor, and that the operas were not properly staged until the Bayreuth production of the complete *Ring* in 1876.

II

ALTHOUGH occasional single performances of the individual operas are given, it is as a complete and indivisible entity that Wagner's *Ring* is best approached. The composer wanted the four parts of the tetralogy to be performed, ideally, on four successive evenings, but the demands it makes on its performers and, for that matter, on its audiences are such that, even under festival conditions, a gap of one or two days between operas is the norm in productions of *The Ring*. The total playing time of the entire work is about fifteen hours.

Its story, drawn by Wagner from a number of disparate sources in German and Norse myth, legend and history, follows in broad outline the prose sketch which the composer had written in 1848: the *Ring* cycle had a gestation period of immense length. The 1848 sketch begins thus:

> From the womb of night and death was spawned a race that dwells in Nibelheim (Nebelheim), in gloomy subterranean clefts and caverns. Nibelungen, they are called. With restless nimbleness they burrow through the bowels of the earth, like worms in a dead body. They smelt and smith hard metals. Alberich seized the pure and noble Rhine gold, divorced it from the water's depth, and wrought therefrom with cunning art a ring that gave him rulership over all his race, the Nibelungen. So he became their master, forced them to work for him alone, and amassed the priceless Nibelungen hoard whose greatest treasure is the Tarnhelm, which Alberich compelled his own brother Reigin (Mime, Eugel) to weld for him, a head covering which confers upon its possessor the power to assume any shape at will. Thus armoured, Alberich set out to master the world and all that it contains.

The Ring has been subjected to a variety of interpretations, ranging from Bernard Shaw's analysis of the work as a political allegory to Robert Donington's description of it in terms of Jungian psychology. It has been seen both as a history of the world and as a treatise on the corruption of the world. Countless books have been written discussing it as music drama, and relating it to Wagner's theoretical writings, but the work itself remains larger and more mysterious than the sum of all these attempts to explain it. It is so vast that its meaning must inevitably become a question of individual interpretation and temperament. Those who respond fully to *The Ring* are, as Shaw wrote of himself, so helplessly under the spell of its greatness that they 'can do nothing but go raving about the theatre between the acts in ecstasies of deluded admiration'.

The clearest description of Wagner's intentions in composing *The Ring* is contained in a letter the composer wrote to a former Dresden colleague, August Röckel, in 1854:

> ... We must learn to die, in fact to die in the most absolute sense of the word. Fear of the end is the source of all lovelessness, and it arises only where love itself has already faded. How did it come about that mankind so lost touch with this bringer of the highest happiness to everything living that in the end everything they did, everything they undertook and established, was done solely out of fear of the end?
>
> My poem shows how. It shows nature in its undistorted truth, with all its opposites intact, which in their manifold and endless permutations also

contain elements which are mutually exclusive and self-repelling. But the decisive source of the disaster is not that Alberich was repelled by the Rhinemaidens—which was perfectly natural for them. Alberich and his ring could not harm the gods if the latter were not already ripe for disaster. So where is the nub of the catastrophe? Look at the first scene between Wotan and Fricka, which eventually leads to the scene in Act II of *Die Walküre*. The rigid bond that unites them both, arising from love's involuntary mistake of perpetuating itself beyond the inescapable laws of change, of maintaining mutual dependence, this resistance to the eternal renewal and change of the objective world lands both of them in the mutual torment of lovelessness.

The course of the drama thus shows the necessity of accepting and giving way to the changeability, the diversity, the multiplicity, the eternal newness of reality and of life. Wotan rises to the tragic height of willing his own downfall. This is everything that we have to learn from the history of mankind: to will the inevitable and to carry it out oneself. The product of this highest, self-destructive will is the fearless, ever-loving man, who is finally created: Siegfried. That is all.

In detail: the power of evil, the actual poison of love, is concentrated in the gold, which is stolen from nature and misused in the Nibelung's ring. The curse upon it is not redeemed until it is returned to nature, until the gold is once again delivered into the depths of the Rhine. This, too, Wotan does not learn until the very end, at the final goal of his tragic course. What Loge touchingly and repeatedly told him at the beginning, Wotan most overlooked in his lust for power. At first he appreciates only the power of the curse—from Fafner's deed. It is not until the ring destroys Siegfried, too, that he understands that only the return of the stolen gold will atone for the evil, and he therefore associates the terms of his own desired destruction with the atonement of the original wrong.

Experience is everything. Siegfried alone (the male alone) is also not the complete 'man'; he is but one half. It is only with Brünnhilde that he becomes the redeemer. One alone cannot achieve everything; many are needed, and the suffering, self-sacrificing woman is the final true and knowing redeemer, for love is really the 'eternally feminine' itself . . .

It is hardly necessary to trace here in detail all the sources which Wagner consulted: his most important sources in the creation of *Der Ring des Nibelungen* are the *Edda* and the *Nibelungenlied*.

The Poetic Edda, as it is generally known, is a collection of thirty-five poems in Old Norse which originated as oral poetry in Iceland around two thousand years ago. The poems were written down at some time during the twelfth century, but long before this they had made their way south into Europe. It is thought that those stanzas dealing with Siegfried and the Nibelungs may have originated in the valley of the Rhine, eventually to become known in Scandinavia.

Its material derived from the *Edda*, the *Nibelungenlied* (or *Nibelungen Not*— Fall of the Nibelungs—to give the epic its formal title) is an early thirteenth-century poem written by an anonymous poet in German, for performance at the Austrian court. It tells, in thirty-nine chapters, of the mighty King Siegfried who, having won Queen Brunhild for King Gunther in exchange for Gunther's sister Kriemhild, is murdered by Gunther's vassal Hagen. Siegfried's death is finally avenged by Kriemhild. In planning his operatic version of the myth, Wagner ignored the second half of the story, which deals with Kriemhild and her vengeance.

Other sources contributed to the making of Wagner's *Ring*, chief among them the *Saga of the Volsungs*, an Icelandic saga dating from the mid thirteenth century which is, in essentials, a prose version of parts of *The Poetic Edda*. *Deutsche Mythologie* (German Mythology) by Jakob Grimm and *Die deutsche Heldensage* (The German Heroic Sagas) by Wilhelm Grimm were also helpful to the composer. (The Grimm brothers are best known, of course, for their collection of children's fairy tales.) *Deutsche Mythologie*, in particular, provided Wagner with a great deal of background information. Though he derived his characters and his plot chiefly from the Icelandic sagas, it was Grimm's study which helped him to relate these to a German ambience.

After he had written all four libretti, and well before the music of *The Ring* had been composed, Wagner decided to publish the complete text. A limited edition was produced at his own expense, but it was not until several years later that the work was published commercially. The first public edition of the libretto of *The Ring* made its appearance in 1863, still some years before the première of *Das Rheingold*. In a preface, Wagner made it clear that, in his view, a new theatre would have to be built to accommodate performances of his vast music drama. 'My principal concern', he wrote,

> has been how best to achieve . . . a performance free from the influences of the routine repertory of our existing theatres. This consideration rules out any but the smaller cities of Germany. One in a favourable situation with the facilities to receive exceptional guests must be sought, and indeed one where there would be no clash with an existing theatre of any great size nor a confrontation with the usual theatre-going public of a large city and its habits.
>
> Here we would build a temporary theatre, as simple as possible, perhaps just of wood, and with no other consideration in mind but the suitability of its interior for the artistic purpose. I have discussed a feasible plan, with an amphitheatrical auditorium and the great advantage of a concealed

orchestra, with an experienced and imaginative architect. Thither we would then summon outstanding dramatic singers selected from the companies of the German opera houses. They would assemble in early spring, let us say, in order to rehearse the several parts of my stage work without the distraction of any other kind of artistic activity. I have in mind perhaps three performances in all, the invitation to attend which would be extended to the German public as a whole, making the performances available, as is the case already with our great music festivals, not to an audience from one town only, but to all friends of art, near and far. A complete performance, in high summer, of the dramatic poem published here would consist of *Das Rheingold* on one evening, and of the three principal pieces, *Die Walküre*, *Siegfried* and *Götterdämmerung*, on the three succeeding evenings.

The advantages that these conditions would bestow on the performance itself, as the first consideration, seem to me to be as follows. (From a practical artistic point of view I see no other way in which a truly successful performance would even be possible.) With the utter stylelessness of German opera and the almost grotesque incorrectness of its performances, any hope of finding the artistic forces ready to meet a higher challenge in the existing company of one of our major theatres is out of the question. The author who has it in mind to put a seriously meant higher challenge to the benighted public realm of art will find nothing to build his hopes on but the genuine talent of some individual singers, not trained in any school or in any style of performance, and these he will find are few and far between—for this kind of talent is at best rare among the Germans—and left entirely to their own devices. Thus, what no one theatre can offer, might, with luck, be attainable only by uniting dispersed forces, brought together at a particular spot for a particular time.

These artists would benefit in our theatre first of all from having only one challenge to meet for a period of time. They would grasp the character of the work all the more speedily and surely for not being interrupted in their study of it by the distractions of their normal work in an opera house. The success of this concentration of their gifts on one style and one challenge simply cannot be rated highly enough, if one considers how little success could be expected in normal circumstances, e.g. when a singer who performed in a badly translated Italian opera the evening before, has to rehearse Wotan or Siegfried the very next day. This method would moreover have the practical outcome of needing relatively far less time to be spent in rehearsals than would be possible in the context of the ordinary repertory routine; and that in turn would greatly benefit the continuity of study . . .

In due course, Wagner's megalomania was to succeed in bringing into existence the theatre he had always dreamed of, though whether such a theatre is really any more necessary for the successful production of his operas than for the production of those of Mozart or Verdi is debatable. In any case, at the time of the première of *Das Rheingold*, the Wagner Festival Theatre or *Festspielhaus* at Bayreuth was still some years in the future. Meanwhile, even without the co-operation of the composer, the singers, musicians and conductor of the Munich company appear to have done extremely well by Wagner's prologue to *The Ring*.

III

THOUGH its music is continuous throughout, *Das Rheingold* is in four scenes. A good third of the more than ninety motifs which are embedded in the musical texture of *The Ring* are contained within this prologue of an opera. The first scene is set in the Rhine, the primordial depths of the mighty river being portrayed by the orchestra's double basses with a long sustained E flat at the bottom of their range, a note on which is built a chord of E flat major as horns and bassoons join in. Slowly a flowing rhythm is built up in the entire orchestra, denoting the calm, majestic course of the river. Towards the end of this remarkable orchestral prelude of 136 bars based on a gently flowing nature motif (Ex. 17), the curtain rises on the depths of the Rhine. Steep rocks

Ex.17

arise from the bed of the river, above which the flowing water can be discerned through a greenish twilight. Three mermaids or Rhinemaidens, Woglinde (soprano), Wellgunde (soprano) and Flosshilde (contralto), guardians of the Rhinegold, can be seen swimming playfully around the rocks, engaged in carefree banter with one another. The gold cannot as yet be glimpsed in the dim light of pre-dawn, but Flosshilde warns her sisters that they must take more seriously their task of guarding it.

The frolicsome games of the water-nymphs are interrupted by the gruff voice of the Nibelung, Alberich (bass-baritone), arising from the depths. (The Nibelungs are a race of ugly dwarfs who live underground in the realm of Nibelheim, beneath the Rhine.) The hideous Alberich hopes to seduce one or more of the Rhinemaidens, but his advances are met with mocking laughter. Again it is Flosshilde who reminds her sisters that they have been warned to be on their guard against such a foe, but even she joins with them in teasing the strange creature whose flattering words cause the nymphs such amusement.

When Alberich exclaims that his arms would love to enfold one of their slim forms, Flosshilde is relieved. 'Now I can laugh at my fears, for our foe is in love,' she tells her sisters. Woglinde swims down to Alberich who, out of his element in water, is having difficulty in clambering up the rock face. She teases him by eluding his grasp whenever he thinks he has caught her. Next, Wellgunde calls to him, and Alberich turns his attention to her, only to be told, when he gets close to her, that he is a hairy, humpbacked horrid, black, scaly dwarf with whom she will have nothing to do. Flosshilde in turn murmurs caressingly to Alberich in phrases of a convincingly seductive quality, and the Nibelung exchanges tender words of love with her. He realizes he is being mocked again only when Flosshilde professes to be enamoured of what she calls his toad-like form and croaking voice.

Driven to a frenzy by their taunts, Alberich lusts after the Rhinemaidens even more strongly. As he stares up from below, wondering how to seize any one of them, his attention is suddenly diverted by the sun breaking through the waters, revealing at the top of the highest rock a dazzlingly bright gleam of gold, and the orchestra enunciates the motif of the Rhinegold in a brilliant flourish of trumpets (Ex. 18). The Rhinemaidens greet the sight of their gold, singing a beautiful and rapturous trio as they swim around it. When Alberich asks them what it is that gleams so brightly, he is mocked again for being so uncouth as never to have heard of the Rhinegold.

Ex.18

The Rhinemaidens communicate their delight in the gold, at which Alberich retorts that, if it is merely something for them to play with, it is of no interest to him. Incautiously, the nymphs now reveal the wonders of the gold. Wellgunde informs Alberich that the man who could fashion a ring from the gold would win for himself the entire wealth of the world. Here, softly in the woodwind, an adumbration of the ring motif is heard. Flosshilde reminds her sisters that they have a duty to guard the treasure, and not to chatter about it, but Wellgunde points out that the gold is perfectly safe, since only he who forswears the delights of love can attain the magic power to fashion a ring from it. Since everything that lives desires love, no one would forswear it. 'Least of all that lascivious gnome there,' cries Woglinde, and the Rhinemaidens yet again pour their scornful laughter upon Alberich.

The dwarf, however, having been so brutally rejected by the three Rhinemaidens, is not only ready but eager to renounce love if by doing so he can achieve power instead. As he clambers up the side of the rock, the nymphs at first think that he has merely gone mad with lust, but when Alberich reaches the summit he stretches out his arm towards the gold, shouting a curse upon love as he does so. Seizing the treasure, he disappears into the depths with it as the Rhinemaidens lament their loss. Darkness descends, and the scene begins to change, the waves of the Rhine appearing to alter gradually to a cloud formation veiled in mist. The motif of renunciation of love at first predominates in the orchestra, giving way to a confident statement of the ring motif.

The mist slowly disperses to reveal the new scene, an open space on top of a mountain. Lying on a flowery bank, sleeping, are the god Wotan (baritone) and his consort, Fricka (mezzo-soprano). In the background, a castle with gleaming battlements stands on a rocky peak. Between it and the foreground there runs a deep valley through which the river Rhine flows. As the orchestra's trombones and tuba, with an occasional trumpet fanfare, sound the noble, stately motif of Valhalla, home of the gods, Fricka suddenly emerges from slumber. Seeing for the first time the castle, Valhalla, which has just been built for the gods by the giants Fasolt and Fafner, she calls on Wotan to awaken.

Still dreaming, Wotan murmurs in his sleep of the mighty edifice he has commissioned. Awakening, he gazes with joy and pride at the distant castle. '*Vollendet das ewige Werk*' (The everlasting work is completed), he exclaims in an exultant arioso. 'Resplendently soaring above the mountain peak, the stronghold of the gods now stands. A sublime, superb structure, just as my dreams desired it and my will directed it.' But Fricka reminds him of the bitter price to be paid for the castle, upbraiding him for having agreed to reward the giants by giving them Fricka's lovely sister Freia, goddess of youth. Here, as throughout the entire *Ring*, the appropriate motif is heard in the orchestra, this one a theme to be associated with the concept of the treaty.

Fricka accuses Wotan of being willing to sacrifice anything and anyone in his thirst for power, but Wotan asks Fricka if she had been entirely free from that same thirst when she begged him to build such a stronghold. Fricka is forced to admit that she desired Valhalla as a means of keeping Wotan at home instead of wandering through the world in search of adventure. Wotan, however, has turned what she envisaged as a domestic refuge into a castle with battlements, a seat of power. Wotan's reply is that, even though she might wish to keep him in the castle, Fricka must surely realize that his will to influence the world would still be active. 'All who live', he tells her, 'love to roam and to find variety. I cannot change my nature.'

In answer to Fricka's charge that he is willing to barter a loving woman for a mere symbol of might and dominion, Wotan replies that he has great love and respect for women. Did he not sacrifice one of his eyes as a pledge when he wooed Fricka? She is not to fear now, for he has never had the slightest intention of yielding Freia up to the giants. 'Then protect her now,' Fricka demands, as the tempo quickens and the orchestra sounds a note of urgency, 'for here she comes, hurrying to you for help, defenceless and frightened.' And indeed Freia (soprano) now rushes in, exclaiming that the giant Fasolt is pursuing her, determined to bear her away with him. A first suggestion of the giants' motif appears in the orchestra.

Wotan asks Freia if she has seen Loge, god of fire and deceit, on whom he is apparently relying to find a way of extricating himself from the bargain he has made. Fricka is dismayed to hear that Wotan still trusts the god, whom she refers to as a trickster, who has deceived him so often in the past. His dignity affronted, Wotan points out that he has never had to seek help from anyone where simple courage is required. But when craft and cunning are necessary, Loge is the ideal person to give advice. Loge had suggested that Wotan should promise Freia to the giants in return for their building Valhalla, and had assured Wotan that, when the time came, he would find a way out of the bargain. 'And he has let you down,' Fricka exclaims, 'for here come the giants. Where is your crafty helper now?'

Freia calls unavailingly upon her brother gods, Donner and Froh, to come to her aid, since her brother-in-law Wotan appears to have abandoned her, but neither of these gods appears and Fricka unhelpfully comments that all of those who had betrayed Freia have now gone to ground. Accompanied by their appropriately heavy, clumsy but menacing motif, the two giants now arrive upon the scene. Fasolt (bass), as spokesman for the building firm of Fasolt and Fafner, points out that, while the gods were wrapped in slumber, he and his brother had toiled untiringly to build the massive fortress Wotan had commissioned. Valhalla is now completed, and it is time to pay. When Wotan disingenuously asks them to name their fee, Fasolt reminds him that it has already been agreed. They have come now to take Freia home with them.

'Has this contract made you crazy?' Wotan asks. 'Think of some other fee, for Freia is not for sale.' Fasolt warns Wotan against treachery, pointing to the marks of solemn treaty on the god's spear, while his more brutish and quick-tempered brother, Fafner (bass), exclaims that they have been swindled. Fasolt, the more philosophical of the two giants, attempts to reason with Wotan. 'Your power', he explains to the god, 'is limited and well-defined. You are what you are only by the strength and surety of your contracts. You have more wisdom than we, but I will curse your wisdom and defy you if you do not know how to honour an agreement. A stupid giant thus advises you, Oh wise one. You would do well to heed him.'

Wotan now accuses the giants of having pretended to take in earnest what he had proposed only as a jest. 'Of what use is this lovely goddess to you louts?' he sneers. Fasolt adopts an aggrieved tone in response to this, but Fafner takes a stronger line. Freia may not be worth much to the giants, he admits, but her absence will certainly injure the gods, for it is only by eating the golden apples which Freia alone can provide that they are endowed with eternal youth. Deprived of the apples, the gods will grow old and weak. Murmuring to himself that he wished Loge would hurry up and arrive, Wotan brusquely orders the giants to think of another fee. They, however, are adamant. 'No fee but Freia,' Fasolt insists, as he and Fafner move towards her.

Froh (tenor) and Donner (bass) now enter in haste, Donner wielding his hammer, warning the giants to leave Freia alone. Violence is averted only when Wotan reminds Donner, and himself as well, that his spear gives protection to the pact. Freia now feels completely forsaken, and Fricka rails at Wotan's cruelty, when suddenly the arrival of Loge (tenor), to music representing his magic fire, alters the situation. Loge has examined the fortress, and assures Wotan that it has been well and sturdily constructed by the giants. This is not what Wotan wishes to hear. He reminds Loge that he, Wotan, is his only friend among the gods, the rest of whom distrust him. Loge had advised Wotan to agree to the giants' request for Freia by way of fee, and had assured him that, when the time to pay came, he, Loge, would find a way out of the bargain.

Loge denies that he made any such promise. He had merely agreed to give the most serious thought to the question of how to evade payment. The other gods now make their disgust with Loge quite clear, but Wotan counsels patience, for he knows that Loge's advice is all the more valuable when he delays in giving it. The crafty god of fire and deceit explains that he has not been idle, but has been searching throughout the world to find something which the giants might find preferable to the beauty of Freia. Wherever there was life, in the elements of water, earth and air, he had asked what might be prized above the delight and beauty of woman. A gentleness and warmth steal into the music at Loge's first mention of 'Woman's delight and worth'.

Everywhere, Loge's question was derided. But he did, at last, hear of one human being who had foresworn love and thus cared nothing for 'Weibes Wonne und Wert'. (Here the orchestra offers the Rhinegold motif in a minor key, followed by the renunciation motif.) The Rhinemaidens had told Loge their sad tale of how Alberich had robbed them of the Rhinegold, which he prized above the love of women, and Loge had promised them that he would pass on to Wotan their appeal to the god to help them recover the gold and restore it to its rightful place in the Rhine. 'You are mad, as well as malicious,' Wotan tells Loge. 'You see what trouble I am in, myself. How can I possibly help others?'

Fasolt and Fafner are interested to hear of this gold, for Alberich has often harmed them—they do not specify exactly how—and they are curious to know precisely why the gold is of value to him. Loge reveals that, although to the Rhinemaidens it is no more than a toy, if it were fashioned into a ring it would bestow supreme power upon its owner.

At this, even Wotan begins to be interested in the gold, and Fricka enquires if it would serve equally well as an adornment for women. Loge tells her that a wife could ensure her husband's fidelity if she wore the jewels which already the Nibelungs are forging from the gold. But he explains that the knowledge to fashion a ring depends upon the renunciation of love.

Hearing this, Wotan turns away in ill-temper, but Loge continues his line of thought. He points out that neither Wotan nor Fricka would have been likely to renounce love, and in any case they are too late. Alberich has already done so, and now he has the ring. However, since the ring has been forged by the loveless Alberich, it can be easily won now without one's having to curse love. When Wotan asks how, Loge answers, 'By theft.' His suggestion is that what a thief stole should simply be stolen from the thief. 'How can possessions be more easily acquired?' he asks, cynically.

Loge warns Wotan that Alberich is full of guile, and that any plan to wrest the ring from him would have to be very carefully worked out if the gold is to be returned to the Rhinemaidens. However, Wotan repeats that the Rhinemaidens are no concern of his, and Fricka, speaking as the guardian of wedlock, adds that she wishes to know nothing of that watery brood, for they have, to her sorrow, lured many a man away with their seductive sport. As Wotan now considers how best to act in the light of what he has learned from Loge, the other gods fix their eyes on him in mute suspense. Meanwhile Fafner, who has been conferring quietly with Fasolt, has come to the conclusion that the Rhinegold is more desirable than Freia. He tells Wotan that he and Fasolt will be satisfied to have the Nibelung's gold in payment, instead of Freia.

In exasperation, Wotan asks how he can give them what he does not possess, but Fafner merely informs Wotan that he and Fasolt will depart with Freia now, and return that evening with her. If the gold is not waiting for them, however, they will leave again, taking Freia with them forever. Fasolt and Fafner now leave, dragging the helpless Freia after them, while Loge, aided by the orchestra's descriptive account of their journey, narrates the giants' swift progress down to the valley, through the ford across the Rhine, to the boundary of the giants' domain, Riesenheim.

A pale mist, which is gradually becoming more dense, has begun to fill the stage. Pausing in his narrative, Loge glances at his fellow-gods, only to find that they have already begun to droop, the bloom fading from their cheeks and the light from their eyes. Freia's absence is, it seems, having an immediate effect. Loge realizes that this is due to the fact that the gods had not that day eaten Freia's apples, which are even now beginning to wither on the branches of the trees. Her absence hardly affects Loge, for he has always depended less on Freia and her apples, being only half as godlike as the others. But without her, he warns Wotan, the race of gods will die.

Roused to action, Wotan decides to descend immediately to Nibelheim, with Loge as his guide and counsel. Brushing aside Loge's question as to what the Rhinemaidens are to be told, he makes it clear that the return of Freia is what immediately concerns him. When Loge asks if they will take the route through the Rhine to Nibelheim, Wotan replies guiltily, 'Not through the Rhine.' He and Loge begin to descend through a sulphurous cleft in the rocks, Wotan assuring the other gods that they will be back by evening with the gold.

The sulphurous vapour issuing from the rocks now spreads over the entire scene, until the gods are lost from view. Wagner's stage direction requires a black cloud to arise from below, soon to clear and reveal a rocky chasm which continues to rise so that the theatre seems to be gradually sinking into the earth. The orchestra describes at length the journey of Wotan and Loge as they travel down into the lowest regions, the music at first taking on a hammering rhythm which represents the incessant toil of the Nibelungs as they slave to pile up treasure for Alberich. Soon the orchestra gives way to the sound of eighteen tuned anvils tapping out their incessant rhythm. As the clang of the anvils dies away, a subterranean chasm appears which fills the entire stage and seems to open into narrow clefts on all sides. This is Nibelheim.

Alberich enters, dragging his brother, the dwarf Mime (tenor), from a side cleft. Mime has been given the task of forging from the gold a Tarnhelm, or magic piece of headwear which will enable its wearer either to become invisible or to assume any shape he desires. Alberich berates his brother for not having yet completed his task, and the cringing Mime, who has actually finished making the Tarnhelm, which he was planning to keep for himself, is now forced to relinquish it. Seizing the Tarnhelm, Alberich puts it on his head and, as the orchestra's muted horns sound an appropriately mysterious motif, makes himself invisible and begins to give Mime a beating. After exulting in his new-found power, and gloating over the fact that his fellow-Nibelungs are now his slaves forever, Alberich departs.

Wotan and Loge enter to find Mime lying among the rocks, groaning with pain. Loge greets Mime gaily. 'Hey, Mime, you merry dwarf, what is it that torments you so?' he asks. He and Wotan listen, amused, as Mime complains to them of the treatment he has received from Alberich. The Nibelungs, Mime tells them, used to be a race of carefree smiths, creating ornaments and trinkets for their women, and forever laughing as they went about their work. Now, having cunningly wrought a ring for himself from the Rhinegold, Alberich has forced the other Nibelungs to toil for him alone. He, Mime, had been given the most difficult task of all: that of forging a magic helmet under Alberich's detailed instructions. Mime freely admits to Wotan and Loge that it had been his intention to keep the helmet, use it to snatch the ring from

Alberich, and thus become his brother's master instead of his slave.

When Loge asks what went wrong, Mime describes how he was outwitted by Alberich's superior cunning, and Loge assures Mime that he and Wotan will help him to free the Nibelungs from their misery. Alberich, now visible again, returns brandishing a whip and driving before him a crowd of Nibelungs laden with gold and silver handiwork which they heap together to form a large pile. Alberich, who has removed the Tarnhelm from his head and wears it hanging from his belt, shouts abuse at Mime and the other Nibelungs, threatening them with dire punishment if they do not keep at work to increase his wealth. Suddenly catching sight of Wotan and Loge, Alberich castigates Mime for having wasted his time chattering to a pair of tramps. Drawing the ring from his finger, he kisses it and holds it forth threateningly. 'Tremble with terror, abject throng, and obey the Lord of the Ring,' he orders Mime and the crowd of Nibelungs, who scuttle away in fear of him. As they run off, howling and shrieking, the orchestral sound reaches a fearsome climax.

Alberich demands to know what Wotan and Loge are doing in Nibelheim, and Wotan assures him that they have come to marvel at the great wonders of which they have heard. Alberich is suspicious, and is by no means won over by Loge's reminding him that, as god of fire, he has been of use in keeping Nibelheim's forges working. But slowly the dwarf is cajoled into boasting of the treasure he is hoarding, At this point the motif of the hoard, rising sequences on bassoons and bass clarinet, is heard for the first time. Loge cunningly remarks that he is impressed by the power of the ring which Alberich wears, but what would happen if it were to be stolen from him in his sleep? Alberich shows him the Tarnhelm and describes its magical properties, at which Loge expresses his scepticism. Alberich is easily persuaded to give a demonstration. Placing the Tarnhelm on his head, he utters the correct words and is instantly transformed into a giant serpent, while the tubas growl an appropriate motif.

Loge pretends to be terrified of the serpent but, when Alberich resumes his usual form, the wily god says that what would be really impressive, and most useful in escaping danger, would be to change oneself into something very tiny which could hide in a crevice. 'Nothing simpler,' replies Alberich, who immediately turns himself into a toad. 'Seize it quickly,' Loge instructs Wotan, who puts his foot on the toad. Loge grabs the Tarnhelm, and suddenly the gods have a squirming Alberich in their clutches. Binding him tightly, they begin their journey back to the earth's surface, dragging their prisoner with them.

The scene changes as before, but this time in reverse order, and the orchestra again describes the journey. The ring motif fades from a deafening *fortissimo* to a delicate *piano*, to be followed by the renunciation motif. The anvils are heard for a few bars as the way up to the outer world passes close by the forges where the Nibelungs are toiling. Later, the measured tread of the giants suggests that the arrival of Fasolt and Fafner is imminent or that they are at least in the minds of two of the travellers as they approach the surface of the earth. Other motifs, among them those of Valhalla and of Loge, are passed in review. At last, the landscape of the second scene reveals itself to view, shrouded in the pale mist which had descended upon it after the departure of Freia.

Wotan and Loge emerge from a chasm, dragging Alberich with them. Loge taunts the Nibelung, who responds with curses, while Wotan makes it clear to him that, if he is to be set free, he will have to pay a ransom: the Rhinegold and the hoard of treasure which has been increasing as the Nibelung slaves extract more and more of it from the earth. Alberich denounces the gods as a ravenous gang of thieves, but murmurs to himself that as long as he retains the ring he can bear to lose the treasure, for he will be able to amass it anew, and increase it. He will have learned a useful, if painful lesson from this temporary setback. 'Will you yield the treasure?' asks Wotan. Alberich agrees. 'Loosen my hand, and I'll summon it here,' he replies.

When Loge unties the rope from his right hand, Alberich kisses the ring and murmurs a command. He then tells Wotan that he has sent for the gold, and demands to be set free. 'Not until it has all been paid,' is the god's reply. Miraculously, within seconds the Nibelungs begin to emerge from the cleft in the rocks, laden with the gold which they pile up on the ground, while Alberich mutters of his shame that his slaves should see him captured and bound. 'Set the gold down there,' he orders them angrily. 'Don't look over here. Get back to work quickly when you've brought all the gold up, and don't let me catch you idling when I return.' After the gold has all been piled up, Alberich kisses the ring again, and holds it out menacingly. At this gesture, the Nibelungs shriek with terror and rush back into the cleft, accompanied by the orchestral climax with which they had been dispersed by Alberich in the previous scene.

Now that his ransom has been paid, Alberich asks Loge to give him back the Tarnhelm, but the wily god replies that this is part of the treasure, and tosses it on top of the piled-up gold. Alberich calls Loge a thief once again, but consoles himself with the thought that Mime can always be compelled to make another Tarnhelm. He now demands to be allowed to go. 'Are you satisfied?' Loge asks Wotan. 'Shall I set him free?' But Wotan has decided that the ring on Alberich's finger ought also to be part of the hoard, and he now insists on having it. 'Take my life, but not the ring,' Alberich cries in despair, to which Wotan answers chillingly, 'I require the ring. You may do what you like with your life.'

Alberich insists that his life is no more precious to him than the ring, but Wotan accuses him of having stolen from the Rhine the gold from which the ring was made. The dwarf, in turn, accuses Wotan of the basest hypocrisy. 'How gladly you yourself would have robbed the Rhine of its gold if you had possessed the power to forge a ring from it,' he observes bitterly. The argument is cut short by Wotan who, while Alberich is still bound, seizes him and pulls the ring from his finger. 'Now', Wotan exclaims, 'I possess what will make me the most powerful lord of all.' Loge sets Alberich free, dismissing him contemptuously: 'Slink off home. Nothing prevents you. You're free to go.'

Before leaving, Alberich indulges himself in a final outburst of hatred and rage. 'Am I now free, really free?' he asks bitterly. 'Then let me give you my freedom's first greeting.' Since the ring had come to him as a result of his cursing love, so now he curses the ring. 'May its magic bring death to all who wear it. Whoever owns it shall be consumed with care, and whoever does not shall be a prey to envy. All shall desire to possess it, but none shall find pleasure in it. Its owner shall guard it to no avail, for through it he shall meet his executioner!' In Alberich's outburst, two new motifs are heard: a syncopated phrase on cellos, horn and clarinets to represent the Nibelung's hatred, and Ex. 19 which is the curse motif, first sung by Alberich to the words 'As it came to me by a curse, so shall this ring be accursed.'

Ex.19

As Alberich scuttles away, the mist which has lain over the mountain-top begins to clear, and Loge observes that Fasolt and Fafner are approaching with Freia. Through the dispersing mist, Donner, Froh and Fricka appear, Fricka anxiously enquiring of Wotan whether he brings good news. 'By both craft and brute force we carried out our task,' Loge replies. 'There lies what will give Freia her freedom,' he tells Fricka, gesturing towards the gold. Fasolt and Fafner now enter with Freia, and Fricka hastens to her sister, only to be restrained by Fasolt, who will not allow Freia to be touched until he and his brother have received their payment. It is only with the greatest reluctance that Fasolt has agreed to return Freia. To be deprived of her, he asserts, will cause him such pain that, if she is to be banished from his mind, the hoard of gold will have to be heaped so high that it hides her completely from his sight.

With the return of Freia, the mountain-top has become completely bright again, and the aspect of the gods has regained its former freshness. However, a misty veil still hovers over the background, obscuring the distant castle, Valhalla.

The two giants now stick their staffs into the ground on either side of Freia, so that they give the measure of her height and breadth, and Loge and Froh hastily pile up the treasure between the staffs. Fafner complains that they are stacking it too loosely, and keeps finding crevices which he insists must all be filled. Wotan expresses to himself his awareness of the shame and disgrace he has brought on the gods, which Fricka is, in any case, not slow to point out to him. Finally, Loge announces that all the gold has been piled up. Fafner, however, is not satisfied. He can still see Freia's hair through a chink, and demands that the Tarnhelm be used to stop it up. Loge obliges, but it is now Fasolt's turn to register his dissatisfaction. He can still see Freia's lovely eyes through a crack in the pile of gold. Loge assures him that there is no more gold to give them, but Fafner points to the ring glistening on Wotan's finger.

Loge attempts to convince the giants that the ring belongs to the Rhinemaidens, to whom Wotan is going to return it. Wotan, however, ruins this story by exclaiming that he has no intention of relinquishing the ring. Despite the entreaties of Freia and Fricka, and even Froh and Donner, who exhort him to give up the ring, Wotan is adamant. Fasolt is about to drag Freia away when suddenly the scene darkens, and his brother restrains him. From a rocky cleft in the ground a bluish light breaks forth, in which Erda, the earth goddess, becomes suddenly visible. Erda half emerges from the cleft, stretching a hand warningly towards Wotan. 'Yield, Wotan, yield!' she commands. 'Avoid the curse of the ring. Its possession dooms you irredeemably to utter destruction.'

When Wotan angrily asks who this threatening woman can be, Erda identifies herself. She knows past, present and future. She is the primeval ancestress of the eternal world, whose three daughters, the Norns, were conceived before time began. She has appeared now because of the danger which threatens the world unless Wotan returns the ring to its rightful owners.

Erda's warning makes use of the Rhine motif which was first heard in the opera's prelude. The theme is inverted to become the motif of the twilight of the gods as she mentions the dark day which will dawn for them if she is not heeded. Ignoring Wotan's request that she reveal more, Erda sinks into the earth and disappears as the angry god attempts to detain her. Froh and Fricka with difficulty restrain him, while Donner calls to the impatient giants to wait and be paid. All now look attentively at Wotan, who at length emerges from deep thought to exclaim decisively, 'You are freed, Freia. Come back and restore our youth to us. Giants, take your ring.' He throws the ring on the hoard, and the giants release Freia, who hastens joyfully to the embrace of her fellow-gods.

As the giants set about gathering up their gold, a dispute breaks out between them. Fasolt demands his fair share, while Fafner maintains that his brother, having cared more for Freia than for the gold, deserves less. Fasolt appeals to Wotan to adjudicate, but the god turns away contemptuously from them both. Loge advises Fasolt to let his brother have the rest of the gold, but to hold on to the ring. Fasolt duly seizes the ring, whereupon a fight ensues which ends with Fafner clubbing Fasolt to death. Fafner then retrieves the ring and calmly resumes packing the hoard, which he drags down the mountainside as the gods watch, horrified. Wotan admits to himself the power of Alberich's curse as its motif sounds in the orchestra.

Wotan expresses a desire to seek out Erda, in order to learn how to dispel the anxiety which threatens to envelop him. He is instead persuaded by Fricka to lead the gods into their new home, Valhalla, although he observes that he has paid for its construction with unclean money. In a stirring passage, Donner calls upon his thunder and lightning to clear the sky, and as he swings his hammer the mist rises to reveal to reveal a rainbow-bridge stretching across the Rhine to the castle, which now gleams resplendently in the sunset. The orchestra paints the serene beauty of the rainbow, and the bridge is described lyrically by Froh. Wotan snatches up a sword which had formed part of the treasure but had been unaccountably left behind by Fafner, and sings in praise of the beauty and splendour of Valhalla (‘*Abendlich strahlt der Sonne Auge*’: The sun's eye gleams in evening light) while, at the climax, there is heard on the trumpet the sword motif (Ex. 20), which will later be associated with the hero on whom the gods will depend for their salvation. Wotan now leads Fricka, Freia, Donner and Froh across the bridge in slow procession to the castle.

Only Loge tarries behind. He considers that the gods are hastening to their end, and is half-inclined to transform himself back into the element of fire. ‘I'll think about it: who knows what I will do?’ he exclaims as he saunters off, carelessly, to follow the others.

Before the procession of gods can cross over the bridge, the plaintive voices of the Rhinemaidens are heard, bewailing the loss of their gold. Ordered guiltily by Wotan to silence them, Loge tells the Rhinemaidens that they must now bask in the gods' newly found radiance instead of the gold. The Rhinemaidens, however, continue to lament. The entry of the gods into Valhalla proceeds ceremoniously to the accompaniment of an orchestral postlude of great splendour, in which the sword motif, which will play so important a part in the later operas of *The Ring*, resounds portentously. The radiant and serene rainbow theme is reprised *fortissimo* as the curtain falls.

Ex. 20

TEN

Der Ring des Nibelungen: 2

Die Walküre

(The Valkyrie)

Music Drama in Three Acts

Dramatis personae
Brünnhilde   (soprano)
Siegmund   (tenor)
Sieglinde   (soprano)
Wotan   (baritone)
Hunding   (bass)
Fricka   (mezzo-soprano)
Gerhilde
Ortlinde
Waltraute
Schwertleite ⎱ (sopranos and
Helmwige ⎰ contraltos)
Siegrune
Grimgerde
Rossweisse

LIBRETTO by the composer

TIME: Legendary

PLACE: Hunding's hut; a rocky height; a rock-strewn mountain-top

FIRST PERFORMED at the Hofoper, Munich, 26 June 1870, with Sophie Stehle (Brünnhilde), Heinrich Vogl (Siegmund), Therese Vogl (Sieglinde), August Kindermann (Wotan), Kaspar Bausewein (Hunding) and Anna Kaufmann (Fricka), conducted by Franz Wüllner.

First performed as part of the complete *Ring* cycle, at the Festspielhaus, Bayreuth, 14 August 1876, with Amalie Materna (Brünnhilde), Albert Niemann (Siegmund), Josephine Schefsky (Sieglinde), Franz Betz (Wotan), Joseph Niering (Hunding) and Friederike Grün (Fricka), conducted by Hans Richter.

I

WAGNER'S life at Triebschen was being maintained through the aid of a pension from King Ludwig, which enabled the composer to live in great style, employing a large household staff of domestic servants and gardeners. There were also dogs, of course, and an aviary of rare birds, and in the gardens two peacocks, Wotan and Frigge.

After the première of *Das Rheingold* in Munich, in September 1869, Ludwig was keen to proceed with the production of the second opera in the cycle, *Die Walküre*. Wagner attempted to play for time, for the idea of a Festival Theatre (or *Festspielhaus*) in a provincial town where nothing but his own works would be performed had now really taken hold of him. He was determined to find a town where he, Wagner, could play the absolute monarch, a place which would be, in his words, 'a kind of Washington of art'. Slowly the idea for a Festival Theatre in the small Bavarian town of Bayreuth began to take shape. The principal advantage of Bayreuth, in Wagner's eyes, was that it possessed a baroque-rococo theatre, built in the mid eighteenth century for the Margrave Friedrich of Bayreuth, with a stage said to be the deepest in Germany. This sounded ideal, and would save Wagner, or someone, the expense of building a new theatre.

Meanwhile, however, there was nothing he could do to prevent a production of *Die Walküre* in Munich, for the ownership of performing rights in the entire *Ring* cycle had been made over to King Ludwig. The first performance of *Die Walküre* duly took place at the Hofoper in Munich on 26 June 1870. After a second performance, *Die Walküre* alternated with *Das Rheingold* for a further three performances of each opera. The new work was greeted enthusiastically by its audiences, and was favourably received by the press in general, though a note of dissent was sounded by the critic of the *Süddeutsche Presse*:

A drama of this kind ought to proceed in simple, sculpturally rounded tableaux. In order to make its point, in order even simply to hold the attention, it ought to be based on morally elevating motives, not on the most dubious aspects of sexual behaviour, not on weakness of character, infidelity and perjury on the part of gods and men alike. . . . In the first act the voices contrive to hold their own with the orchestra, which in the second act they succeed in doing only in places, whereas in the principal scene of the third act, the Ride of the Valkyries, it is barely possible to hear isolated shrieks from the singers through the tumult of the orchestra.

The first act, though for the most part wearyingly long-winded, possesses unity, and its finale glows with wonderfully sensuous colour. The second act drags, being broken into sections which only occasionally spring to life. The third act begins so deafeningly that total stupor would be ensured even if the rest were less long-winded than it is. The overall effect of the music is not agreeable: it is permeated by what one can only call pagan sensuality, and a straining for frivolous naturalism which swiftly suppresses any surges of nobler feeling that occasionally arise, and produces finally nothing but an enervating dullness.

Despite the failure of the *Süddeutsche Presse* to appreciate *Die Walküre*, the first performance of the work had been a triumphant success. Wagner's genius was now universally recognized, and the distinguished audience at the première, which included Brahms, Liszt, Saint-Saëns and the violinist Joachim, acclaimed the opera effusively. Its composer, of course, remained aloof at Triebschen, planning the first integral production of the complete *Ring* cycle.

II

BEFORE one attends a performance of *Die Walküre* it is useful, indeed virtually essential, to know something of what has occurred since those events which were portrayed in *Das Rheingold*. In his book *The Perfect Wagnerite*, Bernard Shaw offers the following helpful and lucid commentary, interpreting the action in terms of nineteenth-century socialism:

Wotan is still ruling the world in glory from his giant-built castle with his wife Fricka. But he has no security for the continuance of his reign, since Alberic may at any moment contrive to recover the ring, the full power of which he can wield because he has forsworn love. Such forswearing is not possible to Wotan. Love, though not his highest need, is a higher need than gold; otherwise he would be no god. Besides, as we have seen, his power has been established in the world by a system of laws enforced by penalties. These he himself must consent to be bound by; for a god who broke his own laws would betray the fact that legality and conformity are not the highest rule of conduct—a discovery fatal to his supremacy as Pontiff and Lawgiver. Hence he may not wrest the ring unlawfully from Fafnir, even if he could bring himself to forswear love.

In this insecurity he has hit on the idea of forming a heroic bodyguard. He has trained his love children as war-maidens (Valkyries) whose duty it is to sweep through battle-fields and bear away to Valhalla the souls of the bravest who fall there. Thus reinforced by a host of warriors, he has thoroughly indoctrinated them, Loki [Loge] helping him as dialectitian-in-chief, with the conventional system of law and duty, supernatural religion and self-sacrificing idealism, which they believe to be the essence of his godhood, but which is really only the machinery of the love of necessary power which is his mortal weakness. This process secures their fanatical devotion to his system of government; but he knows perfectly well that such systems, in spite of their moral pretensions, serve selfish and ambitious tyrants better than benevolent despots, and that, if once Alberic gets the ring back, he will easily out-Valhalla Valhalla, if not buy it over as a going concern. The only chance of permanent security, then, is the appearance in the world of a hero who, without any illicit prompting from Wotan, will destroy Alberic and wrest the ring from Fafnir. There will then, he believes, be no further cause for anxiety, since he does not yet conceive Heroism as a force hostile to Godhead. In his longing for a rescuer, it does not occur to him that, when the Hero comes, his first exploit must be to sweep the gods and their ordinances from the path of the heroic will.

Indeed, he feels that in his own Godhead is the germ of such Heroism, and that from himself the Hero must spring. He takes to wandering, mostly in search of love, from Fricka and Valhalla. He seeks the First Mother; and through her womb, eternally fertile, the inner true thought that made him first a God is reborn as his daughter, uncorrupted by his ambition, unfettered by his machinery of power and his alliances with Fricka and Loki. This daughter, the Valkyrie Brynhild, is his true will, his real self (as he thinks): to her he may say what he must not say to anyone, since in speaking to her he but speaks to himself. '*Was Keinem in Worten unausgesprochen*', he says to her, '*bleib es denn ewig: mit mir nur rat' ich, red' ich zu dir.*' [Those things I tell to no one remain then forever unspoken: I am only keeping my own counsel when I talk to you.]

But from Brynhild no hero can spring until there is a man of Wotan's race to breed with her. Wotan wanders further, and a mortal woman bears him twins: a son and a daughter. He separates them by letting the girl fall into the hands of a forest tribe which in due time gives her as wife to a fierce chief, one Hunding. With the son he himself leads the life of a wolf, and teaches him the only power a god can teach, the power of doing without happiness. When he has given him this terrible training, he abandons him, and goes to the bridal feast of his daughter Sieglinda and Hunding. In the blue cloak of the wanderer, wearing the broad hat that flaps over the socket of his forfeited eye, he appears in Hunding's house, the middle pillar of which is a mighty tree. Into that tree, without a word, he strikes a sword up to the hilt, so that only the might of a hero can withdraw it. Then he goes out as silently as he came, blind to the truth that no weapon from the armory of Godhead can serve the turn of the true Human Hero. Neither Hunding nor any of his guests can move the sword; and there it stays awaiting the destined hand.

III

THE orchestral prelude depicts a turbulent, elemental tempest, cellos and basses representing the relentless wind, with lightning and thunder in the brass. When the storm begins to die down, the curtain rises on the interior of a dwelling-place, in the centre of which stands the trunk of a huge ash-tree whose roots spread themselves over the ground. The upper part of the tree is cut off by the roof, the spreading boughs passing through openings made to fit them. Around the tree, a hut has been crudely built of logs, hung here and there with matting and woven cloth. In the foreground to the right is a hearth, the chimney of which passes through the roof. Behind the hearth is a small store-room, in front of which hangs a half-drawn curtain. At the back is the entrance door to the hut, and on the left another door leads to the sleeping-quarters. A table and some wooden stools comprise the only furniture in the hut.

It is early evening. As the storm outside continues to subside, the entrance door is flung open and Siegmund (tenor) enters hastily. Standing in the doorway for a moment he surveys the room, and then, exhausted, closes the door behind him, staggers to the fireplace and throws himself wearily down on a bearskin. 'Whoever owns this hearth,' he mutters to himself, 'I must rest here.' He sinks back, and remains motionless, sleeping. A moment later, Sieglinde (soprano) enters from the store-room. Startled to find a stranger lying in front of the fire, she approaches him, at which he awakens and asks for water. Sieglinde takes a drinking-horn from the wall, goes out, and returns with it filled with water which she offers to him.

Siegmund drinks gratefully. As he hands the horn back, his eyes fix upon Sieglinde with growing interest. He asks who it is who has so refreshed his spirit and delighted his sight, to which she replies that the hut belongs to Hunding, whose wife she is, and invites Siegmund to rest until Hunding's return. Siegmund tells her he is wounded. Harried by a pack of foes, he had been forced to flee when his spear and his shield were shattered. Sieglinde brings him a horn filled with mead, which he drinks. He then rises quickly, exclaiming that he must go. Bad luck pursues him everywhere, and he would not wish to bring it upon the woman who has befriended him. Sieglinde bids him stay. Bad luck, she says, can hardly be brought into the house in which bad luck already lives. Siegmund, deeply moved, remains standing. 'I named myself Wehwalt [Woeful],' he tells Sieglinde. 'I will wait for Hunding.' They stand, looking meaningfully into each other's eyes, until Sieglinde hears her husband leading his horse to the stable outside. She goes quickly to the door and opens it.

This first scene has been conducted entirely in recitative, but Wagner's recitative throughout *The Ring* is made up of countless melodic fragments. Here, the thematic material is all new, various motifs being introduced: most notably the love motif, which reveals to the audience the feelings which Sieglinde and Siegmund entertain for each other, before they have been expressed verbally.

Heralded by a phrase of dark foreboding in the horns, Hunding now enters armed with shield and spear, as the orchestra thunders forth his menacingly violent motif. Pausing at the threshold when he notices Siegmund, Hunding turns to Sieglinde with a look of stern enquiry. She explains that she had found Siegmund lying exhausted and, asked by Hunding if she had looked after him, admits that she has given him water and treated him as a guest. Siegmund, who has been watching Hunding intently, confirms that Sieglinde gave him shelter and a drink. 'Surely you will not chide your wife for that?' he asks. The taciturn Hunding replies, 'Sacred is my hearth. Treat my house as sacred, too.' Taking off his armour, he hands it to Sieglinde, who hangs it on a branch of the ash-tree. He orders her to serve a meal for the men, which she proceeds to do, bringing food from the store-room. Examining Siegmund's features keenly, Hunding observes to himself that the stranger looks remarkably like Sieglinde. 'That snake-like deceit gleams in his eyes as well,' he murmurs.

As they eat, Hunding asks Siegmund where he has come from, and why he is so exhausted. Siegmund's reply is evasive. He was chased through forests and fields by storms and deep distress. He knows neither where he has come from, where he is going, nor where he is now. He would be glad to know. Hunding informs him that to the west are the wealthy estates of the kinsmen who guard his honour. 'If my guest respects my honour,' Hunding continues, 'he will tell me his name.' Siegmund at first makes no reply, but gazes thoughtfully into space. Sieglinde, who has placed herself opposite Siegmund at the table, stares intently at him. 'If you are wary of trusting me,' Hunding says to Siegmund, 'tell your story to my wife here. See the eager questioning in her look.'

Embarrassed, Sieglinde confesses to Siegmund that she would dearly love to know who he is. Gazing into her eyes, he begins to speak. He cannot call himself Friedmund (Peaceful), and he wishes he were called Frohwalt (Cheerful), but his name has to be Wehwalt (Woeful). His father was Wolfe (Wolf), also known as Wälse, of the Volsung race. (In fact, he was Wotan in human guise.) At his birth, he had a twin sister, but he was prematurely bereft of both mother and sister. One day, while he was still a child, he and his strong, warlike father returned home from hunting to find their house burned to ashes and the body of Siegmund's slaughtered mother lying in the ruins. Of his sister there was no trace. The years of his youth Siegmund had spent in the woods with Wolfe, often pursued by enemies against whom they defended themselves bravely. 'A Wölfing [Wolf-cub] tells you this,' Siegmund concludes his recital, 'and to many I am known as "Wölfing".'

Hunding comments that Siegmund's narrative is a strange and brutal one. He fancies he has heard dark tales of that warlike pair, father and son, though he never knew the names Wolfe or Wölfing. When Sieglinde asks where his father is now, Siegmund continues his narration. Their enemies had begun a fierce attack upon them. Fleeing through the woods, he had become separated from his father. Later, when he searched for him, he found only a wolfskin in the forest. He left the woodland and took up the company of men and women, but wherever he went he was always unpopular. Whatever he thought right seemed wrong to others, and what seemed wrong to him was approved of by everyone else. He ran into feuds everywhere, and yearning for happiness he found only misery. This is why he can only be called Woeful.

'The Norn certainly granted you a wretched fate,' observes Hunding. 'No one is likely to welcome you as a guest.' But Sieglinde asks the stranger to tell them more. How did he come to lose his weapon? Siegmund now brings his story up to date. A young girl forced by her family into marriage with a man she did not love had called on him for help. He had fought and killed the brothers who had been oppressing her, but was surprised to find that the girl then lamented the death of her siblings. Their kinsmen rushed to the spot, thirsting for vengeance, but the girl would not move from the corpses of her brothers. He had protected her for as long as he could, until his spear and shield were destroyed in the fight. Unarmed and wounded, he saw the girl die, and then fled, pursued by a furious horde of her kinsmen. *'Nun weisst du, fragende Frau, warum ich Friedmund nicht heisse!'* (Now you know, questioning woman, why I do not call myself Peaceful), Siegmund concludes in a phrase of intense yearning, gazing at Sieglinde with a sorrowful fervour as the orchestra announces the motif of the suffering race of Volsungs.

Hunding makes it clear that those whom Siegmund had slaughtered were his kinsmen. He was called to avenge their deaths, but arrived too late. He has now returned home to find in his own house the villain who had fled. The laws of hospitality require him to offer Siegmund shelter for the night, but on the morrow they must fight. 'Arm yourself with stout weapons,' he advises Siegmund, 'for tomorrow you will pay for your crimes.' He orders Sieglinde to leave the room, prepare his night drink and wait for him to come to bed. Before she goes, Sieglinde attempts to indicate to Siegmund silently with her eyes a particular spot on the trunk of the ash-tree, while the sword motif from *Das Rheingold* (Ex. 20) sounds quietly in the orchestra, first on the bass trumpet and then on the oboe. A sudden violent gesture from Hunding drives

Sieglinde from the room. With a final warning to Siegmund to be on his guard the next day, Hunding follows Sieglinde into the bedchamber. The closing of a bolt is heard from within.

It has become quite dark. Siegmund sinks on to a bench by the fire, and begins to muse upon his misfortunes. He remembers his father telling him that, in his hour of greatest need, a sword would be given to him. He has come now, without a sword, to the house of his enemy, but it is the woman he has found there who has brought an enchanting fear to his heart. Where, he asks, is the sword that was promised to him? (*'Wälse! Wälse! Wo ist dein Schwert?'*: tenors have been known to hold the G flat of the first 'Wälse' and the G natural of the second for an unconscionably long time.) Suddenly Siegmund notices the firelight shining upon a spot in the trunk of the ash-tree which Sieglinde had been attempting to indicate to him, and where now the hilt of a sword gleams brightly. The sword motif bursts forth on the trumpet as though to give the distressed hero a helpful clue, but the firelight gradually sinks again, and Siegmund imagines it to have been the radiance of Sieglinde's gaze which she left behind her when she went out of the room.

When the fire is completely extinguished, and the room totally dark, the door at the side opens softly, and Sieglinde enters quietly, dressed in a white garment. She whispers to Siegmund that she has placed a sleeping-draught in her husband's drink, and urges the young hero to take the opportunity to flee and save his life. 'I am already saved by your presence,' a joyful Siegmund replies, but Sieglinde urgently directs his attention to the sword in the ash-tree, and proceeds to tell him how and why it was put there.

On the evening of her wedding-feast, when the miscreants who had kidnapped her gave her to Hunding as his unwilling bride, she had sat sadly while the men drank and caroused. At the height of the festivity a stranger, an old man dressed in grey, entered the hall. He wore his hat low on his forehead, hiding one of his eyes, but the glint of stern authority in his other eye brought fear to the hearts of all the men present. To Sieglinde alone, the stranger's eye seemed to suggest a sweet, regretful yearning, sorrow and solace combined. He glowered at the men assembled and, raising his sword, stuck it into the trunk of the ash-tree, right up to the hilt. The sword would belong to whoever could pull it from the tree.

None of the heroes present could wrest the sword from the tree-trunk and, although guests came and went, the sword remained deeply embedded in the tree. It was then, says Sieglinde, that she realised who the stranger must be, and for whom the sword was implanted in the tree. 'Oh, could I find that friend here and now,' she continues, 'my shame and dishonour would be avenged, and I would embrace him as a hero.' The musical interest has begun to quicken with Sieglinde's narrative (*'Der Männer Sippe sass hier im Saal'*: The kinsmen sat here in the hall), which is of such eloquence that it transcends its arioso form to become almost a *bel canto* aria. From this point to the end of the act Wagner's music is at its most beautiful, yet simultaneously obedient to the demands of the drama, hastening it forward with an urgent lyrical flow. It is in this final part of Act I of *Die Walküre* that Wagner's mature genius blazes forth in all its glory for the first time in *The Ring*.

Siegmund's reply to Sieglinde is to embrace her ardently, and declare his love for her. Suddenly, the outer door swings open to reveal a moonlit spring night. 'What was that? Who went out?' asks Sieglinde, startled. 'No one went, but someone has come,' replies Siegmund. 'It is the spring.' In an ecstatic aria (*'Winterstürme wichen dem Wonnemond'*: Winter storms have waned in the wondrous month) he sings rapturously of the passing of winter storms and the radiant approach of spring, which he describes as a brother (spring) in search of his sister (love). 'The sister as bride is freed by her brother. Joyfully the young couple greet one another, and love and spring are at last united,' he concludes in a state of jubilant elation.

'You are the spring for which I longed throughout the frosts of winter,' Sieglinde assures him in her answering aria, '*Du bist der Lenz*.' An urgent outpouring of love ensues, in which each speaks of having recognized the other as in a dream. 'In the stream I saw my own likeness, and now I see it again in you,' exclaims Sieglinde, to which Siegmund replies, 'You are the likeness that I hid in myself.' Once again Sieglinde asks him his name. Is he really called Woeful? 'Not now that you love me,' cries Siegmund. When he tells her that the real name of his father was not Wolfe but Wälse, Sieglinde exclaims 'If Volsa [Wälse] was your father, you are a Volsung, and it was for you that Volsa thrust his sword in the tree. Let me then name you Siegmund [Victor].'

Siegmund proudly accepts his name. As the sword motif rings out in a triumphant *fortissimo*, he approaches the tree with confidence and succeeds in drawing from it the sword, which he names 'Nothung' (Needful). Turning to Sieglinde, he tells her 'You see Siegmund, the Volsung, woman! He brings this sword as a wedding-gift, and thus weds the fairest of creatures.' 'If you are Siegmund, I am Sieglinde who longed for you,' she replies. 'You have won your own sister as well as the sword.' 'Wife and sister you shall be to your brother,' cries Siegmund. 'So let the Volsung blood increase.' The curtain falls on their passionate, incestuous embrace as the orchestra excitedly combines the motifs of the sword and of love.

Though it lacks the musical and dramatic unity of Act I, the second act of *Die Walküre* contains its share of dramatic episodes. A fiercely energetic orchestral prelude combines several by now familiar motifs. It might seem to suggest the feverish flight of the Volsung twins, but at its climax it introduces the rhythm of what will later become the accompaniment of the Ride of the Valkyries. The curtain rises on Act II to reveal a wild, rocky place. In the background a gorge slopes from below to a high ridge of rocks, from which the terrain sinks again to the foreground.

Wotan, fully armed and carrying his spear, addresses his daughter Brünnhilde, the Valkyrie, who is also fully armed. He orders her to fly to the aid of Siegmund and ensure that he wins his imminent fight with Hunding. Shouting her battle-cry ('Ho-jo-to-ho'), Brünnhilde springs from rock to rock up to the highest peak. (The Valkyrie's battle-cry has become so widely known out of context and used for purposes of satire so frequently that its intended effect is not easy now to achieve in performance.) After looking down into the gorge beyond, Brünnhilde calls to Wotan that his spouse, Fricka, is hastening furiously towards them. 'Be careful, Father,' she warns him, lightheartedly. 'Fricka approaches in her chariot drawn by rams. Look how she cracks the golden whip. The poor animals are bleating in fear. I take no delight in this kind of skirmish; the battles of men are more to my taste. I happily leave you to your fate.' And with a further whoop of her war-cry, the fierce Brünnhilde disappears down the slope.

Fricka, in a chariot drawn by two rams, comes up from the ravine to the top of the pass, where she stops suddenly, alights and strides impetuously towards Wotan, who mutters to himself, 'The same old storm, the same old trouble. Yet I must make a stand.' Chiding him for having hidden himself in the mountains in order to avoid her, Fricka tells Wotan that Hunding has sought her aid, and that she, the guardian of wedlock, has promised to avenge him and punish the behaviour of Siegmund and Sieglinde, an impudent, blasphemous pair who have wronged a husband. Wotan attempts to defend the lovers, but Fricka insists that he support her in upholding the sanctity of the marriage vow. She is shocked not only at the adultery committed by the lovers but also at its incestuousness, for she is well aware that Siegmund and Sieglinde are her husband's twin offspring, begotten of a mortal woman.

To Fricka's complaint that he himself has broken his marriage vows time and time again, prowling around the woods like a wolf and coupling with a vulgar human being, Wotan replies that Fricka has never learned to understand actions before they have become accepted. It is convention alone that she understands, whereas Wotan's mind is concerned with deeds not previously attempted. It is imperative, he tells her, that a hero be created who, free from divine protection, will be released from divine law, and thus able to perform the deed which, much as the gods need it, they are prevented by their godliness from doing.

Fricka accuses Wotan of trying to confuse her. Siegmund is no hero, she says, but a creature of Wotan's will. When Wotan insists that he has never sheltered Siegmund, who grew to manhood by himself in bitter sorrow, Fricka pounces on the weakness in his argument. 'Then do not shelter him today,' she orders Wotan. 'Take away the sword which you gave him.' Wotan claims that he did not give the magical sword to Siegmund, who had won it himself in adversity, but Fricka points out that it was Wotan who created the adversity. It was for Siegmund that he had thrust the sword into the tree-trunk, and it was Wotan's cunning which had led Siegmund to find the sword.

Defeated, Wotan agrees not to aid Siegmund in the fight, but Fricka is not satisfied. 'Look me in the eye,' she commands him. 'Don't try any tricks. Keep the Valkyrie away from him too.' When Wotan angrily replies that the Valkyrie, Brünnhilde, will no doubt do as she pleases, Fricka contradicts him. 'Not at all. She carries out your wishes alone. Forbid her to let Siegmund win.' Brünnhilde can be heard approaching as Fricka demands from Wotan his sacred promise that the Volsung, Siegmund, will die in the battle, and that her honour as Wotan's wife will be upheld. Most of this scene has been carried on in dramatic recitative. It is only at the end, when Fricka is confident that she has won her battle of wills with Wotan, that she is able to broaden her utterance into a serene *cantabile* ('*Deiner ew'gen Gattin heilige Ehre*': Your eternal consort's holy honour: Ex. 21). Reluctantly, Wotan gives his solemn oath.

Ex. 21

Dei-ner ew - gen Gat-tin   hei - li-ge Eh - re   be-schir-me heut' ihr Schild!

Brünnhilde has appeared with her horse on the rocky path above. On seeing Fricka, she slowly and silently leads her horse down the mountain path and hides it in a cave. She approaches as Fricka is leaving. 'Your war-father awaits you,' Fricka tells her. 'He will inform you what plans he has made.' As the goddess enters her chariot and drives quickly away, Brünnhilde comes forward anxiously to Wotan, who is now seated on a rock, sunk in a mood of the utmost dejection. When she enquires the cause of his gloom, he erupts in an outburst of shame, rage and despair, describing himself as the most joyless of all living creatures. With loving concern, Brünnhilde lays her head on his breast and embraces him, while Wotan, stroking her hair tenderly, begins to relate to her the history of the Ring.

Wotan's lengthy narration ('*Als junger Liebe Lust mir verblich*': When the delight of young love fled from me) takes in Alberich's theft of the gold from the Rhinemaidens, the subsequent theft of that gold from the Nibelung by Wotan himself with the aid of Loge's cunning, and his payment of the gold, including the magic ring, to Fasolt and Fafner, after receiving Erda's warning. Wotan describes to Brünnhilde how he descended into the bowels of the earth, anxious to learn more from Erda. 'I learned her secrets,' he recalls, 'but she exacted a fee from me.' The world's wisest woman had borne him Brünnhilde and eight other daughters, the Valkyries. The task of these warlike women was to fetch heroes from the world's battlefields to Valhalla, to strengthen the power of Wotan and the gods.

'But we have filled Valhalla with heroes,' Brünnhilde protests. 'I alone have brought you a multitude. What is it that troubles you?' Wotan confesses his concern that the ring, which is still in the possession of Fafner, should not come into the hands of Alberich who, with its power, could bring about the downfall of the gods whom he hates. Since he, Wotan, had made a pact with Fafner, he cannot himself snatch the ring away from him. 'I became a ruler through treaties,' he tells Brünnhilde, 'but now I am enslaved by those treaties.' Only a human hero not helped in any way by the gods, indeed a man opposed to the gods, can perform the deed which Wotan must avoid. How, he wonders, can he bring into existence such a person who, of his own accord, will do what he, the god, desires but must not demand?

When Brünnhilde suggests that Siegmund may be the hero whom Wotan seeks, her father explains to her why this is not so. In a mood of despair, he yearns for the end of everything, exclaiming bitterly that Alberich is working for that same end. Wotan tells Brünnhilde of a rumour he has heard, which is that Alberich had overpowered and seduced a woman who is now about to bear him a child. The god utters an ironic blessing upon Alberich's son.

Wotan's narrative has been long and, of necessity, repetitive, ranging as it does over the entire story of *The Ring*. There is no denying that, in performance, it can seem one of the work's more tiresome *longueurs*, and one might wish that Wagner had found a more musically and dramatically sophisticated method of conveying to audiences the god's dilemma at this point in the action.

Brünnhilde, puzzled, asks what she must do, and is instructed by Wotan to fight on the side of Fricka. When she pleads for Siegmund, whom she knows Wotan loves, he insists that she must bring about the death of Siegmund and procure victory for Hunding. Brünnhilde is bold enough to tell Wotan that she will never be turned against Siegmund by his two-faced orders, at which Wotan angrily reminds his daughter that she is nothing but an extension of his will. Her task that day is to see that Siegmund is defeated. As Wotan departs in a fury at her attempted rebellion, Brünnhilde stands for a long time in confusion. 'O, my poor Volsung,' she murmurs as she leaves slowly and reluctantly, 'I must forsake you in your hour of greatest need.' She ascends to the rocky pass, and looks down into the gorge, where she observes the approach of Siegmund and Sieglinde. After watching them for a moment, she goes into the cave to her horse.

A passionate agitation now enters the music as Siegmund and Sieglinde appear. Sieglinde attempts to hurry on, but Siegmund gently restrains her. Sieglinde is overcome with remorse at having, as she believes, brought shame and disgrace upon her brother and lover. Siegmund tries to comfort her, promising her that the husband whom she detests will soon die, but Sieglinde is alarmed by the horn-calls of Hunding and his followers not far behind them in the valley. She becomes hysterical, imagining she can see Hunding's dogs tearing Siegmund's flesh, and falls to the ground in a faint. Siegmund kneels beside her, cradling her in his arms as the love theme is remembered quietly in the orchestra. The musical interest of this scene is greatly enhanced by the rich colours and pulsating rhythms of the orchestra.

Slowly Brünnhilde, leading her horse by the bridle, emerges from the cave and moves solemnly forward, carrying her shield and spear in one hand. After pausing to observe Siegmund from a distance, she comes closer until she is standing on a ridge just above the spot where Siegmund is seated on the ground with Sieglinde's head in his lap. The solemn motif of death is heard quietly in the brass. After a further pause, Brünnhilde addresses Siegmund in musical phrases of solemn grandeur and beauty ('*Siegmund! Sieh auf mich*': Siegmund! Look on me), announcing that she has come to call him away. When he asks who she is, Brünnhilde tells him that those to whom she appears are doomed to die in battle, and that she will take him to Valhalla and to Wotan. Siegmund asks if he will find his father in Valhalla, and Brünnhilde assures him that he will. The Valkyries, too, will attend to his every wish. But when Siegmund asks if his sister Sieglinde will be able to accompany him to Valhalla, he is told that she must remain behind on earth. Brünnhilde's *Todesverkündigung*, or announcement of death, to Siegmund is one of the musical highlights of the opera.

Before responding, Siegmund bends softly over Sieglinde and kisses her gently on the brow, then he turns again to Brünnhilde. 'Greet Valhalla for me,' he says firmly. 'Greet Wotan, my father Wälse and all the heroes. Greet the beautiful daughters of Wotan. I will not follow you to them.' Brünnhilde attempts to explain to him that he has no choice. 'As long as you live,' she tells him, 'nothing can force you. But death, foolish boy, will force you. I have come here to announce your death to you.' Told that Hunding is to strike the blow that will kill him, Siegmund replies scornfully that Brünnhilde will need to threaten with stronger blows than Hunding's. He shows her his sword, boasting that he who made it promised victory.

Brünnhilde disconcerts him by replying that he who made the sword for Siegmund has now decreed his death, and will remove from the sword its magic power. Siegmund exclaims bitterly that he has been treated shamefully. If he must die, he prefers hell to Valhalla as his final destination, and he will first kill Sieglinde rather than lose her. Moved by his distress, Brünnhilde resolves to give Siegmund her support in the imminent fight. Promising him victory, she hastens away.

It has now grown dark. Heavy storm-clouds sweep across the sky, gradually covering the cliffs, the ravine and the rocky pass. Siegmund lays the still sleeping Sieglinde gently on the ground, and kisses her brow in farewell. Hunding's horn-call is heard, at which Siegmund starts up resolutely, drawing his sword, and hastens to the pass, where he disappears from view. Thunder and lightning awaken Sieglinde, who stares about her in growing terror as she hears the voices of Siegmund and Hunding defying each other.

The two men now appear, fighting. Flashes of lightning intermittently illuminate the scene, as Brünnhilde appears, seeming to float above Siegmund, protecting him with her shield. Just as Siegmund aims a deadly blow at Hunding, a glowing red light breaks through the clouds in which Wotan appears, standing over Hunding, holding his spear out to deflect Siegmund's blow. Brünnhilde, terrified at the sudden arrival of her father, retreats, and Siegmund's sword snaps on Wotan's outstretched spear. Hunding plunges his spear into Siegmund's breast, and Siegmund falls lifeless to the ground. Sieglinde swoons, but Brünnhilde hastens to her, lifts her on to her horse, and immediately disappears with her. Wotan, gazing sadly on the body of Siegmund, kills Hunding by contemptuously ordering him to go and kneel before Fricka. He then erupts in rage against his disobedient daughter, announcing his intention of inflicting a dreadful punishment upon her. As Wotan disappears in more thunder and lightning, the curtain quickly falls and a brief orchestral postlude leaves one in no doubt of the violence of his anger.

Act III takes place on the rocky summit of a mountain. On the peaks, four of the Valkyries, in full armour, are watching the return of their sisters, who arrive one by one, each with a slain warrior hanging over her saddle. Brünnhilde is the last of all to arrive, and when she does it is not a fallen hero whom she brings with her but an unconscious Sieglinde. The famous *Walkürenritt* (Ride of the Valkyries) with which the act begins combines the warlike theme of the Valkyries with Brünnhilde's battle-cry. Its dotted rhythm and pulsating energy contribute to an exciting opening scene.

Brünnhilde appeals to her sisters for assistance, telling them that she is being pursued by the furious Wotan. She explains what has happened, but the Valkyries are too afraid of their father to help her.

Recovering consciousness, Sieglinde exclaims that she needs no help. Death is all she craves. She would far rather have been struck down by the same weapon that killed Siegmund. However, when Brünnhilde tells her that she is carrying Siegmund's child, her attitude changes and she begs the Valkyries to save her and her child. Wotan is rapidly approaching, so Brünnhilde advises Sieglinde to escape quickly and leave her to face the god's wrath. The Valkyries tell of a forest to the east, where Fafner guards the ring and the Nibelung treasure: Wotan dislikes the place, and never ventures there. Brünnhilde gives Sieglinde the broken pieces of Siegmund's sword, which she had gathered up from the battlefield, and tells her to keep them for her son to forge anew. She, Brünnhilde, names the as yet unborn child 'Siegfried' (peaceful in victory). The motif which will be associated with Siegfried is sung by Brünnhilde and repeated by the horns. The eight bars of passionate melody with which Sieglinde responds ('*O hehrstes Wunder*': O greatest wonder: Ex. 22) are among the most affecting in the entire *Ring*. They will be heard only once more, in the closing scene of the entire cycle.

Sieglinde flees just in time, for Wotan now arrives calling for Brünnhilde, whom her sisters have hidden in their midst. The Valkyries plead with their father to deal leniently with her, but Wotan chides them as a soft-hearted bunch of females and accuses Brünnhilde of cowardice in attempting to evade her punishment. At this the music suddenly softens, and a chastened Brünnhilde steps forward humbly, asking Wotan to pronounce judgement on her.

Wotan makes it clear to his favourite child that she has chosen her own punishment. Though she existed only as the agent of his will, she has acted against his will. 'I made you bearer of my shield, but you raised that shield against me,' he tells her sorrowfully. 'I made you the disposer of fates, but you disposed fate against me. I made you the inspiration of heroes, but you inspired a hero to act against me.' Wotan pronounces his sentence sadly, to the theme with which Brünnhilde had announced Siegmund's death to him. Banished from his sight, Brünnhilde is no longer to be a Valkyrie. She will lie on the mountain-top confined in sleep, and will belong to the first man who awakens her.

At this, Brünnhilde's sisters exclaim in horror, and plead with Wotan to rescind his dreadful sentence. But Wotan is adamant. 'She will never again ride with you through the air on horseback,' he tells them. 'Her youth will wither, she will minister to the needs of the husband who wins her, and she will grow old sitting and spinning by the fire, the butt of all jests.' He threatens with the same fate any of her sisters who dare to plead for her. The terrified Valkyries scatter in flight, and Brünnhilde sinks to the ground at Wotan's feet.

After a long pause, Brünnhilde begins to address her father, at first timidly but later with increasing firmness. Was her offence really so shameful, she asks, that she must be so dishonoured? Did she not merely act as Wotan himself secretly desired to act? Was his command to destroy Siegmund not given against his will, at the insistence of Fricka? The music of Brünnhilde's pleading is of a heart-breaking tenderness. But it is precisely because she dared to do what he, the god, could not do that Wotan cannot forgive her.

Brünnhilde begs that, if she must be the slave to a mere human, her master may be no cowardly boaster but a real hero. She prophesies that the greatest hero of all will be born to the Volsung race, at which Wotan angrily interrupts that he has turned against the Volsungs as well as against Brünnhilde. He will offer no protection to Sieglinde or to the child she is to bear.

Wotan tells Brünnhilde that she is now about to be enclosed in deep sleep. At her urging, however, he agrees to encircle her with a ring of magic fire, so that only a fearless hero will be likely to break through it and awaken her. In the orchestra, mysterious chords now introduce the motif of Brünnhilde's magic sleep. Solemnly, Wotan embraces his child for the last time, taking away her divinity with a kiss. His farewell to her ('*Leb' wohl, du kühnes, herrliches Kind!*': Farewell, valiant and glorious child) is immensely affecting. Brünnhilde sinks down in sleep, and Wotan covers her with her shield. Summoning Loge, the god of fire, he conjures up flames from the earth which completely surround the rock on which Brünnhilde lies, while the orchestra conjures up the glorious magic fire music. As Wotan departs slowly and sorrowfully with one final backward look at the daughter he loves most, the fire music begins to fade, and the curtain falls.

DESPITE its occasional *longueurs*, *Die Walküre* is a marvellously rich opera. In *Das Rheingold*, most of the excitement was to be found in the orchestra: *Die Walküre*'s orchestral writing is often thrilling, but by now Wagner has found a way to integrate his voice parts into the overall structure without sacrificing their lyrical independence. Like its predecessor, *Die Walküre* is still primarily a work for solo voices: it is not until the last act of *Siegfried* that we shall hear a real duet, and we shall have to wait until *Götterdämmerung* for the introduction of the chorus. There is, however, an impressive ensemble in Act III of *Die Walküre* when the eight Valkyries are heard together, first in exaltation at the beginning of the act, and then later in fear and dismay.

Die Walküre is best experienced as part of a complete performance of *The Ring*, but it is also popular enough (and sufficiently self-contained) to be frequently staged on its own. Of the four *Ring* operas, it is the one which stands up most firmly outside the context of the tetralogy.

In 1881, when *Die Walküre* was first heard in London, the nature of the relationship between the twin siblings Siegmund and Sieglinde was found distressing by the puritanical British temperament. The critic of *The Era*, taking a short view of this segment of the intensely moral *Ring*, wrote:

> ... The subject may be simply told. It is nothing less than a sudden impulse of sensual passion between brother and sister. There is no mistake about it, no excuse that the relationship is unknown, for the hero openly requests

Sieglinde to become 'his sister and his bride', which the lady consents to without the slightest hesitation, and the climax of the first act is when the guilty and incestuous pair agree to fly at once; the act closing with a duet, the music of which is evidently written to suggest animal passion in its utmost excess.

We have told this brutal and degrading story in as few words as our disgust will permit, but it is not thus told in the scene itself. All the resources of musical, scenic, and histrionic art are employed to make this sensual incident more striking. It is not lightly passed over—not referred to as some painful but necessary incident introduced for the elaboration of the story, but it is brought forward in the most prominent manner possible, as we could prove if we chose to offend the taste of our readers by quoting the libretto. A composer must have lost all sense of decency and all respect for the dignity of human nature who could thus employ his genius and skill to heighten and render more effective a situation which should never again, if our authorities exert their power, be witnessed upon the English stage.

The critic goes on to admit that, although Wagner's lack of taste is lamentable, he is able to supply fine music when the mood takes him. His conclusion, however, is that, despite much in the score that is of musical value, 'nothing can justify the representation of such a story in public. Immoral and unspeakably degrading, it should have no place in true art.'

ELEVEN

Der Ring des Nibelungen: 3

Siegfried

Music Drama in Three Acts

Dramatis personae
Siegfried   (tenor)
Mime   (tenor)
Wotan (disguised as the Wanderer)   (baritone)
Alberich   (bass-baritone)
Fafner (disguised as a Dragon)   (bass)
Erda   (contralto)
Brünnhilde   (soprano)
A Woodbird   (soprano)

LIBRETTO by the composer

TIME: Legendary

PLACE: Various parts of a forest; the foot of a mountain; the Valkyrie's rock on the mountain-top

FIRST PERFORMED as part of the complete *Ring* cycle, at the Festspielhaus, Bayreuth, 16 August 1876, with Georg Unger (Siegfried), Karl Schlosser (Mime), Franz Betz (the Wanderer), Karl Hill (Alberich), Amalie Materna (Brünnhilde), Luise Jaïde (Erda) and Lilli Lehmann (a Woodbird), conducted by Hans Richter.

I

TWO months after the Munich première of *Die Walküre* in June 1870, which he did not attend, Wagner married Cosima. He had completed the composition of *Siegfried* and was already at work on *Götterdämmerung*, from which he temporarily turned aside to compose the *Siegfried Idyll*, a charming piece for small orchestra which he wrote for Cosima's birthday. It was given its first performance on the staircase at Triebschen on Christmas Day.

The following year, to celebrate the defeat of France in the Franco-Prussian War, and the founding of the German Empire, Wagner composed the emptily bombastic *Kaisermarsch* (Emperor March), and wrote a poem, 'To the German Army Outside Paris', which he sent to Bismarck, who wrote from Versailles to thank him. Wagner also completed at last the autobiography which he had begun writing six years earlier. His thoughts now turned increasingly to the idea of a Wagner Festival Theatre, and in May 1871, a visit to Bayreuth having convinced him that the old baroque opera house there would not be suitable for his purposes, the composer formally announced the first Bayreuth Festival and the building of a theatre to house it:

The Stage Festival, *Der Ring des Nibelungen*, will be performed complete, under my personal supervision, on three [sic] consecutive evenings, and will be repeated twice in the two weeks immediately following. The town chosen for the performances is Bayreuth, and the date will be during the summer of 1873. A theatre will be built especially for the performances, the interior construction of which will be in exact accordance with my particular requirements, while its durability and its exterior appearance will depend on the means that are made available to me. I anticipate that the building, and the installation of the special equipment necessary for the performance of my Stage Festival, will occupy the period from the autumn of this year, 1871, to the spring of 1873. After that, the first-rate singers and musicians whom I shall by then have selected will assemble in Bayreuth to rehearse the festival work for the following two months.

Fifteen hundred comfortable seats will be provided for those patrons and benefactors of my undertaking who will have contributed the appropriate finance for the execution of my project, through the medium of a Society of Friends in whose hands I place only this part of the necessary arrangements. These Friends will be known as Patrons of the Stage Festival in Bayreuth, but the realization of the undertaking itself will be entrusted to my experience and skill, and to my endeavours alone. The actual property acquired for this undertaking shall be regarded as being at my disposal for whatever future uses may seem to me appropriate to the aims and to the ideal nature of the enterprise.

I leave all details of the action to be taken in order to raise the necessary finance entirely in the hands of those close friends who have expressed the wish to take this burden upon themselves, and whose endeavours I gratefully salute as an encouraging proof of energy and devotion in the service of German art and, in equal measure, of unanimous confidence in myself.

A year or two earlier, Wagner had met Nietzsche. The twenty-four-year-old professor of classical philology at the University of Basle became a frequent visitor at Treibschen, and it was under the influence of Wagner that he wrote his first book, *The Birth of Tragedy from the Spirit of Music*. The composer, however, made clear to his new young disciple his displeasure that the book was not entirely about him.

Plans for the building of the Wagner theatre at Bayreuth progressed slowly, due to financial difficulties. People were not rushing to donate money to the enterprise as lavishly as the composer had expected them to. In due course, however, though seriously behind schedule, the theatre was completed. Wagner had also decided that a villa should be built in Bayreuth for himself and Cosima. King Ludwig, angry and disappointed that Wagner was obviously never going to return to Munich to live, and not at all appeased by being told that Bayreuth was, at least, within his kingdom of Bavaria, threatened to cut off Wagner's allowance, which, incredibly, in view of the shabby treatment accorded the King by the composer, was still being paid regularly. But Ludwig relented, and even provided additional funds to enable the construction of the Villa Wahnfried to proceed.

Wagner insisted that the theatre was to be a purely temporary structure. 'It would please me', he wrote to a friend in 1872, 'it if were made entirely of wood, like the gymnasia and the halls for the song contests, with no further solidity than to prevent it from collapsing.' (He got his way, and the 'temporary' theatre still stands, though in recent years the wooden beams which comprised the timber frame of the building have been replaced by ferro-concrete.) The foundation stone of the theatre was laid on 22 May 1872, Wagner's fifty-ninth birthday, but its construction took four years. It was completed only a few months before the opening festival performance in the summer of 1876.

While the theatre was still being built, Wagner wrote an essay describing it:

To explain the plan of the Festival Theatre now in course of erection at Bayreuth, I believe I cannot do better than to begin with the principal need I felt, that of rendering the mechanical source of the music, i.e. the orchestra, invisible. This one requirement led step by step to a total transformation of the auditorium of our neo-European theatre.

The reader of my previous essays already knows my views on the concealment of the orchestra, and, even should he not have thought so before, I hope that a subsequent visit to the opera will have convinced him of my rightness in condemning the constant visibility of the mechanism for tone production as an aggressive nuisance. In my essay on Beethoven I explained how fine performances of ideal works of music may make this evil imperceptible at last, through our eyesight being neutralized, as it were, by the rapt subversion of the whole sensorium. With a dramatic representation, on the contrary, it is a matter of focussing the eye itself upon a picture. That can be done only by leading it away from the sight of bodies lying in between, such as the technical apparatus for projecting the picture.

Without being actually covered in, the orchestra was therefore to be sunk so deep that the spectator would look right over it, immediately upon the stage. This at once applied the principle that the seats for the audience must be ranged in gradually ascending rows, their ultimate height to be governed solely by the possibility of a distinct view of the scenic picture. The usual system of tiers of boxes was accordingly excluded; had they begun close to the stage itself, their very height would have made it impossible to prevent their occupants looking straight down into the orchestra. Thus the arrangement of our rows of seats acquired the character of an antique amphitheatre. However, the actual form of the latter, with arms stretched out on either side beyond the full half-circle, could not be seriously contemplated, for the object to be plainly set in sight was no longer the chorus in the orchestra, surrounded for the greater part by that ellipse, but the 'scene' itself. That 'scene', displayed to the Greek spectator in the merest low relief, was to be used by us in all its depth. . . .

A difficulty arose in respect of the side walls of the auditorium. Unbroken by any tiers of boxes, they presented a flat expanse, to be brought into no plausible agreement with the rows of seats. The famous architect [Gottfried Semper] who was first entrusted with the task of building the theatre in monumental fashion had all the resources of his art to draw upon, and made so admirable a use of the noblest renaissance ornament that the bare surface was transformed into a perpetual feast for the eye. But for our provisional theatre at Bayreuth we had to renounce all idea of such adornment, which has no meaning unless the material itself be precious, and were once more faced with the question of how to treat these walls that stood at variance with the actual space for holding the audience. . . .

Now, to mask the blanks immediately in front of our double proscenium, the ingenuity of my present adviser had already hit upon the plan of throwing out a third and still broader proscenium. Seized with the excellence of this thought, we soon went further in the same direction, and found that, to do full justice to the idea of an auditorium narrowing in true perspective toward the stage, we must extend the process to the whole interior, adding proscenium after proscenium until they reached their climax in the crowning gallery, and thus enclosing the entire audience in the vista, no matter where it took its place. For this we devised a system of columns, answering to the first proscenium and broadening with the blocks of seats they bounded. They simultaneously disguised the square walls behind them and admirably hid the intervening doors and steps. With that we had settled our internal arrangements. . . .

By treating in the very baldest way our task of erecting an outwardly artless and purely temporary theatre, to be placed on a high and open site, I believe we have at the same time reduced the problem itself to its plainest terms. It now lies naked and distinct before us, the tangible diagram of what a theatrical structure should outwardly express if it has not a common purpose but an ideal one to reveal. . . . There may it stand, on the fair hill in Bayreuth.

II

THE Bayreuth Festival Theatre opened in August 1876, with the first complete performance of *Der Ring des Nibelungen*, two parts of which—*Das Rheingold* and *Die Walküre*—had already been staged in Munich, in 1869 and 1870. The first cycle of performances was given between 13 and 17 August and was followed by two further complete cycles. A vivid description of the town as the day of the opening performance approached is given by Joseph Bennett, music critic of the *Daily Telegraph*:

Bayreuth is, of itself, a negation; a stranger may wander long about its streets without coming into contact with anything suggestive of the living, active, and positive world, unless, indeed, he encounter a big Bavarian soldier. Of all dull towns I imagine Bayreuth, in its normal state, to be the dullest. Moreover, the utter sluggishness of the place has its impression heightened by plentiful signs that, once on a time, there was life here. In the fine old days when Germany grew princes wholesale, Bayreuth had its little court and was a little capital. The potentate whose sway it owned called himself, I believe, a Margrave, and contrived, somehow or other, to keep up a considerable state. He built palaces, whereof two stand in the town, and, though used for a variety of purposes, are decaying with a fit air of dignity. The third, some two miles off, serves to perpetuate the memory of its builders, much as the Brighton Pavilion immortalises our own George the Fourth.

But these edifices are by no means the only signs of Bayreuth's dead-and-gone grandeur. The place abounds in fine old houses; its streets are adorned with some very respectable statues—that, among others, of Jean Paul

Richter, who lived and died here—while numerous fountains are continually pouring out streams of clear water. These fountains, by the way, are a distinctive feature of the town which they serve to ornament as well as to bless. Of course they trace their origin to the Margraves, and the question at once arises why it was that the tyrannous old German princes expiated their bad ways by providing so much water. Once on a time they built churches, but the logic of that course is clear enough, and unless they saw in the 'pure element' a symbol of the 'mystical washing away of sin' I cannot account for the fountains. The Bayreuth churches, let me add, are not remarkable, and it is to be feared that the Margraves cared very little about them.

On the whole, the town has a stately and dignified look, but is woefully faded. It is a tenth-rate Versailles, crossed with a sleepy provincial borough. Sleepy! I should think so, indeed! Even now, when the place has been galvanized into prodigious activity, one can easily distinguish Bayreuthers from the strangers. The native and his favourite beast of draught, the ox, are well matched, both going dreamily through life at the slowest possible pace, and with a constant disposition to lie down and ruminate.

Just now, as I have said, Bayreuth is uncommonly alert, having actually two things on its mind at once—making money in abundance out of the strangers within its gates, and spending a little economically in decoration. The first of these operations Bayreuth will certainly carry out with success, and, as regards the second, a convenient decision has been arrived at to the effect that there is something exhilarating in the appearance of the fir which chances to abound on the neighbouring hills. The result is that Bayreuth has a fir eruption all over it. Great branches, stuck in the ground to resemble trees, line the pavements—or rather the space where the pavements should be—festoons of fir cover the fronts of the houses, and wreaths of the same cheerful material, made more lively by paper flowers, are stuck wherever room can be found for them. Adding to this a crowd of poles, from which in due time—for the Bayreuther is careful of his bunting—flags will fly, and it must be granted that the inhabitants, considering their normal sleepiness, have bestirred themselves to some purpose, even though, like John Gilpin's spouse, they do not overlook the value of 'a frugal mind'.

The most conspicuous figure in Bayreuth life just now is made by strangers who swarm all over the town and are contemplated by the natives with placid wonderment. They are certainly worth contemplating, as being a remarkable crowd of curious people. Let me frankly say that never before did I see so many short-sighted folk, with long hair and 'loud' hats, gathered together in one place. The ambitious literary youth of England used to imagine an intimate connection between genius and the Byron collar, but they had a model which these Wagnerites lack. Why, then, is it that faith in the 'Art Work of the Future' goes in company with spectacles, long hair, and funny head-gear? I confess I cannot tell. There must be a reason, else hardly would the phenomenon manifest itself in men who have come from all points of the compass and have nothing in common save their faith.

An eager race are they, and a splendid contrast to the slow Bayreuther. You may see them flying along the road that conducts to the Wagner Theatre, 'larding the lean earth' *à la* Falstaff, as they go. Or you may see them racing about the streets, stopping suddenly whenever some fresh manifestation of Wagner is made by a shop window, which means stopping every few yards, for upon the man who has given Bayreuth fame Bayreuth, in turn, bestows whatever it can of honour. The whole town is, so to speak, given up to him, and you see him everywhere. In photographs and statuary, on pipe-bowls and tobacco-boxes, on toilet ornaments and album covers— on countless things, indeed, appear the well-known face and form. Nor is this all. Wagner's music floats about the streets. Here a soprano may be heard declaiming at the top of her voice some passage from the *Nibelungen*; here a tenor, and there a bass, labour hard and lustily; or, perhaps, a violinist has got up among the harmonics, or a pianist is hammering out a succession of 'diminished sevenths' which clash against each other in their search for a key never to be found. I declare to you that I have not yet heard in Bayreuth a single quiet melodic phrase. Music, here and now, is nothing if not 'sound and fury'; nor do musicians deserve the name unless they rave and roar. Well, these are times when the world lives fast and has sharp emotions.

Plus ça change . . . At any rate, it would appear that commercialization and what is today vulgarly known as 'hype' did not originate in the United States of America in the mid-twentieth century.

Charles Villiers Stanford, the Irish composer, was present at this first Bayreuth Festival, which he wrote about many years later in his memoirs:

The performances in 1876 were on the whole excellent. The best available singers had come forward to help. Materna, Lilli Lehmann, Brandt were chief among the women; the first masterly, the second winning, the third a genius of the first order. . . . The most amazing feat at the performance was due to her. The singer of the solitary Valkyrie at the close of the first act of the *Götterdämmerung*, a long and exacting scene, fell ill. Brandt, at a moment's notice, sang the complicated part, and so well that not a trace of unfamiliarity or insufficient rehearsal was discernible. The average ability of the women singers was good throughout.

The same cannot be said of the men. Their ranks contained some great, some passable, and some inferior specimens. Amongst the tenors Vogl was easily pre-eminent, but he was unfortunately heard too seldom. Niemann was a great actor, but his voice was nearly gone; he was but a shadow of his former great self. Unger, the Siegfried, who was popularly supposed to be Wagner's especial choice, was unequal to the part, and did not show the ability, either vocal or histrionic, necessary for it. Of the character parts, Mime and Alberich were supremely well filled. Amongst basses, Betz was admirable; so was Gura, in a provokingly small part. But many others were rough, though large of voice. The older singers were well trained; the younger not.

As a principle Wagner seemed to me to differ from his predecessors by portraying ugly characters by ugly music . . . looking back at the work over forty-five years has not changed my opinion. The criminal colouring which Beethoven gave to Pizarro without a note of ugliness, was not there. The Rhinedaughters were beautiful, but Alberich was ugly. It may be a matter of temperament, but I dislike it, as I should the inferior painting of a hateful subject. Verdi has proved, in his characterization of Iago, that it is possible to combine villainy with beautiful music. I did not note this, however, in the *Nibelungen*.

The theory of leitmotives was, to my mind, carried too far, even to annoyance. The motives were so interwoven that they were often of no avail. Less of them would have effected more, and would have heightened their value. As it is, the plethora of over-done phrases of similitude, so valuable in themselves when used with economy, is threatening to destroy what is inherent in opera and which, properly used, is essential to characterization and to situation. Piled as they are in the *Nibelungen* they may give satisfaction to curious porers over the score, but they fail to grip the listener, and often to attract his attention, or to give characterization when it is most needed. In lesser quantities, as Wagner used them in the *Dutchman* and even in the *Meistersinger*, they carry a fuller conviction to the hearer.

The atmosphere in the Festival Theatre on its opening night was described by the critic Isidor Kastan in the *Berliner Tageblatt*:

It must have been about half-past six when the auditorium began to fill. No one who had read detailed accounts of the interior, which had been published widely for months on end, could have been able to avoid a sensation of intense disappointment. It was not that we did not consider the appearance of the interior agreeable, with its rather steeply raked rows of seats, and the lines of Corinthian columns framing the stalls. It was merely that, after the exaggerated descriptions, one had expected something more astonishing. And this was certainly not what we saw. To describe the shouts

226

of the enthusiasts in more sober language, it must be said that we find ourselves in an auditorium which has been constructed and furnished in a manner perfectly suitable for its purpose. Like most theatres, it contains some good seats and some bad seats. Again, like most theatres, it is really quite warm.

Now let us look around at the other members of the audience. We must hurry, however, for the minutes are numbered, and on the stroke of seven an almost total darkness will descend upon the auditorium. Berlin, the capital of our empire, has sent a comparatively large contingent of spectators and distinguished characters of every kind. All those 'music of the future' Amazons, Valkyries in mufti one might call them, are present and accounted for. Frau Marie von Schleinitz seems to be floating on a sea of ecstasy, while her husband, His Excellency the Minister, is able to view the proceedings somewhat more coolly. Indeed, one almost has the impression that a trace of sarcasm plays about his lips. Countess Dankelmann looks around her, as though confident of victory. In the very centre of the auditorium, a group of really astonishingly beautiful women is assembled. One's eyes are inevitably drawn to the delicate form and lovely features of our Countess Dönhoff. Not far from her, we notice the proud, statuesque Hildegard von Usedom, a really classical, Junoesque apparition.

Over there our glance rests upon a lady who, it seems, would prefer not to be seen. It is Marie Seebach. Niemann, our Heldentenor, and his dainty wife, Frau Hedwig Raabe, wave to us, as dear friends from our home town on the green banks of the Spree. The authentic atmosphere of Berlin, however, hovers over one particular corner, where Dohm, Scholtz, Lindau, Ehrlich and others are all met together. . . . Among all these people, the most interesting face, the focus of everyone's attention, is that of Franz Liszt. The extraordinary combination of worldly elegance and priestly demeanour, the flowing grey hair and the venerable black coat of clerical cut, give his everlasting genius a uniquely attractive charm.

However, we are abruptly torn from these musings by an unusual fanfare signifying that the German Emperor has just entered the theatre. All eyes turn to the Royal Box. Kaiser Wilhelm in civilian clothes is certainly an unfamiliar sight to us Berliners and no doubt to most Germans. We are not used to seeing him in anything other than the uniform of a General. In fact, several seconds passed before the audience recognized the Emperor. But then a storm of applause broke out, suddenly filling the huge auditorium like a hurricane. 'Long live Kaiser Wilhelm' rang out, again and again. It seemed that the cheers would never end.

The Emperor stepped forward to the edge of his box, and bowed to the audience in all directions, with a charming smile. As a conscientious reporter I must not omit to report that the waters at Bad Gastein have truly rejuvenated our Emperor. By the youthfulness of his appearance and the firmness of his movements, the Emperor defies his great age. He has become the real darling of the ladies in these last two days. Wherever he goes, one hears such exclamations as 'God, what a handsome man!' and 'I could throw myself into his arms!'

There is no doubt that the first complete performance of *Der Ring des Nibelungen* was an enormous success. There were, of course, mishaps in stage management, and some singers were distinctly better than others. The neck of the dragon Fafner, in *Siegfried*, failed to arrive at Bayreuth in time, and it was discovered only later that the English firm which constructed it had sent it by mistake to Beirut. But the applause at the end of the first cycle was tremendous. When Wagner appeared in front of the curtain to acknowledge it, he told his audience, 'You have just seen what we can do. Now it rests with you. If you desire it, we shall have art!'

The first two operas, *Das Rheingold* and *Die Walküre*, were familiar to many members of the audience. *Siegfried*, however, was being heard for the first time. But the entire cycle was new to the Norwegian composer Edvard Grieg, who had come to Bayreuth to report on the Festival for the journal *Bergensposten*. Of *Das Rheingold*, he wrote that 'long dialogues, such as the gods have, cannot be consistently interesting for, no matter how much the music sustains them, they still remain quite tedious.' In his opinion, Wagner wrote better for the giants and the dwarfs than for the gods and goddesses: 'He does not have the elevated serenity and noble simplicity that the character of Wotan demands.' Grieg describes vividly the performance of *Das Rheingold* on the first night:

> The theatre is hot and packed with people, and this makes the tone of the orchestra subdued, compared with the rehearsals. It also affects the pitch of some of the singers. But it is really wonderful. Of the singers, the most impressive are Vogl as Loge and Schlosser as Mime who is actually applauded after his 'numbers'. Not even Jaïde's fantastic Erda receives such recognition. Though I can sense that the audience becomes tired of the long monologues, when the curtain falls there is a riot of enthusiasm throughout the auditorium. People stand up to applaud and call for Wagner to appear. Even the Kaiser is waiting for him, but the Master is not to be seen.
>
> There are differing opinions about this episode. The Wagner fanatics say it is because he is annoyed with the technical staff for all the minor mistakes that crept into the production. The enemies of Wagner say it is because the composer, since his Munich days, has become used to taking his calls from the royal box, and will not condescend to appear on the stage, considering

it beneath the dignity of an artist of his calibre. I shall leave all that for the Germans to fight about. And indeed they do actually come to blows in the local inns, with beer mugs for weapons. Anyone hit on the head with a *'Töpfchen'* is *hors de combat*.

'The first night of *Die Walküre*', wrote Grieg, 'was . . . a success. Niemann as Siegmund was overwhelmingly good, so adept at combining his vocal and acting abilties on the stage that he is among the very best singers I have seen. Even in passages where Wagner relies on the orchestra alone to express the inner sense of the drama, Niemann acts with conviction and sensibility.' Grieg continued:

Scheffsky as Sieglinde was convincing too, although her acting ability is not to be compared with that of Niemann. Betz as Wotan was actually disappointing, perhaps because expectations were high and the part so difficult to bring off. Wotan is a strange kind of god: so weak, and so ready to yield to the provocations of his wife. Even if Materna as Brünnhilde does not give as much as she does later in *Götterdämmerung*, she is, nevertheless, impressive vocally. Her cries of 'Ho-jo-to-ho' were impeccable, her pitch faultless in the difficult intervals, and her trills flawless throughout. The 'Ride of the Valkyries', one of the most inspired scenes Wagner has ever written, was completely realistic and overwhelmingly beautiful. I left the Festspielhaus feeling that I had witnessed the true genius of Richard Wagner.

Of the new opera, *Siegfried*, Grieg wrote:

The performance was delayed one day because of the bass, Betz, who was creating trouble. Not that any of the audience complained, for all of us needed the extra day's rest. Every performance is so exhausting emotionally that it leaves one quite worn out. The four o'clock starts and the late finishes are physically very tiring, despite the lengthy intervals, and these intervals themselves are usually hard enough to endure. What with fighting to get out of the Festspielhaus, and then fighting to get back in again, it is no easy struggle.

Once again it is Schlosser as Mime who strikes me as a special kind of artist. He declaims more than he sings, which brings out the words of the text more distinctly. This is perhaps the way to perform music drama. Unger as Siegfried is not much to write home about, although he does not actually ruin anything. It is said that Wagner chose him for his fine appearance rather than for his talent, and I dare say he regretted it afterwards. Betz as the Wanderer made a good impression as the god on earth, meddling in the destinies of the mortals. However, here again the stage properties jeopardise the drama by being so realistic. It is almost impossible to construct a dragon that does not look a bit ridiculous, and this one certainly did that. When Wagner puts so much emphasis on these props, and highlights them as he does, he poses some difficult problems. Even if he does have these stage properties constructed by the best people in London, the question remains: why make them so realistic and so obvious? In, for example, *Don Giovanni*, much is left to the audience's imagination instead of being openly displayed on stage. This forces the audience to use its imagination to create devils and demons in its own mind.

After each act there is tremendous applause, especially after the second with its 'Forest Murmurs' in which Wagner has surpassed himself. He is, however, hard on his singers in these scenes, for they have nothing to sing for long periods and they have to act out their roles to the music of the orchestra alone. It always surprises me how well they manage it. Once again, Materna sang Brünnhilde like a true goddess.

III

SIEGFRIED is, in structure, the simplest of the *Ring* components, an opera consisting of nine dialogues, three in each act, for various combinations of characters. In the three scenes of Act I these dialogues are between Mime and Siegfried, Mime and the Wanderer, and finally Mime and Siegfried again. *Siegfried* is also, to a certain extent, the *scherzo* of the *Ring* symphony, the first two of the opera's three acts a brilliantly coloured contrast to the more sombre orchestral colouring of the other parts of the cycle. Its prelude, however, begins in dark mood, the bassoons portraying Mime brooding on the events that have passed, and dreaming of the gold which he is determined to acquire.

The ring motif and that of the Nibelungs hammering away are heard as the curtain rises on a rocky cavern in a forest, containing a naturally formed smith's forge. The dwarf, Mime, brother of the Nibelung Alberich, is seated at an anvil, attempting to forge a sword. He soon gives up, and begins to complain that, as often as he makes a sword, the youth for whom he has done so immediately breaks it and flings it aside. From Mime's soliloquy (*'Zwangvolle Plage'*: Enforced drudgery) one learns that the youth is Siegfried. Mime has brought the boy up, in the hope that one day he will slay the dragon Fafner who lives deep in the forest, guarding the Nibelung gold, the Tarnhelm and the ring. 'There is a sword', Mime broods, 'that he would not be able to break, but alas I have not the strength or craft to weld its fragments together.' This is Nothung, the shattered sword of Siegfried's father, Siegmund, the fragments of which Sieglinde, who had died in giving birth to Siegfried, had preserved. With Nothung, Siegfried would certainly be able to kill Fafner, and then Mime would gain possession of the ring. Meanwhile, Mime can only continue to forge swords for Siegmund which will be contemptuously discarded. If he does not keep on forging, Siegmund ill-treats him.

The youth Siegfried now enters, playfully driving a large bear before him which he sets on Mime, who hides behind his anvil in terror, to the amusement of Siegfried, who encourages the animal with cries of 'Gobble up the hideous smith! Ask him if he's made me a sword!' Siegfried's music brings a new lightness, confidence and energy with it, to contrast with the dwarf's whining. When Mime convinces him that he has been at work, Siegfried drives the bear off into the forest. He tells the still quivering dwarf that he had brought the creature home, as he was looking for a better companion than Mime. When he is given the sword Mime has finished forging, Siegfried examines it critically and then, striking it upon the anvil, breaks it. 'I ought to have broken it across your skull,' he says to Mime, complaining that, although the dwarf is forever prattling on about giants and mighty battles, he is unable to perform the simplest task.

Mime attempts to wheedle himself into Siegfried's favour by reminding him of all that he has done for the youth. He offers Siegfried some meat he has roasted, and a bowl of broth, but the only response he gets is, 'I've roasted some meat for myself. Swallow your swill on your own.' Mime continues to mutter about how he clothed Siegfried as a baby, made him toys and a splendid horn, and gave him a warm bed to sleep in, but Siegfried replies that, although he has been taught many things by Mime, he has been unable to learn how to tolerate the dwarf, whom he thinks ugly and evil, and whom he is often tempted to kill. 'If you are so wise, Mime, perhaps you can tell me why it is', Siegfried continues, 'that, although I cannot endure the sight of you, and continually run off into the forest to escape your presence, I always come back to you. Every beast, bird, tree and fish I encounter is dearer to me than you are. Why do I return?'

That it is the natural love of a child for its parent which leads Siegfried to return home is a suggestion scornfully dismissed by the youth. He has observed the birds and beasts pairing off together, the father bringing food to the nest or lair while the mother suckles their young. Siegfried's music is tenderly lyrical in this episode. Where, he asks Mime, is the dwarf's wife? Where is the female whom Siegfried can call mother? The musical motif which pervades the score here is quite beautiful. Mime brushes these thoughts aside with the remark that Siegfried is neither bird nor fox, but the youth's curiosity is now aroused. 'You say you brought me up and gave me warm clothes, but where did I come from?' he asks Mime. 'Did you really make me without a mother?' When Mime replies, 'You must believe what I tell you. I am both your father and your mother,' Siegfried reacts angrily. He has seen his own reflection in the sparkling streams of the forest, and he is well aware that he is as like Mime as a glittering fish is like a toad. 'A fish never had a toad for a father,' he tells Mime.

It now occurs to Siegfried that the reason he keeps returning to the cave and to Mime is to discover from the dwarf who his father and mother are. He demands an answer, and when Mime attempts to brush the question aside Siegfried seizes him by the throat. 'Out with it, you shabby scoundrel,' he repeats. 'Who are my father and mother?' Mime is forced to reveal how he had once come across a woman weeping in the forest. He had taken her into his cave, where she had borne a child. She died in giving birth, but not before she had bidden Mime call the child Siegfried, and had given him the fragments of a sword which, she said, had been carried by the child's father in his last fight.

Siegfried manages to drag from Mime the name of the woman, Sieglinde. When he demands proof of the story, Mime produces the fragments of the sword, Nothung. In great excitement, Sigfried insists that Mime immediately set about forging a sword from the pieces of steel. 'Only in these fragments do I place my trust,' he exclaims, insisting that he must have the sword that very day. When Mime asks why, Siegfried replies that he is determined to make his way from the forest out into the world, never to return. Mime is not his father, nor is this cave his home. As soon as he has his father's sword, he will be off, and will never see Mime again. Siegfried rushes out of the cave in a state of great exhilaration, leaving Mime to bewail his situation. How can he keep the youth from leaving him? How will he lead Siegfried to Fafner's cave? More immediately, how on earth is he going to succeed in forging a sword from the stubborn pieces of steel he sees before him? Mime's lament is heartfelt, though hardly calculated by Wagner to win any sympathy for the obnoxious Nibelung.

Numerous reminiscences of *Die Walküre* have pervaded this first scene. Now, as Mime sits brooding on his misfortunes, a disguised Wotan enters, wearing a long cloak and with a broad-brimmed hat pulled low over his forehead to conceal his distinctive eye-patch. Horns and cellos give him dignity and stature as he greets Mime courteously and asks for hospitality, but the dwarf is suspicious, and wonders if the stranger is some enemy who has been following him through the forest. Wotan tells Mime that he is known as the Wanderer, for he has wandered widely over the earth's surface. Mime rudely advises him to continue his wandering, at which Wotan observes that good men usually offer him shelter. It is only the misanthropes who seem to expect misfortune at every turn.

Mime finds himself drawn, against his will, into conversation with the Wanderer, who, after making himself comfortable at the hearth, pledges his head as security if he cannot give Mime useful advice in answer to any questions he may wish to ask. Telling himself that he must ask artful questions in order to be rid of this insidious spy, Mime accepts the wager and allows himself three questions. First, he asks Wotan to tell him, since he has wandered so widely throughout the world, the name of the race which dwells in the depths of the earth. Wotan's answer is a very full one. 'The Nibelungs dwell in the depths of the earth,' he tells Mime, 'and their land is known as Nibelheim.' He goes on to describe Alberich, whom he refers to as Black Alberich (*Schwarz-Alberich*), and his theft of the Rhinegold.

The stranger confidently awaits Mime's second question: 'Which race dwells on the surface of the earth?' Again he answers in detail, naming the giants, their chiefs Fasolt and Fafner, and their home, Riesenheim. He recalls how the two giants won the gold and the ring, and how Fafner slew Fasolt and transformed himself into a dragon to guard the treasure. It is not difficult to predict Mime's third question: 'Which race dwells on the cloudy heights?' The Wanderer answers it by telling of the gods, of Valhalla, and of Wotan, whom he calls Light Alberich (*Licht-Alberich*). He describes Wotan's spear, and the solemn treaties carved in its shaft by which the god assumes custody of the world.

Mime admits that the Wanderer has redeemed his head, and invites him to be on his way. But the stranger merely observes that Mime should have asked about things he really needed to know. It is now his turn to ask questions, and by the rules of contest Mime's head is forfeited if he cannot answer them. The Wanderer's first question is, 'Which race is sorely oppressed by Wotan, although they are dear to him?' Mime has no difficulty in answering this. The Volsung twins, Siegmund and Sieglinde, he tells his questioner, are the children whom Wotan fathered and loved tenderly. They produced Siegfried, the strongest of the Volsungs.

Pleased with himself for having been able to answer, Mime more confidently awaits the second question. 'A wise Nibelung takes care of Siegfried, whom he hopes will slay Fafner for him and obtain the gold,' says the Wanderer. 'Tell me, what is the sword which he must use?' Able to name Nothung, and to describe its provenance, Mime is now beside himself with glee. The stranger congratulates him on his wit and wisdom, and asks his third and most carefully loaded question: 'If you are so clever as to exploit the young hero to serve your own dwarfish desires, tell me who will weld together the splintered fragments of the sword Nothung?'

This last question throws Mime into a panic, for he knows well that it is certainly not he who will succeed in welding the sword. He is unable to answer. Repeating that Mime should have asked more intelligent and practical questions, the Wanderer takes his leave, but not before giving Mime the answer: 'Only he who has never known fear shall forge Nothung anew.' As he departs, the Wanderer advises Mime to guard his head carefully, for it is now forfeit to the hero who has never learned the meaning of fear. Several motifs from the two previous Ring operas are, of course, heard during Mime's scene with the Wanderer, as between them they have rehearsed the entire story of the Rhinegold and its disastrous effects on all who seek to acquire it.

Left alone, Mime stares after the Wanderer, and then is suddenly seized with a fit of terror, imagining that he is being pursued by the dragon Fafner, whose theme, never far away throughout the entire act, now insidiously creeps closer on the tubas, reducing Mime to a state of abject fear. Siegfried returns, demanding to know if his sword is ready, but Mime is seriously worried that he will lose his head to one who has never learned to fear. He realizes that he has never taught Siegfried to fear, and immediately sets about trying to do so. The attempt seems bound to fail, until Mime decides upon a practical lesson. He will lead Siegfried to Neidhöhle, the lair of Fafner, and confront the youth with the dragon.

Siegfried is impatient to be off to fight the dragon and, he hopes, to learn fear. He demands his sword, and when Mime is forced to admit that only someone who does not know fear can forge Nothung, Siegfried determines to forge the sword himself. He proceeds to do so, after discovering from Mime the name of the sword. Siegfried's great forging song, 'Nothung! Nothung! Neidliches Schwert' ('Nothung! Nothung! Trusty sword) now begins, a celebration of brute strength which dominates proceedings to the end of the act. Mime realizes that Siegfried will certainly slay Fafner. He will then need to be rid of the young hero, so that he can obtain the Nibelung's hoard for himself. He mixes a poisonous brew, and dreams of enslaving his brother Alberich and his fellow Nibelungs, while Siegfried works away at his task. Finally, Siegfried is able to hold Nothung aloft, and bring its blade crashing down to split the anvil in two with a mighty blow. As he lifts the sword again exultantly, and Mime cowers in terror, the curtain falls.

The three scenes of Act II are between the Wanderer and Alberich, Siegfried and Mime, and Siegfried and the woodbird, and they all take place in a clearing in the forest, close to the entrance of Fafner's cave. An orchestral prelude conjures up the darkness of the forest, the tuba representing Fafner the dragon, stirring uneasily in his sleep as he senses the approach of danger. Occasionally the ring motif makes a subdued appearance, and the trombones offer a reminiscence of Alberich's curse. When the curtain rises, it is just before dawn. Alberich is discovered sitting on a rock, keeping close watch on the cave in the hope that, somehow, he will find an an opportunity to gain possession of the hoard. The Wanderer approaches, but is instantly recognized as Wotan by Alberich, who calls him a shameless thief and bids him be on his way. Wotan attempts to assure Alberich that he has come merely as an observer of events, but soon the two are deep in another of those discussions of past events which Wagner has ponderously inserted throughout the Ring. After a round or two of accusation and counter-accusation, the Wanderer tells Alberich that his quarrel ought properly to be addressed to his brother, Mime, who is already leading a youth towards Fafner's cave with the purpose of slaying the dragon. 'Be on your guard,' he warns the Nibelung. 'The youth as yet knows nothing of the ring, but Mime will tell him.'

Reassured that Wotan has no intention of seizing the treasure, and that he has to contend with an adversary no more formidable than his own brother, Alberich agrees to Wotan's suggestion that they should awaken the sleeping Fafner, who, grateful to be warned of the approach of danger, might be willing in return to give up the ring to Alberich, and to keep the remainder of the hoard. Fafner is awakened but, after growling that he is hungry for the youth, goes back to sleep. Wotan, amused, repeats his advice to Alberich to take a strong stand with his brother. He departs, leaving Alberich to await the approach of Mime and Siegfried.

As the day dawns, Mime enters, followed by Siegfried, while Alberich conceals himself. Siegfried observes that they have come a huge distance, travelling throughout the night, simply in order for him to learn fear. Mime points out Fafner's cave, and describes the fierce dragon who could easily gobble Siegfried up at one gulp. The youth replies that he will close the dragon's mouth before he can be bitten. When Mime warns him that the dragon's poisonous spittle would cause his flesh and bones to waste away, Siegfried sensibly decides to keep to Fafner's side. He similarly dismisses Mime's graphic description of the dragon's tail, which could coil around him, crushing him to death. 'Has the dragon a heart?' Siegfried asks, 'and in the usual place? If so, I'll thrust Nothung into it.' He is clearly not going to learn fear on this occasion.

Mime assures Siegfried that, when he actually sets eyes on Fafner, his heart will quake with fear, and only then will he realize how much Mime loves him. Angrily forbidding the dwarf to love him, Siegfried orders him out of his sight for ever. When Mime says he will rest at the nearby stream, Siegfried says he will let the dragon go there, and will plunge Nothung into his guts only after he has devoured Mime. The dwarf takes himself off, muttering that he hopes Fafner and Siegfried will succeed in killing each other.

Siegfried lies down in the shade of a tree to wait for Fafner to awaken. He soliloquizes about the beauty of the day and the coolness of the forest, and expresses his feelings of joy and relief at never, as he thinks, having to look on Mime's loathsome visage again. He wonders what his father was like, and scornfully dismisses the possibility that it was Mime, for the Nibelung would surely have spawned someone as ugly and misshapen as himself. Then he falls to musing on what his mother must have been like. His attention is diverted by the singing of a woodbird in the branches of the tree, and he wishes he could understand the bird's song. He fashions a rough pipe from a reed, and tries to imitate the bird, but without success. Siegfried's soliloquy and the orchestra's contribution make up the beautiful sequence known as the

Waldweben or Forest Murmurs (Ex. 23).

Flinging the pipe aside, Siegfried blows a call on his horn, which awakens Fafner, who emerges from his cave calling 'Who's there?' Surprised to encounter a beast able to speak, Siegfried replies that he is someone who does not know fear. Can the dragon teach it to him? 'Is this bravado?' asks Fafner. After they have exchanged taunts, Siegfried and Fafner fight, and Siegfried plunges his sword deep into the dragon's heart. Musically this is a disappointing episode, Wagner's orchestra depicting the fight loudly and clumsily. Fafner, as he lies dying, asks Siegfried who he is. Siegfried's reply is that he does not really know. With virtually his last breath, a rather long, Wagnerian breath, the dragon tells the youth that he has murdered the giant Fafner, who had killed his brother Fasolt for the accursed gold they had acquired from the gods. He warns Siegfried that he who prompted him to this deed is even now plotting the hero's death. Siegfried asks Fafner to tell him something of his, Siegfried's, origins, since the dragon seems so wise at the moment of death. 'Tell me where I came from,' he asks. 'You will know from my name, Siegfried.' But Fafner merely repeats the name 'Siegfried' weakly as he dies.

A little of Fafner's blood has splashed on to Siegfried's hand, which now burns like fire. When he puts his hand to his mouth to suck the blood away, he discovers that the dragon's blood has given him the ability to understand the song of the woodbird. The bird informs him, in a high, light soprano voice, that the Nibelung's treasure, which he will find in the cave, is now his. If he takes the Tarnhelm, it will enable him to perform magical deeds, but if he can find the ring he will become the ruler of the world. Siegfried thanks the bird for its friendly and helpful advice, and enters the cave.

The orchestra's gentle depiction of the forest's murmuring is interrupted by jagged woodwind figures as Mime reappears and makes his way towards the cave, only to be intercepted by Alberich, who has observed everything from his hiding-place. The two brothers begin to quarrel over the Rhinegold, and especially the ring. Mime claims it as his because he has devoted so many years to bringing up Siegfried to retrieve it, but Alberich snarls that he would rather see the ring belong to a mangy cur than to a shabby slave such as Mime. He also rejects out of hand Mime's offer to give up the ring in exchange for the Tarnhelm, for he realizes that he would never be able to feel safe if Mime had the power to make himself invisible. Mime next threatens his brother with Siegfried, who now emerges from the cave holding, as the brothers angrily observe, both the ring and the Tarnhelm. Alberich thinks it prudent to make himself scarce, muttering as he leaves that in due course the ring will return to its rightful owner, by whom, of course, he means himself.

Siegfried does not realize the significance of either the ring or the Tarnhelm, having taken them simply on the advice of the woodbird, which now makes its voice heard again, warning him not to trust Mime. Having tasted the dragon's blood, Siegfried will now be able, according to the woodbird, to understand Mime's unspoken thoughts. And indeed, the hypocritical words of affection which Mime intends to utter now reach Siegfried's ear as threats. Poor Mime finds himself telling Siegfried that he is going to drug him and then cut off his head while he is sleeping. 'So you want to slay me as I sleep?' Siegfried asks calmly. 'I want what? Is that what I said?' replies Mime. 'No, I only want to hack off your head, because even if I didn't hate you so much, how else could I gain hold of the treasure?'

Unable to bear any more of this, Siegfried in a sudden access of loathing takes his sword and kills Mime with a single blow. Nearby, the sound of Alberich's laughter can be heard, as Siegfried drags Mime's body into the cave and places it on top of the gold, blocking the entrance to the cave with the corpse of the dragon.

Exhausted, Siegfried now lies under the shade of a tree to rest, and listens to the woodbird. A new motif, expressing Siegfried's yearning for love, is heard in the orchestra, as he asks the woodbird to find him a faithful friend. The bird tells him that a marvellous woman awaits him, and describes Brünnhilde sleeping on her rock, encircled by fire, and destined to be the wife of the hero who breaks through the flames to awaken her. When Siegfried asks if he will be able to do this, the woodbird answers that only someone who knows no fear will win Brünnhilde. Siegfried happily recognizes himself in this description. Led by the bird, who flies on before him, he sets out in the direction of Brünnhilde's rock as the act ends.

The three dialogues in Act III are between the Wanderer and Erda, the Wanderer and Siegfried, and Siegfried and Brünnhilde. The prelude to Act III weaves several appropriate motifs into its fabric, its restless mood depicting the momentous thoughts of Wotan, the Wanderer, as he travels on, attempting to retain control of the gods' destiny. When the curtain rises, a wild spot at the foot of a rocky mountain is revealed. It is night, and a violent storm is raging, which gradually subsides, although lightning continues flashing intermittently among the clouds. The Wanderer stands at the mouth of a cave in the rock, calling upon Erda, the earth goddess, to awaken from her slumbers and appear. 'I sing you a waking song', he declaims, 'to arouse you from your brooding sleep. Omniscient one, awaken!'

Presently, as the woodwind section of the orchestra gently breathes the sleep motif, Erda (contralto) appears at the mouth of the cave, looking as though she is covered in hoar frost, her hair and garments giving off a shimmering glitter. Erda demands to know who has disturbed her sleep of wisdom and, while the orchestra supports him with the appropriate motifs, Wotan describes himself as someone who has wandered far, roaming the world in search of knowledge. He flatters Erda by telling her that he realizes that no one is wiser than she, but she replies that, while she has been meditating in sleep, the Norns are awake, weaving the world's rope and zealously spinning Erda's knowledge. Why does he not consult the Norns? 'Because', says the Wanderer, 'the Norns are subservient to events which they are unable to influence.' His desire is to alter the actual course of events.

Erda's next suggestion is that the Wanderer should question Brünnhilde. 'Conquered by Wotan,' she says, apparently unaware, despite all her great knowledge and wisdom, that it is Wotan whom she is addressing, 'I gave birth to a wish-maiden. Why do you not seek enlightenment from her, the child of Erda and Wotan?' The Wanderer finds himself telling Erda how Wotan was forced to punish Brünnhilde by putting her into a deep sleep from which she can be aroused only by a mighty hero. 'How would it help me to question her?' he asks, reasonably.

Erda is clearly confused at this news. 'Does he who taught defiance now punish defiance?' she asks. 'Does he who is responsible for a deed feel anger when the deed is done?' She asks to be allowed to return to her slumber, but the Wanderer still requires to know how to overcome his cares. 'You are not what you call yourself,' exclaims Erda, to which the Wanderer replies, 'You are no longer what you believe yourself to be.' He tells her that her wisdom as the earth mother is drawing to a close. Tacitly admitting his identity, he says that he has resigned himself to the fact that his omnipotence as a god is also ending, indeed that he himself has willed it. A new and important motif appears in the orchestra here: that of the inheritance of the world (Ex. 24). Wotan tells Erda that he has bequeathed the world to the valiant Siegfried, who, without any help or advice from him, has gained possession of the Nibelung's ring. 'Brünnhilde, the child whom you bore me,' he continues, 'will awaken to Siegfried, and will perform a deed which will redeem the world.' He releases Erda to return to her slumbers in the depths of the earth.

Ex.24

It is now daylight, and the storm has completely subsided. As Erda disappears, the Wanderer looks into the distance and perceives the approach of Siegfried. Preceded by the cheerful song of the woodbird, the young hero duly arrives. Having guided him to this spot and indicated the way to the mountain-top, the woodbird flies off. Siegfried is about to begin his ascent of the mountain when the Wanderer steps forward and begins to question him. Asked where he is going, Siegfried says that he seeks a rock surrounded by fire, on which there sleeps a woman whom he intends to awaken.

'Who told you of this woman and made you yearn for her?' asks Wotan, in reply to which Siegfried describes the bird whose speech he was able to understand only after he had tasted the blood of a dragon he had slain. 'Who induced you to fight this fearful dragon?' asks his relentless interrogator. Siegfried answers honestly and without guile, but after Wotan has asked him who forged the sword and who made the splinters from which the sword was forged, pointless questions to which the Wanderer already knows the answers, Siegfried understandably loses his patience, calls Wotan an old gossip, and orders him either to point out the direction of Brünnhilde's rock or else hold his tongue and get out of the way.

Wotan advises Siegfried to show more respect for his age, but the youth replies that he has just got rid of one old man who had always obstructed him, and that the stranger will share Mime's fate if he is not careful. He laughs at Wotan's broad-brimmed hat, and asks why it hangs over his face. Wotan tells him that it is for protection against the wind, but Siegfried peers underneath the brim and notices that one of Wotan's eyes is missing. 'No doubt someone struck it out when you barred his way,' he suggests. 'If you don't take yourself off, you might lose the other one.' Wotan answers this obscurely, but Siegfried, impatient to be on his way to Brünnhilde, pays no heed and attempts to move on.

Aware that the hero who wins Brünnhilde will thereby deprive him of his power for ever, Wotan attempts to scare Siegfried away from the task by describing the fire which now can be seen raging around the rock at the top of the mountain. 'Go back, rash boy,' he advises, to which Siegfried replies, 'Go back yourself, braggart!' Wotan now tries to bar the way with his spear. 'My hand still holds the symbol of sovereignty,' he asserts. 'This shaft once shattered your sword. It will do so again.' Thinking that he has encountered the man who killed his father, Siegfried strikes Wotan's spear with his sword, shattering it as a flash of lightning darts from the spear and a clap of thunder is heard. 'Go forward, then. I cannot stop you,' Wotan admits, as he picks up the pieces and quickly leaves. Momentarily annoyed at having let his father's enemy escape, Siegfried now notices the glow of the flames on the mountain-top. Blowing his vigorous horn-call, he advances confidently towards the fire, eager to find the bride who awaits him.

The light now begins to fade, gradually giving way to a dissolving cloud illuminated as though by the red glow of dawn. The cloud in turn becomes a fine, rose-coloured veil of mist which divides so that the upper part entirely disappears above, and the rocky mountain-top now becomes visible, looking just as it did at the end of *Die Walküre*. The sleeping Brünnhilde can be seen, lying in full armour, with her helmet on her head and her shield covering her, surrounded by a ring of fire. The fire-music and sleep motifs have been heard in the orchestra, rising to a climax and then subsiding. Siegfried, as he approaches from below, looks about him. The slumber motif has now given way to the melody in which Loge, in *Das Rheingold*, had sung of 'Woman's delight and worth'. Siegfried sees Brünnhilde's horse, Grane, sleeping in the nearby forest, and stops in surprise when he catches sight of Brünnhilde. Despite what he has been told, he at first mistakes her for a man, even after he has removed her helmet and released her long, golden hair, whose beauty gains his appreciation. It is only when he has lifted up her shield that he exclaims, '*Das ist kein Mann!*' (That's no man), a line with which tenors sometimes experience difficulty. The orchestra's lyrical reminiscence of several motifs accompanies the scene of Brünnhilde's awakening.

Startled at this first encounter with a female, Siegfried at first invokes his mother to help him. But then nature puts it into his head to awaken Brünnhilde with a kiss. He does so, and slowly Brünnhilde awakens to greet the glorious light of day once more, the orchestra depicting her gradual awakening in a nobly radiant passage in which the high shimmering strings sing of the ecstasy of warmth and life, while Brünnhilde greets the sun and the light of day: '*Heil dir, Sonne! Heil dir, Licht!*' (Hail to thee, sun! Hail to thee, light!) To the theme of the fate motif, she asks who has awakened her, and Siegfried tells her his name. Overjoyed, Brünnhilde explains to him that she loved him even before he was born, for she had protected his mother, Sieglinde, when she was carrying Siegfried in her womb. Together, they bless the mother who gave birth to him.

The hero's kiss has awakened not only Brünnhilde but also, it seems, her horse, the sight of whom reminds her of her glorious past. She tries to explain something of the history of the ring to Siegfried, but he can only gaze at her, enraptured.

When he attempts to embrace her, Brünnhilde begs Siegfried to leave her in peace, overcome as she is by shame at having lost her godlike condition. But he insists that she awaken fully to love and to him, and finally she succumbs. To the gracious theme which Wagner had used as the main subject of the *Siegfried Idyll* (Ex. 25), heard first in the orchestra, Brünnhilde begins to melt in tenderness: '*Ewig war ich, ewig bin ich, ewig in süss sehnender Wonne*' (I always was, I always am, always in sweet yearning bliss). 'I will be yours for ever,' she cries, as passion awakens within her.

Wagner, from a group photograph taken in 1881

Wagner's first wife, Minna, painted in 1835

opposite: Wagner and Cosima with their son, Siegfried, in 1873

Wagner and canine friend, Munich, 1865

Ex.25

'The fear you almost taught me I have forgotten,' Siegfried replies as he takes her in his arms. Brünnhilde bids a light-hearted farewell to the resplendent pomp of the gods as she and Siegfried greet the day, the sun, the world. With their ecstatic love duet, the opera ends exultantly. 'You are for ever my own, my all, you are radiant love and laughing death,' they assure each other in the C major final section of their duet, Brünnhilde ending on an exuberant high C as the orchestra gives forth with a combination of motifs involving love, Siegfried and the inheritance of the world.

UNLESS the character of Wagner's 'superman' hero strikes one as being unpleasant, arrogant, brutish and murderous enough to qualify as a proto-fascist, *Siegfried* can be the most appealing of the four music dramas of *The Ring*, rather than the most appalling. Fresh in conception, it is full of music which represents Wagner at his most lyrical, and it is less burdened than either *Die Walküre* or *Götterdämmerung* with redundant or dull passages. Its score is the the most joyous and orchestrally colourful of the entire tetralogy.

TWELVE

Der Ring des Nibelungen: 4

Götterdämmerung

(Twilight of the Gods)

Music drama in a Prologue and Three Acts

Dramatis personae
Siegfried   (tenor)
Gunther   (baritone)
Alberich   (bass-baritone)
Hagen   (bass)
Brünnhilde   (soprano)
Gutrune   (soprano)
Waltraute   (mezzo-soprano)
The Three Norns   (contralto, mezzo-soprano, soprano)
Woglinde   (soprano)
Wellgunde   (soprano)
Flosshilde   (mezzo-soprano)

LIBRETTO by the composer

TIME: Legendary

PLACE: The Valkyrie's rock on the mountain-top; Gunther's castle on the Rhine; a wooded area by the Rhine.

FIRST PERFORMED as part of the complete *Ring* cycle, at the Festspielhaus, Bayreuth, 17 August 1876, with Georg Unger (Siegfried), Eugen Gura (Gunther), Gustav Siehr (Hagen), Karl Hill (Alberich), Amalie Materna (Brünnhilde), Mathilde Weckerlin (Gutrune), Luise Jaïde (Waltraute), conducted by Hans Richter.

I

GRIEG attended the dress rehearsal of *Götterdämmerung*. 'There is no doubt', he wrote,

> that *Götterdämmerung* is the most effective of the dramas and the one with the most compelling action. In it, all that has gone before is resolved, and the fates of the gods and of men are fulfilled. The use of a chorus seems to involve all of mankind—and what an effect it makes! By allowing the Rhinemaidens to recover the gold in the end, Wagner underlines the message that, in the hands of man, it is a force for evil and intrigue. It further shows that *Der Ring des Nibelungen* is the only possible title for the cycle.
>
> I cannot say that any part of the music is better than any other, for it is all divinely composed. To select any one passage at random is to select a pearl.
>
> I want to start by considering the opening scene with the three Norns where the orchestra spins out the rope of fate for them. I once heard this piece played at a concert in Berlin, without voices, and it seemed just as effective as it was here with them. I mention this because I think that the voice parts play only a secondary part in the Ring. The orchestra is all, and of primary importance. Why is it that Wagner does not make more use of the voices, and why, when he does use them, do they not convey more of the text? The human voice must have an opportunity to express everything which goes on in the innermost soul of the character, failing which it should not be used at all. It is a pity that Wagner has got such peculiar concepts about the employment of the human voice, because he does prevent his works becoming coherent and lucid, and thereby expressing his ideas properly.
>
> Beethoven was not the most accomplished writer for voices, but even so he chose to use them to heighten the climaxes in his music. Who could possibly tolerate a performance of the Ninth Symphony without the vocal and choral parts? Nevertheless, I do not wish to disparage the work of Wagner; I merely express how it all appears to me.
>
> It is the mortals in the *Ring* that interest and move us. Wagner's portrayal of these characters is more sympathetic than that of the gods. We identify with them from start to finish. I marvel at the differences in the portrayals of the two characters, Hagen and Siegfried. When Hagen summons his vassals I can detect, in this powerful music, a fundamental Nordic force, and this although I am now hearing it for the very first time. But most enchanting of all to me is the song of the Rhinemaidens. And then there is Siegfried's Funeral March. I do not think there is anything to measure up to it other than Beethoven's 'Eroica'. It is simply incredible.

244

Götterdämmerung

After the first public performance of *Götterdämmerung*, Grieg had this to add:

Yesterday's performance of *Götterdämmerung* made a great and profound impression. Just as in the case of *Die Walküre* with its great use of the forces of nature, so in the case of the final work of the *Ring*, it impresses by its tragic power and thus becomes equally moving. . . . When the final curtain came down at the end of the last act in which the Master had demonstrated his great creative abilities, I thought the theatre would come down too, so great was the outbreak of cheering! The whole house resounded with the call for Wagner. Finally, he came out in front of the curtain and gave his thanks for the ovation. . . . Whatever the shortcomings of detail, one thing is certain. Wagner has created a great work, full of audacious originality and dramatic merit. He has, in his new lively way, brought out old material, little known in Germany, and by means of his clever musical-dramatic treatment has breathed new life into it. Many of these profound legends, for most people a closed book, will be opened up and made popular by Wagner's work. As in a child's picture book, the eye comes to the assistance of the mind. It may also be a good tonic for people nowadays, when parties and factions rule, to witness these great heroes and personalities with their strong passions, selfless actions and complete lives.

The ethical background that Wagner has given the material, one that is in harmony with current philosophies, may also be of importance for the future of the work outside its own sphere of music theatre. . . . An important new chapter in the history of the arts has been written by Wagner. The thousands who have taken part in this Festival will be able to tell the world that German art at Bayreuth has celebrated a triumph that is unique of its kind.

II

THE first act of *Götterdämmerung* is preceded by a Prologue. An orchestral prelude begins with two chords in the wind instruments reminiscent of those with which Brünnhilde saluted the world on her awakening at the end of *Siegfried*, followed by the arpeggios which earlier characterized the Rhine. Other motifs are woven into the orchestral texture: throughout *Götterdämmerung*, Wagner's motifs proliferate to such an extent that it is hardly profitable to attempt consciously to separate and identify them.

When the curtain rises after about eighteen bars of prelude, the scene is Brünnhilde's rock, as it was at the end of *Siegfried*. It is night. There is a gleam of firelight from the background, which serves to illuminate the three Norns, tall women in dark, veil-like drapery, who weave the rope of fate on which the future of the world depends. The first and oldest Norn (contralto) lies under a fir-tree in the foreground, while the second (mezzo-soprano) sits on a rock in front of the cave, and the third and youngest (soprano) on another rock further off. As they weave the rope of the world's destiny, the Norns tell one another what all three of them presumably already know—the story of Wotan, his spear and its runes, the ring and its history. Finally, their rope snaps as the curse motif is insisted upon by the bass trumpet. The three Norns start up in terror, grasping the pieces of broken rope, which they use to tie their bodies together. 'Our eternal knowledge is at an end,' they lament. 'The world will know nothing more of our wisdom.' They vanish into the depths to return to Erda, the earth mother.

The scene with the Norns has been comprised almost entirely of motifs from *Das Rheingold*. As dawn approaches, the orchestra paints its picture of sunrise, beginning with a long cello melody which is interrupted by phrases characterizing the newly transfigured Siegfried (tranquilly, on the horns) and Brünnhilde (on clarinet). It is broad daylight when the music rises to a more impassioned level and the lovers emerge from the cave, he fully armed and she leading Grane, her horse, by its bridle. Brünnhilde and Siegfried embrace as they reaffirm their love for each other, and he places on her finger the fateful ring. In return, she offers him her horse to bear him away into the world to perform great deeds. When their duet has reached its exultant climax, which takes the soprano to a final sustained high C, Siegfried leads Grane down from the rock. Brünnhilde is left standing alone, watching their descent into the valley. Siegfried's horn is heard from below, and Brünnhilde continues to watch, waving rapturously to him until he is lost from her sight. In the orchestra, the motifs of Brünnhilde and Siegfried ring out, as well as, finally, the theme of the love duet with which *Siegfried* had ended.

Wagner directs that the curtain be quickly lowered as the orchestra begins its description of Siegfried's boisterous journey down the Rhine, an episode well-known outside the opera house because of its frequent concert performances. In due course, the more ebullient motifs of Siegfried's journey give way to darker harmonies, foreshadowing the malevolent plotting of Hagen. When the curtain rises on Act I of *Götterdämmerung*, the scene has changed to the hall of the tribe of Gibichungs on the Rhine, beyond which one glimpses the shore of the river, surrounded by rocky heights. Gunther and his sister Gutrune share a throne, with drinking-vessels on a table in front of them. At the other side of the table sits their half-brother Hagen, the son of Alberich. Gunther, the legitimate head of the tribe, concedes that the wise member of the family is Hagen, whose advice he now seeks. He wishes to be reassured that he has properly maintained the glory of the Gibichungs, and when Hagen points out that Gunther has, as yet, no wife, nor Gutrune a husband, Gunther asks how this situation may be remedied.

Hagen tells Gunther of Brünnhilde, whom he describes as the finest woman in the world, waiting on her rock for a suitor who can break through the ring of fire which surrounds her. Gunther will not have the strength to accomplish this task, but Siegfried, strongest of heroes, is destined to do so, and he is the man whom Hagen would wish to see Gutrune marry. He describes how Siegfried slayed the dragon Fafner and won the Nibelung hoard. Gunther is upset at having his desire aroused for a woman whom he cannot win, but Hagen reveals his plan by which Siegfried could be made to bring Brünnhilde to Gunther. It will be necessary for Gutrune to capture the hero's heart. She doubts her ability to do this, but Hagen reminds brother and sister that he possesses a magic potion which will make Siegfried forget any other woman he may have loved, and will turn his desire towards Gutrune. In exchange for Gunther allowing him to wed Gutrune, Siegfried will have to help him win Brünnhilde.

Gunther and Gutrune approve of this plan. When Gunther asks how they are to find Siegfried, a horn-call is suddenly heard from the distance. After it has sounded a second time, closer, Hagen goes down to the shore and calls back to the others that a warrior and a horse in a boat are swiftly proceeding against the current. The robust strength with which the young warrior wields the oar suggests that this must be Siegfried. Hagen calls to to the hero, and invites him ashore. When he arrives in the hall, Siegfried reveals that he had been searching for Gunther. 'From far along the Rhine, I have heard of your fame,' he tells the Gibichung. 'Now fight with me or be my friend.'

Gunther sensibly chooses friendship. While Hagen leads Grane away to be stabled, Gutrune goes off to prepare the magic potion, and the two new friends exchange vows of alliance. Gunther offers his inheritance, his land and his people to Siegfried, who replies that in return all he can offer is the aid of his mighty sword. Returning, Hagen asks if Siegfried is not also lord of the Nibelung treasure. Siegfried says that he had almost forgotten that. He left the gold lying in Fafner's cave, and took only a piece of chainmail, which he wears in his belt, and a ring which he has already given to a wondrous woman. Hagen explains to him the significance of the Tarnhelm, which he has only to put on his head to be immediately transported to wherever he wishes to be, and which will also enable him to assume any shape or disguise.

Gutrune now returns with a filled drinking-horn, which she offers to Siegfried as a cup of welcome. He bows courteously to her, holds the horn in front of him and murmurs, 'Brünnhilde, to you I drink this in token of my faithful love.' The potion has an immediate effect for, as he hands the horn back to Gutrune after drinking from it, Siegfried addresses her in passionate terms and offers himself to her in marriage. Gutrune feigns modest confusion and leaves the hall, while Gunther agrees to give his sister to Siegfried if the hero will help him win the maiden of his choice, who dwells high upon a rock, surrounded by fire which Gunther is not strong enough to break through. At mention of Brünnhilde's name, Siegfried seems to be making an intense effort to remember something which eludes him. But it is clear that he now has no recollection of Brünnhilde, despite the orchestra's promptings. He agrees to break through the flames, in the guise of Gunther, whose shape the Tarnhelm will enable him to assume, to win Brünnhilde and to bring her to Gunther.

Gunther and Siegfried swear an oath of blood brotherhood by pricking their arms with their swords and holding them for a short time over the mouth of a horn before drinking from it. A new motif, that of the vow, is introduced, but is soon followed by the two warning chords of Hagen's motif. Hagen has declined to join in the oath, claiming that his cold and sluggish blood would taint their drink.

Siegfried invites Gunther to accompany him as far as the foot of the Valkyrie's rock. 'For one night you will have to wait by the bank in the boat,' he tells the Gibichung. 'Then you can lead your wife home.' Gunther and Siegfried quickly leave in Siegfried's boat, while Gutrune excitedly looks forward to her marriage with the hero, and Hagen sits guarding the hall and dreaming of the ring which he intends to acquire when Siegfried brings it and Brünnhilde back with him. His solo passage, known as Hagen's Watch, is pervaded by the spirit, and indeed the motif, of his father, the Nibelung Alberich. At the conclusion of Hagen's brooding monologue, the curtain is lowered. After a brief, sombre orchestral interlude, the scene changes back to the rocky summit as in the Prologue. Brünnhilde sits at the entrance to the cave, contemplating the ring which Siegfried had given her, covering it with kisses as she recalls their happiness together and the appropriate motif is heard in the orchestra. A sudden burst of thunder and a flash of lightning in the distance draw her attention to a dark cloud approaching the rock, bearing a winged horse. The voice of one of Brünnhilde's sisters, the Valkyrie Waltraute (mezzo-soprano), is heard calling her, and Brünnhilde hurries down to the edge of the cliff to greet Waltraute, returning immediately with her.

Brünnhilde hopes that her sister has come to tell her that Wotan's anger with her has abated, but in a long narrative Waltraute pours out a sorry tale of the decline of the gods. After his sword had been shattered by Siegfried, Wotan had returned to Valhalla. He had ordered the world ash-tree to be felled, and the logs from its trunk to be piled in towering heaps around the sacred hall of the gods. There Wotan sits on his throne, speaking not a word and refusing Freia's apples. Waltraute had heard him whisper that the gods and the world could be freed from the weight of the curse placed on the ring only if Brünnhilde were to return it to the Rhinemaidens. Throwing herself at Brünnhilde's feet, Waltraute begs her to do this and bring the torments of the gods to an end.

She pleads in vain, for Brünnhilde tells her sister that Siegfried's love means more to her than Valhalla and the glory of the gods. She will never part with the ring which Siegfried had given her. Waltraute rushes off in anger and despair, and soon her receding thunder-cloud can be seen racing away across the sky.

Night has now fallen, and Brünnhilde observes that the wall of flame around her rock is leaping up furiously. Thinking that this denotes the return of Siegfried, she hurries to the edge of the rock, but is halted by the sudden appearance of Siegfried wearing the Tarnhelm, which gives him the form of Gunther. She shrinks back in fear as Siegfried, in a baritonal timbre instead of his usual tenor, announces himself as a suitor who, unafraid of the flames, has come to claim Brünnhilde as his bride. He tells her that he is Gunther, a Gibichung, and that she must now follow him.

Brünnhilde threatens him with the power of the ring, but Siegfried seizes her and they struggle violently. As the motif of the curse rings out, Siegfried tears the ring from Brünnhilde's finger, at which she gives a piercing scream and sinks, as if crushed, into his arms. With an imperious gesture, he drives her before him towards the cave. Several appropriate motifs are now combined in the orchestra: those relating to the oath Siegfried has sworn with Gunther, the sword Nothung, Wotan's treaty, and Hagen. As Brünnhilde sadly and with faltering step enters the cave, Siegfried draws his sword, Nothung, which he declares he will place between him and Brünnhilde in order to keep faith with Gunther. He follows her into the cave as the curtain falls to a violent flurry of motifs in the orchestra.

Act II has been described as Wagner's finest achievement. Its music is certainly of great dramatic power throughout, based on an intricate weaving of the work's musical motifs. After a brooding orchestral prelude depicting the plotting of Hagen and Alberich, the curtain rises to reveal a scene close by the Rhine, in front of the hall of the Gibichungs. Wagner's stage directions, rarely adhered to in modern productions, describe the open entrance to the hall as being on the right with, on the left, the bank of the Rhine from which a rocky eminence, intersected by several mountain paths, rises diagonally towards the background. An altar-stone dedicated to Fricka can be seen, and above it a larger one for Wotan. At the side is another stone erected to Donner. It is night. Hagen, with his arm around his spear, sits sleeping with his sword by his side, leaning against one of the pillars of the hall. The moon suddenly throws a vivid light on the sleeping man and his surroundings, revealing Alberich crouching before him, leaning his arms on Hagen's knees.

The apparition of Alberich penetrates Hagen's slumber. 'Are you asleep, Hagen, my son?' Alberich asks. 'Do you not hear me?' Hagen, apparently still sleeping, although his eyes are open, replies softly, without moving, 'I hear you, hateful gnome. What have you to say in my sleep?' What Alberich has to say, of course, is a recital of the story of how the ring was stolen from him by Wotan. He and Hagen can now inherit the world from the gods, for Alberich has bred Hagen for the express purpose of avenging him and retrieving the Rhinegold. A new motif, that of murder, is heard in the orchestra as the Nibelung unfolds his familiar tale. Hagen swears to obtain the ring, and Alberich gradually disappears from sight, his voice fading with his image as he orders Hagen to remain loyal and faithful to him.

Hagen retains his position without moving, as day begins to dawn and the orchestra takes on a warmer tone. Suddenly, Siegfried emerges from a bush close to the shore. He removes the Tarnhelm which he has been wearing, hanging it from his belt as he steps forward to greet Hagen, whom he informs that he has been transported back from Brünnhilde's rock by the Tarnhelm in a split second, while Brünnhilde and Gunther are following more slowly by boat. Hagen calls Gutrune, who enters from the hall, and Siegfried tells them both how he wooed Brünnhilde for Gunther, walking through the fire with ease because of the strength of his desire for Gutrune.

Not surprisingly, Gutrune wishes to hear the story in more detail. 'So you overcame the intrepid woman?' she enquires. 'She surrendered—to Gunther's strength,' is Siegfried's tactful reply. 'And then you married her?' Siegfried's answer this time can hardly avoid sounding evasive. 'Brünnhilde', he tells Gutrune, 'submitted to her husband throughout the bridal night.' Gutrune is puzzled. 'But you passed for her husband?' she asks. 'Siegfried remained here with Gutrune,' he replies. Gutrune is even more perplexed. 'Yet Brünnhilde was by his side?' is her next question.

Siegfried explains that, on the next morning, Brünnhilde had followed him down to the Rhine where, in a trice, Gunther changed places with him. Through the Tarnhelm's magic power, Siegfried swiftly wished himself back in the hall of the Gibichungs, leaving Brünnhilde and Gunther to make a more stately progress along the Rhine. Their boat is now sighted by Hagen, and Gutrune departs with Siegfried to call her women to greet the lovers, asking Hagen to summon the vassals to attend the wedding-ceremony.

Climbing on to a high rock in the background, Hagen turns away from the river to the surrounding countryside, blows a rough series of notes on his cowhorn, and announces not so much an invitation to a celebration as a call to arms. 'Take up your weapons,' he commands, 'for there is danger. Rouse yourself, Gibich vassals!' Hunting-horns answer from various directions, and along the mountain paths armed men begin to hurry towards the hall, at first singly, and then in increasing numbers. When they are gathered together on the shore in front of the hall, they address Hagen as a chorus. With the exception of the Valkyries in *Die Walküre*, who do not really function as an ensemble, this is the first time that a chorus has been heard in Wagner's *Ring*.

In a rough, boisterous outburst, accompanied at first by their own motif, the vassals ask Hagen why they have been called to arms. What foe is approaching? Is Gunther threatened? Hagen explains that they must greet Gunther, who is bringing home a formidable wife. 'Are the woman's hostile family in pursuit?' the vassals wish to know. They are not. Has Gunther, then, overcome them already? No, Siegfried the dragon-slayer protected him. 'Then why are we needed?' ask the vassals. 'To slaughter steers on the altar of Wotan, to kill a boar for Froh, a goat for Donner and a sheep for Fricka,' Hagen tells them. 'And then what should we do?' they ask. 'Drink until drunkenness overcomes you, in honour of the gods so that they may bless the marriage,' Hagen replies. In another wild choral outburst, the vassals tell one another that prosperity has indeed come to the Rhine if grim Hagen can be so merry.

Hagen, already plotting the downfall of Siegfried, now comes down among the Gibichung vassals. Pointing to the Rhine, he orders them to welcome Gunther's bride, Brünnhilde, to serve her loyally and, if she is ever wronged, to be quick to avenge her. When the boat carrying them comes alongside the river bank, Gunther and Brünnhilde disembark and are greeted by the vassals in a huge chorus based on the theme of the Gibichung tribe.

Gunther leads his bride, who follows him slowly with her eyes cast down, into the hall to meet Siegfried and Gutrune. It is only when he mentions Siegfried's name that Brünnhilde, startled, raises her eyes and sees her beloved. She gazes at him in astonishment, while all wonder at her strange behaviour, and the orchestra emphasizes the significance of the dramatic situation with its combination of the motifs of Siegfried, the sword and Hagen. 'Is she demented?' the vassals wonder, while the orchestra already busies itself with the motif of vengeance (Ex. 26). Siegfried innocently asks what troubles her, and when Brünnhilde, scarcely able to control herself, asks who Gutrune is, he replies that she is Gunther's gentle sister, married to him as Brünnhilde is to Gunther.

Ex.26

Brünnhilde staggers and is about to faint. 'Does Siegfried not know me?' she asks feebly. Then, as she notices the ring on his finger, she asks how it got there. 'This man', she exclaims, indicating Gunther, 'snatched it from me.' Siegfried answers that he did not get it from Gunther, Brünnhilde demands that Gunther claim the ring back from him, while a bewildered Gunther protests that he did not give it to Siegfried, and wonders how Brünnhilde comes to know the ring. The orchestra here is at its most eloquent, fiercely quoting a number of motifs, among them those of the ring, the curse, vengeance and Valhalla, at the appropriate moments. Hagen, meanwhile, has been moving among the vassals, urging them to note well Brünnhilde's complaint. She now furiously accuses Siegfried of having forcibly taken the ring from her. All look expectantly at Siegfried, who can only remember that he took it from the dragon's cave after he had slain Fafner.

Stepping between Brünnhilde and Siegfried, Hagen tells Brünnhilde that, if she really recognizes the ring as the one which Gunther took from her, then Siegfried must have obtained it by trickery, for which he must atone. Though she does not clearly understand exactly what happened, Brünnhilde now accuses Siegfried, to whom she considers herself married, of having broken his vows to her. Astonished, Siegfried insists that his sword, Nothung, lay between them, but of course this is not the occasion to which Brünnhilde refers. There is general consternation, which Siegfried attempts to quell by swearing an oath, on Hagen's spear, that Brünnhilde's accusation is false, and that he has not broken faith with his blood-brother, Gunther (Ex. 27).

Ex. 27

Hel - le Wehr, hei - li-ge Waf - fe! hilf mei - nem e-wi-gen Ei - de!

Pushing Siegfried's hand away from Hagen's spear, Brünnhilde grasps the point and, using the same melodic phrases as Siegfried but doubling the tempo, swears an oath of her own. 'Spear-point, mark my words,' she exclaims. 'I dedicate your great power to his downfall, for he has broken his oath and has now perjured himself.' Siegfried, however, maintains an even temper. Taking Gunther aside, he suggests that he had probably not been completely disguised by the Tarnhelm, and that this must be the cause of Brünnhilde's anger. Advising Gunther to give her time to calm down, he leaves, gaily calling to the women and the vassals to accompany him to the feast.

Brünnhilde, Gunther and Hagen now remain behind, and the trio with which they bring Act II to a conclusion is magnificent in its passionate intensity. When Hagen offers to avenge Brünnhilde by killing Siegfried, she scornfully remarks that a single flash of Siegfried's eyes would make Hagen quake with fear. However, accompanied in the orchestra by music of the deepest feeling, she tells Hagen how he can overcome the valiant hero. Unknown to Siegfried, she had enveloped the young hero in her magic, protecting him from all wounds. However, she did not protect his back, for she knew he would never turn away from an enemy. No weapon, therefore, can harm Siegfried in combat, but if he were to be struck in the back he would be vulnerable.

Though at first reluctant to join in a conspiracy against the man with whom he has sworn blood-brotherhood (as the orchestra's horns now ironically remind him by repeating the musical theme to which he and Siegfried had sworn), and by no means completely convinced that Siegfried has betrayed him, Gunther is finally persuaded to agree to Siegfried's death, on being reminded by Hagen of the immense power which will be his when the Nibelung's ring is in his possession. At Hagen's suggestion it is agreed to keep the truth from Gutrune, who will be told that Siegfried has been killed by a wild boar during the next morning's hunt. As the three of them swear to put this plan into action, the bridal procession emerges from the hall, with Siegfried carried on a shield and Gutrune on a chair. At Hagen's urging, Gunther and Brünnhilde take their places in the procession, which moves on towards the altar-stones on the summit, servants following with beasts to be sacrificed. Conveying a sense both of the nuptial celebration of the crowd and of the murderous plotting of the three conspirators, the orchestra excitedly combines several motifs, among which those of Gutrune and of revenge are most prominent. The curtain falls.

Beginning with Siegfried's horn-call, which is answered by the cowhorns of the Gibichung hunting-party in the distance, the orchestral prelude to Act III moves on through the flowing Rhine motif to a hint of the song of the Rhinemaidens. When the curtain rises on the first scene, it reveals a wild, partly wooded, partly rocky valley by the Rhine, the river flowing past a steep cliff in the background. The three Rhinemaidens, Woglinde, Wellgunde and Flosshilde, rise to the surface and swim, circling around one another as though in a dance. They pause in their swimming to sing to the goddess of the sun, asking for her rays to illuminate the depths of the Rhine as once they did. Hearing Siegfried's horn-call in the distance, they stop to listen, and then renew their plea to the sun, begging now for the arrival of the hero who will restore their gold to them. Their bitter-sweet melody sets the mood of the Rhinemaidens' subsequent scene with Siegfried, one of the few instances of comparative relaxation and charm in *The Ring*.

Siegfried's horn is heard again from the cliffs above, and the Rhinemaidens quickly disappear into the depths of the river as Siegfried himself appears on the cliffs in full armour, having lost his way while hunting. He grumbles that an elf must have led him astray, at which the Rhinemaidens suddenly rise again to the surface of the water to engage him in teasing banter. He has so far been unsuccessful in the hunt, and the Rhinemaidens offer to find some quarry for him, but ask what he will give them in return. Wellgunde draws attention to the golden ring gleaming on his finger, and the three Rhinemaidens ask for it. Siegfried points out, however, that he slew a dragon to get it. Do they expect him to give it up in exchange for a paltry bearskin?

When they accuse him of being mean, Siegfried resorts to the excuse that his wife would scold him were he to part with the ring. The Rhinemaidens laugh at the idea of a hero who fears his wife. Flirtatiously lamenting that so handsome, strong and desirable a youth should be such a miser, they dive below. Amused by their antics, Siegfried decides to let them have the ring. Taking it from his finger, he holds it out over the water and calls to the Rhinemaidens, who come to the surface again, but this time in a less skittish mood. They solemnly warn him of the curse attached to the ring, and of the evil that is in store for him unless he relinquishes it. Siegfried replies that their threats are even less effective than their wheedling. A dragon once warned him of the curse, but did not teach him to fear it. He would give up the ring for love but never in response to threats. The Rhinemaidens swim away, prophesying as they leave that a proud woman will that day inherit the ring and will give them a better hearing.

Siegfried tells himself that he is learning much about the ways of women, both on land and in the water: when their cajoling does not succeed, they resort to threats. And yet, he tells himself, if he had not already pledged himself to Gutrune, he would happily have chosen one of those pretty nymphs for himself. He is aroused from these reflections by horn-calls and the approach of the hunting-party, consisting of Hagen, Gunther and the vassals. They descend from the cliff-top to join him, bringing with them the spoils of the hunt, and producing drinking-horns and skins containing wine. Siegfried admits he has caught nothing, not even the three wild waterbirds who have told him that he would be slain that very day. Gunther looks gloomily at Hagen on hearing this, and in the depths of the orchestra there is a reminder of the oath of vengeance sworn against Siegfried.

Asked by Hagen if it is true that he can understand the song of birds, Siegfried replies that some time has passed since he heeded their chirping. Hagen gives Siegfried a drinking-horn filled with wine, which Siegfried shares with Gunther, noticing that he is in low spirits. Siegfried offers to cheer Gunther up by singing stories of his boyhood days. Encouraged to do so, he embarks upon a narrative involving Mime, the forging of Nothung, the slaying of Fafner, the advice of the woodbird, and Siegfried's scornful felling of Mime, each episode bringing with it the appropriate motif. At this point, Hagen refills Siegfried's drinking-horn and adds to it the juice of a herb, telling him that its magic will awaken his remembrance of things he had forgotten. As Siegfried sings, recollection slowly returns to him. Gunther listens with astonishment, which turns to horror as Siegfried describes how he burst through the magic flames to awaken the sleeping Brünnhilde with a kiss.

Two ravens fly up from a bush, circle above Siegfried, and then fly off towards the Rhine. 'Can you understand the cry of those ravens?' Hagen asks. When Siegfried turns to gaze after the birds, Hagen plunges his spear into the hero's back, shouting 'To me, they cry revenge.' Gunther, too late, attempts to restrain Hagen. Siegfried lifts his shield up high with both hands to bring it down upon Hagen, but his strength fails him, the shield drops behind him, and he falls back upon it as the orchestra contributes, *fortissimo*, a motif which will become the germ of Siegfried's Funeral March. The horrified vassals ask Hagen what he has done, to which he replies that he has avenged perjury, and calmly walks away into the now darkening twilight. A grief-stricken Gunther and the vassals tend the dying Siegfried, whose last words are of Brünnhilde, with whom he confidently expects to be reunited in death. The phrases to which she had awakened to his kiss are heard as he first breathes her name, followed by motifs associated with their love, and finally by the sombre strains with which Brünnhilde had announced the imminent death of Siegmund to him in *Die Walküre*.

Siegfried falls back and dies. At a silent command from Gunther, the vassals lift Siegfried's body on his shield, and solemnly carry the dead hero towards the hill-top, with Gunther following sorrowfully. The moon breaks through the clouds, throwing an increasing light on the funeral procession as it reaches the summit. Then mists rise from the Rhine, gradually filling the whole stage until the cortège is invisible and the stage completely veiled in mist, as the noble, tragic music of Siegfried's Funeral March sounds forth. Almost unbearably moving in its context, the march reviews the dead hero's life and character, using the appropriate motifs.

When the mists disperse, the hall of the Gibichungs is revealed to view as in Act I. It is night, and moonlight is reflected on the Rhine. Gutrune, her motif issuing sadly from the orchestra, anxiously awaits the return of Siegfried with the hunting-party, and voices her disquiet at the odd behaviour of Brünnhilde, whom she had glimpsed earlier walking down to the river bank. About to return to her room, Gutrune pauses when she hears the voice of Hagen outside, loudly calling for torches and announcing that the spoils of the hunt are being brought back, while the orchestra offers a reminder of the vengeance motive. 'Arise, Gutrune, and greet Siegfried,' Hagen calls to her. 'The mighty hero is coming home.'

Terrified, Gutrune asks him what has happened, for she has not heard Siegfried's horn. 'The pallid hero can blow it no more,' Hagen replies grimly, as Gunther and the vassals enter, bearing Siegfried's body, which they set down on a dais in the centre of the hall. As Gutrune screams and falls upon the body, Hagen announces that Siegfried was the victim of a wild boar. Gutrune, however, accuses her brother Gunther of having murdered him, at which Gunther places the blame firmly upon Hagen: 'He is the accursed boar who savaged this noble hero.' Hagen freely acknowledges the deed, and demands Siegfried's ring as a reward, but Gunther regards the ring as family property. 'Would you steal Gutrune's inheritance, you shameless son of a dwarf?' he cries, at which Hagen draws his sword.

The two men fight, and Gunther is killed. But when Hagen goes to Siegfried's body and attempts to remove the ring, the dead hero's hand rises threateningly while all stand transfixed with horror. The motif of the downfall of the gods, heard first from Erda in *Das Rheingold*, now reappears as Brünnhilde enters. She has learned the truth from the Rhinemaidens, and assumes the status of grieving widow, to the fury of Gutrune, who accuses her of having brought disaster upon the Gibichungs. Brünnhilde calmly announces that Siegfried had sworn his eternal love to her long before he ever saw Gutrune, at which Gutrune vents her anger upon Hagen, who stands leaning on his spear in silent defiance.

Brünnhilde now begins her great final scene. Bidding the vassals to stack and light a pyre by the shore of the Rhine, she delivers Siegfried's funeral oration, remembering him lovingly, and castigating Wotan for having sacrificed him. As the vassals lift Siegfried's body on to the funeral pyre, Brünnhilde takes the ring from his hand and places it on her own. She will wear it, she exclaims, as she rides her horse Grane into the flames of Siegfried's pyre, and the Rhinemaidens can reclaim it from her ashes. Snatching a torch from one of the vassals, she calls to Wotan's ravens to fly home to their master and recount what they have observed by the Rhine. She then hurls the torch on to the pile of wood, which quickly ignites.

Two ravens fly up from the shore and disappear into the sky, as Grane is led in. 'Do you know, my friend, where I am leading you?' Brünnhilde addresses her horse. 'Radiant in the fire, there lies your lord, Siegfried, my blessed hero. Are you joyfully neighing to follow your friend? Do the laughing flames draw you to him? Feel my bosom too, how it burns. My heart yearns to embrace him, to be enfolded in his arms, united with him in the most powerful love. Greet your master!' With a final cry, 'Siegfried, see, your wife blissfully greets you,' Brünnhilde mounts Grane and rides into the burning pyre.

Motif has tumbled over motif in Brünnhilde's great scena, a magnificent apotheosis in which all the most important themes of *The Ring* pass in review. The moving theme of redemption by love (Ex. 22), first enunciated by Sieglinde in Act III of *Die Walküre*, is sounded quietly in the orchestra as Brünnhilde addresses Grane, to become more expansive as she sings of the blissful reunion with Siegfried which she confidently anticipates.

The end is described in Wagner's stage directions. The flames immediately blaze up, so that the fire fills the entire space in front of the hall, which it appears to seize on as well. The terrified vassals and women press to the foreground. When the stage is completely filled with fire, the glow suddenly subsides, leaving only a cloud of smoke which drifts towards the background, where it lingers on the horizon. At the same time, the Rhine overflows its banks in a mighty flood which inundates the fire, and the three Rhinemaidens are seen swimming on its waves. Hagen, who has been watching Brünnhilde with growing anxiety, is filled with the greatest alarm at the appearance of the Rhinemaidens. Hastily throwing aside his spear, shield and helmet, he plunges, as though insane, into the flood with a cry of 'Keep back from the ring!'

Woglinde and Wellgunde twine their arms around Hagen, drawing him with them into the depths as they swim away, while Flosshilde, swimming in front of the others, exultantly holds aloft the ring which they have recovered. An increasingly bright glow breaks through the bank of cloud on the horizon, in whose light the Rhinemaidens can now be seen swimming in circles, happily playing with the ring in the calmer waters of the Rhine, which has gradually returned to its natural level. From the ruins of the Gibichung hall, the vassals and women watch the growing fire in the sky with increasing apprehension. When the light reaches its brightest, there becomes visible in the distant sky the palace of Valhalla in which the gods and heroes sit assembled, as described by Waltraute in Act I. The fire appears to envelop Valhalla and, as the gods become completely hidden from view by the flames, the curtain falls. The orchestra has followed this dénouement with a magnificent outpouring of all the relevant motifs. But after the doom-laden motif of the twilight of the gods as Valhalla is consumed by fire, the consoling theme of redemption by love (Ex. 22) wells up in the orchestra to spread its balm over all. The immense *Ring des Nibelungen* ends on an uplifting note.

Ernest Newman and other Wagner commentators have pointed out that the ending of the great tetralogy is distinctly confusing. As Wagner's friend August Röckel wrote to the composer, 'Why, since the gold is returned to the Rhine, is it still necessary for the gods to perish?' The reply Röckel received was unsatisfactory, for there could be no logical answer. Wagner the poet had initially planned that Siegfried's death and Brünnhilde's return of the ring to the Rhinemaidens would lead to a new and happier era for gods and mankind. Musically, however, he was drawn inexorably to the tragic conclusion of 'das Ende'—the end of everything, as wished for by the world-weary Wotan in *Die Walküre*. As composer, Wagner nevertheless contrived to ensure the softening of this tragic conclusion by the consoling power of music. His concept of redemption through love is really redemption through the art of music: art consoles as life ends. One must hope so.

Der Ring des Nibelungen took Wagner more than a quarter of a century to create, from 1848 to 1874. It it, therefore, hardly surprising that the work is stylistically inconsistent, and musically uneven. Its composition is the result of an immense, if not indeed an unparalleled, act of the creative imagination, for which the work's occasional *longueurs* are by no means too high a price to pay. Nevertheless, Wagner's prolixity can be tiring. In *The Ring*, most instances of it are the result of the manner in which the text was constructed through the years, with characters having constantly to summarize the plot for the benefit not so much of new listeners as of new players in the game. As a composer, Wagner always had a tendency to be long-winded, more than somewhat ponderous at dramatic moments, and rhythmically monotonous. Ernest Newman, in his *Wagner as Man and Artist*, makes these points with admirable succinctness:

> Music, let it be said again and again, is primarily an emotional art, and the less it has to do with mere dramatic explanation, the better. We can never tire of Wotan pouring out his heart in loving farewell to his child; but we can hear Wotan tell the long story of his financial and matrimonial troubles once too often. We could listen as often to Kundry's story of Herzeleide [in *Parsifal*] as to the slow movement of the Ninth Symphony or the 'Kleine Nacht-Musik' of Mozart; but wild horses could not drag us to the theatre merely to listen to old Gurnemanz's too-often-told tale of Amfortas and Klingsor, and how the sacred spear was lost. Yet though the poet Wagner is generally answerable for the occasional tedious quarters of an hour in the operas, the musician Wagner is not wholly free from blame. He never managed to get quite rid of the slow-footedness that was characteristic of his music from the first; to the very end he sometimes takes rather longer to drive his points home than is absolutely necessary; and in these more rapid and impatient days that goes against him sorely.

A different attitude to Wagner's occasional shortcomings is displayed by Robert Donington in *Wagner's 'Ring' and its Symbols*, an examination of the work from the point of view of Jungian psychology. Of the repetitive passages in *The Ring*, Donington asserts that

> most of them are necessary parts of the emotional and artistic structure. In *Götterdämmerung* particularly we are told in narrative much that we have already seen in action during the previous three operas; but this does not mean either that these operas could have been dispensed with, or that they make the recapitulatory narrative redundant. Myths themselves are full of such recapitulations, which are part not only of their form but of their technique for emphasising the most crucial implications.

Of course, it is possible to enjoy and appreciate *Der Ring des Nibelungen* without being concerned with either the Jungian mysticism of Donington or the nineteenth-century socialism of Bernard Shaw. One of the earliest and more modestly equipped of Wagner commentators, Cuthbert Hadden, writing at the turn of the century, contributed a certain blunt common sense to the endless debate on the meaning of *The Ring*, although his argument begs a number of questions:

There is no need to make any mystery about the subject; no need to involve it in cloudy discussions about philosophy and metaphysics and all the rest. It is a subject not necessarily implying any great strain on the imagination such as is too often assumed. In plain language, it shows the struggle of free love and human impulse against the fetters of conventional laws, and against the sway of wealth and splendour. It is essentially a drama of today, though dressed up in all the heathen paraphernalia of gods, giants, dwarfs, water-maidens, Valkyries etc. The spectator will readily recognize in it a picture of the world through which he is himself fighting his way. The dwarfs, giants and gods may be regarded as dramatizations of the three main orders of mankind—dwarfs, the instinctively lustful, greedy, grabbing people; giants, the patient, industrious, stupid money-lovers; gods, the clever, moral intellectuals, who make and rule states and communities. The Rhinemaidens are the nature-lovers who admire the gold for its beauty, not for its commercial value. Alberich is the capitalist, who forswears the love he cannot win by reason of his unamiable personality. He carries off the gold to turn it into money and the means of acquiring vast wealth through the labour of millions driven by starvation to accept his terms.

The giants, on the other hand, are willing to buy love and gold honestly, with patient, manual drudgery in the service of the higher powers. These higher powers, who, in comparison with the dwarfs and giants, may be called gods, are the talented moral beings whose aims reach beyond the mere satisfaction of their appetites and personal affections. In order to carry out their projects for the advancement of the world from a state of savagery, they make laws and enforce them by the punishment of the disobedient. In time these laws cease to be in accordance with the ever-widening and developing ideas of the gods. But their law must be preserved at all costs, even when it no longer represents their thought; otherwise their subjects will respect neither law nor law-givers. Thus gradually the gods become entangled in a network of statutes made by themselves, which they must obey in order to maintain their authority.

... *The Ring* is one vast web of motives, many of which rivet themselves at once upon the listener's attention. It must not, however, be supposed (the mistake is often made) that the scores are compounded of a string of disconnected phrases, arbitrarily formed and capriciously titled. The scores are symphonic in their scope. That is to say, the motives are welded together and worked up in such a way as to produce the effect of a united whole, rich in variety, beauty and meaning—a glittering texture of harmony and counterpoint, of which the pianoforte score can give but a faint conception. If the listener can pick out the various motives as the drama proceeds, it will add immeasurably to his intellectual and artistic pleasure. But Wagner's music . . . makes the right mood-pictures even for him who does not know the guiding themes, and this is one of the best proofs of the composer's greatness.

Ideally, the four parts of *Der Ring des Nibelungen* should be heard complete and consecutively: the entire work demands a greater degree of concentration from the listener than any other opera by Wagner, or by anyone else. This is not simply because of the system of leitmotivs woven into the giant work, but also because of the complex nature of the ideas inherent in it, and because of the variety of interpretations to which it is susceptible. Considered as an old Norse saga of gods, heroes, dwarfs, dragons and giants, reworked by Wagner into frequently bad and repetitive verse, *The Ring* is obviously a flawed and unsatisfactory affair. However, its power to move an audience lies elsewhere: in the ability of Wagner's music to bypass its listeners' intellectual and aesthetic responses, to communicate directly with the deepest recesses of the psyche. The naïve absurdities of its plot, the antiquated trappings of the old saga, all fade into insignificance before the emotive force of Wagner's music.

In a sense, *The Ring* fails as a vindication of its composer's theory of the *Gesamtkunstwerk*, or total work of art, for its message is delivered by the music alone: not even, to any significant extent, by the voices, but by Wagner's orchestra. Whether *The Ring* is completely successful as theatre or as music drama may be debatable. What is beyond question, however, is that it provides the listener with a great musical experience, one that in some mysterious way transcends the art of music alone to become almost a spiritual or psychic experience.

It is by no means easy to describe the effect of this masterwork upon the receptive intelligence, and one takes grateful refuge in Wagner's reply to August Röckel: 'You must feel that something is being enacted that is not to be expressed in mere words—and it is wrong of you to challenge me to explain it in words.' But, elsewhere in the same letter to Röckel, Wagner comments on the meaning, for him, of the myth of *The Ring*:

The development of the whole poem sets forth the necessity of recognizing and yielding to the change, the many-sidedness, the multiplicity, the eternal renewing of reality and of life. Wotan rises to the tragic height of *willing* his own destruction. This is the lesson that we have to learn from the history of mankind: *to will what necessity imposes,* and ourselves bring it about. The creative product of this supreme, self-destroying will, its victorious achievement, is a fearless human being, one who never ceases to love: Siegfried. That is the whole matter. As a question of detail, the mischief-making power, the poison that is fatal to love, appears under the guise of the gold that is stolen from nature and misapplied—the Nibelung's Ring, never to be redeemed from the curse that clings to it until it has been restored to nature, and the gold sunk again in the depths of the Rhine. But it is only quite at the end that Wotan realizes this, when he himself has reached the goal of his tragic career; what Loge had foretold to him at the beginning with a touching insistence, the god consumed by ambition had ignored. Later in Fafner's deed he merely recognized the power of the curse; it is only when the Ring works its destroying spell on Siegfried himself that he realizes that only by restoration of what was stolen can the evil be annulled, and he deliberately makes his own destruction part of the conditions on which must depend the annulling of the original mischief.

Experience is everything. Moreover, Siegfried alone (man by himself) is not the complete human being: he is merely the half; it is only along with Brünnhilde that he becomes the redeemer. To the isolated being not all things are possible; there is need of more than one, and it is woman, suffering and willing to sacrifice herself, who becomes at last the real, conscious redeemer: for what is love itself but the 'eternal feminine' [*das Ewigweibliche*]?

Such is the power of Wagner's music in certain parts of *The Ring* that one simply has to forgive and forget the garrulity and tedium of others. Such, too, are the scale and nature of the vast enterprise that it remains possible to interpret *The Ring* in terms of sociology, politics, economics, history, psychology or moral philosophy. It would be as unfair to blame the composer for the fanatical enthusiasm with which Nazi Germany adopted him and his *Übermensch* Siegfried as the embodiment of their ideals as it would be to ignore the distinct probability that Wagner himself would have been delighted by the adulation of Adolf Hitler. The fervent keepers of the flame in Bayreuth certainly referred to Wagner in the festival programmes of the 1930s as a spiritual member of the Nazi Party, and compared the advent of Hitler to Parsifal's final act of redemption.

One thing is clear: *The Ring* is not a work to be dismissed—or accepted—lightly.

THIRTEEN

Parsifal

A Festival Play to Dedicate the Stage, in Three Acts
(Ein Bühnenweihfestspiel in drei Akten)

Dramatis personae
Amfortas (baritone)
Titurel (bass)
Gurnemanz (bass)
Parsifal (tenor)
Klingsor (bass)
Kundry (soprano)
First and Second Knights of the Grail (tenor, bass)
Four Esquires (sopranos, tenors)
Klingsor's six Flowermaidens (sopranos, altos)

LIBRETTO by the composer

TIME: The Middle Ages

PLACE: Montsalvat, Spain, in and near the castle of the Holy Grail

FIRST PERFORMED at the Festspielhaus, Bayreuth, 26 July 1882, with Hermann Winkelmann (Parsifal), Theodor Reichmann (Amfortas), Emil Scaria (Gurnemanz), Amalie Materna (Kundry), August Kindermann (Titurel) and Karl Hill (Klingsor), conducted by Hermann Levi.

I

THE Bayreuth performances of *The Ring* had undoubtedly been successful in the sense that they brought Wagner's name to a wider public. However, that first Bayreuth Festival ended with a huge deficit of more than 120,000 marks. As soon as it was over, Wagner travelled to Sorrento to rest after his exertions, and from there he sent out appeals to his several patrons to help reduce the loss. His suggestion that Ludwig II should nationalize the Bayreuth Festival Theatre fell on deaf ears, and the composer was forced for a time to return to the life of a touring conductor in order to raise funds. In the spring of 1877 he visited London, where a Wagner festival of twenty concerts had been planned to take place at the Royal Albert Hall. However, attendance fell below expectations, and only eight of the concerts were given, with Wagner and Hans Richter conducting half of each concert. There were no profits.

In 1878, King Ludwig came once again to the aid of Bayreuth. An agreement was made whereby Wagner's liabilities would be transferred to the state of Bavaria under certain conditions, one of which was that Wagner's next opera, *Parsifal*, whose libretto the composer had completed the previous year before going to London, should be performed only at Bayreuth, and 'never desecrated by contact with any profane stage'. Now in somewhat failing health, Wagner proceeded to devote himself to the composition of *Parsifal*, which he had begun the previous September. During the *Ring* performances in Bayreuth, he had embarked upon what was to prove the last of his love-affairs, with Judith Gautier, daughter of the French poet and novelist Théophile Gautier, and wife of the poet and critic Catulle Mendes. Cosima, more diplomatic than her predecessor Minna, made no difficulties. Now, while he worked on his new opera, Wagner wrote regularly to Judith to keep her informed of his progress. 'The name [Parsifal] is Arabian', he told her:

> The old troubadours no longer understood it. 'Parsi-fal' means: 'parsi', think of the Parsees, the fire-worshippers, 'pure'; 'fal' means 'foolish'. In an elevated sense it means a man who is untutored but possessed of genius. ('Fellow' in English appears to be related to this Oriental root.) You will perceive (rather, forgive me, you will learn!) why this naïve man bore such an Arabian name! Farewell, my dearest, my *'dolcissima amica'*.

'You will see it [the opera] soon enough, and you will like it,' he tells Judith Gautier in one of his letters. 'But what if you do not? Even if you do not want me to, I shall kiss you just the same. Oh, I have a pretty little thing, and its name is Judith.'

Partly at the Villa Wahnfried in Bayreuth, and partly in Italy, the music of *Parsifal* was slowly urged into existence, its composer working away at his task while swathed in his indispensable silks and satins, and sprinkled with

264

exotic perfumes. Simultaneously with the composition of *Parsifal*, a deeply religious work, Wagner found time to continue his purely literary activity. He founded a magazine, the *Bayreuther Blätter*, appointed a wealthy young Prussian, Hans von Wolzogen, to edit it, but filled its pages with his own scurrilous anti-Semitic tracts. One of the most extraordinary of these, '*Heldentum und Christentum*' (Heroism and Christianity), which Wagner wrote in the summer of 1881, is really an explanatory essay on *Parsifal*. (It is discussed in section II of this chapter.)

In Rome, several months after the Bayreuth *Ring* première, Wagner had met Count Gobineau. Joseph-Arthur Gobineau ('Count' may have been a title of his own devising) was a French diplomat who had propounded his racialist theories in a four-volume work, *Essai sur l'Inégalité des Races Humaines* (Essay on the Inequality of the Human Races), published in 1853–5. Wagner enthusiastically embraced Gobineau's views, and the two men became friends, the composer echoing the author's opinions even more obsessively and violently. The theories of Gobineau were to be embraced, fifty years later, by Hitler and the German National Socialist Party.

Wagner's health was now rapidly deteriorating. Minor heart attacks, a skin disease and consistent rheumatism all plagued the composer while he continued to devote his energies to the completion of *Parsifal*. At the end of 1879 he and Cosima fled from the German winter to instal themselves in a villa in Naples. They remained in Italy for ten months. On the way back to Bayreuth, Wagner visited Munich, where he conducted a private performance of the Prelude to *Parsifal* for Ludwig, who in return guaranteed the composer 300,000 marks to pay for the opera's production at Bayreuth, and also offered him, free of charge, the chorus and orchestra of the Munich Opera.

After deciding that *Parsifal* would have its première at Bayreuth in the summer of 1882, Wagner spent the summer of 1881 preparing for the event by auditioning singers and supervising arrangements for costume and stage designs, as well as continuing to work on the score, which he had not yet completed. At the end of the summer he returned to Italy, finishing the orchestration of the opera in Palermo on 13 January 1882. In the spring, he moved on to Venice, and thence back to Bayreuth to stage *Parsifal* in the summer.

King Ludwig's chief conductor in Munich was now Hermann Levi, the son of a rabbi. Wagner, furious that Ludwig had apparently rejected the anti-Semitic message of *Parsifal*, attempted with the utmost passion to turn Ludwig against Levi. Ludwig's comment that religious and racial differences were unimportant compared with the essential brotherhood of mankind was an especially bitter blow to the composer, who had no alternative but to accept Levi, for whose musical ability he had nothing but the highest praise, as conductor of *Parsifal*. Official tolerance of Jews, however, he regarded as certain to bring about Germany's ruin. He professed himself appalled that Jews were now allowed full citizenship, fearing that they would soon 'consider themselves in every conceivable respect to be Germans, just as Negroes in Mexico are encouraged to regard themselves as white'.

Ludwig had defied Wagner to the point of insisting that, unless Levi were to conduct, there would be no performance of *Parsifal*. Wagner now resorted to other tactics: he made himself personally so offensive to Levi that the conductor asked to be relieved of his task, and had to be coaxed back. Finally, when he realized that he was defeated, Wagner wrote to Ludwig, disingenuously agreeing that he would accept Levi as conductor of *Parsifal* without enquiring into his religion! When the King's response again indicated his distaste for racial intolerance (Ludwig's new soul-mate was the twenty-four-year-old Austrian Jewish actor, Josef Kainz), Wagner spewed forth a foul letter in which he informed Ludwig that he considered the Jewish race to be 'the born enemies of pure mankind and all that is noble in it'.

It was against this background that Hermann Levi conducted the first performance of Wagner's sacred Christian drama, *Parsifal*, at the Bayreuth Festival Theatre on 26 July 1882, with Hermann Winkelmann as Parsifal, Amalie Materna as Kundry, and Emil Scaria as Gurnemanz. Sixteen performances were given, with Levi conducting the Munich chorus and orchestra, the latter augmented to 107 players. The production was directed by Wagner himself, and designed, to the composer's close specifications, by a thirty-one-year-old Russian painter, Paul von Joukowsky, who had become a member of Wagner's entourage a year or two earlier, and who had travelled in Italy with the composer. There were, of course, several cast changes during the run. At the final performance, on 29 August, Wagner made his way into the orchestra pit and conducted the final scene. It was said (and has been repeated in countless books and articles) that Levi had suddenly become ill, and that Wagner took the baton from him, but in fact the composer appears to have planned that he would conduct the last scene of the last performance of what he must have known would be his last opera, as a letter to Rabbi Levi from his son, the conductor, reveals:

> During the transformation music the master came into the orchestra, pushed his way up to the podium, took the baton from my hand, and conducted the performance to the end. I remained standing next to him because I feared he might make mistakes. But this was an idle fear: he conducted with the certainty of one who might have spent his entire life only as a Kapellmeister. At the end of the work, the public broke into a jubilation defying description.

After the première, at which the music was frequently interrupted by applause, Wagner had let it be known that he would prefer the work to be heard to the end without interruption, but that the audience could express its appreciation of the performers at the final curtain call. Despite this, the audiences of 1882 continued to applaud at the end of each act. It was only after the composer's death that the custom developed in Bayreuth of applauding only Acts II and III. Today, entire performances of *Parsifal* are sometimes received in devout silence, which is certainly not what its composer intended. He himself on one occasion shouted an enthusiastic 'bravo' at the flowermaidens in Act II, only to be angrily silenced by the surrounding Wagnerians.

The Viennese critic Eduard Hanslick, he who had been caricatured as Beckmesser in *Die Meistersinger*, was present at the first performance of *Parsifal*, which he reviewed for the newspaper *Die Neue Freie Presse*. Hanslick was as impressed by the visual aspect of the production as by the music:

> Now comes the wonderfully effective Transformation scene. This master-piece of scenic art receives only step-motherly musical support. Until their arrival in the Temple of the Grail, Parsifal and Gurnemanz march to heavy, tiresomely monotonous chords. From here on, the composition gets under way and rises to significant realization, supported by the magnificent and original impressions of the setting. Admirable in their effect are the solemn unison song of the knights, the chorus of the young men, and finally, floating down from above, the promise, '*Durch Mitleid wissend—der reine Tor*' [Made wise through pity—the pure fool]. In this surprising blend of pure high voices the promise motive makes exactly the desired impression; in itself the rather empty ascending theme in fifths would hardly appear original or interesting.
>
> The Holy Communion of the Knights of the Grail in the vaulted hall, with the three singing groups of knights, youths and boys (above in the cupola), and the heavy ringing of the bells, the strange walls like paintings, the solemn unveiling of the Grail—all this combines to make a wonderful picture. The finale belongs unquestionably among those dazzling musico-scenic achievements in which Wagner has no rival.

Cosima Wagner attempted to restrict productions of *Parsifal* to Bayreuth until thirty years after Wagner's death, i.e. the year 1913. However, despite her wishes, the work was staged in New York (1903), Boston (1904), New Orleans (1905), Amsterdam (1905) and several other towns. Concert performances were given as early as 1884 in London, and 1886 in New York.

II

ALTHOUGH it was not until 1877 that he produced a verse libretto for *Parsifal*,

Wagner had begun to think seriously about the Knights of the Grail as the basis of an opera as early as 1857. In April of that year he wrote his first prose synopsis of *Parsifal*, and in May 1859, in a letter to Mathilde Wesendonk, he set forth his thoughts on the subject:

Parsifal is bound to be another very nasty job. Considered strictly, Amfortas is the centre and principal subject. There you have a pretty Parsifal tale at once. To myself all of a sudden it has grown too appallingly clear: Amfortas is my Tristan of the third act, but even more so. With the spear wound—yet again—in his heart, the poor man knows but one longing in his fearful anguish, a longing for death. To achieve that uttermost bliss, again and again he craves a sight of the Grail, in the hope that it might close his wound, since every other aid is impotent. But nothing serves. Again and again the Grail simply confirms to him that he cannot die. Seeing it only multiplies his torments, giving them an immortality.

Now the Grail, as I see it, is the cup of the Last Supper, wherein Joseph of Arimathea gathered the blood of the Saviour on the cross. See what a terrible import is gained by Amfortas's relation to this wondrous cup: he, stricken with the selfsame wound, dealt him by the spear of a rival in a passionate love adventure, for his only sustenance must yearn for the blessing of that blood which once flowed from the Saviour's similar spear wound when, renouncing the world to redeem it, he suffered for us all on the cross. Blood for blood, wound for wound. But from here to there, what a gulf between this blood, this wound!

... Whom does it not thrill with the most affecting and most sublime feelings, to hear that the goblet whence the Saviour pledged his last farewell to his disciples—and wherein the Redeemer's deathless blood itself was gathered and preserved—is still extant, and that the elect, the pure, may gaze at and adore its very self? How incomparable! And then the other meaning of the same vessel, as chalice at the holy eucharist—unquestionably the Christian cult's most lovely sacrament. Thence, too, the legend that the Grail (Sang Real–hence San[ct] Gral) alone sustained its pious knighthood, and gave them food and drink at mealtimes. And all this is so senselessly passed over by our poet [Wolfram von Eschenbach, author of the medieval romance *Parzival*] who merely took his subject from the sorry French chivalric romances of his age, and chattered gaily after them like a starling!

Then think of all that I should have to set about with Parsifal himself. For with him, too, Wolfram does not know what to do. His despair of God is absurd and unmotivated, and his conversion is even more unsatisfying. That matter of the 'question' is too entirely flat and meaningless. Here, accordingly, I should have to invent absolutely everything.

There is a further difficulty with Parsifal: as the longed-for saviour of Amfortas, he is wholly indispensable, but if Amfortas is to be given the importance due to him he acquires such intensely tragic interest that it becomes almost impossible to set up another main interest beside him. Yet Parsifal must be accorded that main interest, unless he is merely to come on at the end as a damping *deus ex machina*. Consequently Parsifal's evolution, his sublimest purification, albeit predestined by his entire pensive, profoundly compassionate nature, has to be placed in the foreground once more. And for that, I cannot choose the kind of spacious outline that Wolfram had at his disposal. I must so compress the whole into three main situations of drastic intent that the deep and wide-ranging contents may yet stand forth sharp and clear. After all, to operate and represent in this manner is precisely my art.

Wagner had first read the German medieval romance *Parzival*, by Wolfram von Eschenbach (whom the composer had included as a character in his opera *Tannhäuser*) in 1845. Eschenbach's work is a lengthy account in verse of the history of the knight who became Lord of the Grail. As Wagner noted in his letter to Mathilde Wesendonk, in Christian mythology the Grail is the cup from which Christ drank at the Last Supper, a legend familiar in English literature from the fifteenth-century *Morte d'Arthur* by Sir Thomas Malory and the nineteenth-century *Idylls of the King* by Tennyson.

However, in Wolfram von Eschenbach's poem the Grail is a precious stone with no specific Christian significance. Wagner, even in his earliest thoughts about the opera he hoped to write, was determined to restore the Christian element to the story. Wolfram von Eschenbach remained his principal source, but the libretto which the composer fashioned from the medieval poem, first as a prose scenario in 1865, with a second draft in February 1877 and the entire verse libretto a month or two later, developed not only Parsifal but also the other characters of the story along lines which were certainly never envisaged by Wolfram.

The libretto of Wagner's opera can be briefly summarized. In a castle in Spain in the Middle Ages, a band of knights preserves and worships the Grail and the spear which wounded Christ. The leader of the knights, Amfortas, is suffering from a wound which will not heal. He had taken the holy spear with him to fight the evil Klingsor, but had been seduced by the temptress Kundry, had lost the spear to Klingsor, and had been wounded by it.

The aged knight Gurnemanz tells two young novices that Amfortas's wound will heal only when a guileless fool, made wise by pity, is found. A young man, Parsifal, appears, having killed one of the sacred swans. At first Gurnemanz thinks Parsifal may be the promised saviour, but when the youth fails to understand the significance of the communion service in the Temple of the Grail, the old knight angrily dismisses him.

Parsifal visits Klingsor's magic garden, withstands the blandishments of Kundry, and wrests the spear back from Klingsor. Years later, Parsifal returns to the knights of the Grail, re-encounters Kundry, who had been under the spell of Klingsor, and forgives her. He heals Amfortas's wound, gives the spear back to its rightful protectors, orders the Grail to be unveiled and blesses the knights.

A study of the libretto in relation to Wagner's various prose writings makes it clear that one of the composer-dramatist's main concerns was to 'Aryanize' Christianity by divorcing it from its Jewish beginnings. In his essay 'Heldentum und Christentum' (Heroism and Christianity), which he wrote in 1881 as a polemical appendage to *Parsifal*, he explains how the Aryans, the Teutonic leaders of mankind, sprang from the gods, only the lesser races being descended from the apes. Christianity's worship of a Jewish tribal God, made flesh in the Jewish Christ, appalled him. In *Parsifal*, Wagner recreated Christ in his own, supposedly Gentile, image. Parsifal is an Aryan Christ.

Another of Wagner's aims in *Parsifal* was to make Germany aware of the threat to its racial purity, already seriously drained by its tolerance of lesser breeds. The knights of Montsalvat, the composer's essay reveals, are an élite and racially pure group of Aryans, and the evil Klingsor represents Judaism. Wagner, incidentally, had now become a vegetarian, which meant that not only all the members of his household, but also his followers, his 'disciples', as well, were instructed to give up meat. Flesh-eating was an evil introduced by those 'former cannibals', the Jews.

In another essay, 'Religion and Art', Wagner voiced very strong doubts as to the Jewishness of Christ, and also took God to task, both for being Jewish and for being anti-vegetarian. The evil Klingsor, Wagner informed Cosima, represented not only the tainted blood of the Jew but also the Jesuit. The luxurious, voluptuous garden of *Parsifal*'s Act II, which the composer thought of as representing Jewish art, is made to disappear by the magical power of the Aryan cross. In the third act of the opera, the pure blood of an Aryan Jesus glows with desire to rejoin the blood in the sacred cup. Amfortas, who had allowed his blood to mingle with that of the racially inferior Kundry, is redeemed, while Kundry is reduced to that menial grovelling which Wagner sees as her proper condition. Like Gobineau, he separated mankind into master-races (*maîtres*) and slave-races (*esclaves*). Is it surprising that Wagner's absurd polemical essays were declared by Hitler to be his favourite reading? 'Whoever wants to understand National Socialist Germany', said the Führer, 'must know Wagner.' (Cosima noted in her diary for 19 December 1881 that Wagner 'makes a drastic joke to the effect that all Jews should be burned at a performance of *Nathan*.' *Nathan the Wise* is a play by Gotthold Lessing (1729–81), about a Jew at the time of the Crusades who regards all religions as facets of the one truth.)

It is also possible to view *Parsifal* merely as a sickly, *fin-de-siècle* homoerotic fantasy about a group of knights who allow no woman to invade their realm; a slow-moving opera, the extreme length of which is disproportionate to its musical and dramatic worth. On the surface, it is a work of pious Christianity, although Wagner had come to detest Christianity as an offshoot of Judaism. But *Parsifal*, whatever else it may be, is a complex work of art. If it can be seen as an attempt to give aesthetic validity to the violent and demented racial prejudice of the composer's articles in the *Bayreuther Blätter*, it can also be seen as the portrait of a soul on its journey towards maturity. Whether it is, in the words of the American Wagner critic Robert Gutman, a 'brooding nightmare of Aryan anxiety' or a celebration of high-minded homosexuality, *Parsifal* seems now to be very much a product of its time, more so than *Tristan und Isolde*, *The Ring*, or even *Die Meistersinger*.

Parsifal's purity was threatened both racially and sexually. Is it fanciful to trace a connection between the monastic homosexuality of the knights and what Gutman calls the 'not dissimilar fellowship of Ernst Rohm's troopers'? The simplistic answer is that art is art, life is life, and never the twain shall meet. But *Parsifal* deserves to be considered on a more complex level of response than this. Properly allowing of fewer varieties of interpretation than *The Ring*, it has nevertheless been subjected to many, by those desirous either of emphasizing Wagner's anti-Semitism or of diverting attention from it.

The music of *Parsifal* is, at least intermittently, as powerful and compelling as anything Wagner ever composed. To those who sentimentally equate great art with great morality, it stands as an uncomfortable reminder that art and morality are often not on speaking terms. The philosopher Nietzsche described *Parsifal* as 'a work of malice, of vindictiveness . . . a bad work . . . an outrage on morality'. He also recognized the power and beauty of much of its music. However, if it is accepted that the arts can influence human behaviour, then presumably they can influence it for evil as well as for good. One is inclined to believe that music, as an art, is essentially innocent, and that only when it is allied to text or drama can it corrupt. But corruption is itself a question-begging concept: it is safer to proceed no further than the declaration that, to some temperaments, *Parsifal* is an uncommonly persuasive work of art.

III

THE Prelude to *Parsifal*, a solemn and slow-moving piece (as, indeed, is almost the entire work), introduces some of the opera's principal motifs. It begins with the motif of the sacrament (Ex. 28), which will be heard again during the communion services in Acts I and III. After it has been repeated, enhanced by

Ex.28

arpeggio harmonies, it is followed on the brass by the motif of the Grail (Ex. 29), for which Wagner made use of the ancient phrase known as the 'Dresden

Ex.29

Amen', which he would have heard countless times in Dresden (and which Mendelssohn used in 1830 in the first movement of his 'Reformation' Symphony). Now trumpets, and later trombones, announce a third motif, that of faith (Ex. 30). The second part of the Prelude depicts the sufferings of Amfortas. Finally, the strings soar gently to their highest register, fading into silence, and the curtain rises.

Ex.30

There are fewer leading motifs in *Parsifal* than in the operas of *The Ring*. A contrast is made between the pure, spiritual motifs associated with the Grail and its keepers, and those earthier ones which represent the magical, sensuous world of the evil Klingsor.

The action of the opera takes place in Spain, in the mountainous region of Montsalvat. When the curtain rises on Act I, it reveals a shady forest with a clearing in the centre. To the left there rises a path leading to the castle of the Grail, while at the back the ground slopes away to a deep-set forest lake. It is dawn. Gurnemanz (bass), an elderly but vigorous knight of the Grail, and two youthful esquires lie sleeping beneath a tree. When a solemn reveille on trombones sounds forth from the castle, Gurnemanz awakens immediately and rouses the two esquires from their slumber. All three kneel in prayer, after which Gurnemanz reminds the youths of their duty to attend on the King's daily bath in the lake.

Two knights enter, and Gurnemanz enquires after the health of the King, Amfortas, who has received a wound from the sacred spear of the Grail, snatched from him by the evil magician Klingsor. The wound will not heal, and every day Amfortas seeks relief in the cooling waters of the lake from the pain it brings him. Gurnemanz wonders if the herb recently collected for Amfortas by Gawain has brought any relief, and is told that it has not. The aged knight sadly declares that they are all fools to search through the world for cures, since one thing alone, indeed one man alone, can help Amfortas. When asked to name him, however, Gurnemanz changes the subject.

The orchestra here changes, too, to a livelier tempo with a succession of phrases announcing the frenzied approach of Kundry (soprano), a strange witch-like creature who, to the accompaniment of her motif (Ex. 31), now

arrives breathlessly upon the scene, bringing yet another herb which she has travelled to distant lands to gather in the hope that it will relieve Amfortas's pain. Pressing the herb upon Gurnemanz, Kundry flings herself to the ground in utter exhaustion as a train of esquires and knights arrives bearing the litter on which Amfortas lies. The litter is set down, and Amfortas (baritone) calls for the knight Gawain, only to be told that Gawain, disappointed that the herb he had brought was of no use, has already sped away to seek another. Amfortas recalls a vision in which he was told that only a pure fool made wise by pity ('*durch Mitleid wissend, der reine Tor*') would bring him relief. He now believes this to be but a description of death.

Urged by Gurnemanz to try the herb brought from Arabia by Kundry, Amfortas thanks her and gives a signal to his knights to bear him away to the lake. The orchestral texture here is at its most beautiful. As the retinue leaves, two more knights arrive and speak harshly to Kundry, whom they consider to be a heathen sorceress. They are reproved by Gurnemanz, who reminds them that Kundry has always shown excessive zeal in her devotion to the knights of the Grail. He thinks that she may be under a curse, or that she is atoning for past misdeeds by her service to the brotherhood. He has observed that, whenever she has left them for any long period, evil has befallen the knights. Kundry had first been found many years ago by the old King, Titurel, father of Amfortas, while he was building the castle. She was lying in the undergrowth as though lifeless.

Gurnemanz now recalls that he himself had found Kundry in similar condition more recently, at the time when 'the evil one across the mountains'—Klingsor—had brought disgrace upon them. He asks Kundry why she had not helped the knights then, to which Kundry replies gruffly that she never helps. If she is so powerful, asks one of the esquires, why not send her to find the missing holy spear? Gurnemanz replies that this cannot be. He tells them how Amfortas had ventured forth, carrying the holy spear, to fight the evil sorcerer, Klingsor, but had been bewitched by a beautiful woman. As Amfortas lay in her arms, Klingsor appeared, seized the spear and thrust it into Amfortas's side. Klingsor then disappeared with the spear, and the wound he had inflicted upon Amfortas is one that will never heal. In this passage, Klingsor's motif (Ex. 32) makes its first appearance.

The two esquires who had accompanied Amfortas to the lake now return to report that the King's bath has given him some temporary relief. Urged to tell the story of the wound in more detail, Gurnemanz relates the entire history of the Grail. This sacred vessel from which Christ had drunk at the Last Supper, and into which his blood had flowed from the cross, had been placed by heaven into the keeping of old Titurel, together with the spear with which a Roman centurion had pierced Christ's side. To house these holy relics, Titurel had built the castle of the Holy Grail at Montsalvat, and had formed the brotherhood of knights of the Grail from among those whose purity of spirit gained them access to the castle.

Klingsor, repenting of his licentious ways, had attempted to join the knights. Though he castrated himself as a symbol of his desire to live a pure life, the knights refused to admit him, and so he turned to sorcery, transforming a wilderness on the southern slopes of the mountain—the side facing Moorish Spain—into a magic garden, filling it with flowermaidens with whom he hoped to seduce the knights away from their holy office. (Here the orchestra anticipates the motif of the flowermaidens from Act II.) When Titurel, in his declining years, handed authority over to his son, Amfortas, the young King left the castle armed with the holy spear to do battle against Klingsor. The unfortunate result of that episode is already known to the esquires. Klingsor is now in possession of the holy spear, and Amfortas has been told in a vision emanating from the Grail that for deliverance he must await 'the pure fool made wise by pity'.

Much of the music of *Parsifal* moves at a stately, reverent pace, interest being sustained by the occasional use of the various motifs. But Gurnemanz's long narrative is, it must be admitted, one of the opera's especially enervating passages, its motifs trotted out mechanically and the old knight's discursive vocal line dully repetitive. At the end of his expository address, when Gurnemanz sings the words of the King's vision, he introduces the prophecy motif (Ex. 33), which the esquires begin to repeat after him.

Ex.33

Suddenly, shouts are heard from the direction of the lake. A wild swan, pierced by an arrow, flutters on to the scene, followed by some of Amfortas's esquires and knights, who are shocked that anyone should have attempted to kill a bird in the precincts of the castle, where all life is held to be sacred. As the bird sinks exhausted to the ground and dies, a knight explains that the King had hailed its flight over the lake as a happy omen when suddenly an arrow flew through the air and the bird fell. Other knights and esquires bring in a youth (tenor) who admits to having killed the swan. 'I hit everything that flies,' he boasts.

The youth, whose name we shall discover in Act II to be Parsifal, brings

Ex.34 *Lebhaft und schnell*

275

with him not only a reference in the orchestra to *Lohengrin*, but also his own motif, joyous and free (Ex. 34). Led to feel ashamed of himself by Gurnemanz's words of admonition, which are sung to a broad and noble melody, the youth snaps his bow and hurls the arrow away. When questioned, he appears to know neither his own name nor that of his father. After the others have departed, bearing the swan off on a litter of twigs, Gurnemanz turns again to the youth and begins to question him further. The lad knows only the name of his mother, Herzeleide (Heart's sorrow), but Kundry, who has been lying in the undergrowth throughout the preceding scene, is able to provide further information. She informs Gurnemanz that, when the lad's father, Gamuret, was slain in battle, his mother reared him in the forest.

The youth now takes up the story, describing how, one day, he had seen a brave company of knights riding through the forest, and had wanted to join them. They laughed and rode on, but he followed in the direction they had taken, travelling for days and keeping himself alive by killing game. Gurnemanz observes that the youth's mother must be worried about him, at which Kundry reveals that the woman is dead. 'I was riding past, and saw her die,' she tells the youth, 'and she bade me greet you, fool.'

The youth springs at Kundry in a rage, gripping her by the throat, but is restrained by Gurnemanz, who assures him that Kundry never lies. When the youth is seized with violent trembling and is about to faint, Kundry hastens to a spring and returns with a horn of water which she sprinkles over him and then gives him to drink. Gurnemanz praises her good deed, but Kundry mutters that she never does good. She then creeps wearily towards a thicket, both yearning for and fearful of the sleep which soon overcomes her.

When Amfortas and his followers return from the lake on their way back to the castle, Gurnemanz, acting on an impulse, leads the youth slowly in the direction the others have taken, assuring him that, if he is pure, the Grail will give him food and drink. The lad does not know what the Grail is, but Gurnemanz tells him he may well be the chosen one, for no one could have found his way to the castle unless led by the Grail. As they walk, the tolling of bells introduces a powerful orchestral interlude known as the Transformation Music, incorporating the Grail and faith motifs and that of Amfortas's repentance. Behind the old knight and the youth, the scene begins slowly to change.

By the time the Transformation Music reaches its climax and dies away again to be followed by a statement of the sacrament motif, the woods have disappeared, and Gurnemanz and the youth pass through a gateway. As trumpets sound and bells continue to peal, they enter the great hall of the castle of the Grail to the sound of the sacrament motif on the trombones. Knights, esquires and youths enter, chanting, and take their places at long dining-tables as the orchestra contributes processional music based on the bell motif. The Grail motif is heard as Amfortas is brought in on his litter, and four esquires bear the veiled shrine of the Grail, which they place upon a stone table.

From the depths of a vault behind the couch on which Amfortas lies, the voice of his dying father, Titurel (bass), issues forth as though from the grave, begging for one final glimpse of the Grail. Amfortas implores his father not to force him to look upon the Grail, the sight of which now brings Amfortas only agony. He asks Titurel to unveil the Grail himself, but the old King, already lying in his coffin and kept alive only by the power of the Grail, is too weak to do so. Amfortas's long and impassioned monologue ('*Wehvolles Erbe*': Woeful lot) is accompanied by several references in the orchestra to the motifs already introduced. When boys' voices from the cupola intone the prediction '*Durch Mitleid wissend . . .*', Amfortas raises himself slowly and painfully and unveils the chalice, which has been lifted from its shrine by boys. Voices from above now begin to chant the words of the communion service as Amfortas bows in silent prayer before the Grail.

In the deepening twilight, a dazzling ray of light from above falls on the crystal goblet, which glows brilliantly as Amfortas raises it aloft and proffers it to all. As he sets it down again, the Grail's light grows dimmer, and the boys replace it in the shrine. Wine and bread, which had been consecrated by Amfortas with the chalice, are now distributed to the kneeling assembly, as the voices of knights, youths and boys continue to chant the words of the holy communion, higher boys' voices floating down from above, reinforced by lower boys' voices and tenors. Gurnemanz gestures to the young stranger to sit by him and participate in the service, but the lad remains standing to one side, motionless as though entranced.

During the service, Amfortas has collapsed in pain, his wound bleeding afresh. He is carried out while various motifs make their way through the orchestra, and the assembly disperses, leaving only Gurnemanz and the youth remaining. When Gurnemanz asks him if he has understood what he has seen, the youth clutches at his heart and nods his head, but says nothing. Annoyed, Gurnemanz calls him a fool and pushes him out by a side door, advising him in future to leave the swans in peace. As the old knight slams the door, the words of the divine prediction are repeated from on high by a solo alto voice, followed by other voices from the top of the dome and the middle height intoning a blessing which fades into silence as the curtain falls to the soft pealing of the bells.

Act II takes place in Klingsor's magic castle. A tempestuous orchestral prelude begins with the sinister motif of the evil magician himself (Ex. 32), leading through other motives to that of the wild Kundry (Ex. 31). The curtain rises on the inner keep of a tower, with side steps leading up to the battlement at the top. The space is filled with magical and necromantic paraphernalia. Seated in front of a metal mirror, the magician Klingsor (bass) gazes into its depths, in which he discerns the approach of 'the fool', Parsifal. Klingsor summons from the sleep in which she is held by his curse a woman whom he addresses as 'the original she-devil, rose of hell, Herodias and the other names you were, Gundryggia there, Kundry here'.

At his words, the figure of Kundry emerges from the darkness below and utters a terrible cry. Though she replies to Klingsor, she appears still to be asleep. He mocks her devotion to the knights of the Grail, whom he knows she visits on those rare occasions when she can escape from his spell, to the power of which, however, she must always return. Klingsor now reminds her that it was she who, under his instructions, lured Amfortas to the castle and exerted her wiles upon him. No man has been able to resist Kundry, except Klingsor himself as he reminds her. And he was able to do so only by a desperate act of self-emasculation.

Kundry yearns for salvation, but Klingsor points out that she can be set free only when a man appears who can resist her. 'Try it on the handsome youth who now approaches, who is already climbing the stronghold,' he advises her. Klingsor's warriors have proved unable to stop Parsifal from scaling the ramparts. The youth has slashed one of them in the arm, and another in the thigh, and now stands gazing down at the enchanted garden. All this Klingsor sees in his mirror. Kundry now vanishes to do Klingsor's bidding, and the magician himself sinks rapidly from view with the entire tower. In its place, a magic garden rises into view, bounded at the back by the battlements of the castle on which Parsifal stands, gazing down in wonder. From all sides, Klingsor's beautiful flowermaidens, clad in diaphanous veils, rush into the garden as though suddenly aroused from sleep. The dramatic and tempestuous music of the Klingsor–Kundry scene now gives way to more mellifluous tones, and Parsifal's motif (Ex. 34) is heard in the orchestra to establish the identity of the youth who has gained entry to the magic garden.

At first the flowermaidens bewail the injuries inflicted upon their lovers. When they catch sight of Parsifal they upbraid him, but his response, as he leaps down into the garden, is to claim that he was forced to strike the warriors who would have barred his way to the maidens. Parsifal has acquired a more sophisticated manner since Act I, and his bantering tone with the flowermaidens is reminiscent of Siegfried addressing the Rhinemaidens in the last act of *Götterdämmerung*. At his words, the flowermaidens change their attitude and begin to flirt with him. Several of them slip away behind the flower-beds, and return looking like flowers. They throw themselves at Parsifal, while some of the other maidens express their annoyance at their sisters' guile and leave the scene to bedeck themselves similarly. Their style, here, also has much in common with that of the playful Rhinemaidens, and

Ex.35

p Komm'! Komm'! Hol - der Kna - be!

their tones are sweetly sensuous (Ex. 35). Soon the flowermaidens are all quarrelling over Parsifal, who gently repulses them. He is about to flee when he hears the voice of Kundry calling, 'Stay, Parsifal.' It is one of the most arresting moments in the opera.

Suddenly remembering that his mother had once called him by that name in a dream, Parsifal looks about him as Kundry's voice orders the flowermaidens to leave him and to tend the wounds of their lovers. The maidens disappear laughing into the castle, and through a gap in the hedge of flowers Kundry can be seen lying on a bed of flowers, no longer hag-like in appearance but a young woman of great beauty clad in a seductively revealing garment. Kundry tells the youth that, while he was still in his mother's womb, he had been named Parsifal or 'Falparsi', foolish pure one, by his dying father. She proceeds to recount in detail the story of Parsifal's childhood, of the loving care lavished upon him by his mother, Herzeleide, and of Herzeleide's sorrow and eventual death of a broken heart when he left her. '*Ich sah das Kind*' (I saw the child), Kundry's lengthy narrative, is a voluptuous outpouring of feeling, part erotic and part quasi-maternal. The same ambiguity of mood is continued in the duet scene between Parsifal and Kundry which follows.

Shocked and overcome with pain and remorse, Parsifal sinks at Kundry's feet. Kundry consoles him with caresses and finally presses her lips to his in a lingering kiss. But Parsifal breaks away from her and leaps to his feet with a gesture of fear. His innocence or foolishness immediately lost, he clutches at his heart as though in pain, and exclaims, '*Amfortas! Die Wunde!*' (Amfortas! The wound!). He now realizes the significance of what he had seen in the Temple of the Grail, and indeed understands the nature of the Grail itself. Falling to his knees again, he prays that his sins be forgiven. His long solo outburst is an extraordinary depiction of a soul in torment.

When Kundry again attempts to kiss him, Parsifal realizes that it must have been thus that she had ensnared Amfortas. Kundry confesses that she has been cursed for all eternity because she had laughed at Christ on the cross. (The two syllables of '*lachte*' (laughed) are screamed in a phrase that falls nearly two octaves from the soprano's B above the stave to her C sharp below it). Kundry can be saved only by him who can withstand her charms, but she must nevertheless continue to attempt the seduction of Parsifal, even though she suspects he may be the means of her salvation.

Although tempted, Parsifal does not succumb. In a fury, Kundry calls on Klingsor for help, and the magician suddenly appears on the ramparts with the sacred spear poised for flight. He aims the spear at Parsifal and throws it, the flight indicated by a harp glissando, but it comes to rest above the youth's head. Grasping the spear, Parsifal makes the sign of the cross with it, at which the castle collapses, Klingsor disappears and the garden shrivels to a desert. Kundry utters a shriek of despair and, as he hastens away, Parsifal pauses to look back at her. 'You know where you can find me again,' he calls. Kundry raises herself and gazes after him as the curtain falls, the orchestra's passionate colours fading to a bleakness descriptive of spiritual emptiness within the space of a few bars.

From its very opening bars (Ex. 36), the brief Prelude to Act III paints a desolate picture of the wanderings of Parsifal in search of the way back to

Ex.36

Montsalvat and the Grail. When the curtain rises, it reveals a spring landscape in the vicinity of the castle of the Grail. Flower-filled meadows adjoin a forest, and there are a spring and a hermit's hut nearby. It is early morning, and Gurnemanz, now grown very old, emerges from the hut, having heard a sound of groaning nearby. He approaches a thicket, in which he discovers Kundry whom at first he fears is dead. However, he rubs her hands and temples, and eventually revives her.

Kundry is dressed in the coarse robes of a penitent. (Wagner adds, in his stage directions, 'as in Act I', having forgotten that Kundry's wild demeanour and attire then were anything but that of a penitent.) Her face is now paler, and the fierceness has gone from her looks and her bearing. After gazing at

Gurnemanz for a long time, she rises to her feet, arranges her dishevelled hair and garment, and moves away, her attitude that of someone engaged in service. Indeed, the first word she utters is not one of thanks to Gurnemanz for having found her, but merely '*Dienen*' (service). In fact, this is her only utterance throughout Act III. Gurnemanz informs her that there will be little need for that, as the brotherhood of the Grail is now in a state of decline, the knights subsisting on what herbs and roots they can find in the forest. But Kundry, without answering, enters the hut, emerging again with a pitcher which she carries to the spring. Glancing into the forest, she perceives someone approaching from the distance, and turns to point this out to Gurnemanz, as Parsifal's motif makes a solemn appearance in the orchestra on horns, trumpets and trombones.

Kundry re-enters the hut, and a man emerges from the forest in a black suit of armour, the vizor of his helmet down, and carrying a spear. He comes slowly forward, his head bowed as though in dejection, and seats himself on a grassy mound. He does not speak in answer to Gurnemanz's questions, but merely nods or shakes his head. When the old knight tells him he should lay his weapons aside in so holy a place, especially as it is Good Friday, the stranger rises, thrusts his spear into the ground, and lays his shield beneath it. Removing his helmet, he kneels in silent prayer before the spear.

Gurnemanz and Kundry, who has come out from the hut, now recognize him as the foolish youth who had once killed a swan. Kundry gazes fixedly but calmly at Parsifal, as Gurnemanz, in great emotion, recognizes the spear. His prayer concluded, Parsifal now greets Gurnemanz and describes his fruitless attempts over the years to find his way back to the castle of the Grail. An evil curse had caused him to lose his way, and countless battles and conflicts had deflected him from the true path, but now at last he has reached the domain of the Grail, where his mission is to cure Amfortas's wound with the aid of the holy spear.

Overcome with joy that Parsifal has finally achieved his aim, Gurnemanz declares that the brotherhood is in great need of his help, for Amfortas has hardly strength enough to unveil the Grail and longs only for death and release. Titurel has died, and the knights are all ageing and preparing themselves for death. Parsifal blames himself and his sinfulness for all this. He is about to fall, exhausted, to the ground, but Gurnemanz supports him and helps him sink on to the mound, while Kundry, on the old knight's instructions, hastily fetches water from the holy spring. Gurnemanz reveals that Titurel's funeral is to be held that day, and that Amfortas has promised to unveil the Grail for the last time. Kundry bathes Parsifal's feet, while Gurnemanz sprinkles the holy water on his head. Now Kundry draws a golden phial from her bosom, pouring part of its contents over Parsifal's feet, which she dries with her hair. At Parsifal's request, Gurnemanz anoints his head with balsam from the phial. As he does so, he blesses Parsifal, hailing him as King of the Grail. The music of this scene of benediction is gravely beautiful.

Unnoticed, Parsifal has scooped up water from the spring, which he now pours over the head of Kundry, baptizing her as a token of her redemption. Kundry weeps passionately. Parsifal and Gurnemanz talk of the significance and beauty of Good Friday, and Parsifal kisses Kundry gently on the forehead. The dialogue of the two men is accompanied in the orchestra by music of an ineffable serenity. The gentle theme of the Easter landscape, heard on the oboe (Ex. 37), introduces this Good Friday Music, as it has come to be known in concert performance. Tranquil and lingering, it exudes a rare spiritual quality.

Ex.37

A distant pealing of bells is heard, and Gurnemanz announces that it is midday. The hour has come. 'Permit, Lord, your servant to lead you,' he says to Parsifal, whom he and Kundry now invest with the mantle of the knights of the Grail. Solemnly Parsifal takes up the spear, and all three make their way slowly to the castle of the Grail, the scene changing gradually as it did in Act I.

The pealing of the bells increases in intensity as they approach the great hall. From one side a procession of knights enters with Titurel's coffin, while from the other side Amfortas is borne in on his litter, preceded by the covered shrine of the Grail. The knights implore Amfortas to uncover the Grail, but he cannot bear to do so. Titurel's coffin is opened, and all cry out in grief at the sight of his body. Amfortas beseeches his father's soul to intercede with heaven to grant him his own death. When the knights again beg him to reveal the Grail, Amfortas springs up in a state of frenzy and tears open his garment, revealing his wound and asking them to plunge their swords into his side and end his torment.

'One weapon alone will suffice,' declares Parsifal, who has entered, unobserved, with Kundry and Gurnemanz. He holds the spear out, so that its point touches Amfortas's side. Immediately the wound is healed, and Amfortas's face shines with holy rapture. Holding the spear aloft, Parsifal advances to the Grail, which he uncovers and before which he kneels in prayer. The Grail glows brightly, a ray of light falls from above and a dove flutters down to hover above Parsifal's head. Kundry, her last gaze fixed on

Parsifal, sinks lifeless to the ground. Amfortas and Gurnemanz kneel in homage before Parsifal, who waves the Grail in blessing over the worshipping knights. The curtain slowly falls.

The music of this final scene, in which the Grail motif is, of course, prominent, makes use too of the motifs of faith, of prophecy, and of the sacrament. With the exception of the somewhat hectoring chanting of the knights of the Grail at the beginning of the scene, it can be extremely moving in performance, especially the ethereal harmonies of the faith and Grail motifs in the closing bars of the opera.

Parsifal is surely the most static of all operas, and the pure fool himself the most passive of heroes. Wagner, of course, never thought of the work as an opera: to him it was the theatrical representation of a sacred rite. Other views of *Parsifal* have been mentioned in this chapter; perhaps the oddest is that of John Runciman, who, in a monograph on Wagner published in 1905, referred to the composer's final work for the stage as a 'disastrous and evil opera' and summarized its plot thus: 'At Montsalvat there was a monastery, and the head became seriously ill because he had been seen with a lady. In the long run he is saved by a young man—rightly called a "fool"—who cannot tolerate the sight of a woman. What it all means—the grotesque parody of the Last Supper, the death of the last woman in the world, the spear which has caused the Abbot's wound and then cures it—these are not matters to be entered into here. Some of the music is fine.'

AFTER the Parsifal performances at Bayreuth in the summer of 1882, Wagner and Cosima left in September for Venice, where they and their entourage, which included the painter Paul von Joukowsky, occupied part of the splendid fifteenth-century Palazzo Vendramin. Various friends, among them Franz Liszt, paid visits to the composer, whose heart was now in a weak condition. On 13 February 1883, Wagner died. A week later, Joukowsky sent an account of his death to Liszt:

Wagner got up on the morning of 13 February, saying to his valet, 'I must go carefully today.' In spite of that, he had coffee with his wife and began to work on his new essay on 'Male and Female' ['The Feminine Element in Humanity']. He stayed in his room until midday. At two o'clock he sent us word that he had his usual cramps, and that we should not delay lunch for him. We were in our usual high spirits. In the middle of the meal, the maid came to tell Frau Wagner that he was asking for her.

The children and I waited in the salon for their parents until four o'clock. Dr Keppler had already arrived at three, which had set our minds completely at rest. But at around four we began to worry again, for we were all supposed to be going out with Wagner. . . . Suddenly we heard cries of despair, and we were brought the truth: he died in his wife's arms. He fell asleep without pain, for he died of heart failure caused by the strain imposed by his usual cramps. By the time the doctor came it was too late.

Wagner was buried in Bayreuth, in the garden of his Villa Wahnfried, his coffin lowered into its grave to the sound of Siegfried's Funeral March from *Götterdämmerung*.

Short Bibliography

John Culshaw: *Reflections on Wagner's Ring* (London, 1976)

Robert Donington: *Wagner's 'Ring' and its Symbols* (London, 1963)

H. F. Garten: *Wagner the Dramatist* (London, 1977)

Robert W. Gutman: *Richard Wagner: The Man, His Mind, and His Music* (New York, 1968)

Robert Hartford (ed.): *Bayreuth: the Early Years* (London, 1980)

Robert L. Jacobs: *Wagner* (London, 1947)

Ernest Newman: *The Life of Richard Wagner* (London, 4 vols, 1933–47)

Ernest Newman: *Wagner as Man and Artist* (London, 1914)

Ernest Newman: *Wagner Nights* (London, 1949)

Charles Osborne: *The World Theatre of Wagner* (Oxford, 1982)

Charles Osborne: *Wagner and His World* (London, 1977)

Bernard Shaw: *The Perfect Wagnerite* (London, 1898)

Geoffrey Skelton: *Wagner at Bayreuth* (London, 1965)

Richard Wagner: *Mein Leben* (Munich, 1911)/*My Life* (London, 1911)

Richard Wagner: *Stories and Essays* (ed. Charles Osborne; London, 1973)

Richard Wagner: *Wagner on Music and Drama* (ed. Albert Goldman and Evert Sprinchorn (London, 1970)

ILLUSTRATION ACKNOWLEDGMENTS

The publishers would like to thank the following for permission to reproduce photographs:

Between pages 48 and 49:
i) *Rienzi* and *Der fliegende Holländer*: Mander and Mitchenson Theatre Collection (M & M)   ii) *Der fliegende Holländer*: Opera Magazine (OM)   iii) *Lohengrin* (*left*): OM; (*right*): OM (photo: Enar Merkel Rydberg)   iv) *Die Meistersinger von Nürnberg*: Zoë Dominic

Between pages 112 and 113:
i) *Tristan und Isolde* (*above*): M & M; (*below*): OM (photo: Donald Southern)   ii) *Das Rheingold*: OM (photo: Winnie Klotz); *Die Walküre*: M & M   iii) *Die Walküre*: National Archive of Richard Wagner, Bayreuth (NA/RWG); *Siegfried*: OM (photo: Winnie Klotz)   iv) *Siegfried* (*above*): OM (photo: Winnie Klotz); (*below*): NA/RWG

Between pages 176 and 177:
i) *Götterdämmerung* (*both*): OM (photos: Winnie Klotz)   ii) *Parsifal*: OM (photo: James Heffernan)   iii) *Parsifal* (*above*): OM (photo: James Heffernan); (*below*): NA/RWG   iv) *Parsifal* (*above*): NA/RWG; (*below*): M & M

Between pages 240 and 241
i–iv) (*all*): NA/RWG

Index